AFRICAN CINEMA AND HUMAN RIGHTS

STUDIES IN THE CINEMA OF THE BLACK DIASPORA

Michael T. Martin and David C. Wall

AFRICAN CINEMA
AND HUMAN RIGHTS

Edited by Mette Hjort and Eva Jørholt

Indiana University Press

This book is a publication of

Indiana University Press
Office of Scholarly Publishing
Herman B Wells Library 350
1320 East 10th Street
Bloomington, Indiana 47405 USA

iupress.indiana.edu

Library of Congress Cataloging-in-Publication Data

Names: Hjort, Mette, editor. | Jørholt, Eva, [date] editor.
Title: African cinema and human rights / edited by Mette Hjort and Eva Jørholt.
Description: Bloomington, Indiana : Indiana University Press, 2019. | Series: Studies in the cinema of the black diaspora | Includes bibliographical references and index.
Identifiers: LCCN 2018049708 (print) | LCCN 2018055027 (ebook) | ISBN 9780253039460 (e-book) | ISBN 9780253039422 (cl : alk. paper) | ISBN 9780253039439 (pb : alk. paper)
Subjects: LCSH: Human rights in motion pictures. | Africa—In motion pictures. | Motion pictures—Africa—History and criticism. | Documentary films—Africa—History and criticism.
Classification: LCC PN1995.9.H83 (ebook) | LCC PN1995.9.H83 A37 2019 (print) | DDC 791.43/6586—dc23
LC record available at https://lccn.loc.gov/2018049708

1 2 3 4 5   24 23 22 21 20 19

To Gaston Kaboré and Edith Ouédraogo,
with gratitude, affection, and admiration

Contents

Acknowledgments

Mᴄᴴᴀᴇʟ T. Mᴀʀᴛɪɴ and David C. Wall, editors of *Black Camera: An International Journal*, saw a book in what we initially had thought of as a special issue. We are grateful to them both for including *African Cinema and Human Rights* in the Studies in the Cinema of the Black Diaspora series. Three anonymous reviewers, one of them a human rights specialist, read the book with a generous eye. Their insightful and constructive comments helped us improve the book. We are most grateful to our authors for their unfailing support for the project, and to the many practitioners who were generous with their thoughts and time.

African Cinema and Human Rights finds a starting point in personal histories of transnational friendship and collaboration that deserve to be acknowledged in detail. More broadly, the book explores film's justice- and fairness-oriented world-making capacities in the context of African realities, practices, strategies, policy-making, and institution-building. This goal can be traced to a very specific site of training and capacity building—the alternative film school, IMAGINE, in Ouagadougou, Burkina Faso—and to the vision and networks of the two people who created it: the internationally prominent Burkinabè filmmaker Gaston Kaboré and his wife, Edith Ouédraogo, a pharmacist and businesswoman.

A unique institution, IMAGINE not only offers short courses in various aspects of filmmaking, but also provides a precious and unusually vital space for musical performances, exhibitions, and colloquia. During the biannual FESPACO festival, long-term friends of IMAGINE from near and far—scholars, festival organizers, film producers, trainers, filmmakers, and film funders—gather around meals and in connection with talks and performances to discuss issues that Kaboré sees as especially important: African visual arts traditions and their global influence, human rights filmmaking in the African context, and the challenges of building sustainable filmmaking communities in the absence of well-established film industries. Included in the group of regularly returning friends is Michael T. Martin. A leading scholar of African cinema who has also embraced the practice of filmmaking (as director of the documentary *In the Absence of Peace*, 1988), Martin's staunch support for the current project has been all-important. Exchanges between Hjort and Martin at IMAGINE, and shared experiences of various events at this unique institution, are without a doubt part of the background here.

IMAGINE is a site of extraordinary solidarity and friendship. The long-term collaboration between Kaboré and Rod Stoneman provides an especially clear example of strong transnational ties based on a shared vision of film's most

ix

valuable contributions, both actual and potential. Stoneman, who has contributed both a chapter and an interview with Kaboré to the present volume, was until recently the director of the Huston School of Film & Digital Media at the National University of Ireland in Galway. He previously served as the chief executive of the Irish Film Board. Of even greater significance in the present context is Stoneman's earlier role as a deputy commissioning editor in the Independent Film and Video Department at Channel 4 Television. During his years with Channel 4, Stoneman was involved in commissioning, buying, or funding more than fifty African feature films. In his Channel 4 capacity, Stoneman consistently emphasized what he calls "direct speech." His insistence on experimentation, artistic values, independence, and the possibility of an authentic voice reflecting cultural specificity was widely supported by African filmmakers. A source of trust and respect, Stoneman's ethos arguably provided the basis for collaboration with Kaboré at a much later stage, within the context of IMAGINE.

Together, Kaboré and Stoneman have launched a number of short courses at IMAGINE, including a Newsreel project that saw student filmmakers from across Africa making documentary shorts about FESPACO. As a means of highlighting the capacity-building efforts of IMAGINE and the talents of its young filmmakers, the films were shown on TV during the festival, as well as in the cinemas, ahead of some of the main features. In 2011 and 2013, Hjort joined Stoneman in Ouagadougou to assist with the subtitling of the Newsreel productions. In 2011, Hjort, Kaboré, and Stoneman organized a one-day colloquium at IMAGINE entitled "Film Training and Education in Africa: Challenges and Opportunities." In 2013, these same three collaborators organized an event that offered an opportunity to discuss human rights filmmaking within the safe space of IMAGINE. Announcements for the occasion were carefully worded so as to avoid undue attention from the authorities in Burkina Faso. A key participant in the human rights event was Jean-Marie Teno, a Cameroonian filmmaker whose efforts to use the camera to expose the long-term effects of human rights violations, many of them perpetrated by colonial powers, have been tireless. Teno is also part of the present volume; his interview, like Kaboré's, highlights some of the failings of a politics- and power-driven international human rights regime.

Hjort's presence at IMAGINE in both 2011 and 2013 was supported by a grant from the Research Grants Council of the Hong Kong Special Administrative Region, China (RGC Ref. No. 340612/CB1384, Lingnan University, 2013-16).

AFRICAN CINEMA AND HUMAN RIGHTS

Filmmaking on the African Continent

On the Centrality of Human Rights Thinking

Mette Hjort and Eva Jørholt

Since 1950, December 10 has been Human Rights Day, commemorating the United Nations General Assembly's adoption of the Universal Declaration of Human Rights in 1948.[1] In December 2016, the Centre for the Study of Human Rights at the London School of Economics featured an especially probing talk, entitled "The Populist Challenge to Human Rights." The speaker, Philip Alston, John Norton Pomeroy Professor of Law at New York University, delivered a number of clear messages and calls to action. He said that the project of defending human rights has always been a matter of struggle, yet current challenges to its legitimacy are especially threatening. Proponents of this project must rethink their strategies and alliances and must find ways of expanding the perceived relevance of human rights. Finally, intellectuals, most notably scholars and teachers, must recognize that the challenges of the times are such that there can be no room for the pursuit of personal recognition through attention-grabbing skepticisms about the very legitimacy of human rights (Alston 2016).

Explaining the seriousness of current challenges to human rights thinking, institution building, and practices, Alston's talk highlighted not only the rise of authoritarian leaders and populist movements, but also the impossibility, moving forward, of relying on traditional lines of defense: "An increasingly diverse array of governments have all expressed a desire to push back against key pillars of the international human rights regime." Alston remarked that "governments of many different stripes" are likely to find common cause in challenging and diluting "human rights standards" and in undermining "existing institutional arrangements" that "threaten to constrain them in any way." Whereas initiatives of this ilk were met by "some push back" in the past, Alston described "the prospect of effective pushback in the future" as "evaporating before our eyes" in what are indeed critical times. Political changes in the United States, Western Europe, and Latin America were described as illustrative in this regard (Alston 2016).

Rejecting despair and despondency as inappropriate responses to an essentially dire state of affairs, Alston sought to identify ways in which the articulation and implementation of the human rights project can be substantially improved. A central claim was that human rights advocates have failed to take inequality and exclusion seriously. In societies struggling with growing inequality, human rights practitioners are increasingly seen as being principally (and wrongly) concerned with the rights not only of "minority" groups but also of "felons" and "terrorists." What is required, claimed Alston, is a new and more capacious "human rights agenda," one capable of redressing the injustices of the social inequality that globalization generates. To succeed, the human rights project needs broad support, yet the current situation is one where the "majority in society feel they have no stake in human rights."

As for the third point mentioned above, referring to the responsibilities of those who write and teach, the message is especially hard-hitting: "It has become fashionable to beat up on human rights. This is not what we need. These are challenging times. We all need to do our bit. More so now than ever before." Failures of responsibility can be found in intellectual movements (e.g., deconstruction and postmodernism) that subjected concepts of truth, justice, knowledge, and progress to excoriating critique. Radical critique leads students and others to what Alston, quoting an influential but unnamed speaker, called "the abyss." For those with a long-term commitment not to theorizing but to doing actual human rights work, intellectual "guidance" of this sort can have a profoundly paralytic and thus negative effect (Alston 2016).

The titles of influential publications by scholars across the disciplinary spectrum—ranging from history to international relations to philosophy to law—suggest that skepticism about human rights is indeed a significant trend: *Human Rights as Politics and Idolatry* (Gutmann 2001), *The Last Utopia: Human Rights in History* (Moyn 2010), *The End of Human Rights* (Douzinas 2000), *The Endtimes of Human Rights* (Hopgood 2013). At the same time, it should be noted that these interventions are not reducible to an outright rejection of the human rights project. Stephen Hopgood, for example, advocates mounting a critical challenge to the recent usurpation of the human rights project by American interests, power, and money. Following Hopgood, the effects of this particular phase in the history of human rights include not only a noticeable loss of legitimacy for the very concept of human rights, but also a destruction of the bases for an international rule of law. Yet the skepticism that the very term "endtimes" evokes by no means encompasses the entirety of the human rights phenomenon. What is rejected is the coopting of an international human rights regime by governments—especially that of the United States—with little or no concern for the effects of double standards. Hopgood's critique is not entirely negative, for he seeks to identify the locus of a human rights project that has genuine legitimacy by virtue of certain constitutive motivations and goals, including compassion and a commitment to fairness and equality.

For Hopgood, there is reason to be hopeful about the activities of activist networks and grassroots movements. His account, then, highlights the human rights issues faced by specific communities and the solidarities that emerge in response to them. This point is highly relevant in the present context, given that the idea of sustaining meaningful organic ties to a given collectivity functions as a guiding principle for the vast majority of filmmakers who operate independently. In the context of Africa, the focus of this volume's discussions, there is an especially strong desire among filmmakers to take up issues that go to the heart of what defines, constrains, and potentially liberates a community. This desire moves filmmakers onto the terrain of human rights, broadly construed.

A collectivist project bridging disciplinary divides and bringing theory and practice together, *African Cinema and Human Rights* finds a starting point in the strongly held conviction that moving images play a significant role in advancing the causes of justice and fairness. This, we believe, is the case whether it is a matter of a narrow construal of "images" as representations, or a broad construal of the term, one emphasizing specific practices of production and reception. There is a long history of moving images either evoking (through fact-based fictions) or actually documenting (in nonfiction works) violations of rights that were clearly articulated in the "Universal Declaration of Human Rights" (Bradley and Petro 2002). Especially significant in this regard are the following articles: article 3 ("Everyone has the right to life, liberty and security of person"), article 4 ("No one shall be held in slavery or servitude"), article 5 ("No one shall be subjected to torture or to cruel, inhuman or degrading treatment or punishment"), and article 9 ("No one shall be subjected to arbitrary arrest, detention or exile"). Moving images may thus be designed to document human rights abuses and thereby to support the claims of victims, but they can also support goals of truth and reconciliation as these relate to a larger community. By documenting human rights abuses—often violations of the right to the security of the person—film- and video-makers typically attempt to give victims a voice. As their works reach viewers, witnessing publics may arise across national borders, and this can be an important factor in achieving redress (Torchin 2012). Yet, as some of the contributions to *African Cinema and Human Rights* make clear, the process of depicting abuses with an eye to achieving justice can be fraught with complexity, including the possibility of misunderstanding and unintended consequences.

Moving images' potential contributions to the realization of human rights extend well beyond effective documentation and its implications for justice in a given case. Moving images, more specifically, help legitimate, and thereby solidify, an expanded scope for human rights. Thus, for example, films and videos focusing on the ever-present dangers to which members of the LGBT community are exposed in specific cultures can help accelerate positive change in areas ranging from the legal to the psychological, especially if the argument-driven images are supported by well-designed distribution strategies. Finally, moving image production may, through the development of the cultural sector, promote the realization of social and economic rights. This is especially the case if the creative activities in question are supported by policies that are designed to be inclusive and to alleviate poverty. Moving image production without any narrowly defined intent to document human rights violations may in fact serve to advance a broad human rights agenda, one ranging well beyond civil and political rights.

So why have we selected Africa as the continent on which to explore these arguments? Clearly, Africa has had, and still has, its share of social injustices and human rights abuses, but the same can be said of all other continents. Our focus on Africa, then, does not aim to highlight how dire things are on "the dark continent." Quite the contrary, in fact, for this volume is motivated by the positive fact that despite constraints of all sorts, Africa can boast a large number of filmmakers who use the medium of film, in its many varieties, actively to engage with all kinds of social injustice. The volume explores a conception of filmmaking that finds clear expression in the work of Gaston Kaboré, the pioneering Burkinabè filmmaker who in 2003 founded the alternative film school IMAGINE in Ouagadougou. As Kaboré puts it, "Any film in Africa is a testament somehow. It's so rare to be able to make a movie here because of the lack of money. So when you have this opportunity, I think any filmmaker wants to say as much as possible. And we're mostly so voiceless, so when we are given the possibility to speak, we're very aware of it. We need to use that possibility to maximum effect with issues of social, political, and cultural responsibility in mind" (interview with Kaboré, this volume). Statements such as these suggest a deep affinity between African filmmaking, as shaped by the circumstances of its production, and community-based human rights thinking of the sort that Hopgood would have us value highly. "Children's rights," "women's rights," "cultural, social, and economic rights"—these terms all point to norms that will typically have much to offer the filmmaker who seeks to pursue a progressive agenda based on analysis of a given community's needs and its prospects for productive change, for movement toward greater justice and fairness.

Emerging from a context of collaboration as explained in detail in the acknowledgments, *African Cinema and Human Rights* is centrally concerned with the issue of direct speech. The aim, overall, is to highlight the voices of African filmmakers, of those practitioners who, in establishing the traditions, styles, and genres of African cinema, have helped define the public value and contributions of filmmaking on the African continent. The importance of direct speech is immediately apparent in the interviews with Jean-Marie Teno and Gaston Kaboré, with both filmmakers adopting a position of considerable skepticism with regard to the deployment in Africa of human rights thinking by Western regimes and funders. In addition to interviews, *African Cinema and Human Rights* features contributions by leading African scholars. Originally from Nigeria, Senegal, and Tanzania, respectively, Nwachukwu Frank Ukadike, Samba Gadjigo, and Martin Mhando have played a critical role in developing African Studies, in part through the academic platforms that well-established American and Australian institutions offer. Based in Ekpoma, Nigeria, Osakue Stevenson Omoera is well able to identify reasons why social and economic rights require far greater attention from the human rights community. Included along-side important instances of "direct speech" from members of the African community are interventions by carefully selected scholars from a number of other cultural backgrounds. Much like Ukadike, Gadjigo, and Mhando, Kenneth W. Harrow, Alessandro Jedlowski, and Melissa Thackway have been committed to developing the field of African Studies.

In the case of Mark Gibney, John Erni, Rod Stoneman, Ashish Rajadhyaksha, Tim Bergfelder, Eva Jørholt, and Mette Hjort, the engagement with African cinema, literature, or history is not explicitly situated within the disciplinary scope of African Studies. It is driven, rather, by a strong interest in a range of related issues: the value of film in a human rights context (Gibney), the expansion of rights through film (Erni), the creation of the conditions in which independent filmmaking voices can emerge (Stoneman), the transnational dynamics of Third Cinema (Rajadhyaksha), the challenges of celebrity activism (Bergfelder), the ethics of representing clandestine migration (Jørholt), and soft power development policies that enable transnational capacity building on a North / South basis (Hjort). Here too the relevant research often evidences a commitment to the idea of direct speech, several of the authors having collaborated with practitioners in specific filmmaking sites in Africa. Relevant in this regard are Bergfelder's involvement in developing research links between the University of Southampton and Addis Ababa University, based on shared interests in film heritage and curatorship, and Hjort and Stoneman's recurring contributions to talent development at Kaboré's film school, IMAGINE.

One task that *African Cinema and Human Rights* takes up has to do with the very place of storytelling within a justice-oriented project. Whether they are works of fiction or nonfiction, the videos and films discussed in *African Cinema and Human Rights* all develop some sort of narrative or story. As Paul Gready points out in the special issue of *Journal of Human Rights Practice* that is devoted to the issue of "Responsibility to the Story," human rights work has "two primary points of reference, the law" and "the story" (Gready 2010, 177). Whereas the law involves well-established bodies of "knowledge and expertise," when it comes to the story, "there is no clear road map" (Gready 2010, 178). Gready rightly sees the lacuna in question as requiring attention, for ethical reasons that are consistent with the norms purportedly being advanced by human rights practice: "The person whose human rights have been violated may be left with little more than their story with which to communicate their hopes and fears" (Gready 2010, 188). In the present context, the term "story" encompasses not only narratives based on first-person experiences of human rights violations, but also fictions with a general rather than specific connection to such realities.

How stories are structured has clear implications for what Murray Smith calls viewers' "alignment" and "allegiance" (1995). Whereas the former term identifies viewers' access to characters' perceptions, beliefs, and desires, the latter indicates viewers' moral assessment of one or more characters as meriting an attitude of sympathy. Speaking in his capacity as the head of communications and fundraising at DIGNITY—Danish Institute Against Torture, Christoffer Glud Grønlund called attention to what he regards as a worrying post-9/11-tendency to foster sympathy, through film, for the perpetrator, rather than the victim of torture (see also Flynn and Salek 2012).[2] Political scientist Darius Rejali has taken issue with the "convenient truths" about torture—for example, the "truth" that torture is effective—that are peddled to audiences by filmmakers with box office appeal and broader ideological concerns in mind: "Audiences accept these cinematic features as substantive truths about torture, and they don't think too hard about them. 'Real enough' fits certain understandings we have of the world. . . . When this is done well, movies achieve semidocumentary status" (Rejali 2012, 223).

With public opinion increasingly shifting toward the affirmation of torture (International Committee of the Red Cross 2016), films that are properly grounded in scientific facts regarding torture's lack of efficacy become one means of building continued support for the Convention against Torture and Other Cruel, Inhuman or Degrading Treatment or Punishment (see, for example, Shane O'Mara's *Why Torture Doesn't Work: The Neuroscience of Interrogation*, 2015). A striking example of such a film is South African filmmaker Gavin Hood's *Rendition* (2007, USA). Based on the case of Khalid El-Masri, a German citizen of Lebanese origin who was tortured at the behest of the CIA and subsequently awarded compensation by the European Court of Human Rights, *Rendition* foregrounds, among other things, the irrationality of violating citizens' human rights in life-threatening torture sessions that have little chance of producing reliable intelligence.

Given that moving images have a great capacity to shape viewers' beliefs and attitudes, Paul Gready is surely right to contend that the responsibilities weighing on filmmakers when they venture onto the terrain of human rights need to be better understood. The examination of successful and less successful instances of human rights filmmaking has much to offer in this respect.

African Cinema and Human Rights also takes up the important task of examining the very concept of human rights, with reference to its history and implications in the African context. Are human rights a Western invention, created at the height of the colonial era and later imposed on the continent? Should we rather speak of "social injustices"? Each in his or her own way, the volume's contributors call for nuanced thinking about how the cinema not only plays a role in challenging human rights orthodoxies, but also can initiate or support change that genuinely and legitimately advances the causes of justice and fairness.

With *African Cinema and Human Rights*, we seek to create the basis for interdisciplinary, transnational, and intercultural exchanges about cinematic representations, as these relate to issues such as rights-based policy making, institution building, advocacy, and claims making. This aspiration is clearly reflected in the design of the volume, including the combined profiles of the selected contributors. The latter include two scholars whose expertise brings together legal studies with other disciplines. Mark Gibney's research is situated at the intersections of humanistic studies and human rights and humanitarian law; in John Erni's work, we find an expansion of the scope of cultural studies, through the pursuit of human rights legal criticism, especially with reference to ethnic and sexual minorities. Erni's interventions as a cultural studies scholar-activist are informed by his legal training at the University of Hong Kong (partly under the prominent Kenyan constitutional lawyer Yash Ghai).

An interdisciplinary approach should be not merely about mobilizing a variety of theoretical perspectives, but also about bridging the often unproductive divide between theory and practice. Practitioners' agency is a core concern in *African Cinema and Human Rights*, with scholar-filmmakers Martin Mhando, Rod Stoneman, and Samba Gadjigo making crucial contributions and two filmmakers (Jean-Marie Teno and Gaston Kaboré) reflecting on their practices within the context of some of the more questionable aspects of the implementation of international human rights thinking. Tanzanian Martin Mhando has succeeded in combining theory and practice, having for years been a teacher and researcher at Murdoch University in Australia, even as he developed and managed the Zanzibar International Film Festival and continued to be involved in film production. Mhando's early feature films—*Mama Tumaini* (1986, Tanzania / Norway) and *Maangamizi* (2001, Tanzania / USA)—attracted awards and international recognition. At the time of writing, Mhando is contributing to initiatives that are designed to realize the potential of an ever more vital Tanzanian film sector, especially with reference to the advancement of social and economic rights. Rod Stoneman has held key institutional roles within the film sector, as deputy editor of independent film and video at Channel 4 and as chief executive of the Irish Film Board, just as he has pursued research through a professorial appointment at the National University of Ireland, Galway, and filmmaking on an independent basis. In his capacity as director, Stoneman has emphasized documentary filmmaking (*Ireland: The Silent Voices*, 1983, UK; *Italy: The Image Business*, 1984,

UK; *12,000 Years of Blindness*, 2007, Ireland; and *The Spindle: How Life Works*, 2009, Ireland). Samba Gadjigo, originally from Senegal, teaches French and African literatures at the liberal arts institution Mount Holyoke College and has also pursued filmmaking in collaboration with Ousmane Sembène, the Senegalese director who was widely seen as, in his own words, *l'aîné des anciens*, the oldest of the pioneers. In 2015, Gadjigo codirected the award-winning documentary *Sembène!* (Senegal / USA).

African Cinema and Human Rights is divided into two sections. The seven chapters that make up the first one—"Perspectives"—discuss overall perspectives and differences of perspective pertaining to Africa, human rights, and human rights filmmaking. The second section—"Cases"—presents eight contributions that take up more specific case studies, either through analyses of individual films or by investigating cinematic renderings of specific areas of human rights violations. In "Human Rights, Africa, and Film: A Cautionary Tale," which opens the "Perspectives" section, Mark Gibney cautions against Hollywood's way of representing Africa as an unending story of human rights tragedies. Usually following a "Savages-Victims-Saviors" matrix that has white Westerners save uncivilized or helpless Africans in the name of international human rights law, such films fuel the stereotypical image of Africa as the "dark continent" and may lead to a certain compassion fatigue in their Western target audiences. Gibney, however, points to a number of films—African and non-African alike—that eschew this pattern and take up human rights violations in "intelligent, provocative, balanced, and meaningful" ways.

In his contribution "African Cinema: Perspective Correction," Rod Stoneman discusses the concept of human rights in a historical context, focusing on how it entails "inherently contradictory demands: the right to equality and the right to difference." The concept, he claims, must be seen in relation to a disparity of power and resources. Against Western perceptions of generality and universality, African and diasporic films typically present more subtle and complex constellations of sameness and difference, Stoneman argues, both within the continent and between Africa and the West. He also points to the advent of digital technologies that promise to overcome African cinema's historical distribution problem, thus facilitating African "direct speech" and a radical pluralism of voices.

In an interview with Stoneman, Gaston Kaboré emphasizes the importance of making young Africans proud of their heritage and conscious of their own strengths. Against the prevailing notion, even among Africans, that the continent has always lagged behind Europe, Kaboré points to the fact that "in certain domains, [Africa was] in advance of Europe, but nobody was interested in acknowledging that." One such domain is human rights, as testified by the thirteenth-century Charter of Mandé, which predates the American Declaration of

Independence and the French Declaration of the Rights of Man and the Citizen by some five hundred years.

It makes intuitive sense that documentaries would be at the forefront of African cinema's engagement with human rights issues. In "Toward New African Languages of Protest: African Documentary Films and Human Rights," Alessandro Jedlowski, who in 2012 and 2013 took part in a continent-wide, team-based research project on the state of the documentary film industry across Africa, explains why, until quite recently, this has not in fact been the case, barring a few notable exceptions. Based on a large-scale research project, he presents the main infrastructural, economic, and political challenges faced by African documentary films across Africa. At the same time, he calls attention to the dilemmas with which the continent's filmmakers must contend. These include the necessity of engaging with human rights topics that some see as part of an imperialist agenda on the part of foreign funding bodies. Affordable digital technologies, however, have sparked a new and dynamic documentary scene and an exploration of possible African languages of protest, as exemplified by Jean-Pierre Bekolo's docu-fiction *Le président—comment sait-on qu'il est temps de partir?* (*The President*, 2013, Cameroon / Germany).

One documentary filmmaker who has indefatigably and against all odds used his camera to reveal social injustice, political repression, and violence is Jean-Marie Teno. In an interview with Melissa Thackway, he takes issue with human rights filmmaking and prefers to describe his own films as "a cinema that challenges injustice." While he does welcome the use of his work within a framework of human rights advocacy, he makes clear that he has never consciously associated himself with human rights as such. To him, the human rights discourse is far too often used cynically and hypocritically to further Western agendas. Not only does he draw attention to the fact that the so-called "Universal" Declaration of Human Rights was adopted at a time when Africa—and other parts of the world—was still under colonial domination, Teno also notes how Western countries tend to "loudly defend human rights in negatively defined parts of the world, but don't question the issue within their own societies."

Acknowledging the skepticism voiced by many African filmmakers with regard to human rights filmmaking, Mette Hjort, whose current research revolves around transnational talent development and capacity building, makes a case for "critically minded practices that do not turn human rights into a mantle of shining virtue for highly suspect ideologies, hypocrisies, and power dynamics." In her chapter entitled "In Defense of Human Rights Filmmaking: A Response to the Skeptics, Based on Kenyan Examples," she distinguishes between, on the one hand, NGOs and other nonfilm groups that use film for specific advocacy projects, and, on the other, filmmakers who are not primarily political activists but who are forced to seek funding from (often foreign) bodies that give priority to "social justice films." In the first case, she argues, there is no cause for skepticism; in the latter, the human rights framework does impose a focus on content rather than form, but it also gives the filmmakers the opportunity to make films about issues that they do actually regard as important. The chapter provides an in-depth analysis of the work of Kenyan filmmaker Judy Kibinge and her partnership with the Danish Center for Culture and Development.

The goal of making especially the younger generations aware of their rights is central to the Zanzibar International Film Festival (ZIFF). In his contribution— "The Zanzibar International Film Festival and Its Children Panorama: Using Films to Socialize Human Rights into the Educational Sector and a Wider Public Sphere"—Martin Mhando, who was the festival's director for almost a decade, explains how ZIFF's Children & Film Panorama provides an environment for children and young people that enables them to speak out about their personal experiences with social injustice and human rights abuses. Mhando's chapter focuses in particular on a screening program that took place in 2016. Five carefully chosen films were shown in ten secondary schools across Zanzibar, each of them followed by a workshop in which facilitators led the youngsters' discussion of the films. The point was to encourage the young viewers to draw connections to their own lives, and the results of this process were spectacular.

The "Cases" section starts out with a chapter on the pioneering Senegalese filmmaker Ousmane Sembène's last film, *Moolaadé* (2004, Senegal / Burkina Faso / Morocco / Tunisia / Cameroon / France). Throughout his career, Sembène addressed what many would see as human rights issues, but in "Ousmane Sembène's *Moolaadé*: Peoples' Rights vs. Human Rights," Sembène expert and biographer Samba Gadjigo argues that unlike the individual-based Western human rights discourse, Sembène was primarily concerned with peoples' rights and the power of collective action. This is brought out in *Moolaadé*, in which the tradition of female excision clashes with "moolaadé"—the duty to offer protection to those suffering from persecution and oppression—when a group of village women decide to shelter young girls from the cutters' knives. Protection is granted for the sake of the young girls, but the action has implications for future generations of women.

Almost 30 years earlier, another African film pioneer, Haile Gerima, made the landmark film *Harvest: 3,000 Years* (1976, Ethiopia). Produced in the heyday of celluloid, it carries the vestiges both of a time of political turmoil in Ethiopia and of the 1970s upsurge of revolutionary black filmmaking in the United States. In his chapter, "Haile Gerima's *Harvest: 3000 Years* in the Context of an Evolving Language of Human Rights," Ashish Rajadhyaksha, a leading expert on Indian and Third Cinema, argues that the film's multilayered realism produces a new kind of active spectatorial gaze that opens up a space for ethical considerations. Seen in retrospect, he contends, *Harvest: 3,000 Years* is "about a present thrice represented": a historical present framing a distant past, a nation-state coming to grips with its history, and an African diaspora mobilizing Africa's past.

Ethiopia is also the setting for the British documentary *Schoolgirl Killer* (Charlotte Metcalf, 1999) and the Ethiopian diasporic feature film *Difret* (Zere-senay Mehari, 2015), which both take up the real-life story of Aberash Bekele, a schoolgirl who in the 1990s stood trial for killing a man who forcibly abducted and raped her when she was only fourteen. In "Abducted Twice? *Difret* (2015) and *Schoolgirl Killer* (1999)," Tim Bergfelder compares the two very different render-ings of the same event and discusses the legal skirmishes that followed the release of *Difret*, which were mainly about the rights to Bekele's story.

With its story about contemporary jihadists who impose a regime of ter-ror in the ancient Malian city of Timbuktu, Abderrahmane Sissako's *Timbuktu* (2014, Mauritania / France) takes a clear stance against jihadism. But Kenneth W. Harrow, inspired by Aimé Césaire's "man of hatred," takes issue with Sissako's adoption for this film of a classic narrative dichotomy between protagonists and antagonists, leading toward closure and a final moment of truth. In his chapter, "*Timbuktu* and 'L'homme de haine,'" Harrow reflects on the risks of a Manichean alignment, of pitting "us" against "them." "What risks being lost," he argues, "are the qualities of openness that are threatened when one becomes 'un homme de haine.'"

The Sudanese documentary *Beats of the Antonov* (2014, Hajooj Kuka, Sudan / South Africa) showcases the amazing resilience of inhabitants of the Blue Nile and Nuba Mountains who found themselves on the "wrong" side of the border when Sudan was divided into two separate nations in 2011. Constantly under attack by government airplanes, these civilians counter persecution, massacres, and forced Arabification with collective song, music, and dance. In "*Beats of the Antonov*: A Counternarrative of Endurance and Survival," N. Frank Ukadike brings to light how the episodically structured film draws on traditional African values—primarily oral storytelling and music—and on a multiplicity of voices to support cultural diversity in the face of oppression.

In "Human Rights Issues in the Nigerian Films *October 1* and *Black November*," Osakue Stevenson Omoera takes up two Nollywood films that deploy "protest aesthetics" to denounce, in one case, the sexual abuse of children, and, in the other, the government's and multinational oil companies' violations of human and environmental rights. If the immensely popular Nollywood produc-tions were to frame human rights issues *as* human rights issues on a more general basis, Omoera argues, these films could play a decisive role in making Africans more aware of their rights and obligations.

The volume's last two chapters look at cinematic representations of two phenomena that are integrally connected with human rights: homophobia in Uganda and the flow of African migrants toward Europe. At a time of increasing ambivalence about the usefulness of human rights, John Nguyet Erni, a cultural studies scholar-activist based at Hong Kong Baptist University, suggests that queerness should be seen as "the discursive lens through which to mark this ambivalence." In "The Antiecstasy of Human Rights: A Foray into Queer Cinema on 'Homophobic Africa,'" he provides a queer analysis of two documentary films on homophobia in Uganda—*God Loves Uganda* (2013, Roger Ross Williams, USA) and *Call Me Kuchu* (2012, Malika Zouhali-Worrall and Katherine Fairfax Wright, USA / Uganda). Erni argues that state-sanctioned political homophobia and antiqueer religiosity may, ironically, prompt particular queer affects and thus contribute to new forms of queer worldings.

International news media routinely portray African migrants as a pitiful, anonymous mass of passive "sufferers," and while European films on the subject may give some migrants a voice, they typically do not address the root cause of African migration toward Europe: a general lack of opportunities induced by global neoliberalism. In "Refugees from Globalization: 'Clandestine' African Migration to Europe in a Human (Rights) Perspective," Eva Jørholt, whose research is situated at the intersection of African cinema and immigration films, looks at four West African feature films that make palpable the "social death" prompting many Africans to become migrants. Jørholt's claim is that the films invite audiences to reflect on the fact that the pursuit of happiness is not considered a universal human right.

As is the case with any collective project, decisions regarding inclusions, exclusions, and foci can be questioned. We are aware, for example, that *African Cinema and Human Rights* does not feature case studies of North African or South African films. The aim of the "Cases" section has not been to cover the entire African continent, but to examine a number of especially significant films that in one way or another illuminate general points made in the "Perspectives" section. The sheer scale and complexity of African cinema are, however, acknowledged through various chapters in the "Perspectives" section. For example, Mark Gibney, Rod Stoneman, and Alessandro Jedlowski all evoke films from northern and southern Africa, albeit in the context of more general arguments.

It is our hope that, with its interdisciplinary scope, attention to practitioners' self-understandings, broad perspectives, and particular case studies, *African Cinema and Human Rights* offers questions, reflections, and evidence that will prove helpful when considering film's ideal role within the context of the more rigorous but also more capacious human rights project that Philip Alston so rightly describes as necessary.

METTE HJORT is Chair Professor of Humanities and Dean of Arts at Hong Kong Baptist University. She is editor (with Ursula Lindqvist) of *A Companion to Nordic Cinema*.

EVA JØRHOLT is Associate Professor of Film Studies at the University of Copenhagen and former Editor in Chief of the Danish Film Institute's journal *Kosmorama*. She is coeditor (with Mette Hjort and Eva Novrup Redvall) of *The Danish Directors 2: Dialogues on the New Danish Fiction Cinema*.

Notes

1. Hjort's contribution to this introduction was fully supported by a grant from the Research Grants Council of the Hong Kong Special Administrative Region, China (RGC Ref. No. 340612/CB1384, Lingnan University, 2013-16).

2. Christoffer Glud Grønlund's intervention took place at the University of Copenhagen, in the context of the Media, Cognition and Communication MA course "Film and Audiovisual Aesthetics," March 27, 2017.

Filmography

12,000 Years of Blindness, 2007, Rod Stoneman, Ireland.
Ireland: The Silent Voices, 1983, Rod Stoneman, UK.
Italy: the Image Business, 1984, Rod Stoneman, UK.
Maangamizi: The Ancient One, 2001, Martin Mhando, Tanzania / USA.
Mama Tumaini, 1986, Martin Mhando, Tanzania / Norway.
Rendition, 2007, Gavin Hood, USA.
Sembène!, 2015, Samba Gadjigo & Jason Silverman, Senegal / USA.
The Spindle: How Life Works, 2009, Rod Stoneman, Ireland.

References

Alston, Philip. 2016. "The Populist Challenge to Human Rights." London School of Economics. Accessed April 2, 2017. http://www.lse.ac.uk/Events/2016/12/201612oltl83ov SZT/The-Populist-Challenge-to-Human-Rights.

Bradley, Mark Philip, and Patrice Petro, eds. 2002. *Truth Claims: Representation and Human Rights*. New Brunswick, NJ: Rutgers University Press.

Douzinas, Costas. 2000. *The End of Human Rights*. Portland: Hart Publishing.

Flynn, Michael, and Fabiola Salek. 2012. "Screening Torture: An Introduction." In *Screening Torture: Media Representations of State Terror and Political Domination*, edited by Michael Flynn and Fabiola Salek, 1–17. New York: Columbia University Press.

Gready, Paul. 2010. "Introduction—Responsibility to the Story." *Journal of Human Rights Practice* 2 (2): 177–190. doi:https://doi.org/10.1093/jhuman/huq008.

Gutmann, Amy, ed. 2001. *Human Rights as Politics and Idolatry*. Princeton, NJ: Princeton University Press.

Hopgood, Stephen. 2013. *The Endtimes of Human Rights*. Ithaca, NY: Cornell University Press.

International Committee of the Red Cross. 2016. "Global survey reveals strong support for Geneva Conventions but growing indifference to torture." Last modified December 5, 2016. Accessed April 10, 2017. https://www.icrc.org/en/document/global-survey -reveals-strong-support-geneva-conventions-growing-indifference-torture.

Moyn, Samuel. 2010. *The Last Utopia: Human Rights in History*. Cambridge, MA: Belknap Press.

O'Mara, Shane. 2015. *Why Torture Doesn't Work: The Neuroscience of Interrogation*. Cambridge, MA: Harvard University Press.

Rejali, Darius. 2012. "Movies of Modern Torture as Convenient Truths." In *Screening Torture: Media Representations of State Terror and Political Domination*, edited by Michael Flynn and Fabiola Salek, 219–237. New York: Columbia University Press.

Smith, Murray. 1995. *Engaging Characters: Fiction, Emotion, and the Cinema*. New York: Oxford University Press.

Torchin, Leshu. 2012. *Creating the Witness: Documenting Genocide on Film, Video, and the Internet*. Minneapolis: University of Minnesota Press.

Part I
Perspectives

1 Human Rights, Africa, and Film

A Cautionary Tale

Mark Gibney

One of the great concerns for a Western scholar writing about human rights films and Africa is that, with rare exception, the only films that reach Western audiences are those with a strong human rights theme—and, quite naturally I suppose, a Hollywood star (or two). I would include in this category *Blood Diamond* (2006, Edward Zwick, USA / Germany), starring Leonardo DiCaprio and Jennifer Connelly as opponents of the civil war–inducing gem industry, as well as *The Constant Gardener* (2005, Fernando Meirelles, UK / Germany / USA / China), in which Ralph Fiennes and Rachel Weisz play star-crossed lovers caught up in the greed and corruption of multinational drug companies that use unsuspecting Africans as human guinea pigs. This category would also include *Hotel Rwanda* (2004, Terry George, UK / South Africa / Italy, with Don Cheadle, Nick Nolte, and Joaquin Phoenix), which presents an international, mainstream version of the 1994 Rwandan genocide. *Sometimes in April* (2005, Raoul Peck, France / USA / Rwanda), the so-called "African" depiction of these same events, was in large part ignored by Western audiences although it was a far superior film. On the other hand, it had only one Hollywood star in the cast, and a fading one at that (Debra Winger).[1]

The larger point is that there is seldom any counterweight to these films. Instead, what is shown—virtually all that is shown—are films that make the "Dark Continent" look that much darker and that much more hopeless as well. To be sure, there are exceptions to every rule, but the vast majority of films that reach a Western audience will be intent on highlighting some human rights tragedy.

Manohla Dargis (2007) of the *New York Times* has described a certain fatigue the viewer is sure to experience from all the harrowing images of Africa now being shown at the local Cineplex, and she asks why and for whom such films are made. Her answer is that they are made because they are "important," and they make those who make these films, not to mention those who star in them, "important" people. She slyly writes: "Most American films about Africa mean well, at least those without Bruce Willis,[2] and even openly commercial studio fare like *Blood Diamond* wears its bleeding, thudding heart on its sleeve. But what, exactly, are we meant to do with all their images, I wonder?"

Dargis continues: "It is exhausting having your conscience pricked so regularly. It may also be counterproductive to the stated aims of the people who make these films. It's an article of faith that social-issue movies are worthwhile, important, even brave, as people in Hollywood like to insist. But it is naïve to think that these films, including a fair share of the documentaries, are being made on behalf of Africa and its people; they are made for us."

In her view, such films ultimately provide little more than an evening's entertainment, although they might also help Western viewers think outside the box for a few short hours. Dargis describes these films as being little more than a "balm for our media-saturated fatigued hearts and minds" rather than serving to aid Africa or Africans. But even more damning, she believes that such films may actually work to shield us (meaning Western audiences) from the "chilling world that is outside."

In a similar vein, although he was not writing about film as such, African scholar Makau Mutua (2001) condemns much of human rights scholarship because it is based on a simplistic (and racist) Savages-Victims-Saviors (SVS) metaphor. *Savages* are invariably dark-skinned people outside the bounds of civilization. The *Victims* are also dark-skinned but are invariably portrayed as passive and helpless. Finally, the *Saviors* are white Westerners waving the banner of the United Nations and the body of international human rights law.

The storyline of the thriller *Tears of the Sun* (2003, Antoine Fuqua, USA), for instance, involves Bruce Willis (nicknamed LT) as the head of a Special Forces unit and his battle-hardened crew: Slo, Zee, Red, Lake, Doc, and a few other soldiers with equally silly-sounding nicknames all intended to show the camaraderie of the unit. Their assignment is to rescue Dr. Lena Kendricks (Monica Bellucci), who is working in an area of Nigeria about to be taken over by a group of rebels (Savages). There are plenty of (long) shots of villagers (Victims), usually with missing limbs or scars on their skulls. At first, the (Savior) crew rescues only Kendricks, but LT has a change of heart (what a surprise!) and decides to do the "right" thing and to evacuate the rest of the village. In the process, he and his force of about twelve men take on a guerrilla force that seems to measure in the thousands. Needless to say, LT and his men lead the refugees and the good doctor to safety. The film closes with wildly cheering Africans who all claim that they will never forget what LT and his brave men have done for them.

The more commercially successful *Black Hawk Down* (2001, Ridley Scott, USA / UK) is based on a real event during the 1992–93 humanitarian crisis in Somalia where upward of three hundred thousand people died of starvation. The story told in the film occurs over the course of less than a day. A small force of US troops has entered Somalia with the mission of capturing or killing the brutal

Somali warlord Mohammed Farrar Aidid whose militia is seizing international food shipments and attacking Red Cross distribution centers. The man in charge of this operation is General Garrison (Sam Shepard), who makes General Custer seem like a military genius. After "intel" locates Aidid, the rough-and-tumble soldiers go into action, all the while maintaining the Savior stereotype they had been assigned from the outset of the film. But what is most interesting is the depiction of Africans. As in *Tears of the Sun*, you cannot imagine how many of them there are, particularly when compared to the rather puny force of American soldiers. With two minor exceptions, they remain nameless, and all seem to have gone for the do-rag look. They repeatedly walk right into barrages of bullets, suggesting that life means little to them. What is surprising is that the Victims are virtually nowhere to be found until a brief and rather bizarre scene near the end of the film: as the Saviors are able to escape from danger and run for safety, a small group of bystanders cheers them on—the first Africans in the film who are not shooting at them.

In this way, many Western films on Africa, including those that take up human rights issues, perpetuate some of the core paternalistic tropes that were forwarded by the imperial powers to justify the idea of the "White Man's Burden." Today the so-called "civilizing mission" has been replaced by a "rescuing mission," and the white Savior has taken the place of colonial archetypes like the Great White Hunter or the equally great white doctor, missionary, or district commissioner. Yet somehow Dr. Livingstone's conviction that it is "on the Anglo-American race that the hopes of the world for liberty and progress rest" (in Pieterse 1992, 65) still seems to sustain most of these essentially Eurocentric films. While some of them are probably not intended as anything but plain entertainment fare set in a continent "known" for its many dangers and conflicts, others appear to be guided by liberal good intentions. But, as Ella Shohat and Robert Stam point out, "Media liberalism . . . does not allow subaltern communities to play prominent self-determining roles, a refusal homologous to liberal distaste for non-mediated self-assertion in the political realm" (1994, 206).

Against this background, it is of course crucial that African filmmakers present their own visions of, dreams for, and critiques of Africa, and their own views on human rights. This is not to say that non-African filmmakers should be prohibited from addressing human rights issues in an African context. If it is indisputable that human rights violations should be disclosed wherever they occur, then Western filmmakers should use their much better funding opportunities and in general much easier access to producing films to do so. In addition, well-funded Western films stand a considerably better chance of reaching Western audiences, and, especially in those cases where the human rights abuses result from international policies, this is not unimportant.

The best way forward is not clear for such films. Although much of what Westerners view and read about human rights and Africa is simplistic, racist, and self-serving, ignoring atrocities is certainly not the answer either. Perhaps the key is to not moralize and to not portray matters in such black-and-white terms (literally). More balanced human rights–based films include Forest Whitaker's stunning portrayal of the genocidal Idi Amin in *The Last King of Scotland* (2006, Kevin Macdonald, UK / Germany), or Idris Elba's mesmerizing performance as a cruel warlord in *Beasts of No Nation* (2015, Cary Joji Fukunaga, USA). And evil is not restricted by color, as is perhaps best evidenced by Nicolas Cage's maniacal portrayal of Yuri Orlov in *Lord of War* (2005, Andrew Niccol, USA / Germany / France). The reader might recall the opening of the film where Cage / Orlov casually informs the audience that one in twelve people on the planet owns a weapon—and that his goal is to sell arms to the other eleven, although he seems to concentrate most of his efforts where they are needed least: Africa.

What follows is an analysis of a number of films that address Africa from a human rights perspective, grouped according to general subject matter. Some of them are made by African filmmakers and some by Westerners, but as a general rule they are far less familiar to Western audiences than the SVS Hollywood matrix described above. I present this analysis with an acknowledgment that the focus of my scholarship is neither Western nor African cinema. I am a human rights scholar, and my main interest is in films that deal with human rights issues, either directly or indirectly. When teaching human rights, I now base my courses around film. For most Americans, including college students, abuses of human rights invoke a theoretical stance—we tend to view them as what I refer to as "distant horribles." Film helps break through this protective veneer. The aim here is not to confront the viewer but to help make students aware that human rights work is, above all else, about protecting human beings. Thus, I look for films that are intelligent, provocative, balanced, and meaningful (Gibney 2014). Fortunately, there are a number of outstanding films on Africa that achieve these standards, and we now turn to these.

Colonialism

Given colonialism's enormous importance in terms of the development of Africa (Ferguson 2011)—or the continent's lack of development (Rodney 1974), depending on one's point of view—it is surprising that there are not more films that deal directly with this issue. One explanation, of course, is that today's "Saviors" would not respond well to their depiction as "Savages."

Although there is a relative dearth of films on colonialism, there are some standouts. First among these is *La battaglia di Algeri* (*The Battle of Algiers*, 1966, Gillo Pontecorvo, Italy / Algeria). This faux documentary on the Algerian independence movement is notable for its depiction of colonialism from the perspective of the Algerians and not as a vehicle to show Europeans enjoying the colonial experience. One of the most unsettling aspects of watching this film now is that the audience is allied squarely behind those who would be considered "terrorists" under the present definition of the term. Perhaps it is not appropriate to speak for others on this matter, but I felt absolutely no qualms when the revolutionaries purposely targeted French civilians in the film. They were, after all, part of the cruel and oppressive colonial enterprise. In contrast, the scenes of torture of the Algerians leave an indelible mark on all those who watch this film. As disturbing as the still photos of Abu Ghraib are, they still do not fully capture the barbarous nature of these practices. The torture scenes from *The Battle of Algiers* do.

Indigènes (*Days of Glory*, 2006, Rachid Bouchareb, Algeria / France / Morocco / Belgium) is a feature film depicting France's call to arms of its colonial soldiers after the country fell to the Germans in World War II. These volunteers faced systematic racism, or worse, as they were repeatedly sent out on the most dangerous missions and treated as whatever the French term for "cannon fodder" happens to be. There is a nice scene at the end of the film when the townspeople of a liberated village acknowledge the bravery of these men in ways that French military officials were simply not capable of. In the epilogue the viewer learns (and is by no means surprised) that the raw racism depicted in the film continued for decades thereafter in the form of pensions to the colonial soldiers that were substantially less than those given to "French" soldiers. However, on a positive note, the film did serve as a catalyst in finally changing this racist policy.

The World War II experience in Francophone Africa has also been explored in two powerful films directed by the Senegalese filmmaker Ousmane Sembène. *Emitaï* (1971, Senegal) opens by showing how service in the French military was anything but voluntary. Rather, all the young men in the village are kidnapped and sent off to fight, first for Vichy France and later for the de Gaulle–led government. But the cruelties of the colonial authorities extend even further when a rice tax is imposed on each African household, purportedly as a way of feeding these conscripts. The women in the village refuse to comply and are held captive. In the face of this show of force, the men eventually capitulate. However, nothing prepares the viewer for the final scene where those who have peacefully delivered the tax tribute are slaughtered.

Camp de Thiaroye (1988, Senegal / Algeria / Tunisia) relates the experiences of a group of soldiers who survived the horrors of the war and are now back on African soil, about to be decommissioned. They find that the makeshift camp where they are being housed is a cross between a prisoner-of-war camp and a concentration camp. They also find that nearly all of the white officers will cheat them and, later, brutally murder those who dare to stand up for the rights these soldiers believed they had fought for.

Figure 1.1. After having fought for France in World War II, Senegalese tirailleurs are placed in a detention camp by the French army. Framegrab from *Camp de Thiaroye* (1988, Ousmane Sembène, Senegal / Algeria / Tunisia).

It is not easy to categorize the documentary *Om våld* (*Concerning Violence*, 2014, Göran Olsson, Sweden). The film uses a series of quotes from Frantz Fanon's essay of this name, dramatically read by Lauryn Hill and combined with a montage of old video footage. These film scenes range from a well-meaning Swedish couple setting up their ministry in some small African village, to labor leaders at a mine who are summarily dismissed for their union activities, to French troops who indiscriminately kill both wildlife and African citizens alike. By the standards of today, these are all disturbing images. But what is most disturbing is how "white privilege" is so blithely assumed throughout the film.

Another outstanding documentary is *We Come as Friends* (2014, Hubert Sauper, France / Austria), which uses the bloody creation of the new state of South Sudan as a way of exploring the horrors of colonialism and the manner in which they still afflict much of the African continent. The Global North was and is certainly greatly enriched by colonialism. And for Africans? As pointed out in the film, they were taught how to march in military formation, how to shoot a rifle, and how to perform dangerous and backbreaking work. Meanwhile, many in South Sudan and elsewhere are forced to live in environmental hellholes that are the natural aftermath of the rape of the continent's resources.

Another successful effort is the feature film *The First Grader* (2010, Justin Chadwick, UK / USA / Kenya), based on the true story of a former Mau Mau rebel who had fought against British colonialization in Kenya in the 1950s, a fight that eventually led to the country's independence. Decades later, at the age of eighty-four, Maruge became the oldest grammar-school student in the world. The film reminds the viewer, not to mention Kenyan society itself, of the enormous sacrifice and bravery of these anticolonialists.

Heritage Africa (1989, Kwaw Ansah, Ghana) is marred by over-the-top acting and a simplistic plot, but what does ring true is its depiction of how colonialization perpetuated itself by selecting the most talented of the local population and brainwashing this elite in such a way that they became the staunchest defenders of the status quo. *Sambizanga* (1972, Sarah Maldoror, Angola / France) provides a small window into the cruel practices of Portugal's rule in Angola. The story revolves around the plight of Domingos, an illiterate worker who is arrested and later killed by the authorities as his long-suffering wife tries to learn of his whereabouts. Once again, many of the atrocities are carried out by locals whose only avenue for advancement is to do the dirty work of the colonial power.

Lumumba (2000, Raoul Peck, France / Belgium / Germany / Haiti) presents the story of the tragic assassination of Patrice Lumumba a short time after the Belgian Congo achieved independence. Lumumba was the country's first prime minister, but his time in office was short-lived. African independence is one thing, but as this story shows, it was to be done on the terms of the colonial power. Lumumba was thought to have socialist tendencies, and for that reason he was eliminated in a plot directed by Belgian and American interests. What followed is reason enough to return to this story: decades of corruption and brutality, which continue to this day.

A nice companion piece is *King Leopold's Ghost* (2006, Pippa Scott and Oreet Rees, USA), based on the outstanding book with the same name by Adam Hochschild (1998). *King Leopold's Ghost* goes further back into the history of the Congo, into the brutal rule of King Leopold of Belgium when upward of ten million Africans were killed and many more times that dismembered. Much to its credit, the documentary brings the tragic history to the present time by showing how the killing has continued unabated in the decades since Lumumba's assassination.

Xala (1975, Senegal) is certainly not Ousmane Sembène's best film. However, many of the early scenes capture colonialism perfectly. The movie opens on the day of national independence. The country's black leaders march into the offices of the soon-to-be-deposed white officials and make a great display of throwing them out. But it is not long before the whites come back, now with briefcases full of cash, and for all intents and purposes, they are back in charge. Except for skin color, the new order is no different from the old order, and it is not even clear that there is any new order as such.

Finally, let me close this section by mentioning two excellent films that take up the issue of colonialism from the more personal level. The first is *Chocolat* (1988, Claire Denis, France / West Germany / Cameroon). In this film a white woman reflects back on her experience growing up in a colonial household in rural Cameroon. What drives the story is the emergency landing of an aircraft with a group of colonialists aboard who are now forced to stay with the young girl's family. I will not attempt to more fully summarize the plot. However, the moral of the story is simple enough: never trust white people, especially the "nice" ones.

The second is *La noire de . . .* (*Black Girl*, 1966, Ousmane Sembène, Senegal / France). The plot itself is quite simple. A young Senegalese girl (Diouana) arrives in Antibes, France, to work for the white French couple she previously had worked for in Senegal. However, she immediately senses something dramatically wrong. For one thing, although she was hired to be a nanny, their young son is nowhere to be found, at least initially. Moreover, the couple, particularly the wife, harass Diouana mercilessly. Although they had promised that she would be exposed to France in all its glories, Diouana is little more than an indentured servant, or worse, a novelty to show off to their friends. Once a colonialist, always a colonialist.

Poverty

I am of the opinion that *Darwin's Nightmare* (2004, Hubert Sauper, Austria / Belgium / France / Germany) is one of the greatest films ever made. The documentary takes place entirely in an impoverished village in Tanzania on the shores of Lake Victoria. There are no talking heads; and the story unfolds slowly. The local inhabitants are in the business of catching Nile perch and selling them to a fish processing firm from India. The fish are fileted and frozen and then sent on airplanes bound for the shops and restaurants of Europe. However, it is not clear how long this will continue because the Nile perch, which is not indigenous to Lake Victoria, is eating all of the other species of fish, thus killing the lake itself.

Due to their extreme poverty, the villagers are not able to afford to eat the fish they have caught. Rather, they live on fish entrails, and the scenes of the maggot-filled cauldrons where fish skeletons are cooked are not for the faint of heart. The viewer also comes to know through radio reports overheard in the background that Tanzania is experiencing a famine that might claim up to two million lives. This, however, does not put a halt to the fish-selling business. As the film progresses, the viewer comes to realize that these planes are not arriving from Europe empty, as so many people claim. Instead, each one is stocked with advanced weaponry that will fuel the various civil conflicts in the African continent. In sum, a country experiencing a famine is sending food out while importing arms. All of the trade ministers—European and African alike—seem quite pleased with this arrangement, but the viewer's eye and attention cannot leave the desperate street children. In what way have they benefited?

An equally impressive film is *Bamako* (2006, Abderrahmane Sissako, Mali / USA / France). This leisurely but angry film takes place in the middle of a small village in the capital city of Mali. In a local courtyard, laundry is done, food is

Figure 1.2. Poor Tanzanian fishermen loading Nile perch for Europe while the villagers themselves are starving. Framegrab from *Darwin's Nightmare* (2004, Hubert Sauper, Austria / Belgium / France / Germany).

cooked, and young children run all about unattended. What the viewer sees— but only if the viewer wishes to see it—is an Africa that Western audiences almost never are exposed to: life without violence or famine. Yet all is not what it seems to be. In the middle of this sleepy African village, a trial against the International Monetary Fund and the World Bank is being carried out. Both institutions are accused of perpetuating poverty rather than taking measures to alleviate it, and the arguments against these international financial institutions are quite damning. *Bamako* is an extraordinarily thought-provoking film, one that might be contrasted with the documentary *The End of Poverty?* (2008, Philippe Diaz, USA), narrated by a shrill Martin Sheen and populated with any number of important-sounding talking heads espousing all kinds of pseudo-Marxist dogma.

Worth mentioning also is *Hyènes* (*Hyenas*, 1992, Djibril Diop Mambéty, Senegal), which relies on metaphor to depict the selling out of African populations. In this scenario, the (post-)colonial powers do not need to apply any kind of force. Rather, the local Africans readily and greedily go after the small crumbs that international institutions are willing to give them, which only serves to keep the population distracted and suppressed.

AIDS

The African continent has been devastated by AIDS. Two films that deal with the topic intelligently but also poignantly are *Yesterday* (2004, Darrell Roodt, South

Africa) and *Life, Above All* (2010, Oliver Schmitz, South Africa / Germany). The former tells the story of a woman whose husband has contracted AIDS. When he returns home, the entire village is fearful that they will also become infected, and they insist that he no longer live there. Yesterday, his wife, proceeds to build a makeshift hospice for him just outside the village, and he dies there. However, Yesterday then discovers that her husband has passed the disease along to her, and she understands that this is her death sentence. Her biggest concern is the caretaking and the education of her daughter. But at this point things come full circle: schoolteachers she befriended in the film's opening scene promise Yesterday that they will dedicate themselves to this task.

Life, Above All is another deeply moving feature film on the AIDS crisis, particularly the shame associated with HIV infection and the enormous efforts that families will go through to hide the disease. In this story, Chanda, a twelve-year-old girl, hears rumors that her mother has gone away because she has AIDS. She then goes to bring her home, and the confrontation that ensues with the neighbors who oppose this is truly a classic.

Children

Nongovernmental organizations learned a long time ago that the best way to grab the public's sympathy on an issue is to focus on the plight of children. A recent example of this phenomenon is the critically acclaimed Netflix original *Beasts of No Nation* (2015, Cary Joji Fukunaga, USA), which tells a nightmarish tale of child soldiers. *Soldier Child* (1998, Neil Abramson, USA) is a documentary that focuses on the efforts to rehabilitate these devastated children who have grown accustomed to carrying out all kinds of atrocities in the bush. Although the film is workmanlike in its approach, what the viewer witnesses is the difficult struggle these children are put through to essentially be children once again.

Invisible Children (2006, Carol Mansour, Lebanon) begins like an African version of *Bill and Ted's Excellent Adventure* (1989, Stephen Herek, USA), where the viewer is introduced to a small group of clueless American college students who seem intent on nothing more than having an "African adventure." However, the documentary soon turns into a serious and probing portrayal of how young children in northern Uganda are making every effort to remain out of the clutches of the Lord's Resistance Army (LRA). In the nighttime scenes, the town's young people seek sanctuary any place they can find it and end up literally sleeping on top of one another, readily bringing to mind depictions of living conditions on slave ships. Far less successful was *Kony 2012* (2012, Jason Russell, USA), the follow-up project to *Invisible Children* that sought to create a worldwide effort to have Joseph Kony, the leader of the LRA, arrested and in custody by the end of 2012. The problem is that by soliciting people to sign up to participate in this effort—and sending them a Kony 2012 hat and a Kony 2012 bracelet and whatnot for their "efforts"—this human rights movement took on the worst aspects of telemarketing. And let it also be pointed out that Joseph Kony remains free.

It is difficult not to be fully absorbed by *War / Dance* (2007, Sean Fine and Andrea Nix, USA), a documentary shot mainly in Uganda's war zone, which uses as a backdrop the country's national musical competition. The story focuses on three youngsters, all of whom have a harrowing story to tell about the LRA. But what drives the film is the dedication to music, which results in the youngsters' first trip to the capital city. I will not give the ending away, but let it be said that the viewer witnesses a joy that these children might well be experiencing for the first (and perhaps only) time in their lives.

ABC Africa (2001, Abbas Kiarostami, Iran) is a rather straightforward account of the kinds of poverty experienced by so many children on the African continent. What keeps the documentary from falling into pathos is the exuberance of the children and their constant mugging in front of the camera. These children need food, they need an education, they need adequate housing, they need health care—but perhaps the most startling and effective aspect of the film is the shared humanity. These are, above all else, just like our children. I would go even further and say that under the International Covenant on Economic, Social and Cultural Rights, which mandates that all states parties engage in "international assistance and cooperation," these truly are our children.

Repression, Oppression, and Corruption

As mentioned at the outset, most of the films on Africa that reach a Western audience deal with repression, oppression, and corruption in some way. Thus, the lawless gem trade and its relationship to Africa's civil wars were the focus of the Leonardo DiCaprio project *Blood Diamond*. How much truth there is in the plotline in *The Last King of Scotland* is debatable. However, what is not debatable is Forest Whitaker's incredible portrayal of the murderous Idi Amin. An equally bizarre film is the documentary *Général Idi Amin Dada: Autoportrait* (*General Idi Amin Dada: A Self Portrait*, 1974, Barbet Schroeder, France / Switzerland), where the viewer gets to see the "real" Idi Amin in all his sociopathy.

A much different and quieter form of oppression is shown in *Timbuktu* (2014, France / Mauritania), a feature film directed by Abderrahmane Sissako and set in a small town in Mali that has come under the rule of Muslim fundamentalists. Not much happens in the village, but that is exactly the point: the "life" of the village has been choked away by rules, regulations, and all manner of religious edicts. The title of the documentary *Al midan* (*The Square*, 2013, Jehane Noujaim Egypt / USA / UK) refers to Tahrir Square in Cairo, which was the central meeting place for those opposing the Mubarak dictatorship and later the oppressive (and short-lived) rule of the Muslim Brotherhood.

The insightful documentary *Big Men* (2013, Rachel Boynton, UK / Denmark / USA) tells the story of the massive levels of corruption in Nigeria and the manner in which the country's oil reserves have actually retarded economic growth. Of course, it takes two parties to engage in corruption, and what the viewer sees here are Western concerns that are more than willing to do business with anyone and everyone—as long as the price is high enough. One of the more interesting aspects of this film involves the pirates in their small boats who literally dip into the oil supply lines. They do so for private gain—Robin Hood has not yet appeared in the Delta region—but it is encouraging to see citizens who are not passive in the face of the government's kleptocracy.

The short documentary *Fuelling Poverty* (2012, Ishaya Bako, Nigeria) concerns itself with the government fuel subsidy in Nigeria that was originally scheduled to last for only six months but that has now been in place for decades, lining the pockets of the ruling elite. When the Nigerian people staged protests throughout the country in the early part of this decade, the subsidy was temporarily removed, but the cost of everything—fuel in particular—went through the ceiling. Life is miserable with the subsidy, but the government will make life even more miserable if the people insist on its removal.

But the people of Nigeria persevere, and nowhere is this so gloriously shown as in *Finding Fela!* (2014, USA), an explosive documentary by Alex Gibney on the musician and social critic who was for so long a thorn in the side of the Nigerian ruling elite. The viewer witnesses a man who might easily have peacefully enjoyed all the trappings of success, but who risks all of this for a political cause. It is a cliché to say that the music alone is reason to watch *Finding Fela!*. Rather, it is the combination of the music, the politics, the stagecraft, and Fela's riveting personality that makes this such a compelling film. What also should be noted is that the play of this name had a long run on Broadway.

The titular character in *Le président* (*The President*, 2013, Jean-Pierre Bekolo, Cameroon / Germany) has been in power for forty-two years when he suddenly disappears, prompting the media in Cameroon to keep up their breathless coverage of this dictator. In a unique way, this feature film explores the corrupt world of a dictator who has lost all touch with the people. Unfortunately, even with his removal from the scene, it is by no means clear that life will get any better for the citizens of that country. Those who live by the sword will eventually die by the sword, although the real victims are those who remain mired in poverty and despair.

The thrilling documentary *The Ambassador* (2011, Mads Brügger, Denmark / Sweden) can best be described as Michael Moore meets James Bond. The setup is that the Danish journalist Mads Brügger poses as a businessman who, for a healthy sum of money, has obtained diplomatic papers allowing him to operate almost unfettered in Africa. Although he is white, Brügger's cover is that he is a Liberian diplomat who is interested in establishing a match industry in the Central African Republic (CAR). But his real prey is the country's diamonds, and there is no shortage of people both inside and outside of government who come forward to do business with him. It is easy to conclude that there is not a single person (aside from Brügger's two pygmy assistants) in either the CAR or Liberia who is not knee-deep in corruption or worse. But the corruption is by no means limited to Africans, as evidenced by the thousands of Europeans who hold similar diplomatic papers as Brügger does, all arranged by European companies.

Private Violence

Not all oppression comes at the hands of the government. *Born This Way* (2013, Shaun Kadlec and Deb Tullmann, USA / Cameroon) shows just a small slice of the hatred and danger faced by gays in Cameroon. The Cameroon government has a responsibility to protect individuals from private violence, and, as is evident in this film, it has failed miserably in this task. Yet the viewer retains some hope from the manner in which the LBGTQ community bands together. *Call Me Kuchu* (2012, Katherine Fairfax Wright and Malika Zouhali-Worrall, USA / Uganda) tells a similar story in Uganda against a backdrop of proposed legislation that would make engaging in homosexual acts punishable by death. The opposition is led by the indomitable David Kato, an openly gay man, who by involving himself in this political struggle literally puts his life on the line. The bravery of the LBGTQ community is matched only by the brutality of the other side.

In the Shadow of the Sun (2012, Harry Freeland, UK / USA) shows the terrible danger facing albinos in Tanzania. The documentary tells the story of two people. One is Josephat Torner, a middle-aged albino man who decides to confront the violence head-on by traveling to villages throughout the country and speaking to assembled masses, nearly all of whom believe that the bones of an albino will provide them with eternal life. This certainly has overtones of Daniel in the lion's den, only in this case there are literally hundreds of would-be "lions." Still, Josephat thrusts himself into danger as he calmly and convincingly shows his hostile audience that, skin color apart, he is the same as they are. In the end, Josephat decides to bring his awareness campaign to new heights, literally, when he embarks on a trip to climb Mount Kilimanjaro. The other story involves Vedastus, a teenage boy who wants nothing more than to go to school but who is excluded because he is albino. The boy's loneliness is made that much worse after his mother dies of AIDS, but he finally gets the opportunity that should not be denied to anyone.

Female genital mutilation (FGM) is one of the great scourges of Africa. *Finzan* (1989, Cheick Oumar Sissoko, Mali) is an older film that deals with this issue, but the acting in the film is of poor quality, and the story line one-dimensional.

A vastly better cinematic portrayal of the issue can be found in the feature film *Moolaadé* (2004, Ousmane Sembène, Senegal / Burkina Faso / Morocco / Tunisia / Cameroon / France). The story line is straightforward. Four young girls who are about to be "circumcised" beg one of the mothers of the village for protection— or moolaadé. This throws both village life and family life into turmoil. After all, the argument goes, this is a long-standing tradition, and no man would want to marry a woman who had not undergone the procedure. Although Sembène's sympathies are quite obvious, the subject is treated in an intelligent and sympathetic fashion. *Mrs. Goundo's Daughter* (2009, Barbara Attie and Janet Goldwater, USA) is an intriguing documentary dealing with FGM. The daughter in the title is just a few months old and never utters a line, but still, she is the point of attention (and contention) as her mother files an asylum claim in the United States in an attempt to ensure that her child will never be sent back to Western Africa to face FGM.

War

War is certainly no stranger to the African continent, although except for the seemingly never-ending conflict in the Democratic Republic of the Congo, in nearly every instance what we are speaking about is civil war and not a war between states. For whatever reason, including systematic racism, only two wars have received much attention in the West. The first involves the atrocities in the Darfur region of the Sudan. The other is the 1994 genocide in Rwanda.

The Devil Came on Horseback (2007, Ricki Stern and Anne Sundberg, USA) is a documentary about how the conflict in Darfur came to worldwide attention in the first place. It centers on Brian Steidle, formerly a soldier in the US military who was serving as a peacekeeper in the Sudan. Steidle not only personally witnessed the massive atrocities in Darfur but also happened to take a number of pictures of these events. When Steidle returned to the United States, he showed many of these images to family and friends—and soon thereafter, Steidle became something of an international celebrity. As ironic as this might sound, it was only after a white American showed visual images of the atrocities that Darfur entered into the popular lexicon.

Darfur Now (2007, Ted Braun, USA) brings the star power of Don Cheadle and George Clooney. The documentary uses several intersecting stories, but the organizing theme is that in 2004 the United States recognized that genocide was taking place in the Sudan—and yet did nothing about this. A separate subgenre involves the so-called Lost Boys of the Sudan, a group of adolescent refugees who escaped from the Sudan in the 1980s and then spent upward of a decade warehoused in a refugee camp in Uganda as the fighting between the Arab north and the African south dragged on. The only reason they are well-known is that several thousand were admitted to the United States as refugees. *Lost Boys of*

Sudan (2003, Megan Mylan and Jon Shenk, USA) could have limited itself to the collision of the Old and New Worlds, and there is some of this, at least at the outset of the film. However, the movie morphs into a poignant portrayal of the struggles of two young Sudanese men who are desperately trying to make a go of it in the United States.

Sierra Leone's Refugee All Stars (2005, Zach Niles and Banker White, USA) is one of the more uplifting films you will find on the ravages and displacements of war. This documentary tells the story of a group of musicians who form a now world-renowned band while in a refugee camp in western Africa. At the end of the film they return home, and where there had been brutality there is now peace. The music itself is fantastic. Yet the part of the story I found most instructive concerns the one musician who simply cannot go back to Sierra Leone. It was there that rebels forced him to crush the skull of his newborn child, and this one, quiet scene reminds the viewer of the ravages of war. Other documentaries do this more directly. *Lumo* (2007, Bent-Jorgen Perlmutt and Nelson Walker III, USA / Congo) and *The Greatest Silence: Rape in the Congo* (2007, Lisa F. Jackson, USA) show us the horrors of rape in wartime.

Two films that provide at least some measure of hope are *Pushing the Elephant* (2010, Beth Davenport and Elizabeth Mandel, USA) and *Pray the Devil Back to Hell* (2008, Gini Reticker, USA). The former tells the story of Rose Mapendo, who with nine of her ten children was able to escape the Democratic Republic of the Congo (DRC) and make a new life in the United States. Her daughter, Nangabire, was in a different part of the DRC when the family fled, and the film tells the story of their eventual reunification. The title comes from Rose's description of seeking peace in the DRC as "pushing an elephant," and as the continuing conflict shows, this might be a gross understatement. But the documentary is not just a feel-good story of a sister reuniting with a family that has become completely American- ized. Rather, the film also highlights Rose's enormous courage in returning to the DRC and her tireless efforts to see if, somehow, she can get the elephant to move.

Pray the Devil Back to Hell is Girl Power to the extreme. The documentary tells the amazing story of a group of women from Liberia who decide that after years of warfare, they have had enough. They essentially crash the peace negotia- tions between the Liberian government and rebel groups—a peace process that was going nowhere, fast—and they refuse to allow the men involved in the pro- cess to leave until peace is achieved. It is an incredible story of grit, patience, and supreme determination.

As mentioned before, except for the Darfur crisis, most of the warfare in Africa gets virtually no attention in films that reach Western audiences. The other exception to this is the 1994 genocide in Rwanda, where an estimated eight hundred thousand people were killed in a span of one hundred days. Most people are familiar with *Hotel Rwanda*, which I referred to earlier. The film stars Don

Cheadle as Paul Rusesabagina, a hotel manager. Rusesabagina is a Hutu, and his wife is a Tutsi. Until the genocide broke out, intermarriages such as theirs had been possible, despite the division between the majority Hutu population and the minority Tutsi population. However, when the killing began, all moderate Hutus and every single Tutsi were targeted for extermination. In the midst of this incredible genocide, the film shows us some of the best in human nature as Rusesabagina does everything in his power to protect Tutsi and Hutu alike.

Sometimes in April (2005, Raoul Peck, France / USA / Rwanda) looks at the Rwandan genocide from an African perspective. The plot revolves around two brothers. One is Honoré Butera, who works for Radio Television Libre des Mille Collines, which became infamous due to the incendiary messages it broadcast likening Tutsis to "cockroaches." The other brother is Augustin Muganza, a captain in the Rwandan army who is married to a Tutsi woman with whom he has two sons.

There is a host of documentaries on the Rwandan genocide, but of particular note is *Shake Hands with the Devil* (2007, Roger Spottiswoode, Canada), which focuses on Romeo Dallaire, the UN commander in Rwanda before and during the genocide. The film uses the ten-year anniversary of the genocide—the first time Dallaire returned to Rwanda—to reflect on how Western governments and the United Nations itself abandoned the Rwandan people.

South Africa

There have been a number of outstanding films on the apartheid regime in South Africa. *Cry, the Beloved Country* (Zoltan Korda, UK) was released in 1951, a short time after apartheid became official state policy; the seeds of separation and the subsequent oppression of blacks are evident even then. *Cry Freedom* (1987, Richard Attenborough, UK) and *A Dry White Season* (1989, Euzhan Palcy, USA) are excellent feature films, both with all-star casts. The former film stars Denzel Washington, whose intelligence and charm bring Stephen Biko to life. Kevin Kline plays Donald Woods, a newspaper editor who, like seemingly all whites in South Africa at that time, cannot conceive that the government is capable of the kinds of cruelties that Biko assures him take place. However, after Biko invites Woods to visit him in a township so he can observe conditions firsthand, Woods becomes a changed man. Perhaps the most dramatic moment in the film is a courtroom scene where Biko makes the presiding judge look like nothing more than an apologist for the apartheid regime. The authorities see Biko as a threat to their well-being—and in that, they are correct—and he is beaten and killed. Woods then attempts to bring this to light, but at this point he is viewed as an enemy of the government, and, most certainly, a traitor to his race. One of the most effective aspects of the film is in the closing credits where the names of those who fought against apartheid and were killed while in police custody are shown. The list seems to go on forever.

A Dry White Season stars Donald Sutherland as Ben du Toit, a headmaster at a school, who, like many whites, would consider himself a "liberal." And like many liberals, he inherently trusts the government, and he refuses to believe that there is no good reason why the son of one of the groundskeepers at the school has been arrested. Believing that there is some unfortunate mix-up, du Toit makes some inquiries, which only makes matters worse. But in doing this, he begins to see some of the injustices that have been around him his whole life.

There are two spectacular scenes in the film. One involves a confrontation between du Toit and his wife where she tells him that his affiliation with black Africans has to stop and that he needs to realize that whites have to stick together. She eventually leaves him. The other is a courtroom scene where Marlon Brando, playing an antiapartheid attorney, completely exposes the cruelties and hypocrisy of the apartheid regime, but to no avail—just as he had told du Toit would occur.

On the surface, *District 9* (2009, Neill Blomkamp, South Africa / USA / New Zealand / Canada) has nothing to do with race. Rather, the film pretends to be about extraterrestrial beings living in extreme poverty in an isolated outpost in South Africa called District 9. Of course, the film has everything to do with race and the country's apartheid system. But the film also beautifully explores what it means to be a human being and how perceived differences between "us" and "them"—in this instance between humans and prawns—are simply social constructs.

There are also any number of documentaries on South Africa under apartheid. *Long Night's Journey into Day* (2000, Deborah Hoffmann and Frances Reid, USA) explores the country's Truth and Reconciliation Commission (TRC). The film uses four different stories to explore the relationship—but also the tension—between social progress and justice. As a general rule, the TRC process prioritized the former in the sense that virtually all political crimes would be amnestied if the perpetrator came forward and told the truth—no matter how gruesome and cruel these practices happened to be.

One of the themes repeatedly shown in the film is the enormous contrast between rich and poor—and white and black. Without explicitly saying so, these scenes could be read to say that white South Africans have made out well. Yes, whites no longer run the government as they did under apartheid; but otherwise little has changed for them. Most still live in magnificent homes, and they still remain the economic elite of the country. The lack of postapartheid advancement for blacks is taken up directly in the documentary *Dear Mandela* (2012, Dara Kell and Christopher Nizza, South Africa / USA), which uses the country's continuing housing crisis to explore how little South Africa has changed. The new South African Constitution is the most progressive in the world in the sense that it guarantees economic, social, and cultural rights—including the right to housing. However, as this fine documentary shows, the reality is very different.

Amandla! A Revolution in Four Part Harmony (2002, Lee Hirsch, South Africa / USA) is a moving (and melodious) tribute to the role that music and later marching played in the fight against apartheid. The scenes with former revolutionaries excitedly breaking into song are certainly inspiring to witness. But the film also shows the manner in which politics can never be isolated from the social life of a country.

We will close this section with two films on Nelson Mandela. *Mandela: Long Walk to Freedom* (2013, Justin Chadwick, UK / South Africa) stars the incredible Idris Elba, who plays Mandela from his early twenties, when he was a swaggering lawyer, to the day he assumes the presidency of the new South Africa. There is not much physical resemblance between Elba and Mandela, but that simply does not matter. In this wonderful performance, you can begin to understand how and why Nelson Mandela was such a magnetic and revolutionary force.

Invictus (2009, Clint Eastwood, USA) might be written off as nothing but a "sports" film, but it is far more noteworthy than that. Mandela is played by Morgan Freeman in a role that he seems born for. The story line involves the Rugby World Cup, which is being hosted in postapartheid South Africa. Rugby is considered to be a sport for whites, while soccer (or football) is the game that blacks play. Recognizing this sharp racial divide, Mandela befriends Francois Pienaar (Matt Damon), the captain of the Springboks (the South African national team), and he convinces him of the political role that rugby can play in transforming the country. Based on true events, the film ends on an optimistic note when South Africa wins the World Cup by defeating the heavily favored All Blacks of New Zealand.

Justice

Earlier I mentioned the film *Bamako*, in which the World Bank and the International Monetary Fund are put on trial for their failure to alleviate the oppressive poverty in Africa. Unfortunately, such proceedings have never taken place. Nor has there been any justice for the Rwandan people against the Belgian government and other Western states for abandoning them in their hour of need. Nor will the French government ever be held to account for its corrupt practices in the Central African Republic, on full display in *The Ambassador*.

However, there has been some effort to bring justice to the African people. Perhaps the best example of this is the topic of *The Dictator Hunter* (2007, Klaartje Quirijns, Netherlands), which focuses on the long-standing international effort to prosecute the former dictator of Chad, Hissène Habré. Although the documentary ends on a rather pessimistic note, there have been some positive developments since then; most notably, in May 2016 Habré was given a life sentence by the Extraordinary African Chambers in Dakar, Senegal.

War Don Don (2010, Rebecca Richman Cohen, USA)—literally, the war is over—is a splendid piece of filmmaking on the proceedings of the Special Tribunal for Sierra Leone against Issa Sesay for war crimes and crimes against humanity. One of the more interesting aspects of the documentary is the way it shows the conflicted feelings of the people of this country. They certainly want to see justice done. However, they are also of one mind that the enormous amount of money being spent on these proceedings by the international community might better have been spent to alleviate the crushing poverty all around them.

Finally, *My Neighbor, My Killer* (2009, Anne Aghion, USA / France) allows the viewer to witness the informal so-called gacaca (i.e., "justice amongst the grass") proceedings in Rwanda where victims confront some of those who carried out genocide in 1994. In many instances what we see is neighbor confronting neighbor. The question is whether justice is being served. But perhaps the better question is whether justice for these atrocities would ever be possible.

Conclusion

The starting point for this chapter was a piece by the *New York Times* film critic Manohla Dargis entitled "Africa, at the Cineplex," which was critical of all the "important" movies on Africa that Hollywood has been turning out. In each of these films Africa is depicted as a dark and forbidding place. Or to quote LT, the character played by Bruce Willis in the dreadful *Tears of the Sun*, "God left Africa a long time ago."

The reality, of course, is not nearly as simplistic as it comes across in mainstream Hollywood fare. There are some great movies out there that take a much less black-and-white approach to human rights issues on the African continent. Some of them are made by Africans, some by Westerners, some are documentaries, some are feature films, but what the ones I have focused on here have in common is that, for the most part, they are provocative, intelligent, insightful, and accurate.

MARK GIBNEY is Belk Distinguished Professor in Humanities at the University of North Carolina–Asheville and was the inaugural Raoul Wallenberg Chair of Human Rights and Humanitarian Law at the Faculty of Law, Lund University. His most recent book is *International Human Rights Law: Returning to Universal Principles.*

Notes

1. The film came out long before Idris Elba became a megastar.
2. The Bruce Willis reference is to *Tears of the Sun* (USA 2003, dir. Antoine Fuqua), costarring Monica Bellucci.

Filmography

ABC Africa, 2001, Abbas Kiarostami, Iran.
Amandla! A Revolution in Four Part Harmony, 2002, Lee Hirsch, South Africa / USA.
The Ambassador, 2011, Mads Brügger, Denmark / Sweden.
Bamako, 2006, Abderrahmane Sissako, Mali / USA / France.
La battaglia di Algeri (*The Battle of Algiers*), 1966, Gillo Pontecorvo, Italy / Algeria.
Beasts of No Nation, 2015, Cary Joji Fukunaga, USA.
Big Men, 2013, Rachel Boynton, UK / Denmark / USA.
Bill and Ted's Excellent Adventure, 1989, Stephen Herek, USA.
Black Hawk Down, 2001, Ridley Scott, USA / UK.
Blood Diamond, 2006, Edward Zwick, USA / Germany 2006.
Born This Way, 2013, Shaun Kadlec and Deb Tullmann, USA / Cameroon.
Call Me Kuchu, 2012, Katherine Fairfax Wright and Malika Zouhali-Worrall, USA / Uganda.
Camp de Thiaroye, 1988, Ousmane Sembène and Thierno Faty Sow, Senegal / Algeria / Tunisia.
Chocolat, 1988, Claire Denis, France / West Germany / Cameroon.
The Constant Gardener, 2005, Fernando Meirelles, UK / Germany / USA / China.
Cry Freedom, 1987, Richard Attenborough, UK.
Cry, the Beloved Country, 1951, Zoltan Korda, UK.
Darfur Now, 2007, Ted Braun, USA.
Darwin's Nightmare, 2004, Hubert Sauper, Austria / Belgium / France / Germany.
Dear Mandela, 2012, Dara Kell and Christopher Nizza, South Africa / USA.
The Devil Came on Horseback, 2007, Ricki Stern and Anne Sundberg, USA.
The Dictator Hunter, 2007, Klaartje Quirijns, Netherlands.
District 9, 2009, Neill Blomkamp, South Africa / USA / New Zealand / Canada.
A Dry White Season, 1989, Euzhan Palcy, USA.
Emitaï, 1971, Ousmane Sembène, Senegal.
The End of Poverty?, 2008, Philippe Diaz, USA.
Finding Fela!, 2014, Alex Gibney, USA.
Finzan, 1989, Cheick Oumar Sissoko, Mali.
The First Grader, 2010, Justin Chadwick, UK / USA / Kenya.
Fuelling Poverty, 2012, Ishaya Bako, Nigeria.
Général Idi Amin Dada: Autoportrait (*General Idi Amin Dada: A Self Portrait*), 1974, Barbet Schroeder, France / Switzerland.
The Greatest Silence: Rape in the Congo, 2007, Lisa F. Jackson, USA.
Heritage Africa, 1989, Kwaw Ansah, Ghana.
Hotel Rwanda, 2004, Terry George, UK / South Africa / Italy.
Hyènes (*Hyenas*), 1992, Djibril Diop Mambéty, Senegal.
In the Shadow of the Sun, 2012, Harry Freeland, UK / USA.
Indigènes (*Days of Glory*), 2006, Rachid Bouchareb, Algeria / France / Morocco / Belgium.
Invictus, 2009, Clint Eastwood, USA.
Invisible Children, 2006, Carol Mansour, Lebanon.
King Leopold's Ghost, 2006, Pippa Scott and Oreet Rees, USA.
Kony 2012, 2012, Jason Russell, USA.
The Last King of Scotland, 2006, Kevin Macdonald, UK / Germany.
Life, Above All, 2010, Oliver Schmitz, South Africa / Germany.

Long Night's Journey into Day, 2000, Deborah Hoffmann and Frances Reid, USA.
Lord of War, 2005, Andrew Niccol, USA / Germany / France.
Lost Boys of Sudan, 2003, Megan Mylan and Jon Shenk, USA.
Lumo, 2007, Bent-Jorgen Perlmutt and Nelson Walker III, USA / Congo.
Lumumba, 2000, Raoul Peck, France / Belgium / Germany / Haiti.
Mandela: Long Walk to Freedom, 2013, Justin Chadwick, UK / South Africa.
Al midan (The Square), 2013, Jehane Noujaim, Egypt / USA / UK.
Moolaadé, 2004, Ousmane Sembène, Senegal / Burkina Faso / Morocco / Tunisia / Cameroon / France.
Mrs. Goundo's Daughter, 2009, Barbara Attie and Janet Goldwater, USA.
My Neighbor, My Killer, 2009, Anne Aghion, USA / France.
La noire de… (Black Girl), 1966, Ousmane Sembène, Senegal / France.
Om våld (Concerning Violence), 2014, Göran Olsson, Sweden.
Pray the Devil Back to Hell, 2008, Gini Reticker, USA.
Le président (The President), 2013, Jean-Pierre Bekolo, Cameroon / Germany.
Pushing the Elephant, 2010, Beth Davenport and Elizabeth Mandel, USA.
Sambizanga, 1972, Sarah Maldoror, Angola / France.
Shake Hands With the Devil, 2007, Roger Spottiswoode, Canada.
Sierra Leone's Refugee All Stars, 2005, Zach Niles and Banker White, USA.
Soldier Child, 1998, Neil Abramson, USA.
Sometimes in April, 2005, Raoul Peck, France / USA / Rwanda.
Tears of the Sun, 2003, Antoine Fuqua, USA.
Timbuktu, 2014, Abderrahmane Sissako, France / Mauritania.
War / Dance, 2007, Sean Fine and Andrea Nix, USA.
War Don Don, 2010, Rebecca Richman Cohen, USA.
We Come as Friends, 2014, Hubert Sauper, France / Austria.
Xala, 1975, Ousmane Sembène, Senegal.
Yesterday, 2004, Darrell Roodt, South Africa.

References

Dargis, Manohla. 2007. "Africa, at the Cineplex." *New York Times*, February 4.
Ferguson, Niall. 2011. *Civilization: The West and the Rest*. New York: Penguin Press.
Gibney, Mark. 2014. *Watching Human Rights: The 101 Best Films*. Boulder, CO: Paradigm Publishers.
Hochschild, Adam. 1998. *King Leopold's Ghost: A Story of Greed, Terror and Heroism in Colonial Africa*. Boston: Houghton Mifflin.
Mutua, Makau. 2001. "Savages, Victims, and Saviors: The Metaphor of Human Rights." *Harvard International Law Journal* 42: 201–45.
Pieterse, Jan Nederveen. 1992. *White on Black: Images of Africa and Blacks in Western Popular Culture*. New Haven, CT: Yale University Press.
Rodney, Walter. 1974. *How Europe Underdeveloped Africa*. Washington, DC: Howard University Press.
Shohat, Ella, and Robert Stam. 1994. *Unthinking Eurocentrism: Multiculturalism and the Media*. London: Routledge.

2 African Cinema

Perspective Correction

Rod Stoneman

We connect, and we separate, in expression of a right granted by our
humanity.

(McHugh 2011, 261)

Aғтεʀ а sεʀιεs of engagements with African filmmaking over quite a long
period, I think a key issue is the persistence of significant misperception and misunderstanding of Africa in the West linked to representation that has consistently
been imposed from outside. No matter how well-intentioned, Western perspectives often misconstrue the experience and perspective of other parts of the
world, once called "third," now called "developing," "the Global South," or simply
"the South." In fact, all these euphemisms work to contain the actual disparities
of power, prosperity, and life conditions between different places on the planet.
Europe and America tend to construct Africa as a place of disrepair and disorder
in order to grant themselves interpretive mastery over it.[1] In such a construction,
human rights advocacy can be deployed to play the role of moral rescuer.

Reflecting on diverse versions of African cinema that have emerged over the
last fifty years, it becomes clear that most films from Africa cut across American
and European expectations formulated in the Western image system. It is not
only the most obvious argumentations in socially engaged films that challenge
the self-righteous complacencies of the West. In diverse ways all versions of African filmmaking insist on differences of perspective and perception. As Alexie
Tcheuyap suggests, the multiple, contradictory, and hybrid identities of film language are a starting point even within the broad Pan-African label of a continent
with a range of cinemas (Tcheuyap 2011, 231).

"African Cinema: Addressee Unknown" (Stoneman 1993) was originally
drafted as a tentative taxonomy for a symposium at the 1992 Carthage Film Festival in Tunis, outlining some of the determinations on films made with Western
funding and for audiences in the West.[2] Revisiting the essay now, it is apparent

that, with the important exception of digital production and reception of popular cinema, not much has changed in the dynamics of African cinema in the last twenty-five years. Since the early 2000s, experiences in various workshops in the Maghreb, Vietnam, West Africa, and the Middle East have been formative and revelatory for me.[3]

To some extent all forms of indigenous production outside the industrialized film industry in America contribute to the possibility of a reflexive, politicized "human rights of filmmaking" disrupting a global monoculture, specifically offering alternative filmic and digital versions of the moving image. In Africa any such exploration supports a pluralist celebration of differences across a diverse continent. The selected representations in an African film not only create new presences, they also implicitly bring attention to the absence of certain histories and memories, lacunae which influence our understandings of the present.

A description of a politicized aesthetics relevant to human rights filmmaking could start by examining the productive interdependence among at least three distinct levels of engagement between film and politics, each with different forms and audiences: filmmaking may function at the level of agit prop, propaganda, or the theoretical / experimental. Agit prop is immediate and urgent, addressing short-term, specific local issues and audiences. Propaganda works with longer-term subject matter and broad ideas. Theory, at its most productive, is often for a small audience and linked to experimentation using radical form to open new configurations and practices. All three levels are necessary, although, as Peter Wollen explained in a 1974 interview, "the problem for political films is [that they are] often posed in terms of one against the other" (Mulvey and Wollen 1974, 131). The taxonomy is still useful if understood in terms of the interdependency and unexpectedly porous movement between versions of radical filmmaking in this domain, refusing "documentary" and "fiction" as categories of separation.

Thinking through the scale, temporality, and target audiences involved in different forms of filmmaking in Africa involves calibrating the various ways films make meaning for their audiences at home and abroad. For African filmmakers, the politics of their activities must raise considerations about the delineations of identity—about the borders between "inside" and "outside." This affects the way in which their images circulate both within their specific African countries of origin and elsewhere on the African continent (and beyond). Possibilities for the reception of indigenous production in the South are also affected by the political economy of their funding and distribution contexts.

Diasporic work made by Africans or those of African descent in Europe or America moves within and between African cultures in the West, but also has an occasional presence in Africa through festivals and digital circulation. It is important to be clear about the relational perspective (described in 1980's film theory as *"d'où je parle"* / "from where I speak"). I remember when John Singleton, fresh from the success of *Boyz n the Hood* (1991, USA) remarked, "It feels like I have returned home" to Ousmane Sembène during the Panafrican Film and Television Festival of Ouagadougou (FESPACO). Sembène replied with a graceful welcome and said carefully, "But let's be clear—you live and work in Los Angeles; you are very welcome here, but it is not your home."[4] There is a longer-term hope to expand the interaction of filmmaking from the diverse cultures and continents of the South, across relevant domains in Asia and Latin America. For diasporic filmmakers who are conscious of the relation between Africa and Europe / America and the representational practices generated within these regions, this intercultural space encourages an interaction of difference and hybridity, "home" seen from afar—and immersion within the global image system and a direct sense of intervention in it. In crossing multifaceted and unstable boundaries, their work involves both identity and otherness.

There is no reason to preemptively confine theoretical / experimental filmmaking to a lesser scale of audience: there are smaller audience engagements in galleries, but the spectacular three-screen projection of John Akomfrah's *Vertigo Sea* (2015, Ghana / England) has the potential to reach wide audiences. My experience commissioning and programming films for the British television station Channel 4 in the 1980s taught me that, carefully positioned and presented, there are significant audiences for "difficult" work. And the same director's *Handsworth Songs* (1986, UK), transmitted on Channel 4 in 1987, was an early indication of the potential for reaching significantly wider audiences with formally innovative, politically relevant experimental film.

On occasion a different frame exists for filmmakers working in specific circumstances in Africa and elsewhere. For example, a workshop for advocacy filmmaking held in August 2014 at the IMAGINE Institute in Burkina Faso involved the calibration of images and sounds so that political ideas could be communicated to the audience without crossing a line that risked provoking intervention from a repressive state apparatus. Daoda Zallé's *The Price of Commitment* (2014, Burkina Faso) mentioned the assassination of independent journalist Norbert Zongo in 1998. Zongo had begun an investigation of a politically sensitive murder, and he died in a car accident that is thought to have been organized by then-president Blaise Compaoré's regime. While mentioning Zongo as a *cause célèbre*, the video avoided specific reference to Thomas Sankara, the revolutionary leader whose assassination led to Compaoré's succession in October 1987. This adjustment was consciously attuned, for at the time the film was made, the regime contained the officially sanctioned memory of Sankara through statues and streets named after him, while unauthorized memories or invocations were suppressed. Zallé's short film indicated an undertow of resistance to the regime, but without inviting the dangers of an explicit provocation. It turned out to be a dramatically accurate premonition: just two months later, the popular uprising implicitly called for by the film erupted in the streets of Burkina Faso and ended Comparé's twenty-seven-year rule.

Critiques of Human Rights

"Africa" is a continent that calls its own historiography into question—the versions of its history over the last half century have been turbulent and contested. Like the Western discipline of anthropology, the writing of African history has developed a self-reflexive dynamic as it has encountered social and political change. As Didier Awadi asserted in *Le point de vue du lion* (*The Lion's Point of View*, 2011, Senegal): "As long as lions do not have their own historians, tales of hunting will always glorify the hunter."[5] Any attempts to tell the histories of the continent implicitly ask: What elements of the past can be selected or disinterred? What material—archaeological, anthropological or cultural—allows such narratives to be built? From what point of view is the historical account articulated? What are the determinations and interests at play behind the specific historical descriptions? As the Burkinabè filmmaker Gaston Kaboré suggests in the interview reproduced in this volume, "Africans should know about their history" because "if you want to know where to go, you need to know where you are coming from."

The assumption that the continent possesses an essential unity and therefore an integrated identity is based on the dominance of shared aspects and effacement of differing ones. As Kaboré's interview makes clear, there are direct connections between the politics of representation and the struggles for material gain in a history of exploitation. In a monoculture that is made elsewhere, "Africa" as concept suffers misperception and patronage, which inflicts psychological damage on African people. As a region condemned to successive humiliations as well as poverty, such a conception places Africans in a defensive starting point—one of refutation and self-justification. Most African countries are trapped in a structure that starts in international markets and financial centers and ends in every detail of its citizens' lives. The assumptions confine Africa to a depleted potential—to export commodities including culture and tourism. These activities are welcome and tradeable, but few would extrapolate from these starting points and arrive at the tacit suggestion in the 2013 exhibition *Le Don de l'Afrique au Monde / Africa's Gift to the World* at the IMAGINE institute, Ouagadougou, that Africa is a continent that built the past and also can shape the future.

There are various frameworks for the understanding of human rights both in Africa and more broadly. Western-centric versions of the perceived history of those rights are founded on myopia and amnesia. *Africa's Gift to the World* gave some prominence to the thirteenth-century *Charter of Mandé / Kurukan Fuga* (Center for Linguistic & Historical Study of Oral Tradition [CELHTO] 2008). In

1235 Soundjata, the ruler of the Mali empire, established a constitution, a moral code dealing with social organization, property rights, and personal responsibilities. Preserved for nearly eight hundred years by oral repetition, it was reconstituted in Kankan, the Republic of Guinea, in 1998 with a gathering of griots who facilitated the transcription of a charter that had been preserved via word of mouth—literally "direct speech."[6]

The edicts begin by asserting that "Everyone has a right to life and their physical integrity"—a clear and fundamental affirmation (paragraph 5). Toward the end of the proclamation, the charter offers the sage advice "Just help those in need," an orientation toward mutual support and perhaps the still radical notion of a society based on use value rather than exchange value (paragraph 31). The detail also deals with the humane treatment of slaves: "Do not ill-treat the slaves. You should allow them to rest one day per week and to end their working day at a reasonable time. You are the master of the slaves, but not of the bag they carry" (paragraph 20).

Importantly, the charter also proposes that "Women, apart from their everyday occupations, should be associated with all our governments and managements" (paragraph 16). This is a version of ancient African history that lies many generations before the contemporary feminism of, for example, Nigerian writer Chimamanda Ngozi Adichie's intervention with a TEDx talk in December 2012, "We Should All Be Feminists," and its subsequent publication. The charter is a clear precedent of the French Declaration of the Rights of Man and of the Citizen in 1789 and the UN Declaration of 1948, and it should be seen as a primary statement of the various endeavours to establish rights and reciprocal human responsibilities. Indeed, it seems sensible to summon all relevant precedents.[7] More recently there have been risible competitive attempts to relocate the beginning of human rights to a later date and place; American academic Samuel Moyn, for instance, desired to establish a year zero for human rights from 1970, locating it in the USA (Moyn 2010).

To suggest that the "human rights community" is rarely cognizant of the complexities and contradictions of the term and its operations is not to underestimate the effectiveness of the many specific political interventions that have been supported by human rights discourses. The ideology of human rights does not amount to a systematic form of politics. A contemporary surrogate for what had once been enunciated within the ideals of socialism, it introduces progressive ideas and political engagement to a wider public space than do specific political assertions.

The avowal of rights that are *human* suggests they apply across race, class, gender, and nation, their provenance and application being outside of any specific time and place. The strength of this discourse is its ostensible irrefutability—it takes the notion and operation of rights toward generalized ethical and political principles. But there are clear problems with deployments that bring with them the disingenuous ahistorical assertion of universalism, for "humanity" and "human rights" rely on an absolute and generalized equivalence. Contemporary versions often work to conceal their ideological bias through naturalization as Western universal values, despite precedents in other cultures.

"The same, but different" formulates the tension at the center of concepts of human universality. The phrase indicates a necessary double movement—cultural, social, but also ethical. In principle, humans exist with equivalent rights, but very clearly these rights, whether respected and supported or repressed and repudiated, exist in widely different dispositions. The source of human rights gives rise to inherently contradictory demands: the right to equality and the right to difference. There exists a disparity of power and resources between each concrete historical situation.

Contemporary examples of this construction forget that rights are relative and enable quite contradictory short-term arguments to appropriate the notion of a "right." Charlotte Rampling defended the Oscar selections in 2016 and suggested any criticism of the racially skewed selection was "racist against whites." Pressure groups such as "Fathers 4 Families" argue that women have an unbalanced set of overdeveloped rights in family disputes, and bullfighters complain about their lack of human rights.[8] The issue of power that remains in place is effaced, and we see discursive manoeuvres that reconfirm those in a position of relative dominance through the invocation and inversion of rights. We can always ask, "How does a specific discourse function?" and "Who does it serve?" As Michel Foucault suggested, "The facts of power, the relations of domination and exploitation . . . insinuate [themselves] in the tissue of reality" (Morris and Patton 1979, 24).

A wider framework of politics is needed to place the deployment of human rights arguments in context to counter the "ostensibly depoliticized politics" as Slavoj Žižek argued in "Against Human Rights" (Žižek 2005). In historical terms the elaborated set of political categories came into being after 1968. That year was a formative political moment for the second half of the twentieth century for a whole generation contributing to the consolidation of the agenda of the New Left. A range of disparate historical events that year led to new appraisals and a resetting of a range of ideas:

- May, Paris—students and workers challenge the French state, presenting a critique of the social order in a "developed" Western democracy.
- The Prague Spring—a premonition of the end of Stalinism in Eastern Europe.
- The Tet Offensive in the Vietnam War—a turning point in the most visible of the myriad anticolonial struggles taking place in the third world.

- Feminist and gay social movements build their presence and consolidate their critique of the reigning social order acknowledged by decriminalization in the United Kingdom and marked by the Stonewall Riots a year later.

The above can be seen as the starting point for a set of coordinates for thinking about several issues. Importantly, the factors involved—the politics of race, class, gender, and colonialism—interact in specific circumstances, but they should not be set in any kind of a preemptive hierarchical order. Since the 1960s the previous versions of class-based politics that contended for power and ownership on behalf of the working class have connected with "identity politics" in new and productive ways. We see an ensemble of coordinates adapting to the new histories we inhabit with the potential to provide a basis for the building of broad alliances for change. The factors in question are not fixed or resolvable in advance, but they constitute a starting point for resolving the contending claims of human rights that designate the precise space of a genuine politicization. For instance, this wider frame of reference is necessary in order to address the impasse that has arisen between arguments for and against abortion: feminist pro-choice advocacy of the rights of the mother are fiercely disputed by pro-life counterarguments for the rights of the unborn, on behalf of the fetus. These disagreements, which came to the fore in the altercations of the Abortion Referendum held in Ireland during May 2018, are only resolvable with recourse to arguments outside the disputed sets of "rights."

These contradictory deployments are not a retraction or abandonment of human rights arguments; rather, they constitute a wider, necessary context for the positioning of human rights explanations (which are socially constructed and not abstract legalisms) in attempts to situate rights in a wider political framework, in practice. Discussing the constraints of human rights discourse for social movement activists, David Landy argues for a "more complex understanding of human rights discourse as a negotiation between situated local contention and universalist claims" (Landy 2013). The instability of a set of relevant coordinates, which refuse to settle into a rigid hierarchy, offers a more flexible and rigorous basis to respond to the specificities of African cultural politics in all its different parts and measures. But, as Haitian filmmaker Raoul Peck noted, "We live in a world that does not encourage complexity."[9]

Representation: Negotiating Relations between the North and the South

There is a productive contrast between a wider range of representations of Africa originating from indigenous filmmakers and most of the perspectives that prevail elsewhere. However, these more or less subtle differences in politics and perception are visible and effective only if African films are accessible on a broad basis.

The Western perceptions of generality and universality were manifest in the 1955 photographic exhibition "The Family of Man," launched in New York by Edward Steichen. It took place in the same significant phase as the UN Declaration of Human Rights—in the backwash of World War II and in the first stages of the Cold War. The fault lines in that historic moment of confrontation were deliberately effaced, as were significant differences in wealth and power relations, in order to assert a generalized and unified humanity. A New York taxi driver was juxtaposed with a Vietnamese peasant; children playing in England were next to representations of motherhood and the Masai in Kenya—all elements were connected in the formation of a faltering humanist optimism. Roland Barthes described the exhibition in *Mythologies*: "from this pluralism a kind of unity is magically produced" (Barthes 1973, 100–2).

The imposed unity of "The Family of Man" exhibition can be contrasted with the confirmation of self-representation and its deft movement of separation and connection evident in the example of Thomas Sankara's reinvention of his country's name in 1984, which was integral to a process of remaking its identity at a moment of revolutionary change. The country had been originally called Haute Volta / Upper Volta by the French, and this nomenclature continued after independence in 1960. Sankara proposed its renaming as Burkina Faso in August 1984. "Burkina" means "dignity" in Mooré (spoken by the Mossi ethnic group); "Faso" means "house of" in Diula (spoken by traders and originating from the second city, Bobo Dioulasso). The suffix of the name for an inhabitant, "Burkinabè," is in Fulani and means "Land of the upright men / people of integrity." The main rivers—the White, Red, and Black Voltas—were also given back their original names: Nakembè, Nazinon, and Mouhoun. By combining elements of West African cultures and languages from the constituent groups, the country took a unified name of judiciously articulated hybridity for all to embrace internally and asserted an ethical / ethnic identity by self-description.[10]

Focusing on the example of a feature film made in that country four years later, further cultural and political subtleties emerge. The film touches on issues that are described in the West as "human rights" but integrates them into a more complex set of cultural images and narratives. Gaston Kaboré's *Zan Boko* (1988, Burkina Faso) contains a sequence that effortlessly enacts the cultural difference implicit in a domestic ritual. In the film there is a moment when two women sit outside their huts in a village to talk. One woman has a baby that she hands to an elder daughter to look after as they chat: "How's the baby?" "How are things going with your husband?" As they talk there is a lilting sound, for each of them makes a gentle background hum under the other's words; when one is talking, the other is going, "Mmmm . . . aahh." Each of their voices hums under the other's speech, and we sense the exquisite granularity of a culture, a moment of recognition—but also of dissimilarity.

What the two women are doing is perfectly recognizable in many cultures. It is an intimate instance of the everyday tenderness that flows between people. Everywhere around the world, women friends have intimate conversations with each other about how their lives and homes are going, how their babies are doing, and the circulations of their domestic spheres. Whether it is in Caracas or Manhattan, Rome or Hong Kong, forms of those exchanges and conversations continue. But the actual texture of the exchange in Mooré in the village of Tensobentenga in the countryside outside Ouagadougou is completely specific and different, so there is a double movement of something that can be recognized in other cultures but is also a different version of it. It is a noticeably calm, gentle, and affectionate interchange, one that is possibly more difficult to achieve in busy New York or Paris or any other fast-paced metropolis. A short sequence buried in a feature film narrative, the association of both strangeness and recognition is exemplary as one of its significant effects is to relativize and question our habitual practices. It is not just a photograph in a passing parade of humanism, but a piece of substantive work from another culture. The response varies with our cultural context, questioning and curiosity arising in different ways in different places.

This subtle sequence is embedded in a film about an independent-minded local journalist who raises the controversial issue of the encroachment of urbanization (and urban values) when a peasant family is displaced by the new middle class. His attempt to produce a television discussion is thwarted by the interference of a government minister who phones the journalist and presenter while the program is live on air to halt discussion.

But the depiction in *Zan Boko* of tender conversations between neighbors in a village and censorship of an independent journalist in a city does not insist on other substantial differences that lie behind the cultural exchange—those larger-scale disparities of wealth and power both within the country and between the continents. These differences and the underlying structures of exploitation, oppression, and uneven development between continents cannot be completely hidden. The West has little time for commutation tests because the only existence African cultures are granted is at the edge of the frame, as peripheral and strange, an entirely exotic Other, populated by needy victims.

What is denied is the normal articulation of identities and relations between the North and the South of the planet at this moment in their histories, the complex way in which these different parts of the world are configured in terms of prosperity and power, health and wealth. As the middle-class family in the film expands its domain to build a swimming pool and to swallow the village within the city, it is the image of prosperity from the West that has transposed its trappings of success to another culture. An examination of material differentials within and between societies demonstrates unexpectedly wide differences in the average gross national income (GNI) per capita per annum. This is the case even within the European continent, with Armenia at $3,880 and Switzerland at $84,180. And of course there are much wider contrasts in global comparisons: the United States is at $54,960 (average life expectancy at birth: seventy-nine years), and Burkina Faso is at $660 (life expectancy at birth: fifty-nine years).[11] One would be accused of excessive naivety if one asked why people born on one part of the planet should have a significantly extended life expectancy or one hundred times the income of people born on another part of the planet. Perhaps a degree of such "unrealistic" incredulity may be a necessary starting point for reconfiguring our expectations. The extent to which the gap in per capita income between, roughly speaking, the North / West and the South / East of the world has actually deepened after half a century of "developmentalism" suggests that the structure of inequality is interdependent and entrenched. These implicit and underlying relations are a grid of distortion—the level terrain of universalism on which human rights can be developed does not exist. We are unconscious of our starting points—it cannot be a surprise that the place from which we see the world determines what we perceive and what we perpetuate in describing and categorizing other places.

A deceptive misrepresentation is also evident in the rarefied academic and institutional contexts with the terms used to characterize areas of study. In film studies, art history, and musicology, there is reason to question the appearance of relatively new discipline designations: world cinema, world art, and world music. It is important to acknowledge that at this point there is a belated degree of inclusion—at least the relevant instances of wider cultural expression are reaching the curricula—but this often involves the importation of other frames of reference or angles of approach that are already set in a Western framework (Ba and Higbee 2012). We do not even see it as strange that the term "world" actually means everything *outside* the Western mainstream (Stoneman 2012). While most of Anglophone academia uses the term to refer to cinema and music from Africa, Asia, and Latin America, in "An Atlas of World Cinema," Dudley Andrew deploys it to include all non-English language films (Andrew 2004). Lúcia Nagib, in "Towards a Positive Definition of World Cinema," argues that the description of world cinema as non-Hollywood is restrictive and negative. She counters the trend with a proposal to see world cinema as an inclusive domain, a cinema of the world against the binaries and centrism of the dominant paradigm (Nagib 2006), and a notion of "polycentrism" as applied to global film cultures (Nagib, Perriam, and Dudrah 2011). The dominant perspective is powerful and constructs Western meanings in the non-Western.[12] We are always trying to see how the Other can be accounted for and fitted into our conceptualizations. As Youssef Chahine quipped, "The Third World is England, the US and France. I'm from the First World, I've been there for seven thousand years!"[13]

Some of these questions are evident in Richard Mosse's *The Enclave*, Ireland's entry to the Venice Biennale in 2013, which won the £30,000 Deutsche

Figure 2.1. Gallery installation of photographs and film from the Congo, shot on infrared film stock. Richard Mosse, *The Enclave*. Framegrab.

Börse Photography Prize in May the following year. This multiscreen film installation utilized discarded infrared film to recolor the Democratic Republic of the Congo and its relentless civil war. The colors of the scenes on several screens pattern the country's villages, landscapes, and inhabitants in a way that startles but also aestheticizes and exoticizes our sense of the distant world it depicts.

The Enclave is a detached representation of disturbing content without context, representing a pitiless human conflict without depth of political or historical analysis or understanding. Consonant with most mainstream media coverage of the "dark continent," this installation offers a visually spectacular rendition in which "the Africans are killing one another again." The absence of articulation is marked; there is no space for direct speech, explanation, or understanding from those who inhabit that reality. Mosse's piece also raises questions about the basis of involvement and degree of participation by the protagonists in their own representation.[14]

Richard Mosse's work brings a forgotten and distant carnage into white-walled galleries in Europe—a continent that can be said already to be at risk of "compassion fatigue." Understanding its context and effects is a question not of the artist's intentions, but of the inherent way that the work is received and interpreted by the particular audiences that encounter it in Western European galleries.

The implications of these strategies are clear: while Mosse introduces overtly political issues into an art context, there is no discourse, visual or verbal, to contest the assumptions perpetuated by the dominant media that surround these images outside the white walls of a gallery. Like other aspects of "developmentalism," it produces atomized and decontextualized victims who need outside assistance to survive. The doxa of common sense has already established that in darkest Africa gruesome carnage comes as no surprise. There is a lack of argumentation that could intercept unconscious assumptions and engage the images

Figure 2.2. Santigold as a monster devouring a flock of birds. *The End of Eating Everything* (2010, Wangechi Mutu, Kenya / USA). Framegrab.

productively. Contention or counterargument might productively set specific defined meanings in motion, bringing some of the contradictions to the fore.

As Marx suggested in *The 18th Brumaire of Louis Bonaparte* (1852), the peasantry cannot represent themselves, and therefore they must be represented by others.[15] The natives are excluded from discourse and from agency; they just enter Conrad's *Heart of Darkness* to utter the dénouement: "Mistah Kurtz—he dead."

The Enclave can be contrasted with examples from African filmmakers, based in the diaspora, which negotiate the underlying problems and articulate their address to the power of the West in a different way. For example, *The End of Eating Everything* by Wangechi Mutu (2010, Kenya / USA) uses digital means to create and depict a vision of the Anthropocene era.

A Medusa-like female, the face of North American singer Santigold, hovers in the sky in a postapocalyptic landscape. The gorgon's torso is made of a suppurating body of wounds, parts of machines, and limbs; a sharp-toothed head obtrudes from a bleeding figure; her pores spew poisonous smoke; a swarm of birds fly too close and are bitten into shreds. This insatiable monster becomes a cruel hallucination of our own self-destructive consumptions. Crucially, this most dangerous creature is a consolidated combination of all parts of the planet, suggesting humanity working in concert to destroy itself.

Figure 2.3. A three screen gallery installation of *Vertigo Sea* (2015, John Akomfrah, England). Framegrab.

John Akomfrah, whose family came to Britain from Ghana after the 1966 coup, made *Vertigo Sea* (2015, England). It is an epic visual orchestration: a cultural history of humankind's relationship to the sea, both as victims and as perpetrators. Three interacting screens and a complex soundtrack configure fragments of image, text, and music in luscious and polysemic movement around the theme of the "aquatic sublime." Ecological atrocities such as the slaughter of whales and polar bears are placed in juxtaposition with natural history footage. These images sit alongside a historic feature film reenacting the infamous Zong massacre of 1781, an act of mass murder of 133 enslaved Africans thrown overboard from a stranded ship for the purpose of claiming insurance money against their loss. "The way of killing man and beasts is the same."[16]

Deploying Herman Melville's *Moby Dick* and Heathcote Williams's *Whale Nation* as intertexts with archive footage and staged tableaux, *Vertigo Sea* sets collective and personal memories and histories against the West's amnesia. The film utilizes contemporary footage of migrations to argue against what Akomfrah has called "the rhetoric of contagion" that characterizes European fears of immigration. Conjoining examples of filmmaking from the South, Europe, and the African diaspora indicate the complex interaction of place and perspective and suggest some vectors for change.

Cinema's Issues

Any discussion of rights issues in African filmmaking should acknowledge that the approach occurs with and through the specificity of the form. The categories of agit prop and propaganda in political filmmaking mentioned earlier carry their signifying practices through specific forms, fictional as well as nonfictional. To state the obvious, different cultural and political practices have developed in response to the particular possibilities of funding and audience. While African television has been almost entirely absent from support for feature filmmaking, Nollywood in Nigeria has developed an economy for a more continuous and industrial basis for fiction production, focused on decidedly commercial filmmaking for popular African audiences. This industry has proved extremely flexible with great variations of budget and technological shifts (occasionally shooting on celluloid in the most recent period) and has developed a cinema that produces an average of fifty films a week, with a turnover of $600 million per year.[17]

Even with popular successes, the problem of a weakened exhibition infrastructure limits the reach of cinema for national African audiences. In many countries the decline of the film theater as a traditional exhibition space has led to an inevitable increase in viewing on smaller electronic screens.[18] A high proportion of contemporary South African fiction production has also developed on a model of commercial entertainment for popular audiences.[19] Crucially, the economic autonomy and self-sufficiency of this cycle of production and reception avoids the distortions of foreign funding outlined in the original essay "African Cinema: Addressee Unknown" referred to earlier (Stoneman 1993).

As a creative documentary, Didier Awadi's *Le point de vue du lion* emanated from a new generation informed by a wide range of art forms. The director had worked as a rap artist and produced a film with a forceful polemic—a new generation's indictment of their parents' politics and the first fifty years of most African countries' independence.[20]

The opening sequence about African migration in *Le point de vue du lion* connects it with *La Pirogue* by Moussa Touré (2012, Senegal), which chronicles the dangerous journey across the edge of the Atlantic for a motley group of economic migrants. *La Pirogue* is classified as a fiction feature, although, in the director's words, "all African films are documentary"—an appropriate assertion in the case of this cinema's proximity to urgent realities.[21] A powerful narrative with effective digital special effects, *La Pirogue* won prizes in FESPACO and Carthage and was shown in Un Certain Regard at Cannes. Despite these strengths, the film did not impinge on the widespread complacency about the constant haemorrhage of lives in an unfolding calamity. But for those working in film, there is a characteristic overestimation of the power and influence of cinema and images more generally in the public sphere. Even the widely reproduced image of the body of Aylan Kurdi, a three-year-old Syrian child, washed up on a Turkish shoreline in September 2015, did not have a decisive impact. The attempts to reach Europe via North Africa continue without adequate response from European countries.[22] But realism about the difficulty in changing attitudes and policies should lead to more accurate public representation, not pessimism—there is no reason not to continue to contest the image system.

The influence a film from the South can have on Western audiences is limited. Suggestive of the constraints is African and Arab cinema's significantly reduced visibility for a wider public in Britain once Channel 4 ceased to screen a consistent range of films. Festivals have proliferated and certainly help in the marketing of films within the specialist sector of art house cinema exhibition, but the films have a limited social reach in the broader public domain. The proliferation of specialist African cinema festivals outside the continent of Africa is welcome, but the limited circuits of auteur films are most likely to reach a cinephile audience already seeking out Arab and African cinema, displacing the moment of the films' reception to specific niche groups and encouraging a spurious notion of an international audience.[23]

Our epoch has seen mass marketing determine an increasingly limited version of cinema and shift audience taste toward it. Southern audiences are unavoidably influenced by the American modes of cinema that are part of an image system manufactured in the centers of cultural and economic power. In this period a cultural industry has spread across the world: aided by digital technology, popular cinema has itself narrowed and become more formulaic. Contemporary cinema in the West is itself in crisis—it neither apprehends global realities honestly nor is it an aid in imagining a different kind of future. It is suffocated by a set of anachronistic conventions dictated by the agents of commerce. The political economy of the media encourages us to live in a culture of distraction where short-term, superficial narratives are at the center of press attention while serious, long-term issues and determinant forces in the world's ecology and political economy are seen as insufficiently interesting or attractive to enter the frame of our viewing.

In Europe and America, the global South is still represented as the Other, as primitive and dangerous, as exotic and strange; largely unacknowledged is its economic role in securing cheaper manufacturing costs in order to support excessive capital accumulation for a small proportion of the world's population. Among images that are reproduced for recreation and tourism, there is an awful continuity with the earliest encounters in previous epochs in the way that the "otherness" of Africa has always reinforced the identity of Europeans.[24]

Direct Speech and the Digital

Article 19 in the 1948 UN Universal Declaration of Human Rights asserts plainly that "Everyone has the right to freedom of opinion and expression . . . to receive and impart information and ideas through any media and regardless of frontiers." In principle this should counter the imposed monoculture with a diversity of indigenous voices emerging from autonomous Southern production structures. But inevitably these voices have to overcome significant barriers to distribution.

They also have to negotiate the audiences' tastes at home and abroad, when these have been fabricated elsewhere and are reinforced by powerful marketing. The exercise of meaningful freedom of expression involves delivery, distribution, and access to direct speech.

The previously mentioned and short-lived historical example of Channel 4 television represents an attempt to establish this principle within public service television in Europe. I experienced this dynamic moment when working in the Independent Film and Video Department at Channel 4 in the 1980s. At that time, there was a commitment to build direct speech from communities to minimize the processes of mediation from "television professionals" and shift the balance to participatory access and interactivity. This connected with an emphasis on marginalized and voiceless communities in Britain and abroad. For a decade this endeavour was sustained through the various genres of fiction and documentary filmmaking and included an attempt to create a space for direct speech from Africa and other continents in the South for a specific British audience. We moved from initial seasons of purchased films such as *Africa on Africa*, *New Cinema of Latin America*, *Caméra Arabe*, and *Vietnam Cinema* to the weekly "slot" called *Cinema of Three Continents* and began to coproduce by committing to new films in advance of their production. Although Channel 4 funding was a modest contribution to the total budget, it helped build confidence in new projects and, crucially, attract other finance to them. In 1991 we added a television magazine series called *South*. In the words of the launch invitation, *South* was billed as "a new peak time magazine programme that takes a radical approach to global affairs on television and features the work of film makers from Latin America, Africa, the Caribbean, Asia, South East Asia and the Arab world."[25] These elements were in stark contrast to the "parachute journalism" of most existing television coverage. An indication of the success of this strategy within British broadcasting was evident in BBC 2's (implicitly a rival station to Channel 4) increasingly competitive approach to buying films at African film festivals and commitment to staging a season around African culture. For both Channel 4 and BBC 2, these activities faded as part of the gradual debilitation and demolition of European public service television in the early 1990s.

The new infrastructures of the digital age continue to transform the valence of distribution and access as new means of digital production offer a partial and complex shift in cultural forms. We should, however, be skeptical of Western overstatements about the part played by digital means in social change. Examples include the starring role of social media, such as references to Facebook or the "Twitter revolution" used to describe the complex social process of the Arab Spring in different countries. The new communication networks facilitate but do not wholly determine the processes of social contention. Digital distribution has the potential for free expression, but this is often illusory as it depends on the transmission to an audience—posting an independent film on YouTube does not necessarily mean that it reaches an audience or creates public debate.[26]

The dynamic movement between different art forms is made evident through the utopian lyrics from "Silence, on rêve" by Tatouages, present in *Africa Remix: Contemporary Art of a Continent*, a large-scale exhibition staged in Paris and London in 2005, which included music and film among a range of visual arts. "Identities of people, countries and cultures have become a product of marketing . . . we are the spokespeople of the planet with riches that are forgotten by globalization, sold down the river by politicians. But we have the power to transform the world immediately."[27]

A fifth of the continent has access to broadband, and Pan-African connections are fostered through the digital networks, exemplified by the website *Africasacountry.com*, which reviews films from the continent as a whole each month. National interchange can become global as new cultural forms allow African voices direct speech, the possibility of retort, and assertion of counter perspectives. A video by young South Africans articulates a sharp and satirical riposte to Bob Geldof's well-intentioned but patronizing "Do They Know It's Christmas" (a group of high-profile pop stars launched a Christmas single in 2014 to raise money for the fight against Ebola, following the format of the original Band Aid single in 1984). "African Radiator Song to Norway—Support Radi-Aid!" is a mocking parody of the original Band Aid song. In it Africans offer to collect and ship radiators from Africa to Norway, to help Scandinavians keep warm during their harsh winter months. Like Swift's *A Modest Proposal* (1729), a reversal leads to revelation. However, it is salutary to note the relative YouTube viewing figures ("Do They Know It's Christmas" is at 22,419,986 views; "African Radiator Song" is at 111,206),[28] which reinforce the confines of this means of counteraction.

New generations have made a point of taking unexpected variations of political filmmaking as a starting point for their work with moving images. For example, following three FESPACO Newsreel interventions, the 2014 IMAG-INE workshop *Telling Microstories* was an intense ten-day workshop supporting young filmmakers having "something to say in an innovative form." Participants undertook a series of sound and image exercises and experiments leading to the production of short films posted on the internet.[29] Young filmmakers worked to develop new ways of putting together images and sounds using new digital media for production and dissemination. The pieces were poetic, sensitive, efficient, and inspired—aware of new uses of cinematic language. This workshop indicated potentially inventive forms of capacity building and developed models of sustainable filmmaking for a new generation of African filmmakers.

The spectrum of relevant production for contemporary filmmakers extends from the traditional political documentary *Life Is Waiting: Referendum and Resistance in Western Sahara* (2015, Iara Lee, USA / Western Sahara) to the politicized skateboarding short *Jas Boude* (2014, Georgina Warner and Imraan

Christian, South Africa), which chronicles the 20SK8 collective and its attempt to describe the implicit violence of postapartheid spatial geography in Cape Town.[30] The spectrum also includes innovative and substantial films like *Félicité* (2017, Alain Gomis, France / Belgium / Senegal / Germany / Lebanon), which displays an assured complexity that opens the polysemy of Akomfrah and Mutu's installations into a feature film. Set in Kinshasa, the film moves between documentary and fiction forms and uses local and Western musics; its style articulates a new and fluent confidence in African filmmaking.

The imperative at this point should be to support African cinema in all its forms and to circulate direct speech from the South. Engaging with subjects understood as "human rights issues" offers localized moments of cognition and contention translated into a universalized language that both enables and constrains the practice of transnational solidarity. The radical pluralism of new voices will offer, in addition to new narratives and perspectives, different patterns of thought. It is only through the transmission of direct speech in all its forms that we can counter and adjust the misapprehensions of Western media and challenge the unconscious and naturalized assumptions that continue to dominate the field of representation. Hopefully, some of these voices may question the complacency and overdevelopment of the West and its economy of perpetual growth; they can help counter the insularity that undermines the prospect of an equitable and civilized global community.

We have created a scale of prosperity and a consumerist lifestyle which makes disparity and injustice inescapable. For this reason, at this moment of grave economic and ecological crises, it is increasingly imperative to collaborate on a project of mutual reinvention in which the values of all cultures from every part of the world are able to play a full and dynamic role. As we face a concatenation of present anxieties, perhaps African cinema can help us explore the possibility, restated in Gaston Kaboré's *2000 génération d'Afrique* (2009, Algeria / Burkina Faso), that "the African continent still holds the promise of the future for the whole of humanity."

ROD STONEMAN is Emeritus Professor at the National University of Ireland, Galway. He was previously Director of the Huston School of Film & Digital Media, Chief Executive of Bord Scannán na hÉireann / the Irish Film Board, and a Deputy Commissioning Editor in the Independent Film and Video Department at Channel 4 Television in the United Kingdom.

Notes

1. "Cultural domination is more flexible, more effective and less costly" (Sankara 1988, 153).

2. As a tool for understanding, any taxonomy is a provisional provocation which should always be argued with, transformed.

3. The Hanoi Academy of Theatre and Cinema, Vietnam, 2005; a script workshop at IMAGINE, Ouagadougou, Burkina Faso, 2005; Med Film Development, Marrakech, Morocco, 2006–2008; FESPACO newsreel workshops, Ouagadougou, 2009–2013; Beyond Borders, Djerba, Tunisia, 2010; Med Film Factory, Amman, Jordan, 2011–2016.

4. At breakfast in Hotel Silmandé during FESPACO, February 1991, Ouagadougou.

5. A quotation from Chinua Achebe's *Anthills of the Savannah*.

6. Convened by Siriman Kouyaté, CELHTO, March 3–12, 1998.

7. The English might invoke aspects of the Magna Carta in 1215.

8. "Bullfighting Returns to San Sebastián after Three-Year Ban," *The Guardian*, August 12, 2015, accessed January 6, 2017, https://www.theguardian.com/world/2015/aug/12/bullfighting-returns-san-sebastian-after-three-year-ban.

9. Raoul Peck's comment was made during a debate after the screening of his documentary *Fatal Assistance* (2012, Haiti / USA) at the ICA, Human Rights film festival, London, March 16, 2013.

10. Having attended FESPACO in Ouagadougou since 1984, I could not help but notice the misspellings of the country's name in its rare appearance as a caption or on a map on Western television: most often Burkina Fasso, sometimes Bukina or Fasi.

11. All figures are for 2015, available from www.worldbank.org. Accessed December 8, 2016.

12. The question of displacing the "West versus the rest" binary in film studies has also been developed in relation to ideas of transnational cinema. Will Higbee (whose input to the concept and this essay is especially appreciated) coauthored "Towards a Critical Transnationalism in Film Studies" with Song Hwee Lim (2010).

13. Chahine interview in *Caméra Arabe* (1987, Ferid Boughedir, Tunisia).

14. This is in contrast to a short film by Dearbhla Glynn, *The Value of Women in the Congo* (2012, Ireland), that inhabits a different place outside the art world: it is used for advocacy and shown in the context of human rights and the operations of NGOs. It is an uncompromising, clear-headed, and disturbing examination of the effects of the sexual violence perpetrated with impunity against women and girls in war-torn Eastern Congo.

15. Gayatri Spivak's seminal essay "Can the Subaltern Speak?" (1983) develops the historical and ideological factors that obstruct the possibility of being heard for those who inhabit the periphery.

16. John Akomfrah explains that this quote is "a very rough paraphrase of one of Ahab's ramblings from *Moby Dick*" (email to author, January 5, 2017).

17. *The Ticket, Irish Times*, November 18, 2016.

18. A relevant example would be Moroccan cinema, which has seen the number of films produced each year rise from four or five in the 1980s to around twenty in the 2000s. At the same time, cinemas have declined from 285 in 1980 to approximately 40 in 2014. In 1980 the four Moroccan films would have been competing for a share of the box office of about twenty million spectators; in 2014 about twenty films are competing (along with imports from the United States, Europe, and Bollywood) for a reduced share of four million spectators.

19. Examples include *Happiness Is a Four Letter Word* (2016, Thabang Moleya, South Africa) and *Tell Me Sweet Something* (2015, Akin Omotoso, South Africa).

20. In contrast, *Road to Missed Calls* (2016, Tunji Ige, USA / Nigeria) is an inventive self-portrait of a rising rap star that sets aside analysis in pursuit of a commercial perspective.

21. *Imagine FESPACO Newsreel 3*, IMAGINE Institute, 2013.

22. Refugees fleeing from the Syrian civil war follow the victims of British policy in previous centuries. Marx's suggestion that "history repeats itself, first as tragedy, second as farce" may apply when John Russell, as foreign minister, wrote privately in 1860 that he hoped a European intervention against massacres in Syria "may vindicate the rights of humanity, so cruelly outraged in Syria."

23. Another perspective is argued in *Curating Africa in the Age of Film Festivals* (Dovey 2015).

24. Also touched on in *Hauntologies*, a booklet produced to accompany the installation of *Psyche* (Akomfrah 2012, 6).

25. Channel 4 Press Office invitation to launch at the Venezuelan Embassy, London, September 19, 1991. As Michael Grade quipped in his launch speech, "Most British television research into the Third World takes place in Terminal 3 [for intercontinental flights] of Heathrow airport."

26. Cf. the "African Radiator Song" example below and the discussion of *Go Forth* in *Educating Film-Makers: Past, Present and Future* (Stoneman 2014, 301–04).

27. Tatouages is a group of five women from the DRC who sing Afro-gospel. Lyrics from *Africa Remix / AH FREAK IYA*, Sai Sai Productions, Éditions Milan Music 2005.

28. https://www.youtube.com/watch?v=-w7jyVHocTk and https://www.youtube.com /watch?v=q5opSsAYQ3k. Accessed December 11, 2016. "African Radiator Song" was produced by Ikind / K-Cap / SAIH—Students and Academics International Assistance Fund in Durban and Oslo.

29. *Les Larmes de Thérèse / Elle / The Rose / Des voix et des choix*, accessed December 9, 2016, http://www.chraschool.org/chra-videos-1.

30. 20SK8 is a brotherhood formed through skateboarding, originating in the Cape Flats, Cape Town, aiming to "resist gangsterism and drugs, and promote urban street culture," https://vimeo.com/123847322 and https://www.youtube.com/watch?v=4vTCMfNqeTI. Accessed December 11, 2016.

Filmography

2000 génération d'Afrique, 2009, Gaston Kaboré, Algeria / Burkina Faso.
Boyz n the Hood, 1991, John Singleton, USA.
Caméra Arabe, 1987, Ferid Boughedir, Tunisia.
The End of Eating Everything, 2010, Wangechi Mutu, Kenya / USA.
Fatal Assistance, 2012, Raoul Peck, Haiti / USA.
Félicité, 2017, Alain Gomis, France / Belgium / Senegal / Germany / Lebanon.
Handsworth Songs, 1986, John Akomfrah, UK.
Happiness Is a Four Letter Word, 2016, Thabang Moleya, South Africa.
Jas Boude, 2014, Georgina Warner and Imraan Christian, South Africa.
Life Is Waiting: Referendum and Resistance in Western Sahara, 2015, Iara Lee, USA / Western Sahara.
La Pirogue, 2012, Moussa Touré, Senegal.
Le point de vue du lion (*The Lion's Point of View*), 2011, Didier Awadi, Senegal.
The Price of Commitment, 2014, Daoda Zallé, Burkina Faso.
Road to Missed Calls, 2016, Tunji Ige, USA / Nigeria.
Tell Me Sweet Something, 2015, Akin Omotoso, South Africa.

The Value of Women in the Congo, 2012, Dearbhla Glynn, Ireland.
Vertigo Sea, 2015, John Akomfrah, England.
Zan Boko, 1988, Gaston Kaboré, Burkina Faso.

References

Adichie, Chimamanda Ngozi. 2014. *We Should All Be Feminists*. London: Fourth
    Estate. 2012 TEDx talk accessed December 2016. https://www.youtube.com
    /watch?v=hg3umXU_qWc.
Akomfrah, John. 2012. *Hauntologies*. London: Carroll / Fletcher.
Andrew, Dudley. 2004. "An Atlas of World Cinema." *Framework: The Journal of Cinema and
    Media* 45 (2): 9–23.
Ba, Saer Maty, and Will Higbee, eds. 2012. *De-Westernising Film Studies*. London: Routledge.
Barthes, Roland. 1973. *Mythologies*. St Albans, UK: Paladin.
Center for Linguistic & Historical Study of Oral Tradition (CELHTO). 2008. *La Charte de
    Kurukan Fuga*. Conakry, Guinea: L'Harmattan.
Dovey, Lindiwe. 2015. *Curating Africa in the Age of Film Festivals*. New York: Palgrave
    Macmillan.
Higbee, Will, and Song Hwee Lim. 2010. "Concepts of Transnational Cinema: Towards
    a Critical Transnationalism in Film Studies." *Transnational Cinemas* 1 (1): 7–21.
    doi:10.1386/trac.1.1.7/1.
Landy, David. 2013. "Talking Human Rights: How Social Movement Activists Are
    Constructed and Constrained by Human Rights Discourse." *International Sociology* 28
    (4): 409–28. doi:10.1177/0268580913490769.
Marx, Karl. 1852. *The 18th Brumaire of Louis Bonaparte*. Accessed January 2017. https://www
    .marxists.org/archive/marx/works/1852/18th-brumaire/.
McHugh, Peter. 2011. "How the Dead Circulate (in Life)." In *Spectacular Death*, edited by
    Tristanne Connolly, 261–69. Bristol, UK: Intellect.
Melville, Herman. (1851) 2012. *Moby Dick*. London: Penguin Classics.
Morris, Meaghan, and Paul Patton, eds. 1979. *Michel Foucault: Power, Truth, Strategy*.
    Sydney: Feral Publications.
Moyn, Samuel. 2010. "Human Rights in History." *The Nation*, August 30–September 6, 2010.
    Accessed December 2016. https://www.thenation.com/article/human-rights-history/.
Mulvey, Laura, and Peter Wollen. 1974. "*Penthesilea, Queen of the Amazons*—Interview with
    Laura Mulvey and Peter Wollen." *Screen* 15 (3): 120–34.
Nagib, Lúcia. 2006. "Towards a Positive Definition of World Cinema." In *Remapping World
    Cinema: Identity, Politics and Culture in Film*, edited by Stephanie Dennison and Song
    Hwee Lim, 30–7. London: Wallflower.
Nagib, Lúcia, Chris Perriam, and Rajinder Dudrah, eds. 2011. *Theorizing World Cinema*.
    London: I.B.Tauris.
Sankara, Thomas. 1988. *Thomas Sankara Speaks: The Burkina Faso Revolution 1983–87*. New
    York: Pathfinder.
Spivak, Gayatri. 1983. "Can the Subaltern Speak?" In *Can the Subaltern Speak? Reflections on
    the History of an Idea*, edited by Rosalind C. Morris, 21–78. New York: Columbia
    University Press.

Stoneman, Rod. 1993. "African Cinema: Addressee Unknown." *Vertigo*, Summer / Autumn 1993. Accessed January 2017. http://www.kinema.uwaterloo.ca/article .php?id=367&feature.

Stoneman, Rod. 2012. "Isn't It Strange That 'World' Means Everything outside the West?" In *De-Westernising Film Studies*, edited by Saer Maty Ba and Will Higbee, 209–21. London: Routledge.

Stoneman, Rod, and Duncan Petrie. 2014. *Educating Film-Makers: Past, Present and Future.* Bristol: Intellect.

Tcheuyap, Alexie. 2011. *Postnationalist African Cinemas.* Manchester: Manchester University Press.

Williams, Heathcote. 1988. *Whale Nation.* London: Cape.

Žižek, Slavoj. 2005. "Against Human Rights." *New Left Review* 34: 115–31 (July–August).

3 Africa's Gift to the World

An Interview with Gaston Kaboré

Rod Stoneman

About Gaston Kaboré

Gaston Kaboré is a pivotal figure in African cinema, on account of his own films as well as for his various types of engagement to ensure the evolution of filmmaking on the African continent.

Born in Burkina Faso (then Upper Volta) in 1951, Kaboré obtained a master's degree in history from the Sorbonne in Paris, France, in 1972. His interest in the cinematographic portrayal of African history led him to filmmaking and to a diploma from the French film school École supérieure d'études cinématographiques (ESEC) in 1976. Upon his return to his home country, he was appointed director of the newly established Centre national du cinéma (CNC) and started teaching filmmaking and scriptwriting at the Institut africain d'études cinématographiques (INAFEC).

In 1982, he made his debut as a feature film director with the internationally acclaimed *Wend Kuuni*, the very first film to be fully funded by Burkina Faso. Both *Wend Kuuni* and its "sequel," *Buud Yam* (1997), are historical films that draw on the African oral tradition.

From 1985 to 1997, Kaboré served as secretary general of the Pan-African association of filmmakers, FEPACI (Fédération panafricaine des cinéastes); in 1992, he cofounded the bilingual film journal *Écrans d'Afrique / African Screen*, which he directed until 1998; and in 2003, he founded the independent film school IMAGINE in Ouagadougou.

In 2012, Concordia University in Montreal conferred an honorary doctorate upon Gaston Kaboré for "his work promoting filmmaking on the African continent and beyond, and for his dedication to transmitting an appreciation of film, video and multi-media creation to young artists through his teaching." He was awarded an honorary doctorate by Lingnan University in Hong Kong in 2013.

The Interview

When you organized Le don de l'Afrique au monde / Africa's Gift to the World *in February 2013, was human rights one of the themes of the exhibition?*

I think the main focus was not related to human rights, but to try to reestablish some of the basic truths in the history of Africa. Necessarily this is going to touch on problems related to slavery, colonialism, even racial issues, how black people from Africa were seen by Western countries, by Europeans. It tried to be clear about theories and ideologies that have been built up to serve the interests of Europe, about how Africans were not regarded as real human beings.

Many things have been put in place to facilitate the work of the Europeans who wanted to transport us. The people that they captured—young people, girls, boys, women, and men—were sent overseas to create resources; they worked without being paid and were treated like animals; so this must be related to human rights.

But when we decided to do this exhibition, the idea was to try to explain to Africans, particularly to the youth of Africa today, that it's not a terrible fate to have been born in Africa, meaning that they should not see themselves as being punished by destiny because they were born here. Of course Africa today has a lot of problems, but new generations have many reasons to be proud of a long African history. Many things have been invented in Africa. Africans have been able to create philosophy, to create myths and legends. They've been able to define visions of the world, to conceive different forms of artistic expression. It's also important to remind people that the history of humanity started in Africa.

Yes, you also had a replica of the skeleton of "Lucy," which reminds us that the beginnings of the human race are here on this continent.

Yes, more and more we are going to find older proofs of the ancient establishment of humanity in Africa. But even in art, in the cave inscriptions in the Sahara, you see the first attempts of human beings to tell us stories through drawings. All those things are there, but they're not so well-known by Africans. We intended to provide another way of looking at the history of Africa, one that could help rebuild confidence in the minds of young people in particular. We have to pay tribute to a group in Grenoble, France, who worked with many people, NGOs, anthropologists, sociologists, philosophers, artists, scientists—many of them had connected and worked to think about how to describe the relationship between Africa and Europe differently. They decided to call the exhibition that they developed *Ce que nous devons à l'Afrique* / *What We Owe to Africa*.

In relation to human rights, the exhibition draws attention to The Charter of Mandé, *which was developed in the thirteenth century?*

The charter was born when Soundjata, who was a ruler of a vast West African empire, decided to bring all those different ethnic groups together and to have a common law. The fundamental law was intended to keep them together, and what is really striking is that they started by saying, "The life of any one human

Figure 3.1. Gaston Kaboré. Photo: Rod Stoneman.

being equals every other human life." This is really something important. All the griots of the different important ethnic groups were there, and they first contributed to defining the different articles, and then they memorized the charter. I'm also really interested in how the charter survived the ruptures of history. How have all these oral elements been kept intact and transmitted across the centuries? It's a period from at least the thirteenth to the twentieth century, because it's only in the last few years they have started working on it. Today, historians have been reconstructing the oral versions from the very beginning.

It's clear that very few people in Europe could imagine that Africans were able to theorize these philosophical, spiritual, political, and social elements in the thirteenth century. It completely changes ideas about the relationship between "advanced" Europe and its Other, Africa, which is always thought of as "primitive."

Because at that time, from then to now, the question persists—how is Africa going to catch up with Europe? The fact is that in certain domains, we were in advance of Europe, but nobody was interested in acknowledging that. They could not be interested in expressing or accepting that, because if they built up the confidence of Africans, there would be problems—confidence would jeopardize the continued pursuit of European interests.

So we have to do this kind of research because Africans need to know who they are, who they were. If you want to know where to go, you need to know where you are coming from. To suggest that there are a lot of things that Africans should know about their history is not to say that there was some kind of paradise in the past, and that's why we need to look back. No, that would be completely useless.

Is the charter, this early version of regulating relations between people, significantly different from more recent human rights declarations in the West?

I don't even want to think about the issue in that way. I would say since Africa has been stopped in its own timetable, its own dynamics of progress have been halted. The history of its people is not a linear progression. What is essential to keep in mind is that our own capacity to address our own issues has been stifled.

After Africa was invaded by the Europeans, there was an attempt to take European rationalities, conceptions, and visions and to apply them directly in Africa, without taking into consideration who we were and what we had achieved. We were not empty vessels. It's not as if we were without vision, stories, philosophy, and knowledge. But they said, "No, you cannot speak your language, nor practice your own religions. Give up your own rules and adopt new ones from Europe without any process of adaptation." As a result I think people stopped thinking, because if you have ideas and they are not taken into consideration, you stop making proposals, suggestions. You don't have the ability to change things because you are under the domination of someone else.

Then, to use Sembène's phrase, we were studied like insects by the Europeans, and they said, "These Africans are very curious—they don't have this and they don't have that." And nobody cared about who we were and what our heritage on this continent actually was. There is no single culture and set of beliefs in Africa, of course; there are many different cultures in Africa, although we share a very strong common background. But there is a diversity, which is a very good thing in itself.

During the colonial period, they didn't see anything but the blackness of the skin and defined that in terms of late development, compared to Europeans. Today Africans have been completely smashed, and we have somehow accepted that we are not the same. You can hear Africans saying that Africa is unable to develop or all those silly things. Why?

I am listening to Europe with its views on human rights, life in general. I really choose my words carefully because we know that even in Europe there is a lot of inequality between individuals. But it's looked at differently in Africa as though everybody knows very little, and outsiders arrive saying, "Yes, the Africans are this, this, and this; the women are not free, they're exploited . . ." What makes me very angry is those young kids of twenty-two, twenty-three years, as soon as they've finished their studies in Europe, they are sent off to those NGOs that are working here, and the assumption is that of course they know what is best for Africa. They can become experts after six months on the soil of Africa. It's really damaging to the self-construction of Africa because being completely dominated by all those groups and declarations—how could you begin to be a young African? How can you even begin to develop your own ability to think for

Figure 3.2. Ministry for the Promotion of Human Rights, Ouagadougou, Burkina Faso. Photo: Rod Stoneman.

yourself? Because you are completely, I don't know the right word, weighed down by all those ideas. And this is the source of many real problems.

Imposing an Agenda

This is the progress that we must make today, and I prefer not to waste my time making comparisons, because in Africa, when comparisons are drawn, the inevitable conclusion is that we can't reinvent everything. We should ourselves be able to select what's needed and thereby to continue on our path; we shouldn't be dictated to by anyone else.

There's a problem when you hear all those people expressing their anger about the way Europe continues to mistreat Africa. It's not that this is untrue, but I am not blaming the Europeans more than I blame myself and other Africans, because we are responsible for our destiny, and in some ways we must take responsibility for how we let others see us.

It's useless to focus on guilt or culpability because it only creates problems. People show up here; they are paid for it. This is how it works, even within the UN—nobody is really trying to understand and to define justice for Africa. They're defining *their* own interests, nothing else. But at the same time, why should I blame them? We have to do what's right for ourselves. We cannot expect other people to be a charity for us, to be generous to us. We have to address ourselves to the issues that we are caught up in. This will create frictions, confrontations, but it's what we have to do.

Is the attempt to impose a Western human rights agenda a distraction or, even worse, a digression that blocks the development of African thinking and action?

The problem is really central. The agenda is not unreasonable, but there's something wrong with it nonetheless, and that has to do with the fact that we're not empowered to do things ourselves. The organizations come here with money and experts, and when the money stops, everything stops. I think we have to say we don't want this type of cooperation. We need to do things differently. Of course, the worry could be that we're wasting time by not cooperating. Sometimes things do move in the right direction, and in those cases I prefer to do small things, to take steps in the direction of rights as defined by the West, instead of just saying "No, no, no." I have to take what's good to nurture my analysis and continue on my own. That's why I've chosen to teach, to build IMAGINE as a school, to transmit something. I want to bring all the people who have the same vision along with me. So we try to give something to Africa and the world. This exhibition and school will not be able to resolve all the problems, but they can teach us something, and then we have to continue on from there. The frontline is so wide, so extensive.

What is the role of films in the politics of the wider culture and the discourses of human rights?

Human rights is such a huge field that anything you might do, giving people access to knowledge and know-how is also an aspect of human rights. Films allow people to portray themselves, they enable people to recognize themselves in their own images, and this will certainly help to make things less difficult for the majority of people. But I don't like this categorization. I'm very cautious and suspicious of using the term "human rights" in that way. A phrase like "cinema and human rights" doesn't open things up. It shuts things down, narrows something. Because for me, human rights is not only about democracy, politics. What about the relationship between Africa and Europe? This is a big human rights battlefield. Africans are dying daily because of the greed of the companies from Europe, because of their shareholders and how they think about what is good for their profits. And those companies are most often supported by our governments because they think the companies are good for our countries. It's always the same story.

Maybe Africa is the continent where life is cheaper than anywhere else. Why is that? Because a capitalist company buys the raw material at the minimum cost, the lowest price. If they don't get the level of profit they expect, what do they do? They close the operation and fire workers—twelve thousand workers, to them it's nothing. A human being is less than a machine. So, should we accept this way of life, this way of thinking, this way of seeing the world?

There's a tendency to define the problem by putting it in compartments and categories (by developing policies and programs to support women against female genital mutilation, for example)—it's a way of fragmenting reality; in the end one loses a holistic vision, a long-term perspective. We have to look at how certain forms of democracy function, and we'll have to work out priorities that deliver lasting changes in terms of the lives of future populations. These are global problems. Africa is not a laboratory for the West to experiment with.

Women's Rights and *Wend Kuuni*

How can these ideas work within culture, within a fiction film?

I tried in my first movie, *Wend Kuuni* (1982), to show a story where two women decided to refuse the social norms in their tribe. The mother of Wend Kuuni rebels because she's convinced that her husband is still alive, and she wants to wait until he returns. And her revolt leads to a lot of difficulties for her and also her children. And then her son loses the capacity to speak. Another young woman revolts against the seventy-year-old husband she was given to when she was just sixteen; she rebels and tells him, "You're impotent!"—so everybody is scandalized!

As far as I'm concerned, the film wasn't acting out some ideology, but you can see that the two women represent change in a society. Even when a society seems to be absolutely immobile, some ideas are working within it. I prefer if you can interpret and create your own reflections on the film. It's better than taking on a story that has been digested by someone else and just repeating the ideas without really absorbing the elements.

To take another example from your own cinema: Zan Boko *(1988) is a film that touches on many things, but I've heard it discussed in terms of specific human rights—freedom of expression, for example, or the issue of urbanization. That's a narrow way to interpret elements from a film that touches on society and change in a complex way.*

If someone says, "Gaston, you have made a film, you know, on human rights," I'm not going to argue against the claim. But as far as I'm concerned, I didn't sit down and say, this is what I'm going to do. In fact, somehow the words "human rights" make us prisoners. The words we're using have imprisoned us.

Filmmaking and Training

How did you make that decision, quite exceptional for a filmmaker, to divide your time between your own filmmaking and building a new training institute?

Figure 3.3. Accused of being a witch, Wend Kuuni's mother flees her village, carrying her sick son on her back. Framegrab from *Wend Kuuni* (*God's Gift*, 1982, Gaston Kaboré, Burkina Faso).

I think since the beginning the ideas have come in different forms, one after the other. I think I've always been convinced that it's important to transmit something to someone else, to pass on the knowledge. Because I decided to become a filmmaker, this clock inside me started to tick. I started to think about where the knowledge and the know-how could be distributed in a new way. In other words, I like to teach because I like to learn, and because I like to learn, I like to teach. The one who teaches is also the one who learns the most.

Training was one of my main preoccupations when I managed the national film board from 1977 to 1988, and also when I was with the Pan-African Federation of Filmmakers, which I was president of from 1985 to 1997. I was always struggling to see how I could enlarge the scope of training within the country, or regionally, or elsewhere in Africa. I looked for partners and started organizing workshops in 1978.

So then the idea of creating the IMAGINE Institute came to me. I wanted to create this place where people would come, where the youngsters would learn alongside their elders. I wanted to create a place for discussion, a place where ideas, passion, and skills related to the craft of filmmaking could be shared. Even the architecture of this building is part of all that.

Funding, Self-Censorship, and Financial Pressure

Have you experienced the process of applying to European funders for support for either filmmaking or IMAGINE as distorting your aims and intentions?

When you talk to any sponsor or funder, you realize that there are also some expectations from the donor. But if you're a creator, you need to find the balance between the personal project you wanted the money for and the extent to which you can compromise with the agenda of the donors. I've received money to make my films, but I've never felt I've been forced to do what I didn't want to do. Not in any way. It's a question of choice, a question of independence, and sometimes you should simply stop yourself asking for money from sources where you know it's best not to go.

I don't think I've betrayed any of the people who have given me money to make my films, because my project is clear in advance. I've always presented the film as a project, and I've never sought to please anyone, neither during the shooting, the editing, or the process of post-production. But self-censorship is the worst, because sometimes you might find yourself thinking, "If I do that, it won't be accepted." This is for me the worst kind of censorship because we should always try to aim at the maximum, at the extreme of our personal designs, of our convictions.

You should be prepared to be misunderstood sometimes, to disappoint people. When I made *Zan Boko*, for instance, after having made *Wend Kuuni*, some people said, "You're better at doing a poetic or mythic film like *Wend Kuuni*." And I said, "But I'm the same person who made both, and I don't have a preference for any one of my films." In fact, audiences and critics responded very differently to my films, but that's not my business. I make the film I want to make, and I accept that the others see it as they wish and that they will have their opinions. I have to accept that.

In the case of the IMAGINE Institute, it's perhaps not quite as simple. In general, it's always a process of applying for support—you go out there to ask for money. Generally, what's taken into account is the quantity of things, not the quality of things. And we're always defined by figures.

People have to say things like, "Why are you doing that? We're more interested in this or that." But I won't change my program just to please, because if you do that, you'll never get where you are aiming to go. I try to convince funders that what I've chosen to do is the right thing. And then they have to make their decisions.

There is a whole range of cultural, political, and economic contexts, which means that if you make a film in Africa today, it is likely you already have something to say, something urgent to communicate.

Yes, it seems that any film in Africa is a testament somehow. It's so rare to be able to make a movie here because of the lack of money. So when you have this opportunity, I think any filmmaker wants to say as much as possible. And we're mostly so voiceless, so when we are given the possibility to speak, we're very aware of it. We need to use that possibility to maximum effect with issues of social, political, and cultural responsibility in mind. Culture is something important. Culture is not as short-term an issue as the politicians think. In a deep sense, it is the route to the future, a projection of how we understand our future.

Recorded in Ouagadougou, Burkina Faso, on February 21, 2016. Transcription by Yuenlam Li Janice.

ROD STONEMAN is Emeritus Professor at the National University of Ireland, Galway. He was previously Director of the Huston School of Film & Digital Media, Chief Executive of Bord Scannán na hÉireann/the Irish Film Board, and a deputy commissioning editor in the Independent Film and Video Department at Channel 4 Television in the United Kingdom.

Films by Gaston Kaboré

Wend Kuuni/God's Gift, 1982, Burkina Faso.
Zan Boko, 1988, Burkina Faso / France.
Rabi, 1992, Burkina Faso / UK.
Lumière et Compagnie, 1995, France.
Buud Yam, 1997, Burkina Faso / France.
Le loup et la cigogne, 2007, France / Burkina Faso.
2000 génération d'Afrique, 2009, Algeria / Burkina Faso.

4 Toward New African Languages of Protest

African Documentary Films and Human Rights

Alessandro Jedlowski

In the history of African cinema(s), documentary films have long been stand-ing in the shadows of narrative feature films (Ukadike 1995, 89).[1] Often marked by ambiguous relations with political authorities, the documentary format was until recently looked upon with suspicion by most African filmmakers and audi-ences. After having been widely used by colonial administrations and missionar-ies as a tool for propaganda and education (Sanogo 2009; Bloom 2008; Gangnat, Lenoble-Bart, and Zorn 2013), the format was later adopted for similar uses by the newly formed independent governments (Loftus 2012; Tapsoba 1996), as well as by NGOs and international humanitarian organizations (Bryce 2010). In the eyes of many African audiences, filmmakers, and broadcasters, African docu-mentary films have therefore come to be seen either as foreign-funded, boring, message-oriented films, or as equally boring government-funded propaganda fare—good only as a "'bread winning genre', more similar to commissioned films than to films of creation" (Tapsoba 1996, 54, quoted in Akudinobi 2000, 345). A few notable exceptions do exist, of course—think of the works by Samba Félix Ndiaye, John Akomfrah, and Jean-Marie Teno, for instance (Imbert 2007; Eshun and Sagar 2007; Nganang 2005)—but most of these films have been produced by diasporic filmmakers or have circulated almost exclusively on the international festival circuit.

With the introduction of new recording and editing technologies in the late 1990s and early 2000s, things have begun to change significantly. The emer-gence of commercial film industries such as the Nigerian Nollywood, the Tan-zanian Bongowood, and the Ghanaian Ghallywood (Krings and Okome 2013; Garritano 2013; Overbergh 2015) is probably the most visible and talked-about consequence of these transformations, but the field of documentary film pro-duction has also witnessed important growth and diversification (Fronty and

Kifouani 2014). New documentary film festivals have appeared across the continent, new training initiatives have been created, and a new generation of young and dynamic African documentary filmmakers has begun to emerge. Both locally and internationally, this phenomenon is welcomed with enthusiasm by all those who see documentary films as a privileged tool for fostering a more dynamic and politically engaged civil society. Nevertheless, the process of creating and consolidating a viable and solid documentary film production environment still faces numerous challenges, which, in my view, must be the necessary starting point for any thorough discussion of the relationship between documentary films and human rights in Africa today.

This chapter, therefore, takes a closer look at the African film production context in order to pinpoint what key stakeholders across the continent consider to be the main obstacles to creating an independent and economically sound African documentary film industry. Indeed, if there is already an important corpus of African documentary films whose contents and aesthetics can be discussed in a human rights perspective,[2] the documentary genre's mere "conditions of existence" in contemporary Africa are critical. As most interested parties agree, the establishment of genuine economic and political independence across the continent is a precondition for any further discussion about the interaction between documentary films and human rights. Even if it is true that the introduction of affordable digital technologies has made film production easier, quicker, and more accessible, specific infrastructural, political, and economic factors still condition documentary film production in fundamental ways.

In order to tackle these issues, I have divided the chapter into three main sections. The first one is based on a wide range of materials collected between 2012 and 2013 for a continent-wide, team-based research project on the state of the documentary film industry across Africa. The project, which I had the chance to participate in, was financed by the Bertha Foundation as part of the African Documentary Film Fund (ADFF) initiative.[3] A discussion of these materials allows for a comprehensive (although inevitably general) analysis of the main challenges that African documentary filmmakers are facing today, including aspects related to content production, funding, training, distribution, and the lack of infrastructures. This analysis opens up the space for a critical discussion of the interaction between human rights discourses and documentary film production in Africa today, which is the focus of the second section. Human rights discourses have been the object of much scholarly debate in Africa, and a discussion of these debates in relation to the challenges highlighted in the first section will help us better understand the field of tensions within which African documentary filmmakers are operating. This field of tensions is further analyzed in the third and last section of the chapter, which takes a closer look at Jean-Pierre Bekolo's docufiction *Le président—comment sait-on qu'il est temps de partir?* (*The President,*

2013, Cameroon / Germany), one example among many of African documentary cinema's ongoing exploration of new languages of protest.

Producing Documentary Films in Contemporary Africa

Based on the data collected as part of the ADFF initiative, it is possible to draw a portrait of the conditions for contemporary documentary film production in Africa. It is hard to summarize these conditions without resorting to some degree of simplification, for there are important differences between the various regions identified in the reports. Especially Egypt and South Africa deserve to be discussed independently—as indeed they have been in most scholarly work on African cinema—because of the specific historical depth and complexity of their local film industries. In addition, there are fundamental differences between groups of countries that had diverse colonial experiences. It is, for instance, much easier to compare the current state of training and production infrastructures in Nigeria and Kenya, or in Senegal and Mali, whereas the differences are evident when one tries to compare, for instance, Kenya with Mali, or Nigeria with Senegal. However, bearing these fundamental limitations in mind, it is possible to outline a number of common trends and challenges that can be observed throughout the continent, as evidenced by the ADFF research reports.

As mentioned in the introduction, the first major obstacle to documentary film production in Africa is the fact that this format still struggles to find its audience. In most African countries, broadcasters, advertisers, and the audience consider documentary films to be a very marginal product, and directors encounter innumerable difficulties when it comes to having their films screened, not to mention making the exhibitors (television channels, theater halls, etc.) pay for the rights to screen them. The many documentary film festivals that have emerged all over the continent during the past few years are doing an important job in creating an audience for the films,[4] but this is an ongoing process that still needs time and a lot of support in order to be fully achieved. Most audiences, in fact, still connect the documentary format exclusively to NGO films or to the National Geographic style of nature documentaries. During my fieldwork in countries such as Nigeria and Côte d'Ivoire, however, I observed an emerging interest in more politically relevant, creative documentaries, as indicated by the compilations of pirated documentary films that are sold in the street markets of cities such as Abidjan and Lagos. These compilations, however, hardly include any African documentaries but are rather made up of randomly selected films downloaded from YouTube or other free online platforms.

This situation reflects the paucity of documentary films produced on the continent and their difficulties in finding viable circulation networks. In general terms, it is possible to say that while the continent is traversed by widespread dynamism and a number of interesting experiences have emerged over the past few years, documentary film production is still everywhere affected by a general lack of resources, first of all when it comes to funding, but also in terms of professional skills as well as pre- and postproduction facilities. Over the past few years, some countries (such as South Africa, Algeria, Tanzania, Morocco, Tunisia, Gabon, Benin, Burkina Faso, Mali, Nigeria, and Senegal) have developed state-directed initiatives to support film production (such as National Film Funds and National Film Institutes), but the efficacy of these undertakings is often criticized by local filmmakers, who denounce the nepotism involved in the allocation of funds. Local investment is almost absent, and where it does exist, it is related either to the production of electoral and propaganda films commissioned by the politicians in power or to the production of documentary films for limited circulation within corporate business initiatives. Beyond these forms of investments, the only resources available come from external agents, such as NGOs, international television channels (such as BBC, Al-Jazeera, Arte, CCTV, and TV5 Monde), international film funds, and governmental institutions. As I will discuss in more detail below, it is important to underline that the activities of these organizations are often criticized by filmmakers because they do not allow creativity to develop freely, instead imposing specific themes and agendas.

It is worth noting that local broadcasters are almost completely absent from the picture. In the past few years, the situation has begun to change owing to the continent-wide process of digital switchover, which is multiplying the number of local TV channels and boosting their demand for content (Jedlowski 2016).[5] But the troubles created by decades of disconnection between the broadcasting sector and the documentary film production environment are still very much visible on the ground. In most African countries, local television providers hardly ever assume a share of the production expenses. On the contrary, they typically ask filmmakers to buy airtime from them in order to screen the films. The director or producer then has to sell advertising slots in order to recover the relevant expenses. This is, for instance, the model in force (until recently) in Nigeria, Ghana, Guinea, the Democratic Republic of Congo, Botswana, Kenya, and Uganda. Similar dynamics are found in most francophone West African countries, where local television stations (both private and public) in many cases do not sell airtime but pretend to have the right to screen the film for free as many times as they want.

This state of things is the consequence of a number of factors that have plagued the television sector across the continent for the past three or four decades. One problem has to do with the traditional role played by national television stations within the local media environment. More specifically, they have enjoyed an unchallenged monopolistic position, one that has spurred them to disregard commercial fairness. Due to the liberalization processes imposed by Structural Adjustment Programs (SAP), this situation began to change throughout the

1990s and early 2000s, but in most countries the national broadcaster is still in a position of uncontested hegemony with regard to the local market, and acts accordingly.

Another problem has been the lack of an apt legal framework for protecting the interests of local producers (such as, for instance, laws imposing a quota of local productions on the content screened by local broadcasters), which, combined with the unfair behavior of international broadcasters and donors, has made most local networks heavily dependent on foreign content. Indeed, some international broadcasters have offered African television stations package deals that allow them to screen foreign content for free, thus making it practically impossible for local productions to compete. Instead, a problematic state of dependency has been created—the most notable agent in this respect being Canal France International in francophone Africa.[6] The troublesome state of the local advertising market has also played a role. The general underdevelopment of this sector means that it does not mobilize significant revenues for television stations, the result being a lack of purchasing power (see also Alozie 2011). In this situation, local television stations have found it hard to compete with the commercial offerings made available by international satellite TVs that have invaded most African countries over the past few years and that can generally afford to offer much better-quality content than the local television stations themselves.

Another fundamental factor to consider when assessing the situation of the documentary film industry on the continent is the often dilapidated state of various infrastructures, which, as Brian Larkin (2008) has eloquently showed, plays a fundamental role for media production and circulation all over Africa. The first element that comes to mind in this sense is electricity. One of the worst countries in this respect is probably Nigeria (Olukoju 2004), but unpredictable power cuts do happen in most sub-Saharan countries and have multiple impacts on film production. In many cases they increase film budgets since the power necessary for the proper functioning of all technical equipment (on set and during postproduction) has to be locally produced through expensive gas-powered generators. Power disruptions also have a problematic influence on television budgets. In Nigeria, for instance, most television channels, both private and state-owned, have to generate the power they consume, which dramatically reduces the budgets available for content production.[7]

Furthermore, the general infrastructural collapse that occurred in the 1980s and 1990s as a result of the SAP has provoked an almost complete abandonment of existing national archives whose documents (U-matic tapes, celluloid recordings, and so on) needed specific, expensive care in order to be correctly preserved. While a few initiatives of restoration have seen the light over the past few years in countries such as South Africa, Mozambique, and Burkina Faso, in many cases most documents have been lost, which creates a major problem for filmmakers who wish to use archival material as part of their projects (Bensalah 2000; Ndiaye 2011). Today, most African filmmakers who want to include archival footage about their own countries in their works find themselves in the paradoxical situation of being obliged to buy it from TV channels and archives located in the ancient colonial metropoles. As a result, the cost of using archival footage is so high that in many cases film projects relying on archival materials are simply abandoned, or can never achieve official distribution for lack of official authorization to use the images included in the film.[8]

Furthermore, SAP also pushed the majority of African states to privatize most state-owned media infrastructures (film schools, recording studios, theater halls, television stations, etc.). In many cases these infrastructures have been reconverted and put to other uses, thus creating an infrastructural void, the consequences of which are still felt by both documentary and fiction film directors and producers throughout the continent. The main problem concerns distribution and exhibition venues. Except for a few countries such as South Africa, Egypt, Ethiopia, Algeria, and Morocco, most cinema theaters on the continent have been closed down and, in many cases, turned into churches. Some countries such as Nigeria, Ghana, and Kenya are witnessing the emergence of multiplex cinemas, but with their focus on commercial distribution, these venues target elite audiences and screen mainly foreign films. A few projects are emerging that involve the creation of film hubs with access to large film libraries (such as the Lagos Film Society and the Nairobi-based Docubox film hub), and attempts to create networks of community screening centers equipped with digital projectors have also made some progress over the past few years.[9] But in general most people watch films and television in informal places, such as video clubs and neighborhood screening halls.

It is within this context that the introduction of digital technology has opened a new set of possibilities and allowed for the emergence of a new generation of young, often self-trained filmmakers. This has surely revitalized film production all over the continent, but in many countries it has also provoked a generational conflict between, on the one hand, the old school of highly trained celluloid filmmakers and television operators who, because of their somehow nostalgic attachment to expensive celluloid technologies, tend to have a very low rate of production, and, on the other hand, a new generation, which, thanks to the new technologies, manages to produce and circulate a large quantity of films. As most of the ADFF investigations show, older professionals tend to see the new generation as pretentious, undertrained, and often politically superficial, while the new generation considers the old one to be nostalgic and attached to its own privileges.[10] In most cases, the old generation controls the redistribution of the few national resources available for the local film industries, and very often they prefer to redistribute them among the restricted circle of old-school filmmakers, thus provoking the resentment of the emerging talents.

This brings us to the last point worth considering here: training. Formal and well-structured training institutions for documentary filmmaking are lacking in most African countries, and the existing institutions are concentrated in countries with a longer and more established filmmaking tradition such as South Africa, Senegal, Burkina Faso, Ghana, Mali, and Tunisia. Across the continent, the most dynamic and methodologically up-to-date training opportunities are often connected to foreign cultural centers and film festivals. In order to benefit from funding programs related to international cooperation, these institutions usually invite filmmakers from abroad (mainly from Western countries) to offer master classes and workshops to young, aspiring African filmmakers. However, as Jean-Marie Teno has underlined, having "Europeans training Africans to look at and represent themselves raises certain questions, especially if one considers many of these teachers' lack of awareness and sometimes lack of interest in the history of the continent, and particularly the history of African representation" (2011).

Be it because of the interference of governments and local politicians, or because of the intervention of NGOs and international stakeholders, African documentarists have struggled and still struggle to free themselves from the utilitarian perspective of the agencies that fund them. As Charles Acland and Haidee Wasson have emphasized, cinema entertains a complex relationship with institutions, a relationship that sometimes reduces film to an instrument for political transformation or, in other cases, to a tool for maintaining the status quo: "Even as institutions may extol the virtues of technological innovation and progressive change, at one level such actions help preserve and reproduce that institution. Film has long been used in this seemingly paradoxical sense: to both promote change and to resist it" (Acland and Wasson 2011, 4). Contemporary documentary filmmakers in Africa definitely find themselves in this conundrum, and their reliance on external funding networks does not help them gain more freedom. Indeed, this situation has important implications not only for the aesthetic and narrative decisions that filmmakers are forced to make, but also for the specific content and values they can express. In fact, as Jade Miller pinpoints, "no matter what language films are produced in, there needs to be a script produced in a major European language in order for it to go through competitive funding processes" (Miller 2016, 74, quoting Armes 2006). The issue of language occupies a central position in many filmmakers' concerns and goes beyond the straightforward issue of the written language of the script or the spoken language of the film. It also involves the larger question of which cultural values, ethical principles, and narrative models the filmmakers can adopt while talking about human rights in Africa.

Human Rights Discourses and Documentary Filmmaking

Human rights discourses are far from uncontested in Africa. While to some scholars their mobilization is a mainly pragmatic and normative issue related to local social and political practices (Musa and Domatob 2010), others consider human rights discourses themselves to be a "largely untheorized" field in the African context (Duncan 2012, 175), a field that would need to be subjected to "closer historical and political scrutiny" (Shivji 1989, vii). One of the most vocal and explicit critics in this regard is the Tanzanian intellectual Issa Shivji, who has suggested that "'human rights ideology' is an ideology of domination and part of the imperialist world outlook" (1989, 3). And Francis Nyamnjoh reminds us that "political, cultural, historical and, above all, economic realities, determine what form and meaning the discussion and articulation of citizenship and rights assume in any given context" (2005, 17). The production and distribution of documentary films in Africa clearly demonstrate how specific situations determine even the most basic conditions of existence of a given discourse.

It is within this context that the issue of language takes center stage, adding a further layer of complexity to the argument this chapter develops. As Herri Englund asks in his work on human rights talks in Malawian call-in radio programs, "what insight might be gained into rights and obligations if claims expressed in African languages were taken seriously by activists, academics, and policy-makers?" (2011, 2). As documentary filmmakers have to deal with an external funding system, also when discussing human rights, they have found themselves facing what Sinfree Makoni defines as a situation of "theoretical extraversion," in which they "construe their professional work as a space to test Western constructs rather than to develop endogenous knowledge practices" (2012, 1). Following the call to unmask "spurious universals" (Wiredu 1996, 5), many African intellectuals have attempted to find in African languages and cultures the basis for the construction of an African understanding of human rights. Concepts such as those of "ubuntu" in southern Africa (Metz 2011; van Binsbergen 2001), "gada" among the Oromo people in the Horn of Africa (Legesse 2006), and "onipa" among the Akan people in West Africa (Wiredu 1996) have been discussed at length as possible and valuable entry points into specifically African ways of dealing with the issue of individual and collective rights.

At times, this debate has created sharp polarizations opposing "rights talks" to "culture talks," and it has favored a politically dangerous cultural relativism easily instrumentalized to justify various forms of human rights abuses. As Mahmood Mamdani has poignantly asked, "how do we ensure that those who claim to safeguard cultural difference do not turn around to impose a cultural dictatorship on their own communities? Put differently, how do we ensure diversity—not just between cultures but also within cultures—and thus free play for those forces that give cultures their internal dynamism?" (2000, 4).

These questions highlight the extremely complex field of tensions at the heart of any engagement with issues related to human rights in an African context. How are the documentary filmmakers to tackle problems related to social justice, citizenship, minority rights, and other similar issues? Which languages are best at expressing these concerns in ways that are accessible and culturally familiar to local audiences and political authorities? And how are the filmmakers to elaborate an original, culturally specific language within a context of economic dependency on foreign organizations that adopt a vocabulary of "rights" and "wrongs" that is at times ambiguously connected to the imperialist agenda?

Such tensions are particularly visible when it comes to the issue of LGBT rights. As underlined by Patrick Awondo, Peter Geschiere, and Graeme Reid, "the first decade of this century brought a sudden propulsion of 'homosexuality' as a burning issue on the public scene in many parts of Africa" (2012, 147). The increase in public concern about this issue has been a direct consequence of an expanding international activism on the part of both LGBT rights campaigners and conservative, right-wing American Christian parties supporting antigay politics. In addition, the uproar has been reinforced by the rapid growth throughout the continent of both local LGBT organizations and conservative, "traditionalist" movements labeling homosexuality as a "Western import." The imposition of a binary vision of "a global gay identity based on the homo/hetero dyad" has in some cases ended up reinforcing "homophobic reactions" (Awondo, Geschiere and Reid 2012, 160). Within this context, African LGBT people have found themselves prisoners of monolithic discourses, unable to take into account the historical and cultural specificities of African experiences of homosexuality.

Documentary filmmakers who have attempted to discuss these issues have a firsthand experience of such polarizations. A good example is provided by the trajectory of the docu-fiction film *Stories of Our Lives* (2014, Jim Chuchu, Kenya), which consists of a few short, fictive reenactments of real-life LGBT stories collected by members of the Kenyan art collective NEST during a trip around Kenya. The film had a very successful opening at the Toronto International Film Festival in 2014, but soon after it was censored by the Kenyan Film Classification Board and banned for "obscenity, explicit scenes of sexual activities and [for promoting] homosexuality, which is contrary to [Kenya's] national norms and values" (Vourlias 2014). As one of the film's producers told me during an informal conversation, international LGBT organizations proposed to create an international campaign against the Kenyan government and in favor of the film, but the filmmakers refused, for fear that the international intervention might provoke further repression in the country. According to Jim Chuchu, "we sometimes get the sense that countries that are 'over it' [the struggle for LGBT rights] get impatient with the rest of the world. It's almost like a big brother who's done with school and is standing next to you, screaming, 'C'mon already!' The language developed in countries where they've already dealt with LGBT issues is now being imposed to us—already packaged—and I think there's some resistance from people in our

Figure 4.1. The President, played by the Cameroonian actor Gérard Essomba. *Le président— comment sait-on qu'il est temps de partir?* (*The President*, 2013, Jean-Pierre Bekolo, Cameroon / Germany). Copyright: Weltfilm.

part of the world, who want to define things for themselves" (Chuchu, quoted in Harding 2014).

As demonstrated by research on LGBT rights across the continent, many "homophobic reactions are closely related to resentment of Western imperialism" and, as a result, "interventions from outside Africa—whether from politicians or activists—that prescribe certain values can very easily turn out to be counterproductive" (Awondo, Geschiere, and Reid 2012, 159–61). In the case of *Stories of Our Lives*, the filmmakers' refusal to let international organizations intervene seems to have helped the film in progressively finding a local audience and in promoting local debates contradicting the international, media-generated "monolithic image of one homophobic Africa" (ibid., 149).

These examples highlight once again the complexity of the situation within which African documentary filmmakers operate. Interventions by international activists tend to corroborate the widespread impression that "the dominant human rights discourse [is] an initiative with a strongly American flavor that serves a stabilizing and conservative function, as it replaces the discourse of revolution with that of reform" (Duncan 2012, 175). From this perspective, human rights discourses, and the main agents of their circulation across the continent (such as NGOs and other local and international humanitarian organizations), are often considered to be causing a troubling "depoliticization" of the arena within which rights claims can be made. Paraphrasing James Ferguson's classic work (1990), they can be seen as "anti-politics machine[s]" that reduce the space within which local actors can maneuver politically. To counter this situation, Mahmood Mamdani suggests, we should not follow the temptation to abandon the human rights discourse altogether. Rather, we should "go beyond the confines of 'rights talk and culture talk' and embrace the 'language of protest' which bears a relationship to the 'language of power'" (Dicklitch 2001, 618, quoting Mamdani 2000).

New African Languages of Protest

As Jean-Pierre Bekolo has provocatively emphasized, "Cinema always arrives afterwards, to tell us about the Arab Spring for example. Where was the Cinema before? The Cinema must be forward-thinking, open new doors and make the revolutions. I do not want to tell people what happened, I want to inspire those who will make it happen" (Bekolo, quoted in Diao 2012).

These words are, in my view, a powerful translation of Mamdani's definition of emerging "language(s) of protest"—aesthetic and narrative languages that are able to go beyond "rights talks" and "culture talks" to intervene in a given reality by fostering the emergence of autonomous social movements. Bekolo's own work can help us outline some key aspects of such emerging languages of protest within the context of African documentary cinema. While *Le président— comment sait-on qu'il est temps de partir?* can hardly be straightforwardly labeled as a documentary film, its direct reference to the reality that is behind (and all around) the camera makes it a very interesting example of how the documentary format can be pushed to its extreme limits to formulate new aesthetic and narrative languages attuned to the complexity of the contemporary world. Bekolo's film combines elements from the language of TV shows, documentary films, music video clips, and fiction films to imagine the end of Paul Biya's decades-long regime in Cameroon. It attempts to open up a new space for people to imagine alternative futures within a context where even thinking about the future (and thus about a post-Biya era) has become taboo. This is not an easy task since, as Bekolo stressed in the debate after the first public screening of the film (as one of the unofficial side activities of the FESPACO 2013 festival in Ouagadougou), the filmmaker needs to rebuild the very possibility of critical knowledge in a context where the idea of criticism as such has been banned for decades. To Bekolo, it is a process that has to advance step by step, through dialogue rather than radical confrontation. How can the audience be pushed to turn against a figure they have learned to regard almost as a deity? In Cameroon, stresses Bekolo, most people think that criticizing the president means saying that "he's a bad person; but it's not about whether he's good or bad. He's been there too long. This guy was minister when Obama was one year old. It doesn't matter whether he's done good or bad, he might even be a good person. Between him and himself, when does he know when it's time to go?" (Bekolo in Eardley 2013).

Indeed, one of the most amazing things about Bekolo's film is the deep humanity of the character of the president, a humanity that seems to invite the regime to an act of introspection. In the film, Biya's alter ego (played by one of Cameroon's greatest actors, Gérard Essomba) is an old man, over eighty, who decides to disappear not because he is threatened or ill, but because he finds himself immersed in an interior dialogue that drives him to question not only himself, but also the legacy of his government and the future of his people. This is a president who suddenly becomes human, weak, thoughtful, unsure of himself, and determined to explore, for a few days and in disguise, his own country, a country that he stopped being curious about a long time ago. Wrapped in a long traditional robe that makes him unrecognizable, the president wanders across the country, overhears the conversations of his fellow citizens, and sees the despair in the eyes of the young who are unemployed. He even meets up with a young rapper who dared to send him, some years back, a number of open letters in the form of songs—an event that created much agitation in the streets of Yaoundé and Douala. The rapper, Valsero, is a real person and a very well-known musician in Cameroon. In the film he appears as himself and talks directly to the president who, in reality, never answered his letters. The audience is invited to witness a surreal debate between the fictional president and the real rapper, with the rapper throwing the most explicit of his songs at the president's face. He looks straight into the camera and sings: "President, Cameroon is ill / Cameroon is a land of martyrs / We die of hunger, everyone wants to leave / you are responsible."[11] The president tries to defend himself, to reply, but he is clearly tired and weak and does nothing to resist or silence the criticism. On the contrary, he seems to become even more immersed in his own thoughts. "My goal is not to show a bad president," emphasizes Bekolo in another interview, "but a man who wonders about his life. I did not want to condemn the president, but rather pass him the ball" (Bekolo in Hering 2013, my translation).

The president's surreal existential journey is narrated to the audience with salacious irony by the investigative journalist Jo Woo'do, anchorman of a fictitious TV show on one of the many Cameroonian private networks that have emerged over the past few years. But against this background, a number of other storylines intersect. In several sequences, for example, political prisoners are seen secretly exchanging information leaked, from the outside, about the disappearance of the president. The prisoners come across as tense, waiting to decide when to take action in what appears to be a coup plot. Another set of sequences are held in a tone somewhat similar to that of certain sequences in Djibril Diop Mambéty's *Touki Bouki* (1973, Senegal). Here, the camera follows, at length and in a naturalistic way, some young motorcycle taxi drivers in the streets of Yaoundé. In the discussion after the screening of the film in Ouagadougou, Bekolo explained that these young people represent what remains of the energy of contemporary

Figure 4.2. Moto-taxi drivers in *Le président—comment sait-on qu'il est temps de partir?* (*The President*, 2013, Jean-Pierre Bekolo, Cameroon / Germany). Copyright: Weltfilm.

Cameroon, its ultimate survival instinct. Despite their studies and diplomas, most young people's only economic prospect is to buy a cheap Chinese motorcycle and become taxi drivers. This is the zero degree of survival possibilities granted by the regime, a zero level that the youth is ready to defend at all costs, thus unveiling what remains of their instinct for political organization and rebellion. When a few years ago the government tried to impose a new tax on gasoline and expressed its intention to regulate the motorcycle taxi service licenses and enforce stricter safety rules, the youth of the main Cameroonian cities instantly took to the streets to revolt. Insisting on the images of the young motorcycle taxi drivers, their tired and displeased faces, Bekolo pays a tribute to what is left of the Cameroonian capacity to revolt, secretly inviting his fellow citizens to continue doing so.

Through these parallel narrative lines, Bekolo seeks to maintain a moderate, even poetic tone. Rather than explicit messages proposing a specific political project, he uses hints and suggestions to awaken a new hunger for the future in the Cameroonian public. Perhaps that is why the film ends up being deeply revolutionary. For Biya's government it might have been easier to condemn and ban a more openly subversive film. That the regime does not shy away from resorting to extreme violence against its critics was demonstrated in April 2013 when Richard Djimili, a film student at the University of Yaoundé, was kidnapped and tortured for several days by henchmen of the regime because of a short film in which he openly criticized Biya. But Bekolo's unusual approach has put the government in a difficult position. Not only is Bekolo himself a figure of international stature, his film is also more of an invitation than a snub. It does criticize the misdeeds of the government but does not judge the president. Rather, it proposes a dialogue on the possibilities of a post-Biya era, a dialogue that is not allowed in today's Cameroon.

Despite its subtle approach, the film was immediately censored in its home country. Also, institutions and international partners who had accompanied the production, such as the French Cultural Institute (Alliance Française) in Yaoundé and the satellite channel Canal +, decided to withdraw their support, justifying their action by stating that they could not interfere in the internal affairs of the country. Bekolo bitterly commented on these events, which he saw as nothing more than the latest betrayal by institutions claiming to defend human rights, while economically and militarily supporting the worst dictatorships. "Today," he writes, "the plot of these institutions becomes even clearer in light of what we see happening in many African countries. They emptied the African cinema of each substance to make it nothing more than an object to carry around from one festival to the next, for the pleasure of the Western public" (Bekolo 2013, my translation).[12]

Making political cinema in Africa today means engaging in a fierce battle against political persecution and censorship and against the control exercised by international partners and sponsors who are but accomplices of the regimes in power. But Bekolo's film has probably managed to shake something up. Although *Le président* has never been theatrically released or shown on television in any African country, the online interest in the film has gone viral, as evidenced by the numerous comments and reactions on blogs and in journals after it was screened at international film festivals and made accessible on YouTube. If, with this film, Bekolo tried to formulate an effective language of protest and political action for African cinema, the disordered and irritated response on the part of the Cameroonian government and its international partners seems to suggest that his attempt was (at least partially) successful.

Conclusion

If African documentary film is indeed emerging as a new important trend in African cinema, primarily thanks to the introduction of new technologies, the working conditions of African documentary filmmakers are still defined by multiple problems. While digital technology has, unquestionably, made production more accessible, it is debatable whether it has also had an impact on the public's access to content. Internet distribution platforms and web TV channels have multiplied over the past few years,[13] but internet access remains a relatively elitist privilege in many areas of the continent, and wherever it is available and economically affordable, the connection is hardly powerful enough for people to download films and videos (see also Miller 2016). However, as Francis Nyamnjoh puts it, "because Africa is part of the world, and because its backwardness is less the result of choice than of circumstance, ordinary Africans are determined to be part of the technological revolutions of the modern world, even if this means accessing the information superhighway on foot, horseback, bicycles, bush taxis and second-hand cars. . . . This makes the African mediascape a rich and fascinating blend of traditions, influences and technologies" (2005, 4).

Within this interesting as much as challenging environment, African filmmakers are finding their way through the complex web of "rights talk" and "culture talk." African cinema's dependence on foreign funding and distribution networks in combination with the international human rights discourses prompts African artists and intellectuals to explore new languages and new narratives that may have an impact on their realities. The discussion developed in this chapter in relation to Jean-Pierre Bekolo's film is just an example. Across the continent, there is a wide range of initiatives aimed at consolidating a truly autonomous and innovative African documentary film industry, and many more will come.

ALESSANDRO JEDLOWSKI is a Belgian Fund for Scientific Research (FRS-FNRS) postdoctoral fellow in anthropology at the University of Liège and Lecturer in African History at the University of Turin.

Notes

This paper is partly based on research materials collected in relation to the African Documentary Film Fund (ADFF) initiative funded by the Bertha Foundation in 2012–2013 (see Barnes 2014 and http//:adff.org). I wish to thank Joslyn Barnes, Rebecca Lichtenfeld, Steven Markovitz, Don Edkins, and the researchers who conducted the seven regional investigations included in the final report, in particular Judy Kibinge, Josh Mwamunga, Femi Odugbemi, Djo Munga wa Munga, Pedro Pimenta, Marion Berger, Khadidiatou Diallo-Oriach, Ali Essafi, and Patrick Vergeynst. I am also grateful to the Belgian Fund for Scientific Research (F.R.S.-FNRS), which funded the postdoctoral fellowship during which this essay has been written.

This work is dedicated to Milena, Davide, Filippo, and Giuliano, who showed me what it means to resist and fight against all odds.

1. It should be taken into consideration, however, as Jean-Marie Teno has suggested, that for a long time debates about African cinema were dominated by the "impression that the first films by African filmmakers were either documentary in style or of documentary value" (2011).

2. See for instance the analysis proposed by Ukadike (1995), Akudinobi (2000), and Gabara (2003) and recent films such as *Miners Shot Down* (2014, Rehad Desai, South Africa) and the *Steps for the Future* program (which since 2001 has produced more than fifty documentary films on human rights issues in the southern Africa region) (see Ginsburg and Abrash 2003; Levine 2007).

3. The results of these investigations are open to the public in the form of a several-hundred-pages-long report—see Barnes (2014), also available online at http://adff.org/.

4. The most relevant documentary film festivals include Encounters South African International Documentary Film Festival (Cape Town and Johannesburg, South Africa), Dokanema Documentary Film Festival (Maputo, Mozambique), iREP International Documentary Film Forum (Lagos, Nigeria), and Rencontres Internationales du Documentaire Africain (Saint-Louis, Senegal).

5. One example of the positive impact that the multiplication of both satellite television and cable channels can have for the circulation of African documentary films is the emergence of the Afridocs channel, a television channel (recently available also in a mobile-friendly format on the "tuluntulu" app) entirely dedicated to African documentary films and documentary films about Africa, created by the South African production company Steps. See http://afridocs.net/ and http://www.tuluntulu.com/.

6. In the section on Gabon included in the ADFF research report, Djo Munga wa Munga underlines, for instance, that "the partnership signed between Canal France International (CFI), the two (Gabonese) public televisions and the private television TV+, does effectively allow RTG1 to enjoy, free of charge, the complete programming of CFI; and allows TV+ to receive daily news media monitoring. In 2006, for example, 1339 hours of CFI programming were broadcast on the two public channels" (Barnes 2014, 671). Similar data can be found in most reports on francophone Africa countries, providing clear evidence of the role that CFI played in inhibiting local content production in many African countries.

7. In relation to Nigeria, for instance, Jade Miller underlines that "a recent World Bank report estimated that 10 per cent of Nigerian companies' revenues are devoted to private power acquisition" (Miller 2016, 25).

8. A wonderful example in this respect is Jide Olanrewaju's historical documentary *Naij: A History of Nigeria* (2010, Nigeria), which has never achieved official distribution for lack of authorization to use the archival footage included in the film. The film has, however, circulated widely via YouTube.

9. Consider, for instance, the activities of the Sesotho Media and Development association, in Lesotho. See http://www.sesothomedia.org/.

10. A similar generational confrontation took place in relation to Nollywood. See for instance Jedlowski (2011).

11. From the text of Valsero's song "Lettre au Président," which he sings in the film.

12. The point that Bekolo raises here recalls the analysis proposed by the Moroccan anthropologist Aomar Boum (2012) of how Moroccan rap and hip-hop music changed their networks of circulation from the streets to festivals and national televisions—a process Boum describes as a "festivalization of dissent."

13. For a quick survey of the existing VOD platforms and web TV channels distributing African content, see the Mokolo database (http://tv.mokolo.net/).

Filmography

Miners Shot Down, 2014, Rehad Desai, South Africa.
Naij: A History of Nigeria, 2010, Jide Olanrewaju, Nigeria.
Le président—comment sait-on qu'il est temps de partir? (*The President*), 2013, Jean-Pierre Bekolo, Cameroon / Germany.

Stories of Our Lives, 2014, Jim Chuchu, Kenya.
Touki Bouki, 1973, Djibril Diop Mambéty, Senegal.

References

Acland, Charles R., and Haidee Wasson, eds. 2011. *Useful Cinema*. Durham, NC: Duke
    University Press.
Akudinobi, Jude G. 2000. "Reco(r)ding Reality: Representation and Paradigms in Nonfiction
    African Cinema." *Social Identities* 6 (3): 345–67. doi:10.1080/13504630050137660.
Alozie, Emmanuel C., ed. 2011. *Advertising in Developing and Emerging Countries: The
    Economic, Political and Social Context*. Burlington, VT: Gower Publishing.
Armes, Roy. 2006. *African Filmmaking: North and South of the Sahara*. Bloomington:
    Indiana University Press.
Awondo, Patrick, Peter Geschiere, and Graeme Reid. 2012. "Homophobic Africa?
    Toward a More Nuanced View." *African Studies Review* 55 (3): 145–68. doi:10.1017
    /S0002020600007241.
Barnes, Joslyn, ed. 2014. *African Documentary Film Fund*. New York: Abington Square
    Publishing. http://adff.org/the-report/.
Bekolo, Jean Pierre. 2013. "Le président: le complot des institutions." *Le blog de Jean-Pierre
    Bekolo*, June 2. https://bekolopress.wordpress.com/2013/06/02/le-president-le-complot
    -des-institutions/.
Bensalah, Mohamed. 2000. "La mémoire audiovisuelle et cinématographique: un patrimoine
    en péril." *Insaniyat, Revue algérienne d'anthropologie et de sciences sociales* 12: 149–58.
    doi:10.4000/insaniyat.7915.
Bloom, Peter J. 2008. *French Colonial Documentary: Mythologies of Humanitarianism*.
    Minneapolis: University of Minnesota Press.
Boum, Aomar. 2012. "Festivalizing Dissent in Morocco." *Middle East Report* 263: 22–5.
Bryce, Jane. 2010. "Outside the Machine? Donor Values and the Case of Film in Tanzania."
    In *Viewing African Cinema in the Twenty-First Century: Art Films and the Nollywood
    Video Revolution*, edited by Mahir Saul and Ralph A. Austen, 160–77. Athens: Ohio
    University Press.
Diao, Claire. 2012. "Que les blancs reviennent en Afrique—entretien avec Jean-Pierre
    Bekolo." *Slate Afrique*, December 11. Accessed September 10, 2016. https://bekolopress
    .wordpress.com/tag/claire-diao/.
Dicklitch, Susan. 2001. "Beyond Rights Talk and Culture Talk: Comparative Essays on the
    Politics of Rights and Culture by Mahmood Mamdani (Review)." *Canadian Journal of
    African Studies* 35 (3): 618–20.
Duncan, Jane. 2012. "Communication, Culture and Human Rights in Africa (review essay)."
    Journal of Contemporary African Studies 30 (1): 174–7. doi:10.1080/02589001.2012.643008.
Eardley, Megan. 2013. "Everyone Has Their Own Paul Biya." *Africa Is a Country*, August 9.
    Accessed September 10, 2016. http://africasacountry.com/2013/08/everyone-has-their
    -own-paul-biya/.
Englund, Harri. 2011. *Human Rights and African Airwaves: Mediating Equality on the
    Chichewa Radio*. Bloomington: Indiana University Press.
Eshun, Kodwo, and Anjalika Sagar. 2007. *The Ghosts of Songs: The Film Art of the Black Audio
    Film Collective*. Liverpool: Liverpool University Press.

Ferguson, James. 1990. *The Anti-Politics Machine: "Development," Depoliticization and Bureaucratic Power in Lesotho*. Cambridge: Cambridge University Press.

Fronty, François, and Delphe Kifouani, eds. 2014. *La diversité du documentaire de création en Afrique*. Paris: L'Harmattan.

Gabara, Rachel. 2003. "Mixing Impossible Genres: David Achkar and African AutoBiographical Documentary." *New Literary History* 34 (2): 331–52. doi:10.1353/nlh.2003.0018.

Gangnat, Émilie, Annie Lenoble-Bart, and Jean-François Zorn, eds. 2013. *Mission et cinéma. Films missionnaires et missionnaires au cinéma*. Paris: Karthala.

Garritano, Carmela. 2013. *African Video Movies and Global Desires: A Ghanaian History*. Athens: Ohio University Press.

Ginsburg, Faye, and Barbara Abrash. 2003. "Introduction: Essays on *Steps for the Future*." *Visual Anthropology Review* 19 (1–2): 4–7. doi:10.1525/var.2003.19.1-2.4.

Harding, Michael-Olivier. 2014. "The New Movie 'Stories of Our Lives' Dispels the Myths Fueling Kenya's Homophobia." *Vice*, October 5. Accessed September 10, 2016. http://www.vice.com/read/story-of-our-lives-879.

Hering, Tobias. 2013. "Cinéma/Jean-Pierre Bekolo: 'Il ne s'agit pas pour moi de montrer un mauvais président, mais un homme qui s'interroge sur sa vie.'" *Ekang Media Press*, June 6. Accessed September 10, 2016. http://www.nkul-beti-camer.com/ekang-media-press.php?cmd=article&Item=4372&TAB=-1&SUB=0.

Imbert, Henri-François. 2007. *Samba Félix Ndiaye. Cinéaste documentariste africain*. Paris: L'Harmattan.

Jedlowski, Alessandro. 2011. "When the Nigerian Video Film Industry Became 'Nollywood': Naming, Branding and the Videos' Transnational Mobility." *Estudos Afro-Asiaticos* 33 (1-2-3): 225–51.

Jedlowski, Alessandro. 2016. "Studying Media 'from' the South: African Media Studies and Global Perspectives." *Black Camera* 7 (2): 174–93.

Krings, Matthias, and Onookome Okome, eds. 2013. *Global Nollywood: The Transnational Dimensions of an African Video Film Industry*. Bloomington: Indiana University Press.

Larkin, Brian. 2008. *Signal and Noise: Media, Infrastructure, and Urban Culture in Nigeria*. Durham, NC: Duke University Press.

Legesse, Asmarom. 2006. *Oromo Democracy: An Indigenous African Political System*. Trenton, NJ: Red Sea Press.

Levine, Susan. 2007. "Documentary Film Matters: The *Steps for the Future* Media Advocacy Project in Southern Africa." *Critical Arts* 21 (2): 234–49. doi:10.1080/02560040701810024.

Loftus, Maria. 2012. "Kuxa Kanema: The Rise and Fall of an Experimental Documentary Series in Mozambique." *Journal of African Cinemas* 3 (2): 161–71. doi:10.1386/jac.3.2.161_1.

Makoni, Sinfree B. 2012. "Language and Human Rights Discourses in Africa: Lessons from the African Experience." *Journal of Multicultural Discourses* 7 (1): 1–20. doi:10.1080/17447143.2011.595493.

Mamdani, Mahmood, ed. 2000. *Beyond Rights Talk and Culture Talk: Comparative Essays on the Politics of Rights and Culture*. New York: St. Martin's Press.

Metz, Thaddeus. 2011. "Ubuntu as a Moral Theory and Human Rights in South Africa." *African Human Rights Law Journal* 11 (2): 532–59.

Miller, Jade L. 2016. *Nollywood Central*. New York: Palgrave Macmillan.

Musa, Bala, and Jerry Domatob, eds. 2010. *Communication, Culture and Human Rights in Africa*. Lanham, MD: University Press of America.

Ndiaye, Babacar. 2011. "Les archives audiovisuelles en Afrique de l'ouest." *Journal Warbica* 6: 3–4.

Nganang, Patrice. 2005. "Deconstructing Authority in Cinema: Jean-Marie Teno." In *Cinema and Social Discourse in Cameroon*, edited by Alexie Tcheuyap, 139–56. Bayreuth, Germany: Thielmann and Breitinger.

Nyamnjoh, Francis B. 2005. *Africa's Media: Democracy and the Politics of Belonging*. London: Zed Books.

Olukoju, Ayodeji. 2004. "'Never Expect Power Always': Electricity Consumers' Response to Monopoly, Corruption and Inefficient Services in Nigeria." *African Affairs* 103 (410): 51–71. doi:10.1093/afraf/adh004.

Overbergh, Ann. 2015. "Innovation and Its Obstacles in Tanzania's Bongowood." *Journal of African Cinemas* 7 (2): 137–51. doi:10.1386/jac.7.2.137_1.

Sanogo, Aboubakar Sidiki. 2009. "The History of Documentary in Africa the Colonial Era." Unpublished PhD dissertation. Los Angeles: University of Southern California.

Shivji, Issa G. 1989. *The Concept of Human Rights in Africa*. London: CODESRIA book series.

Tapsoba, Clément. 1996. "The African Documentary." *Écrans d'Afrique* 16 (2nd quarter): 45–54.

Teno, Jean-Marie. 2011. "Writing on Walls: Documentary, the Future of African Cinema?" *Africultures*, March 21. Accessed September 5, 2016. http://www.africultures.com /php/?nav=article&no=10003.

Ukadike, N. Frank. 1995. "African Cinematic Reality: The Documentary Tradition as an Emerging Trend." *Research in African Literatures* 26 (3): 88–96.

van Binsbergen, Wim M. J. 2001. "Ubuntu and the Globalisation of Southern African Thought and Society." *Quest* 15 (1, 2): 53–89.

Vourlias, Christopher. 2014. "Kenya Bans Film about Its LGBT Community." *Al-Jazeera America*, October 11. Accessed September 10, 2016. http://america.aljazeera.com/blogs /scrutineer/2014/10/11/kenya-lgbt-film-banned.html.

Wiredu, Kwasi. 1996. *Cultural Universals and Particulars: An African Perspective*. Bloomington: Indiana University Press.

5 Challenging Perspectives

An Interview with Jean-Marie Teno

Melissa Thackway

About Jean-Marie Teno

Jean-Marie Teno is one of Africa's most prolific filmmakers, working almost exclusively within the documentary format. Born in Cameroon in 1954, he studied audiovisual communication at the Université de Valenciennes in France. While working as an editor at the French television network FR3 from 1985 until 1997, he took to making independently produced documentaries in his spare time, starting with *Homage* in 1985, a tribute to his father.

A tireless critic of social injustice, abuse of power, and the lingering effects of colonialism, not least in his home country, Cameroon, Teno has shot several of his films himself, often using an unobtrusive DV camera that has by and large allowed him to pass under the radar of the authorities. His films are typically characterized by a deeply personal, questioning approach to the topics he investigates, often presented in an experimental form that mixes past and present with diverse aspects of, for example, the abuse of power. He produces and distributes his films himself, through the Paris-based Les Films du Raphia, which he co-owns.

Jean-Marie Teno's films have been awarded numerous prizes at international festivals. He was visiting artist at Amherst College, Massachusetts, 2007–2008, and visiting professor at Hampshire College, Massachusetts, 2009–2010.

The Interview

Looking at cinema in Africa, a cinema born out of political independence in the 1960s, and one which has always been strongly rooted in and marked by social issues, how do you account for this commitment to the rights of African people—or, in other words, to human rights—in African film?

I think it's important to clarify something first. I find the notion of human rights problematic—not that it's not important, as it has given a frame to activists around the word to voice their causes—but at a state level. It is incredibly cynical

Figure 5.1. Jean-Marie Teno. Photo: Melissa Thackway.

for certain countries around the world to support rogue governments that abuse their people when those governments serve their interests, yet on the other hand to point the finger at those they dislike in the name of human rights.

Focusing specifically on African cinema, however, I can say without a doubt that our cinema took the rights of the people seriously from its inception and has often had their concerns in mind whether seeking to entertain or educate through images. That may have changed somewhat in more recent times, with the emergence of other filmmaking practices, such, for example, as Nollywood. But perhaps I can most usefully address the question in terms of my own personal experience, my encounter with African cinema.

One of the key and deeply marking moments for me, as I've often said, was seeing my first Cameroonian film, *Pousse-Pousse* (*Tricycle Man*) by Daniel Kamwa (1976). It's a film that addresses a concrete social issue: the practice of dowry. It tells the story of a poor young man's struggle to marry the woman he loves as his future in-laws keep raising the price of the dowry. It's a comedy that addressed a reality, a real social issue that affects a lot of people in Cameroon, raising the question: do poor people have the right to love too? Can they get married like anyone else, without having to face the harshest of situations? For me, this film illustrated the situation in which the majority of Cameroonians found themselves at the time. They were faced with such financial precariousness that it was a hurdle, preventing them from making themselves a life, from getting married, even. A society where people are unable to get married is a society that risks disappearing. This situation where money was taking on an increasingly great place in society was a hangover from the colonial era.

Compare this, for example, to the situation in my own village where, when you reached adulthood, your father, or the head male in your concession, would give you a plot of land. When you'd managed, through your hard work and with the help of others, to build a house on this land, you would go to see your father to ask him to bring some warmth to this house. And he would accompany you to seek a wife. You'd take just a bundle of wood to the house of the woman destined to become your wife, and that was the dowry. It was this bundle of wood that demonstrated that you were asking the woman to join you in your home. In our postcolonial society, this symbolic gesture, this symbolic dowry became a means for families to get rich, to force people to pay more and more before being able to start a family. So, here was a film that really touched people, as it addressed a concrete reality. To the extent, even, that the government of the time—which was hardly a progressive government—decided to pass a law to limit the maximum amount people could set the dowry at—I think it was 50,000 CFA Francs at the time—which was a reasonable sum, an amount people could manage to pay. For me, this was the proof that cinema was really in touch with society.

Not only did people need to see stories that concerned them on the screen, they needed to be represented on the screen. They needed their issues to be addressed. This was the belief of our first, pioneering filmmakers, too, who came together in the late sixties when the Ouagadougou Film Festival (FESPACO) and the Carthage Film Festival were founded, where they met to define the bases of what African filmmaking should be at the time. For them, there were two clear directions: popular education and entertainment. These were the two sides of what they thought cinema should be. Given the high illiteracy rates in the colonial language, which was the official language, many people thought at the time that it would be possible to educate people through images, through films. They believed that cinema had the vocation to entertain and, at the same time, to give people elements to find their bearings in the new postcolonial societies. Naturally, then, cinema had both a social and political dimension. Addressing people's day-to-day problems is what I believe to be a concern for human rights.

Film technology was new, but was this function that filmmaking took on in the newly independent African countries not simply the continuation of a social role that arts played locally, such as storytelling, or popular theater? Was filmmaking a new expression of something that already existed and that was socially and culturally rooted?

It was certainly the continuation of both. We mustn't forget that during the colonial era, the colonial authorities used cinema as a way of influencing minds, of assigning people to "their place," by formulating negative representations of them and their cultures, by valorizing the cultures they introduced and denigrating anything local. So, African filmmakers firstly sought to contest that. But at the same time, in order to contest these representations, they turned to modes of narration or to spaces of transmission that existed within families, in social spaces such as *tontines*, Cameroon's community mutual support cooperatives, in the different spaces where people gather and socialize and exchange, through stories. The cinema became just another such place. And if cinema were to exist amidst all of this, in this new fashionable social space, and if Africans were to make their own cinema, they couldn't completely break away from these existing modes. Just like with music. The major hits of the sixties and seventies were songs whose lyrics had meaning for the people. People didn't write songs that spoke only about love; they were always songs that had some kind of moral or message to them. Stories too. So cinema, naturally, entered that logic too. Except that film, unfortunately, is destined to travel too, to represent the country abroad, to be seen far from its original cultural sphere. How to ensure that local cultural habits will be understood by people who don't necessarily share the same culture? And that's why we later embarked on all these processes of professionalization and universalization, of a dilution and even complete destruction of the very idea of narration, of the very idea of a cinema rooted in the space in which people live.

Marked, then, in its early years, by this desire to participate in the construction of the new postcolonial societies, do you think that it was because the dreams and promises of independence, of freedom, were not in fact delivered that such politically committed themes continued to prevail, as filmmakers espoused and expressed ongoing struggles for freedom of all forms in their work?

If you think about it, you could say that cinema everywhere in the world in that period shared this dimension. If you think of all the committed films of the late sixties and seventies, whether French cinema, Italian cinema, Latin American cinema, American independent cinema. . . . It was a time of great struggle, of social and political struggle, May '68. . . . There were movements and struggles for freedom everywhere trying to resist ongoing imperialism, hegemony, and later the steamroller of neoliberal globalization. I think that at that time, everywhere in the world, there was a desire in cinema to participate in what was going on in different societies. In Africa even more so. In societies where people hadn't had a voice, where they hadn't had the means to represent themselves, this political dimension was even greater. Unfortunately, in Africa, we were in countries where there weren't many spaces of mediation.

It's not as if in many African countries you could easily descend into the streets to demonstrate or go on strike. It's not as if we had parliaments that functioned, or states that had been created with enough trained figures or leaders who could articulate these struggles. Everyone talked about ending underdevelopment in Africa, as it was called then, about improving people's lives, but at the same time, the colonial powers did everything to give the impression that things had changed, without them really changing. Our leaders were up against situations that needed to be changed, and yet the former colonial powers controlled the very workings of our economies. They certainly didn't want things to change and spent their time trying to co-opt this new African ruling elite so that their interests would continue to be protected. A new class, a new bourgeoisie thus emerged, while the people continued to suffer. And there were filmmakers who tried to articulate these problems, to ask questions so that citizens could have a better life, so that their problems would be taken into account. They used the cinema to that end. When someone like Sembène said, for example, that cinema was a weapon to fight against all of this, it was because you could expose a certain number of problems clearly through film, and cinema could help educate people. This was essential because the education system was not at the service of the people; it was designed to keep them at a certain level. In short, in societies where spaces for questioning are limited, this highly seductive popular space called cinema needed to be used to challenge, entertain, and educate the people.

You, then, as a spectator, a film enthusiast, used to watch these early African films, such as Pousse-Pousse, *or Souleymane Cissé's* Baara *(1978), another film that you often cite as a milestone for you, these seventies films that reflect this engagement, denouncing different forms of oppression . . .*

Yes. I'd also add Jean-Pierre Dikongue-Pipa's *Muna Moto* (1975) . . .

. . . After a while you started to make your own films in the eighties. What made you decide to start making films, and what pushed you to constantly address social issues in your work?

Watching all these films, and having witnessed the promises of independence as a child, the independence that our parents fought for, we thought that simply by virtue of being independent, people would start addressing the issues facing us. And the issues facing people were huge. Living in a poor neighborhood in Yaoundé, access to running water was a major issue. I lived in the neighborhood of Nvog ada, where the public water fountain was about a kilometer from my home. If you wanted clean water, you had to take a bucket and go and fetch it. It was a great meeting place. Every day, at about five or six p.m., all the young people would gather there to chat and to flirt! But the water situation posed the wider question of health.

In those days, before wanting to make films myself, I used to love going to the cinema. Before the main feature, they used to screen newsreels, with the omniscient voice of the white man, speaking from France, the voice of authority, telling us how to think about this or that, talking about such and such an inauguration, telling us how beautiful the country was, but never addressing the questions that people were facing. When I was young, I used to love Indian cinema, Bollywood, with stories that always pitted good against evil, all the fairytales. And then I saw the film *Pousse-Pousse* and how it managed to bring change to the dowry question. It really struck me, and I thought to myself, this is a medium worth exploring.

Another thing was that, at that time, life was very difficult for journalists. Whenever they said something that the state didn't like, they were locked up, beaten up. There was a cruel and violent censorship against anyone who didn't toe the government line. So, I started to think that maybe by making films, I could show and denounce things, like all the trash I used to see in the streets while hearing on the radio that our country was the best in the world! I loved the idea of making films. I went to do my studies, and the year I finished my master's in audiovisual communications, I started working for French public television. I bought myself a 16mm camera. I loved filming! I wanted to make comedy—I loved comedy—but when I started making images, when I went home on vacation one time and decided to film my village, I was torn between these two sides of myself, between really knowing what someone living in our neighborhood experiences, and having traveled and seen how things could be so different in other places. I tried to create a dialogue between these two elements, these two sides of myself, while looking at reality. So, the first thing I did when I started filming, when I started making images, was to write filmic essays showing my in-betweenness, my oscillation from one element to the other. That was what we were all about; that was our predicament. We had a local culture; another culture was imposed on top, smashing ours, not solving any problems, and only leaving us with more questions. So, the reason I started making films was to express this in-betweenness I experienced, and that's how my first film *Homage* (1985) came about. When I decided to continue making films, I wanted to laugh. Laughter was a way to cope with our difficult reality. *Yellow Fever Taxi Man* (1985) was a comedy, the story of a taxi driver traveling around picking up customers. Through him we see the city, but even in that film, there was still a consciousness behind the story, because I cannot show things without questioning them further. The political awareness that people around me couldn't speak out, that they didn't have a say, meant that I wanted to show and to voice the issues that people were facing daily.

And so, from these first short films and on to your first feature-length film, Bikutsi Water Blues *(1988), the issues of access to clean water, to decent health and sanitation, to education—fundamental human rights—were already at the heart of your work . . .*

Absolutely, because I was from a place where I was witnessing all that, seeing that these rights were not being provided in a proper way, seeing the corruption, seeing that no one was really addressing these questions, that everybody was turning a blind eye. All my works stem from looking at the environment. The idea for *Bikutsi Water Blues* came from a conversation that I had with a medical doctor in the district where my mother used to live. I used to go and chat with him when he had free time at the health clinic. He told me something that really struck me: that two diseases out of three in the district were the result of unclean water. If the question of giving people access to clean water were solved, two-thirds of his patients wouldn't need to come.

I thought about that and started to ask myself about all the kids in the neighborhood I'd see who were often ill because they drank unclean water because the drinking water fountain was so far away that people would dig wells to get water instead. But these wells were often too close to the latrines they also dug, so everything was contaminated. . . . You can boil water, but people didn't always, and they would dump the trash near the water source. This was a terrible situation. It created another vicious circle, because kids would miss school as they were ill, their education would suffer, and they would drop out because they became too old to go to school. So, you end up with a vicious circle of water, and a social vicious circle that keeps people down, stuck in the same poor neighborhoods, not advancing in life, apart from the exceptionally bright ones. So, I wanted to address this double vicious circle created in society by the poor water system and poor health conditions. That's why I made *Bikutsi Water Blues*. It was a long journey, as it wasn't only a problem in my district; it was a problem in the whole country. I couldn't not ask, "How come we have a problem this huge almost thirty years after independence? How come no one is tackling this issue?", particularly in a country where we had oil, a country rich in natural resources that were bringing revenue into the country. Almost another thirty years later, you can see how much worse the situation has become.

With each film—and we can certainly consider that, taken together, your films constitute a coherent ensemble—we can trace a clear development, a continuity of the sorts of issues that you're interested in and articulate. I'm thinking, for example, in Afrique, je te plumerai *(Africa, I Will Fleece You, 1992), of your exploration of the ties between the state of contemporary Cameroonian society and the country's recent colonial past, the question of political repression, of cultural genocide . . .*

The continuum of *Bikutsi Water Blues* led me to question the issues in *Afrique, je te plumerai* because, not finding any adequate answer to my questions, I started to ask, "What is this culture? What's in the minds of the people running this country? What is it about the history of this country that means that we have rulers who do not even think of providing basic necessities to the people?" That's when I started looking into our colonial history and exploring the questions of abuse, of violence, of the violence of the state whenever people ask questions, when people ask for what they need, for social services, for all these basic rights that other people enjoy elsewhere. In Cameroon, all these issues are highly political, and from our youngest years, our parents warned us not to get involved in politics as it meant trouble and possibly prison or death. If someone asked, "Why don't we have a school in this neighborhood?" they could easily be accused of talking politics and could get in trouble for it.

During the struggles against the colonial system, when people rebelled against colonial oppression, they were met with violence, and that violence was learned. People have learned that violence is how a government functions. Right up until today, the Cameroonian government functions with the same colonial mindset. When people demonstrate to say they want something, the government doesn't invite them to discuss the issue. There's no dialogue; they just send in the police or the army to kill a few demonstrators to set an example. That's what we're witnessing today, in 2016. Recently, there were student demonstrations in Buea, and the students were brutalized, humiliated, simply for demonstrating peacefully, for demanding conditions that students demand everywhere.

You mentioned the word "journey." Your entire body of films is like a journey, as is each individual film, often literally and always symbolically. As I said before, it's interesting to see how these themes develop and are explored, like leitmotifs. Consistently, this question of repression, of the abuse of power—whether governmental, local, or familial—is present in all your films. In questioning and trying to understand why these situations of abuse and repression arise, their root cause, you, as a filmmaker, are also "talking back," to cite bell hooks. You are making a space for your own personal expression, which is manifestly very political. When you first started making films—and even today, some thirty years on—did you consciously think of cinema as a way for you to challenge these problematic situations? Did you consciously think, "I'm going to make committed films"?

When you say "committed films," I can't imagine myself speaking to say nothing, or speaking to just talk about the mood I'm in, to make a bourgeois poetic love story, or anything like that. I just have the feeling that—especially knowing what people are experiencing in certain parts of the world—I don't see myself making a film that would totally ignore such issues. Nor could I set it in a place where it would just give me the opportunity to show how skillful I am at putting elements together. So, when I started making films, I didn't think, "I'm going to make committed films." I was aware that cinema is also entertainment, it's about emotions, but for me, it also had to lead to something, to serve a purpose. I cannot make cinema without emotion, but with the emotion, I also always make films that try to say something meaningful about a person's life, a person's struggle, a person's experience.

In the Cameroonian context, in the African context, it would be hard for me not to make a film about the different forms of violence people live through, that people experience, at the hand of the state. Or injustices in society between women and men, between the generations. Everything in society that seems to me to be unbalanced is an object that I can use to make cinema. So, for me, all this is just material for creation. But within that, I try to tell a story, to be engaging enough so that people can follow me on that journey, identifying with the characters portrayed, feeling, and reacting to the situation, so that they can understand what is really going on. Cinema is emotion, but also emotion related to a situation or an experience. And when people are experiencing terrible things, such injustices, the film exposing their situation becomes a committed film.

It's interesting that, in talking about your films, you talk about "cinema," making no distinction between fiction and documentary. You sound like you're talking about fiction, yet you're known primarily as a documentary filmmaker.

Yes. All my documentary films are constructed as if they were fiction, because I take disparate elements and I organize them to tell a story, a story totally rooted in a reality that is a Cameroonian reality. I don't mean I talk about "the" reality of Cameroon, because, of course, you have many different filmmakers, some of whom are in Cameroon, and who are living very comfortably within the system; they will never make the kind of films that I make because they don't see, or don't want to see, certain things. So, you can have different approaches to the same situation and create different realities, but I personally am constructing a vision of Cameroon that is the Cameroon I know, that is the Cameroon that I wish were different, and I tell stories with people who experience difficult situations.

So, your cinema could be described as a cinema of injustice, one that challenges human injustice?

Yes, a cinema that challenges injustice. One aspect of my cinema is certainly a cinema that challenges, challenging injustice per se, but also challenging stupidity. But I also like to laugh, and I hope that I manage to make people laugh, to gain distance, to step back and to look at and read the world from a different perspective. A cinema, also, of diversity, a cinema that is shifting perspectives and looking at the world from the place of those who don't usually have a say. When I started using first-person narrative in my films, I wasn't using the first person as Teno speaking; for me it was the first person as an African, or a Cameroonian, looking at a situation, being in the colonial space and looking at the stories we were told and reading history from a different place, not from the place of official discourse. The official French discourse completely merged with the official Cameroonian state discourse, and this was what they wanted to impose, as the individuals in the positions of power benefited—and are still benefiting—from this situation, unlike the vast majority of the population. So, by attacking the state, we attack the colonial master, indirectly. And by attacking both, I ended up between a rock and a hard place!

When I started making films, I was often told in France, "Your cinema is not African," as I wasn't showing beautiful, idyllic, apolitical villages and landscapes. And in Cameroon, I was attacked for showing what was happening without hiding anything, giving, according to some, a bad image of the country. Over the course of time, funnily enough, another of the first African films that I saw was *Wend Kuuni* (1982), a beautiful, timeless rural tale. I met Gaston Kaboré at the Three Continents Film Festival in Nantes in 1982, and we got along very well. *Wend Kuuni* was beautifully made, but it was also talking about the stupidity of the group, about intolerance. It was great.

There were many films from West African countries that were dealing with village life. I, from my very first film, was dealing with the city, because that was what I knew. But many people in the West weren't interested in our city scenes. I had read authors like Mongo Beti, who portrayed the chaos of the city, and that's what I was nourished by, not by an idealistic idea of the village. So, my cinema naturally deals with people in this kind of urban context.

In your films, we can identify several overriding themes: the denunciation of violence, be it political or gender violence; the critique of all forms of oppression and abuse of power; the reexamining of history, unmasking forgotten or silenced genocides, etc. Obviously, these sorts of themes resonate clearly with the notion of human rights. If we think of the Universal Declaration of Human Rights, it declares, for example, that people should be free and equal in dignity and rights, that they should be free from arbitrary arrest and detainment—an issue you dealt with in your 1996 film Clando—*and, of course, it advocates freedom of thought and expression, which you, as a filmmaker, clearly claim your right to. . . . There's a strong resonance between the notion of human rights and the sorts of issues you deal with in your films, then. Have you ever consciously thought of your work in a human rights frame?*

Making my films, I've never consciously associated myself with human rights as such, except when human rights film festivals started inviting me to show my films because they felt that my films entered that realm. That gave my films and these issues exposure. It also made people aware of the difficulties of the Cameroonian situation. I started getting calls from lawyers defending Cameroonian

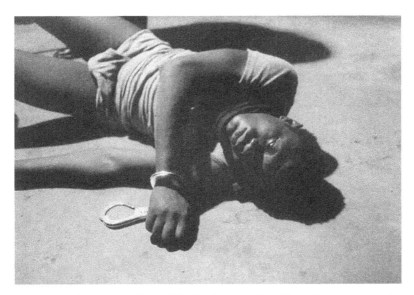

Figure 5.2. Paulin Fodouop in *Clando* (*Clandestine*, 1996, Jean-Marie Teno, Cameroon / France / Germany). Photo: Jean-Marie Teno.

asylum seekers in various countries, who wanted to use my films as evidence to support their cases in court. Which is all fine. I could, in that respect, say that my films enter that frame.

But we also need to go back to that moment when the Universal Declaration of Human Rights was adopted, because we cannot just take this declaration at face value. Everything said in it, every principle defended in it is wonderful. But let's not forget that it was adopted in 1948, at a time when nearly all the African countries and many other places in the world were still under colonial domination. The countries that promoted this declaration, the countries like France that claim to be the first to have written human rights charters, they were colonial powers, dehumanizing a significant proportion of humanity, while simultaneously promoting human rights! So, there was the theoretical discourse on the one hand, and the practice and their economic interests on the other, a difference between discourse and reality.

Even today, how can we talk about human rights when colonization is still going on in some parts of the world, and when the colonizers are considered to be part of the free and democratic world? There's a lot of hypocrisy and cynicism around this notion, as I mentioned earlier, so I take the human rights discourse with a pinch of critical salt. The discrepancy between the discourse and practices of certain states, who so loudly proclaim they defend human rights, who even practice aggressive human rights diplomacy, who bomb or sell weapons in the

Figure 5.3. Ernestine Ouandié in *Une feuille dans le vent* (*Leaf in the Wind*, 2013, Jean-Marie Teno, Cameroon / Gabon / France). Photo: Jean-Marie Teno.

name of human rights . . . they've spread so much suffering around the world in the name of democracy and human rights. Their human rights are often a double standard. The way minorities are frequently treated today in their own countries, in the biggest democracies in the world, is unacceptable. Take Black Lives Matter. How many black men are being shot in the streets of the United States? In France, racism or racial profiling by the police continues to harass people based on the color of their skin. . . . They loudly defend human rights in negatively defined parts of the world but don't question the issue within their own societies. So, the principle of human rights is of course good, but their application, their reality, still leaves a lot to be desired.

How do you interpret the word "universal" in the Universal Declaration of Human Rights?

"Universal" as a concept is part of the whole problem, as some people simply go around the world imposing their values, their views on the rest of the planet and claim them to be "universal." At the same time, in their own societies, they don't leave space for anybody who may have different views or ways of living.

Universalism has often been a way for the dominant group to shape opinion and to exclude so many people, so we need to deconstruct the concept. If one were to be serious about it, the whole human rights concept should first be questioned within Western society, within the countries that initially promoted the Declaration, to see if every citizen in those countries is free from harassment, from abuse, particularly minorities, whether religious, ethnic, sexual, etc. All this needs to be questioned.

To conclude, do you feel that your film work, that the issues you explore and particularly your personal perspective—clearly at the fore in your use of a first-person voice—contribute to decolonizing the human rights agenda?

I hope so! It's vital that we examine the association between human rights, the universal, and colonization, because you could say that the notion of universal is to go from your home all over the world and to try to impose your own view, your own self as the model. That's what colonization is. And in doing so, you deny other people their very existence, their humanity. So, to be able to talk, to be able to understand the question of human rights, you first need to challenge your own idea of humanity, of your own humanity, and where you place your humanity in relation to that of the others around you, who are different from you, who don't have the same culture, color, religion, wealth, education, etc. You have to go deeper and challenge all these assumptions.

By pushing people to question their own place, their ways of thinking, the ways they look at things, my films contribute, I hope, to challenging these questions. And my films also consist in retelling history not from the official standpoint of Europe's so-called civilizing mission, hidden behind all the so-called good intentions, but to show all the damage that this presence has done to other people, to try to get people to put themselves in the place of the populations of the countries where the Europeans went. How would they feel if I, as an African, suddenly came and imposed this or that on them? Would they be happy? By forcing people to shift perspectives, to put themselves into other people's shoes, I hope to challenge official discourse and to contribute to decolonizing the minds of the people in the West, because that's necessary, so they no longer allow their politicians to continue waging ridiculous wars that have led us into the dead end that we are in today in the world.

Paris, December 2016.

MELISSA THACKWAY is Lecturer in African Cinema at Sciences-Po and the Institut des Langues et Civilisations Orientales (INALCO) in Paris. She is author of *Africa Shoots Back: Alternative Representations in Sub-Saharan Francophone African Film.*

Films by Jean-Marie Teno

Hommage (*Homage*), 1985, Cameroon / France.
Fièvre jaune taximan (*Yellow Fever Taxi Man*), 1985, Cameroon / France.
La gifle et la caresse (*The Slap and the Kiss*), 1987, France.
Bikutsi Water Blues, 1988, Cameroon / France.
Le dernier voyage (*The Last Trip*), 1990, Cameroon / France.
Mister Foot, 1991, Cameroon / France.
Afrique, je te plumerai (*Africa, I Will Fleece You*), 1992, Cameroon / Germany / France.
La tête dans les nuages (*Head in the Clouds*), 1994, Cameroon / France.
Clando (*Clandestine*), 1996, Cameroon / France / Germany.
Vacances au pays (*A Trip to the Country*), 1999, Cameroon / Germany / France.
Chef! (*Chief!*), 1999, Cameroon / France.
Le mariage d'Alex (*Alex's Wedding*), 2002, Cameroon / France.
Le malentendu colonial (*The Colonial Misunderstanding*), 2004, Cameroon / Niger / Germany / France.
Lieux saints (*Sacred Places*), 2009, Cameroon / France.
Une feuille dans le vent (*Leaf in the Wind*), 2013, Cameroon / Gabon / France.

Other films mentioned in the interview

Baara (*Work*), 1978, Souleymane Cissé, Mali.
Muna Moto (*Somebody Else's Child*), 1975, Jean-Pierre Dikongue-Pipa, Cameroon.
Pousse-Pousse (*Tricycle Man*), 1976, Daniel Kamwa, Cameroon.
Wend Kuuni (*God's Gift*), 1982, Gaston Kaboré, Burkina Faso.

6 In Defense of Human Rights Filmmaking

A Response to the Skeptics, Based on Kenyan Examples

Mette Hjort

THE CONCEPT OF human rights filmmaking is divisive when evoked with reference to the African continent, or the Global South more generally.[1] Supportive affirmations based on assumptions of virtuous intervention on behalf of justice and the good are to be expected, but so is deep skepticism, even hostility. Advocates see the relevant activity as serving worthwhile goals, including viewers' enhanced understanding of human rights, new or heightened awareness of abuse, and the pursuit of justice on behalf of victims (Bronkhorst 2004; Torchin 2012). However, as far as the skeptic is concerned, "human rights may be implicated in a system of knowledge that . . . has imposed a certain view of the 'human' on the rest of humanity" (Tascón 2015, 4). The "humanitarian gaze" encouraged by human rights filmmaking is seen as reflecting an unequal relationship between "donors / helpers and supplicants," the stories of "urgency and panic" serving, perversely, to reposition "the privileged within their privilege" (ibid., 204).

Speaking with the specificities of African cultures and histories in mind, Burkinabè filmmaker Gaston Kaboré points to a different set of problems, having to do with the dynamics of the filmmaking sector. In response to interviewer Rod Stoneman's question about "the attempt to impose a Western human rights agenda" on African filmmaking, Kaboré says: "The problem is really central. The agenda is not unreasonable, but there's something wrong with it nonetheless, and that has to do with the fact that we're not empowered to do things ourselves. The organizations come here with money and experts, and when the money stops, everything stops. I think we have to say we don't want this type of cooperation. We need to do things differently" (Kaboré 2017, this volume). In giving priority to film practices that promote human rights, Western development policies, it is suggested, generate unintended effects. Kaboré's diagnosis of the ills, in terms of diminished agency on the part of film practitioners and unhealthy dynamics in the creative sector, is, as we shall see, consistent with the views of filmmakers elsewhere on the continent.

It has never been easier to be skeptical about the project of intertwining human rights with film. Bolstering the views of the skeptic is an impressive array of books that raise serious questions about the legitimacy of the discourses and practices of human rights: *The End of Human Rights* (Douzinas 2000), *The End-times of Human Rights* (Hopgood 2013), *Human Rights as Politics and Idolatry* (Ignatieff 2001), and *The Last Utopia: Human Rights in History* (Moyn 2010). The charges leveled against human rights thinking, and the practices and institutions that it has spawned, are many. In the context of North / South interactions, for example, "human rights [discourse] is increasingly seen as the language of a moral imperialism just as ruthless and just as self-deceived as the colonial hubris of yesteryear" (Ignatieff 2001, 20). Human rights institutions appear to critics to be deeply flawed constructions, with the agenda of the International Criminal Court (ICC) in The Hague having been dominated by Africa, resulting in accusations of bias. The ICC is charged, more specifically, with applying "selective standards" in both its focus on "'weak' states on the [African] continent" and its lack of interest in "more powerful states, in particular the United States" (Viljoen 2012, 72).

In *Human Rights, Southern Voices: Francis Deng, Abdullahi An-Na'im, Yash Ghai and Upendra Baxi*, William Twining (2009) identifies further problems. Referring to the concerns of Upendra Baxi, professor of law in development at the University of Warwick, Twining points to a human rights project that is seen as having been hijacked by "technocrats." The result is a human rights discourse that is in "grave danger of losing touch with the experience of suffering and the needs of those who should be the main beneficiaries [of human rights practices]—the poor and the oppressed" (Twining 2009, 2). Costas Douzinas offers a damning picture of these technocrats and their fellow travelers: "Official thinking and action on human rights has been entrusted in the hands of triumphalist column writers, bored diplomats and rich international lawyers in New York and Geneva, people whose experience of human rights violations is confined to being served a bad bottle of wine. In the process, human rights have been turned from a discourse of rebellion and dissent into that of state legitimacy" (2000, 7).

For Stephen Hopgood the problem with human rights can be traced directly to the workings of American power. From the early 1990s to the late 2000s, American foreign policy forged an alliance between money, liberal power, and human rights, leaving "the global human rights regime . . . bereft of moral authority." As a result, "human rights, handmaiden to neoliberal democracy, are unveiled as ideological, opening a legitimacy gap that has allowed their opponents to make increasing inroads against them" (Hopgood 2013, xiii). Yet if Hopgood sees little legitimacy in a Human Rights project driven by American interests, he remains hopeful in connection with what he refers to as human rights work "with lower-case initials" (ibid., viii). Signaling activities undertaken at "tremendous personal cost" by "local and transnational networks of activists" whose efforts are fueled by compassion, human rights work does offer a measure of hope for the future: "The endtimes can never come for this form of 'human rights' in the same way that nothing can stop people banding together to demand their own freedom or justice in whatever language they prefer. These ethical and political claims are rooted in our shared interest in fair and equal treatment" (ibid., viii).

As the references to Hopgood and other notable thinkers make clear, some of the most probing critiques of human rights regimes stop short of rec-ommending a wholesale rejection of the very idea of human rights. What is sought, rather, is better use of the instruments of social justice—that is, critically minded practices that do not turn human rights into a mantle of shining virtue for highly suspect ideologies, hypocrisies, and power dynamics. Douzinas, for example, retains a belief in the ability of human rights to "create new worlds, by continuously pushing and expanding the boundaries of society, identity and law, . . . [thereby bestowing] dignity and protection to novel subjects, situations and people" (2000, 343). And for the celebrated Kenyan constitutional lawyer Yash Ghai, human rights thinking continues, in the context of the multicultural states that increasingly define our current realities, to offer our best hope for a "negotiated understanding of the acceptable framework for coexistence" (Ghai 2009b, 115). Acknowledging the paradox of considerable progress in the develop-ment of "human rights norms" in times of "massive human rights violations" (Twining 2009, 2), Ghai affirms the value of human rights regimes. Approached in a pragmatic and materialist way, the institutional results of human rights thinking offer critically important tools for countering the dehumanizing effects of poverty (Ghai 2009a, 144).

The contrast established by Hopgood between a constructive activist-driven project, on the one hand, and a destructive state-driven pursuit of hegemonic power, on the other hand, offers hope to those who seek rejoinders to the skeptic's view on human rights filmmaking. Yet the distinction may not be as clear-cut as one might hope, for film and media activists often depend on funding from Western nations. And in the case, for example, of Denmark's support for film-making in the Global South, eligibility for funding hinges on a match between projects and the priorities of a human rights–based development strategy.

Focusing on the specific context of contemporary postcolonial Kenya, I seek to pinpoint the specific nature of problems arising from the intersection of moving image work and human rights thinking. To this end, I draw attention to deci-sive differences between the often positively regarded advocacy work of specific human rights organizations and the more ambiguous realities of independent filmmakers who must navigate through a sector shaped by the collective impact of NGO filmmaking.

I consider two quite different examples of advocacy work through film: the first focuses on the rights of sexual minorities and involves collaboration between the artists' collective the NEST and UHAI-EASHRI (the East African Sexual Health and Rights Initiative), an organization that does not typically emphasize the power of moving images; in the second case, involving collaboration between the Endorois tribe, WITNESS—an "international organization that trains and supports people using video in their fight for human rights" (https://witness.org)—and CEMIRIDE (Centre for Minority Rights Development), the focus is on the rights of ethnic minorities. In both cases, human rights filmmaking is a welcome instrument in the context of specific advocacy projects, with the various partners buying into the filmmaking process on the basis of varying degrees of commitment to video- and filmmaking as such.

The problematic aspects of human rights thinking with reference to film mostly arise in connection with filmmakers whose primary identity is that of filmmaker, not political activist. Analysis of the filmmaking career of Judy Kibinge, one of Kenya's, indeed Africa's, most accomplished women filmmakers, sheds light on the failings of a system that gives priority to what she calls "social justice films."[2] An independent filmmaker with a primary commitment to the art of film as culture, rather than as a means of direct political engagement, Kibinge does not regret the experience of having been drawn into social justice filmmaking. She does, however, regard the dominance of the advocacy film as imposing unwelcome limits on creative expression and as encouraging a neglect of issues of quality and form. Designed to achieve specific outcomes in the immediate future, the advocacy film is focused on the message and its intended uptake and effect, not on the cultural or aesthetic value of moving images as a source of quality art or entertainment.

If, as both Kaboré and Kibinge suggest, the true source of problems with human rights thinking in the context of film lies in the dynamics of an entire system, then the policies shaping the sector warrant careful attention. As far as the role of Western nations is concerned, a distinction between different categories of rights must be made. In a limited funding regime, rights-based approaches to development are likely to have a negative effect at the systemic level if exclusive priority is given to what Bronkhorst (2004, 7) calls "integrity rights"—the right to be "protected from torture and arbitrary detention"—or to political and civil rights. These are the categories of rights that encourage justice-oriented work with film where attention is on the sufferings of real-world victims. When the emphasis is placed on economic and cultural rights, on a process of facilitating economic growth and inclusion through culture, the overall effects appear to be far more positive and wide-ranging. In the cultural register, for example, the process of giving children and young people access to filmmaking equipment for the purposes of telling stories that they consider meaningful counts as a rights gain, even when the stories are fictional and eschew issues of justice. Difficulties arising from a broadly cultural approach to rights-based development work have to do, not with inherent weaknesses in the policies themselves, but with limited funding and the long-term sustainability of worthwhile projects. An especially significant factor in this regard turns out to be changing political priorities in the West. When the "money stops," as Kaboré puts it, a regime shift in the Global North may well be the immediate cause.

Video- and Filmmaking in Partnership with Human Rights Organizations

Human rights organizations typically adopt one of two possible stances on filmmaking: (1) some are open to filmmaking projects that are perceived as advancing their specific human rights goals, but have no intention of working with film as a primary means of doing so; (2) others see filmmaking as an integral part of their human rights work. The filmmaking partners also reveal diverse interests, adding further categories to the mix: (3) some see themselves as artists who value filmmaking but are not exclusively committed to it; (4) others embrace the identity of filmmaker on a long-term basis, as in the case of Kibinge, discussed at length below. Finally, there are groups (5) who become part of the filmmaking process for purely instrumental reasons. As victims of human rights abuses, they have come to see moving images as potentially advancing their cause but otherwise have little or no interest in video or film.

Based on a combination of (1) and (3), *Stories of Our Lives* (2014, Jim Chuchu, Kenya), an award-winning anthology film dramatizing true stories from the LGBT community in Kenya, points to human rights filmmaking as a genuinely creative process with social benefits.[3] In her characterization of the collaboration with UHAI-EASHRI (the East African Sexual Health and Rights Initiative), the film's scriptwriter, Njoki Ngumi (a medical doctor and a member of the artists' collective the Nest), identifies a win-win situation based on trust, mutual respect, flexibility, and, crucially, a shared commitment to advancing the cause of sexual minorities in Kenya:

> UHAI is a regional funder for work with regard to marginalized sexualities, as well as sex worker rights. It is difficult work that they do and a lot of it has to do with programs that go directly into empowering marginalized populations, into more activist work. So with us they took a chance, because they hadn't previously worked with a company whose primary purpose is expression, and creative expression at that, in all shapes and forms. So UHAI were pretty cool, in the sense that they just kind of trusted that we knew what we were doing and they were able to give us a bit of money to make the film. They were also

able to help us to get to Toronto when the film was selected by TIFF [Toronto International Film Festival]. (Ngumi 2016)

Ngumi sees the constructive, one-off collaboration with UHAI as consistent with a strategy that emphasizes maximal outreach for the purposes of community engagement and community building:

> For us, at The Nest, we sit in this weird place, where sometimes we go to gatherings with queer organizations, and they say, you guys are not gay, you're an arts organization. Then the arts organizations say, "You're not really this or that, you're queer." And then the film people are like, "Aren't you guys artists or queer?" We're in the middle of being able to reach out to so many different places, and so for us the primary aim is not belonging to any of these things, holistically, but being able to be of use in all these different communities. All the spaces in which we are able to work have different ecosystems that we fit into differently. (Ngumi 2016)

Although the Nest's first film, *Stories of Our Lives*, emerged from a one-off, hands-off, and wholly supportive values-based partnership with UHAI, Ngumi describes the latter as only one of a host of admirable human rights organizations with a commitment to the kind of hopeful community building that the artists' collective promotes. Using positive terms such as "important," "amazing," "beautiful," "creative," and "expressive," Ngumi refers to the work of organizations such as ISHTAR, GALCK (Gay and Lesbian Coalition of Kenya), AFRA (Artists for Recognition and Acceptance), Gay Kenya Trust, PEMA Kenya, and Jinsiangu. Like the Nest, some of these organizations foreground art and culture, while others are more focused on the kind of activist work that UHAI undertakes. Together they constitute an entire ecosystem focused on sexual rights, one that the Nest, with its primary emphasis on the pursuit of a "politics of blackness and otherness" through artistic practices, can access and be part of in various creative ways (Ngumi 2016).

Far from impeding creativity, the partnership with UHAI allowed the Nest to take their cultural work in new directions through filmmaking. The funding provided by the dedicated human rights organization facilitated crucial cultural work that the artists themselves initiated and regard as the very basis for significant social change. Reflecting on the relation between cultural and legal work, Ngumi sees the South African context as indicative of the sorts of problems that arise when culture and the law are insufficiently calibrated. In South Africa, more specifically, "progressive laws" protect the rights of sexual minorities, yet these rights continue to be violated as a result of the prevalence of such abusive practices as "corrective rape." As Ngumi sees it, the cultural engagement that *Stories of Our Lives* represents has the effect of creating the conditions in which positive legal changes can be properly effected. In Kenya, she claims, "There's room for changing legal frameworks" pertaining to sexual minorities. At the same time,

"There has to be commensurate room for changing social frameworks" through cultural work. The latter is "just as important as the legal work" (Ngumi 2016), inasmuch as the processes of implementing and following laws ultimately depend on a certain level of general conviction and belief.

Characterizing the intended audience for *Stories of Our Lives* as decidedly Kenyan, Ngumi articulates a localist perspective on the question of progress in the area of human rights on the African continent. Even the ban[4] that was immediately imposed on the film is seen as "authentic and organic," because it is the outcome of local prejudices that the Nest and others seek to combat. The lifting of this ban, Ngumi insists, must be the result of Kenyans having "decided to unban, and not because they have received pressure from abroad" (Ngumi 2016). *Stories of Our Lives* is the result of a full-blown artists' collective with a commitment to human rights joining forces with a specialized human rights organization with an interest in and respect for the power of moving images. In this film, and in the values and thinking that made it possible, we see evidence of the human rights activities in which Hopgood places great faith. It is difficult to see how the skeptic could make critical inroads against this kind of human rights project or this kind of human rights filmmaking.

Rightful Place: Endorois' Struggle for Justice (2006, Kenya) is the result of a very different permutation, one where the emphasis is on a purely instrumental use of images for the purpose of achieving justice. The short video is the work of Kenyan CEMIRIDE (Centre for Minority Rights Development), in partnership with WITNESS (the video advocacy organization founded by Peter Gabriel in the wake of the Rodney King beating in 1991), and the displaced Endorois tribe of Kenya. CEMIRIDE belongs to category (1) above, inasmuch as moving images represent a strategy that is adopted on a case-by-case basis. WITNESS, by contrast, is a prime example of category (2), video being at the very core of its human rights work. The modus operandi of the not-for-profit organization WITNESS is to aid "its Core Partners (human rights organizations across the globe) in using video technology within an advocacy campaign" (Torchin 2012, 141). To be of use in an advocacy campaign, the videos must convey carefully constructed "finished narratives" that are addressed to the specific audience that has the power to effect justice (Gregory 2010, 192), and it is for this reason that WITNESS has made video training a core element in its mission. The third partner, the Endorois, is the wronged party on whose behalf justice is pursued through the video itself and the advocacy campaign into which it is integrated. Unlike the artists belonging to categories (3) and (4), the Endorois' interest in moving-image making is purely instrumental; their place is thus in category (5).

Just under ten minutes long, *Rightful Place* focuses on the Endorois tribe's 1973 eviction from its ancestral lands by the Kenyan government for the purposes of developing a game reserve and a tourist resort, on the effects of this eviction, on the Endorois' decades-long struggle for justice, and on the tribe's right to the lands due to its occupation of them since "time immemorial."[5] A title in the opening frame in the video establishes its purpose, as "an evidentiary submission to the African Commission on Human and Peoples' Rights (ACHPR)." The video is credited with having played a critical role in achieving justice for the Endorois, the African Union having adopted the ACHPR's decision that the tribe's human rights had been violated. This ruling was precedent setting, inasmuch as it recognized "for the first time in Africa, indigenous peoples' rights over traditionally owned land and their right to development" (WITNESS Blog 2010). The efficacy of *Rightful Place* as a means to a well-defined end was such that the video is now used by WITNESS in the context of its training programs, for example, at a conference in South Africa in 2016, where attendees came from across Africa to discuss responses to "land grabbing and forced evictions by big companies, environmental problems affecting local communities . . . , [and] poor working conditions and sexual exploitation" (Mbaye 2016). If there is a problem with human rights filmmaking, *Rightful Place*, we can safely conclude, is not part of it. Let us turn, then, to the realities of being an independent filmmaker in Kenya, for it is here that the problematic aspects of pursuing rights through moving images become clear.

Cinematic Authorship in a Human Rights-Oriented Funding Regime: Judy Kibinge

Born in Nairobi in 1967, Judy Kibinge is one of Kenya's most prominent filmmakers. With a degree in media and communications from Manchester Polytechnic Art College, Kibinge moved into filmmaking from a successful career in advertising. She is the owner of the independent production house Seven, established in 2006, and founding director, since 2012, of the East African Documentary Film Fund, Docubox. In response to a question about her role in making Kenyan social justice films, Kibinge describes her involvement with this kind of filmmaking as a matter of "coincidence." Recalling her reasons for moving into filmmaking, she foregrounds an interest in meaningful indigenous expression:

> I come from an advertising background, and I used to work for an agency called McCann Erickson, and I worked there for about ten years. And at the time McCann had a lot of the bigger accounts in East Africa. We did a lot of work for Coke, for example, and I think it got to the point where I just got tired of making commercials. It just started to feel a little bit empty. I loved it as a career, loved it completely. It intersects with so many things. It's words, which I love, it's pictures, which I love. It's not one thing. Every client is a different story. Every day you're trying to figure out a new story and yet you're working with photographers and musicians. So to me it was just the most amazing first career. But when I quit, I quit because I wanted to make films. And in Kenya in those days, everything on TV—it's not that much better now—everything was foreign. And so I just wanted to make films that made sense to me. (Kibinge 2016)

Remarking on how her first films—*Dangerous Affair* (2002) and *Project Daddy* (2004)—are "fun, contemporary love stories," Kibinge insists that, years later, having made a significant number of social justice films, she would still welcome the opportunity to make a regular "romantic comedy." Yet, in her career as an award-winning Kenyan filmmaker, it is social justice films, or films probing the fault lines of democratic nation building in a postcolonial multiethnic society, that are especially salient.

Produced by STEPS International as part of the global "Why Democracy?" project, Kibinge's *Coming of Age: Democratic Evolution in Kenya* (2007) provides a subjective take on Kenyan politics, from independence under Jomo Kenyatta, through the Daniel Arap Moi era and the initial period of Mwai Kibaki's regime from 2002 to 2007, to the year when postelection violence threatened to make Kenya a "failed state" (Kibinge 2016). In *Peace Wanted Alive: Kenya at the Crossroads* (2009), Kibinge documents the extraordinary peace-building efforts of Concerned Citizens for Peace, an organization created as an immediate response to the postelection violence of 2007–2008. In *Peace Wanted Alive*, we see Marc Gerzon, president of Mediators Foundation, describing the group's interventions as a true model for active peace building, and initiators of Concerned Citizens for Peace affirming the opportunities that emerged in the wake of violent ethnic conflict. The film, it is clear, is meant to be hopeful and forward-looking.

The fiction film *Something Necessary* (2013) is the result of Kibinge's participation in a joint training initiative by One Fine Day Films, DW Akademie, and Ginger Ink that is exclusively oriented toward African filmmakers and African stories. Produced by Tom Tykwer, with the support of the German Federal Ministry for Economic Cooperation and Development, the German Society for International Cooperation, and the Hubert Bals Fund Rotterdam, among others, *Something Necessary* begins with a text: "Kenya 2007. Following results of the disputed presidential elections widespread violence erupted. Gangs of unemployed youths incited by politicians took to the streets all over the country. The characters in this film are purely fictional. The story is not." Kibinge sees clear continuities between *Something Necessary* and her earlier short film *Killer Necklace* (2009). In both films, young men bereft of opportunities are central to the story, the filmmaker's view being that the root causes of instability in Kenya lie in the marginalization of youths through unemployment and poverty: "I think Joseph's equivalent [in *Something Necessary*] is Boo [in *Killer Necklace*]. He's trying to do the right thing, but the doors are just shut to him and so he goes in the wrong direction. I feel that Joseph is Boo incarnated in a different role. I keep finding these young men, who keep turning up, because they're determining what Kenya is right now" (Kibinge 2016).

Scarred: Anatomy of a Massacre (2015) is a full-blown social justice documentary focusing on the massacre in 1984 of ethnic Somalis by Kenyan security forces in Wagalla, in the northeastern county of Wajir. Kibinge identifies earlier

Figure 6.1. Walter Lagat as the repentant rapist Joseph in Judy Kibinge's feature film about postelection violence in Kenya. Framegrab from *Something Necessary* (2013, Kibinge, Kenya).

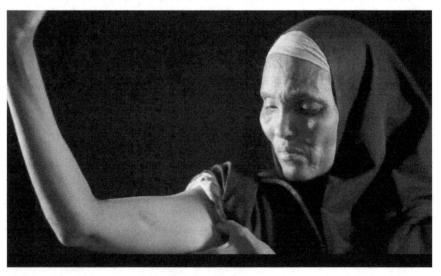

Figure 6.2. Survivors of the 1984 Wagalla massacre display their scars. Framegrab from *Scarred: Anatomy of a Massacre* (2015, Kibinge, Kenya).

work for the Kenya Human Rights Commission—the production of short films about absent landlords in the coastal region, about human rights abuses in the northern region, and about forgotten Mau Mau veterans in the central region—as a motivating factor in the making of *Scarred*. During the trip to Isiola in the north, Kibinge was told the story of the Wagalla massacre by a survivor whom she has never seen since. *Scarred*, she claims, is the realization of the promise she made to him to tell the then largely suppressed story of what happened in 1984.

In *Scarred*, Kibinge uses reenactments; black-and-white photographs of bodies and faces; scenes of survivors testifying about rape, murder, and torture before the Truth, Justice, and Reconciliation Commission of Kenya (TJRC); evocative images of an arid and blisteringly hot landscape;[6] and a haunting soundtrack to create a deeply moving account of the brutality and its still potent aftereffects. In addition to supporting survivors' pursuit of justice, *Scarred* offers a historical perspective that links Kenya's stability in the future to processes of effectively coming to terms with ethnically motivated human rights abuses in the past. Much as in *Something Necessary*, crucial information presented in titles at the beginning of the film sets the stage for the narrative:

> Wagalla town is located in Wajir, Northern Kenya. Northern Kenya refers to the former Northern Frontier District and its people. At first the British called the North their "protectorate", then "colony" and much later it became a buffer zone between Kenya and the present day Somalia. It was given an operative term, the "Northern Frontier District" (NFD). Soon legislations were enacted to isolate and control the NFD further. In 1902 movement in and out of the NFD was restricted. In 1934 the British bestowed on administrators extensive powers of arrest, restraint and detention. Finally collective punishment of tribes and clans was legalized. By independence, Kenya was practically divided in two: North and South. In the 1980s conflict between the Degodia and the Ajuran in Wajir resulted in a demand from the government that both clans surrender their weapons. When the Degodia handed in just 8 guns the administration mounted an operation to disarm them. The stage had long been set for what followed next.

Just as *Something Necessary* links ethnic violence to the irresponsible incitements of politicians and to their neglect of poverty and exclusion, *Scarred* looks to the failings of colonial and postcolonial agency and to policies of ethnic division for the root causes of killings, torture, and rape.

Especially significant, in terms of *Scarred*'s capacity to move and engage the viewer, are the scenes devoted to the women. Indeed, one scene, featuring a woman in whom Kibinge sees "an extraordinary poet," is crucial. Referring to the pride that the women still have as "Somalis" but also to how "beaten" they are, Kibinge recalls how one woman "would lead this song and then they would all start crying." Realizing the power of the song about deep existential loss when it was translated for her, Kibinge decided to make it a central element in the film:

> It's a song about all the things that were taken. And they sing it so beautifully, with such pride. But then the tears are just always one inch away. You just realize that they are walking in this shadow the whole time. I didn't have as many interviewees as I'd have liked to. I felt the film needed a section that really reflected the strength of these women. And that song did it for me. And

Abdla Abey

My lovely soul drifted off

Figure 6.3. Abdla Abey leads the other women in the singing of a song about loss and survival. Framegrab from *Scarred: Anatomy of a Massacre* (2015, Kibinge, Kenya).

that song is also a transitional song that takes us all the way to the hearings in Nairobi. So we're traveling from Wajir as she is singing about all the things they lost, on their way to reclaim themselves, hopefully, through justice. (Kibinge 2016)

As an executive producer, Kibinge has also helped promote the cultural rights of marginalized communities in two of Nairobi's informal settlements, Kibera and Pipeline. Kibinge's participation in the global "Why Democracy?" project led to an introduction, through Mette Hoffmann Meyer (then at the Danish Broadcasting Corporation), to then commissioning editor for the Finnish broadcaster YLE Iikka Vehkalahti. Describing Vehkalahti as a "good friend of Docubox," Kibinge recalls her team's involvement in "Project Story Tent" with great fondness. The concept of simply pitching a tent and inviting people in to share a story from their lives on camera required some adjustment as the project, funded by the Finnish Foreign Ministry, moved from Finland to Africa. Kibinge, for example, draws attention to security issues—the need "to figure the neighborhood out" and "to work with people from the community." The results were also different: "The stories are much heavier, much sadder [than the Finnish ones]" (Kibinge 2016). Kibinge sees the Pipeline stories as especially meaningful, because they come from a space of transience. Unlike the better-known informal settlements, Mathare and Kibera, which have long histories stretching back to the colonial era, as well as families, and a mix of rich and poor, Pipeline is a new urban space, and one of considerable individual uncertainty:

Pipeline is this really Mad Max estate because it's that place of transition when people are coming from up country and they want to come to Nairobi. They get off the bus, with nothing in their pockets and they land up in this sprawl. And it looks very different from Kibera and Mathare. It's these massive high rises that come out of bloody nowhere. And the land is quite swampy, so sometimes they just collapse. You see so many hustlers. Because they're stuck. You can't go back home because you've got nothing, and you can't quite break into the Nairobi that you thought you were coming to. And so you are stuck in this place of transition, with all these windowless buildings that you live in, with everyone selling little bundles of things to people who have no money to buy the bundles of things. It's really a weird place. Pipeline is just hustlers. So we set up our tent there and looked around for some boys who were waiting to rip someone off. They became part of our crew and their job was to get people into the tent. The stories are just unexpected. Some are very sweet, some are very sad. Some are ridiculous. But they are all true. And people don't get paid to tell their stories. The whole pitch is just: Come and tell us something that you've never told anyone before. Story Tent is happening globally. They've done it in Europe, in South America, and so the pitch is: Let's add your voice. If anything, you'll be heard. (Kibinge 2016)

The shorts, with titles identifying the storyteller and the main focus of the story, were screened at Docubox (at Shalom House in Nairobi), as well as at award-winning photo journalist and human rights activist Boniface Mwangi's PAWA254, a "collaborative space" dedicated to nurturing creative industry activities aimed at social impact (PAWA254).[7] With its emphasis on telling a story for the very first time, Story Tent Pipeline brought the voices of marginalized people during periods of difficult transition into a wider conversation. The results of this cultural rights–oriented project, claims Kibinge, were small films that people could really "connect with" (Kibinge 2016).

It is clear that Kibinge's work as a filmmaker is shaped by an understanding of moving images as powerful tools for advancing not only integrity rights, but cultural rights. But if her turn to rights-oriented filmmaking was largely due to "coincidence," then what does the trajectory outlined above tell us about the constraints and opportunities of a creative sector shaped by the priorities of NGOs and the development policies of various foreign ministries? How does Kibinge, as an independent Kenyan filmmaker with broad interests in filmmaking, view her own deepening engagement over the years with social justice films? Kibinge's lucid reflections on the effect of a funding regime that gives priority to social justice films—to human rights films narrowly construed—and on her own involvement with a variety of relevant types of filmmaking, offer nuanced and valuable insights. Indeed, her thinking provides a valuable corrective to recurring skepticism regarding the role of human rights filmmaking on the African continent.

Kibinge's (2016) statements regarding social justice filmmaking in the Kenyan context support a number of quite different theses, ranging from claims about the inherent value of the relevant films to claims about the need, not to limit the opportunities to engage in human rights filmmaking, but to expand the possibilities for other types of expression:

1. Social justice films are inherently important.

    "I really love films like that [romantic comedies]. But I think these other films are just really important, as a way of untangling who we are and what happened in the past and where we are going."

2. Filmmakers gain an enhanced understanding of the value of social justice films by making them.

    "The thing is, the more you do NGO films—which have such a bad rep, because they're often made badly, or boringly—the more you see Kenya and the continent properly. Because you go to places where you'd never go; nothing would ever take you to these places. And so I really started valuing these experiences."

3. In Kenya, social justice issues impose themselves and are thus in a sense necessary and inevitable.

    "These social struggles just keep festering underneath the whole time. Every film can't help but be tinged. Even when I try to do something, it just starts telling itself in a different and more somber way."

4. Social justice films sustain Kenyan filmmakers.

    "A lot of people in Kenya do a lot of these NGO films. And that's another reason why I've ended up doing so much of a certain kind of work, because that's actually how most people pay their rent."

5. Social justice films are also hard to fund.

    "I kept pitching the story [of the Wagalla massacre] and never could find anyone to support it. And lots of years later, like maybe seven years later, I went to Open Society Foundations [OSF, founded by George Soros] and pitched them three completely different stories. And as a second thought, I thought, 'Let me pull out that proposal that nobody is interested in and send it to them.' And strangely they wrote back and said, 'That's the one we're supporting.'"

6. Training programs offer a welcome escape from the dominance of documentary and social justice–oriented filmmaking.

    "As a filmmaker here it's so difficult to get the opportunity to make a film that is not an NGO film and not a documentary. So I applied for One Fine Day Films' training program."

The extrapolated claims are noteworthy because they highlight a rationale for continued commitment to social justice filmmaking, while suggesting changes that would help create a more supportive space for independent filmmaking in Kenya. The main problem with human rights filmmaking, it would seem, is its dominance in an institutional landscape that offers insufficient room for creative diversity, for the unique expressions that a deeply personal drive, vision, and voice can produce. The East African Documentary Film Fund Docubox is a hopeful attempt to bring change to the sector. The relevant efforts are being supported through the kind of government-driven development work that is often met with deep skepticism, on account of an allegedly intrusive prioritization of human rights. As we shall see, however, interactions between Kibinge, as founding director of Docubox, and the Danish Centre for Culture and Development (under the Danish Ministry of Foreign Affairs) reveal an approach to development through art and culture that is flexible and gives considerable weight to local knowledge and the agency of local practitioners, all within a human rights framework.

Docubox and the Danish Ministry of Foreign Affairs' Rights-Based Development Strategies

Kibinge's Docubox initiative is a direct response to the challenges of filmmaking in Kenya. Funded by the Ford Foundation, Docubox's most important feature, as Kibinge sees it, is that "it's a fund for filmmakers, created by filmmakers." Indeed, the fund's provenance in the vision and agency of practitioners makes "all the difference in the world" (Kibinge 2016). For Kibinge, it matters whether the motivation to make a particular kind of film comes from an inner space or from an external prompt. Human rights filmmaking is often driven by the externalities that structure the institutionally available opportunities for filmmakers. Although the resulting process and outcome—the making of a given film and the film itself—may be well worth affirming and may even foster desires to pursue further projects along similar lines, the narrow scope that an external agenda generates is problematic. Filmmakers, for example, cannot fully develop their craft or realize their own creative potential, let alone the narrative possibilities of their history and culture, if the space for individual choice and voice is severely restricted:

> You do all these NGO films, you tell stories because someone commissioned you to tell them, or they ran a competition, like the "Why Democracy?" one. I wouldn't have thought about doing a film about democracy. But because it was a competition, and because you're earning off it as well, then you realize: "Ok, I'm telling an important story." But that's not what made you tell it to start with. All that's not what brought you to that space. We don't have government funds, broadcasters don't give open calls, so how does a filmmaker make a film, especially a documentary? Everyone keeps saying, we have such fantastic stories to tell. But if you want to make a documentary and spend two to three years making it, how are you going to do it? How are you going to support yourself? (Kibinge 2016)

Devised with direct reference to the needs of the sector, the Docubox framework imposes no thematic constraints and encourages a personal vision and voice:

> People often ask you, "What themes do we have to send in?" And I'm like, "It's up to you. What's the story you want to tell?" We don't ask for social justice films. I don't care what people come with, as long as it's told in this authentic, unique voice. The structure is interesting and the story is interesting. But people do tend to lean towards social justice films when they send their stories in. I wish people would be a little more experimental. (Kibinge 2016)

In addition to funding filmmakers' proposed projects, Docubox offers "sparring"—constructive feedback in the context of an emphasis on talent development—and mentoring, networking and community building, and a platform for building an audience for the films.

Kibinge seeks to recruit mentors with a fine-grained understanding of the challenges faced by African filmmakers and with a strong interest in and "connection to the continent" (Kibinge 2016). Mentors who have worked in partnership with Docubox include George Amponsah, a Ghanaian producer and director living in Britain whose directorial credits include the documentaries *The Importance of Being Elegant* (2004), *The Fighting Spirit* (2007), and *The Hard Stop* (2015); producer, director, and screenwriter Laura Nix (*The Politics of Fur* [2002], *Afghanistan: Land in Crisis* [2002], and *The Yes Men Are Revolting* [as writer, 2014]); producer, director, and screenwriter Marc Hoeferlin, who is married to a Kenyan and lives in Nairobi (*Battle for Haditha* [2007], *Albino United* [2010], and *Tales of the Grim Sleeper* [as writer, 2014]); and the South African filmmaker and university teacher François Verster (*Sea Point Days* [2008] and *The Dream of Shahrazad* [2014]).

Verster's own experiences as an African filmmaker operating within an especially difficult institutional environment are seen as offering precisely the guidance that emerging Kenyan filmmakers need: "He was so fantastic, because he understands what it means not to have funding. His films have won all these awards, but he's struggled. So he teaches at Cape Town University, because he can't live off his films, despite being one of South Africa's best known documentary film directors" (Kibinge 2016). As Kibinge sees it, a central task for the community-building efforts of Docubox—through sparring, mentoring, and regular workshops focusing on filmmakers' ongoing projects—has to do with the nurturing of an open, generous, and supportive culture of honest sharing among film practitioners: "As Kenyans we have that culture of politeness. You see something really awful but you don't want to hurt someone's feelings, so you just don't tell them. You don't say anything and then later you say, 'Eh, that thing was bad.' But you won't tell the person. So a lot of it has to do with encouraging constructive criticism in a safe space between filmmakers" (Kibinge 2016). Networking, project development, and the enhancement of skill sets all matter, but so does the quality of the interactions among members of the filmmaking community. With regard to such interactions, trust and the fostering of moral principles governing practices of open sharing are also key. Referring to recurring problems of broadcasters "swiping" the ideas of independent practitioners, Kibinge sees a need for the kind of counterculture that Docubox's framework and practices are designed to facilitate.

In recent years Kibinge's initiatives have received support through the "Kenya Culture and Development Programme (2014–2017)," the Danish Centre for Culture and Development's most recent and, due to government cuts in Denmark, last program in Africa. The DCCD's activities are governed by the Danish Ministry of Foreign Affairs' strategy for culture and development, "The Right to Art and Culture," adopted by the Danish parliament in May 2013. This strategy is itself based on the government's overarching strategy for development cooperation, "The Right to a Better Life," which was adopted in June 2012. In the context of art and culture, the Danish government gives weight to five strategic priority areas:

1. Empowering people through active participation in art and cultural activities
2. Ensuring freedom of expression for artists and cultural actors
3. Enhancing economic growth through creative industries
4. Strengthening peace and reconciliation in postconflict areas through art and cultural activities
5. Promoting intercultural dialogue and intercultural collaboration (CKU 2014, 9; Hjort 2017)

The DCCD designs each of its programs based on the recommendations of a detailed country report. Its responsibilities include selecting the local partners and determining which of the government's priority areas are to be pursued. In the case of Kenya, partnerships were established with Sarakasi Trust, Docubox, Kenya Poets Lounge, and the Nest. Of the five priority areas, 1 and 3 were chosen, with Kenyan lawyer and DCCD program officer Elizabeth Maina pointing out that a conscious decision was made *not* to focus on peace and reconciliation, because the needs in other areas were seen as greater: "It's easier to access funds for filmmaking if the films have a social justice angle, which is why you find a huge focus on screening films in less privileged communities, in low income communities.[8] We have a component in our strategy document where one of our objectives is to promote dialogue between different communities. But it just didn't make sense for us, because there are many other organizations that are doing that" (Maina 2016). Rather than foregrounding the kind of abuse-focused social justice work that many associate with human rights-based cultural development programs, the DCCD's framework for Kenya supports Kenyans' participation in cultural activities and the development of creative industries in Kenya.

Maina's account of the process of both designing and running the Kenyan program points to the inclusion of partners and stakeholders in decision making about how best to spend the available funds. Indeed, the philosophy appears to be consistent with the Danish "arm's length principle" that has long been a pillar of Danish cultural policy, for the emphasis is very much on practitioner's agency and on facilitating the further development of the partner organizations' various goals:

> One thing that we do that most donor organizations don't do is that we let them formulate the project. Then we take it through our systems to see whether it will work, and we work together to tweak the projects so that they'll meet our objectives. But after that they pretty much run it. I do constant monitoring and evaluation. They have to inform us if there are any deviations from the original plan. But we try not to be very in their face. We don't want them to come up with a project or to conduct any activities, just so they can please us as opposed to advancing the objectives of the organization. *The problem is that when you have donor-driven projects, you've spent so much time trying to align everything, to ensure that the donor is happy, that you don't end up doing anything substantial* [emphasis added]. So that's what we've been trying to encourage our partners to do. So, so far it's been fantastic. They've grown a lot. (Maina 2016)

In the case of Docubox, funds were provided not to expand the production work that is already being supported by the Ford Foundation, but to undertake audience building in six counties outside of Nairobi, the point being to "grow interest in documentary filmmaking" (Maina 2016). The hope, on the part of Maina / the DCCD and Kibinge / Docubox, is that audience building over a period of three years will enable Docubox to develop broad interest in films that are creative, personal, and experimental. Also, audience building is seen as a factor in Docubox's ability to attract quality "submissions from all over the country" in response to its calls. In sum, the monies derived from Denmark's rights-based development strategy are effectively being used to expand the filmmaking sector in a variety of ways, among other things by challenging the dominance of the social justice film in its more narrow NGO incarnation. It is hard to find a straitjacket in the rights-based program, or an undermining of local practitioner agency in the specifics of its implementation.

In the DCCD case, the single most striking problem is that the liberal government of Lars Løkke Rasmussen resolved to shut down the center's operations in 2016, with programs being phased out in 2017 at the latest. This decision recalls Kaboré's concerns but does not provide a basis for a generalized skepticism about attempts to combine the pursuit of human rights with filmmaking. It is important to be aware of the diversity and complexity of the realities in question. A generalized skepticism is damaging, for it creates an inhospitable space for the human rights work for which there must and can be no "endtimes" (Hopgood 2013, viii).

METTE HJORT is Chair Professor of Humanities and Dean of Arts at Hong Kong Baptist University. She is editor (with Ursula Lindqvist) of *A Companion to Nordic Cinema*.

Notes

1. The work described in this chapter was fully supported by a grant from the Research Grants Council of the Hong Kong Special Administrative Region, China (RGC Ref. No. 340612/CB1384, Lingnan University, 2013-16). The account of rights-oriented engagements with moving images in Kenya draws on a mix of research methods. One method was *site visits* to Lola Kenya Screen (dedicated to filmmaking for and by children and young people in the context of cultural rights), to Docubox (the East African Documentary Film Fund), and to the informal settlement of Kibera (where the nonprofit organization Hot Sun Foundation, established by the Nairobi-based University of Southern California graduate Nathan Collett, is based). I also conducted face-to-face *interviews* with Kenyan practitioners Ogova Ondego (managing trustee and creative director of Lola Kenya Screen), Judy Kibinge (founding director of Docubox), Elizabeth Maina (program officer, Culture, the Royal Danish Embassy in Nairobi), and, through Skype, Njoki Ngumi (a medical doctor and community builder with the artists' collective the Nest). In Denmark, key interviewees were Louise Friis Pedersen and Vibeke Munk Petersen (previously responsible for program development at the Danish Centre for Culture and Development, under the auspices of the Danish Ministry of Foreign Affairs); in Holland, Charles Liburd (filmmaker and producer at No Money, No Cry) offered insights, through Skype, about the Nollywood-inspired Riverwood phenomenon and his Riverwood 2.0 initiative (see Vourlias 2011 on Riverwood). I conducted *institutional research* focused on policy documents of the Danish Ministry of Foreign Affairs; studies commissioned by the Kenya Film Commission; initiatives of the African Union, especially NEPAD (the New Partnership for Africa's Development); and the workings of the nonprofit sector (WITNESS and InformAction). Finally, I examined a comprehensive *corpus of diverse films and videos* with an eye to issues of production as well as questions of style and content. Not limited to works with a clear human rights focus, this corpus also included Riverwood video productions and nonlocal commercial productions set in Kenya, both recently and in earlier decades (see Slavkovic 2015 for an account of filmmaking in East Africa).

2. I am grateful to the Danish film producer, film commissioner, and talent developer Jakob Høgel for having introduced me to Judy Kibinge, in connection with his Global Film Fund initiative.

3. See the Nest (2015) for the book that complements the film.

4. George Gachara, the film's executive producer, was arrested for allegedly violating Kenya's Films and Stage Plays Act (Prendergast 2014).

5. See WITNESS Blog 2010.

6. Kibinge refers to "trying to imagine and really build up the feeling of heat and nowhere to run to as the film goes on" (Kibinge 2016).

7. The Pipeline films, available on Vimeo, are *Rebecca Moraa—The Kisii way to test a father; Joseph Mutua—My wife, my greatest joy; Ezra Mwiti—One day, one time we would meet; Annfaith Mmasi—Dangerous blackouts; Kevin Kiliru—If we die, we die together; Arthur Jaika—My lovers, three daughters and their mother; Polycup Machuka—Rat poison; Emma Ndunge—Fake abortion pills; Kimani Mwangi—Sugarcane, paperbags and X-rays; Rose Imenza—There was someone under my bed* (links and password provided by Judy Kibinge).

8. An example is the Hot Sun Foundation, which pursues social transformation, poverty alleviation, dialogue, and inclusion by offering marginalized communities tools and opportunities for expression. Having achieved success with the short film entitled *Kibera Kid* in 2006, Nathan Collett, who is also the creative director for the production company Hot Sun Films, has continued to focus on Kibera, an informal settlement on the outskirts of Nairobi. With a population of 250,000, Kibera is not only the "biggest slum in Africa" (Kibera Facts & Information), but the site where the postelection violence of 2007–2008 started before spreading to other parts of Kenya (Sana and Okombo 2012, 2). Kibera is thus a prime candidate for interventions aimed at conflict resolution, reconciliation, and active peacemaking in a multiethnic society.

Filmography

Afghanistan: Land in Crisis, 2002, Laura Nix, USA.
Albino United, 2010, Marc Hoeferlin and Barney Broomfield, USA / Tanzania / UK.
Battle for Haditha, 2007, Nick Broomfield, writer Marc Hoeferlin, UK.
Coming of Age: Democratic Evolution in Kenya, 2007, Judy Kibinge, Kenya.
Dangerous Affair, 2002, Judy Kibinge, Kenya.
The Dream of Shahrazad, 2014, François Verster, South Africa / France / Egypt / the
     Netherlands / Lebanon / Turkey.
The Fighting Spirit, 2007, George Amponsah, USA / UK.
The Hard Stop, 2015, George Amponsah, UK.
The Importance of Being Elegant, 2004, George Amponsah and Cosima Spender, France / UK.
Killer Necklace, 2009, Judy Kibinge, Kenya.
Peace Wanted Alive: Kenya at the Crossroads, 2009, Judy Kibinge, Kenya.
The Politics of Fur, 2002, Laura Nix, USA.
Project Story Tent—Pipeline, 2015, producer Judy Kibinge, Kenya.
Project Daddy, 2004, Judy Kibinge, Kenya.
Rightful Place: Endorois' Struggle for Justice, 2006, WITNESS, CEMIRIDE, and Endorois,
     Kenya.
Scarred: Anatomy of a Massacre, 2015, Judy Kibinge, Kenya.
Sea Point Days, 2008, François Verster, South Africa.
Something Necessary, 2013, Judy Kibinge, Kenya.
Stories of Our Lives, 2014, Jim Chuchu, Kenya.
Tales of the Grim Sleeper, 2014, Nick Broomfield, writer Marc Hoeferlin, UK / USA.
The Yes Men Are Revolting, 2014, Andy Bichlbaum and Mike Bonanno, writer Laura Nix, the
     Netherlands / Denmark / France / Germany / USA.

References

Bronkhorst, Daan. 2004. "The Human Rights Film: Reflections on Its History, Principles and
     Practices." Amnesty International Film Festival.
CKU (the Danish Centre for Culture and Development). 2014. "Kenya Culture and
     Development Programme October 2014 to October 2017."

Douzinas, Costas. 2000. *The End of Human Rights*. Portland: Hart Publishing.

Ghai, Yash. 2009a. "Understanding Human Rights in Asia." In *Human Rights, Southern Voices: Francis Deng, Abdullahi An-Na'im, Yash Ghai and Upendra Baxi*, edited by William Twining, 120–155. Cambridge: Cambridge University Press.

———. 2009b. "Universalism and Relativism: Human Rights as a Framework for Negotiating Interethnic Claims." In *Human Rights, Southern Voices: Francis Deng, Abdullahi An-Na'im, Yash Ghai and Upendra Baxi*, edited by William Twining, 109–120. Cambridge: Cambridge University Press.

Gregory, Sam. 2010. "Cameras Everywhere: Ubiquitous Video Documentation of Human Rights, New Forms of Video Advocacy, and Considerations of Safety, Security, Dignity and Consent." *Journal of Human Rights Practice* 2 (2): 191–207. doi:10.1093/jhuman/huq002.

Hjort, Mette. 2017. "Eyes on the Future: World Cinema and Transnational Capacity Building." In *Routledge Companion to World Cinema*, edited by Rob Stone, Paul Cooke, Stephanie Dennison, and Alex Marlow-Mann, 482–496. London: Routledge.

Hopgood, Stephen. 2013. *The Endtimes of Human Rights*. Ithaca, NY: Cornell University Press.

Ignatieff, Michael. 2001. *Human Rights as Politics and Idolatry*. Princeton, NJ: Princeton University Press.

Kaboré, Gaston. 2019. "Interview with Gaston Kaboré." Interviewed by Rod Stoneman. In *African Cinema and Human Rights*, edited by Mette Hjort and Eva Jørholt. Indianapolis: Indiana University Press.

Kibera Facts & Information. Accessed December 30, 2016. http://www.kibera.org.uk/facts-info/.

Mbaye, Isabelle. 2016. "WITNESS Trains on Video Advocacy at Sustainability and Corporate Accountability Summit in South Africa." Accessed January 14, 2017. https://witness.org/witness-trains-on-video-advocacy-at-sustainability-and-corporate-accountability-summit-in-south-africa/.

Moyn, Samuel. 2010. *The Last Utopia: Human Rights in History*. Cambridge, MA: Belknap Press.

The Nest. 2015. *Stories of Our Lives: Queer Narratives from Kenya, from an Archive of Stories Collected for the "Stories of Our Lives" Research Project*. Nairobi: The Nest Arts Company Limited.

PAWA254. Accessed December 31, 2016. http://pawa254.org/who-we-are/.

Prendergast, Frank. 2014. "Executive Producer of Gay Kenyan Film Arrested." *DailyXtra*, October 15, updated October 21. Accessed January 9, 2017. http://www.dailyxtra.com/world/news-and-ideas/news/executive-producer-gay-kenyan-film-arrested-94358.

Sana, Olang, and Okoth Okombo. 2012. *Taking Stock of Socio-economic Challenges in the Nairobi Slums: An Inventory of the Pertinent Issues between January 2008 and November 2012*. Nairobi: Friedrich-Ebert-Stiftung (FES), Nairobi.

Slavkovic, Milica. 2015. "Filmmaking in East Africa: Focus on Kenya, Tanzania, and Uganda." In *Small Cinemas in Global Markets: Genres, Identities, Narratives*, edited by Lenuta Giukin, Janina Falkowska, and David Desser, 189–214. Lanham, MD: Lexington Books.

Tascón, Sonia. 2015. *Human Rights Film Festivals: Activism in Context*. New York: Palgrave Macmillan.

Torchin, Leshu. 2012. *Creating the Witness: Documenting Genocide on Film, Video, and the Internet*. Minneapolis: University of Minnesota Press.

Twining, William, ed. 2009. *Human Rights, Southern Voices: Francis Deng, Abdullahi An-Na'im, Yash Ghai and Upendra Baxi.* Cambridge: Cambridge University Press.

Viljoen, Frans. 2012. *International Human Rights Law in Africa.* Oxford: Oxford University Press.

Vourlias, Christopher. 2011. "Riverwood tells Kenya's stories. Unassuming Industry Builds a Mountain of Movies." *Variety* 425 (1): 8. Accessed December 28, 2016. http://variety.com/2011/film/news/riverwood-tells-kenya-s-stories-1118045992/.

WITNESS Blog. 2010. "*Rightful Place:* Endorois' Struggle for Justice." February 10. Accessed July 25, 2018. http://www.comminit.com/content/rightful-place-endorois'-struggle-justice-video-advocacy-kenya.

Interviews

Kibinge, Judy. 2016. Shalom House, Nairobi, Kenya, February 22.

Maina, Elizabeth. 2016. The Palacina, Nairobi, Kenya, February 23.

Ngumi, Njoki. 2016. Skype (Hong Kong / Nairobi), May 11.

7 The Zanzibar International Film Festival and Its Children Panorama

Using Films to Socialize Human Rights into the Educational Sector and a Wider Public Sphere

Martin Mhando

Sᴜɴᴄᴇ ɪᴛꜱ ᴠᴇʀʏ beginnings in 1998, the Zanzibar International Film Festival (ZIFF) has encompassed specific educational purposes. ZIFF's mission is "to produce and deliver a film-centered international forum for interaction and engagement through and with the arts and multiculturalism, and maintain in Zanzibar a professional, annual festival of the dhow countries able to provide other artistic and event management services while contributing to regional artistic and socioeconomic growth." Called the Festival of the Dhow Countries, ZIFF uses film to comprehend various worlds (the Indian Ocean World, the African World, the Film World), but it also features three key Panoramas—on Women, Children, and Villages—which seek to create "a culture of interaction with the media, the development of the perception of different types of information, skills analysis and interpretation of media texts, the formation of critical thinking, [and] creativity in the field of media" (Federov 2015, 214).

As a social experiment, the festival adheres to the United Nations' actions regarding human rights education as sanctioned under the UN General Assembly Resolution 49/184 (December 1994). Being a nongovernmental organization, ZIFF allows for less politicized learning environments within the school and community settings, and in these advocacy contexts (called "uanaharakati" in Kiswahili), we are able to focus on social issues such as gender, human rights values, social justice, and development, topics we would not have been able to address under the political regimes of social control. In Zanzibar there are many external sanctions beyond norms and cultural values, such as censorship, expulsion, and limitations of political freedom that the government enforces as a means of social control.

The purpose of the three Panorama programs as regards human rights is thus the socialization of human rights norms into the educational sphere and, through this, the wider public sphere. We continually question whether the principles articulated in the Universal Declaration of Human Rights as well as the UN Convention on the Rights of the Child are practicable and can be put to work, and how they actually affect social behavior within Zanzibari society.

With specific reference to the Children Panorama, our guiding concern is how films can be utilized to explore issues of human rights among children and youth in an African setting and to help society engage with "issues such as poverty, gender, religion and social justice within human rights frameworks" (Simmonds 2014, 142). How can we, in other words, create conditions favorable to the study, understanding, and articulation of the living conditions of the child in Zanzibar and to the implementation of human rights norms?

The Children Panorama program and its work with film as a tool for the socialization of human rights is the main focus of this chapter. After providing a brief general introduction to the program, its background, and its contexts, I concentrate on a specific outreach project that ran from January to June 2016. The project involved dialogues with audiences, evaluation gatherings, and discussions held with film and project facilitators. One of the films was the Tanzanian short film *Faraja* (2014, Nasir Al Qassmi and Yusuf Kisokky) about a young girl facing forced marriage in Zanzibar. The discussions following *Faraja* in particular will be addressed in the final part of the chapter.

The Children Panorama—Background and Contexts

Children's human rights education refers to educational practices in schools and educational institutions that are consistent with the UN Convention on the Rights of the Child. It is a form of education that takes the view that children have human rights, that children are citizens in their own right, and that schools and educational institutions are learning communities where children learn (or fail to learn) the values and practices of human rights and citizenship.

The Children and Youth Panorama program was incorporated into ZIFF in 1999, during the second festival. The original program proposal notes that "[The Children Panorama] introduces young people to the power of the visual medium in conveying messages and as a way of speaking out on their issues; both technical and issue based training is given to children. The screenings' focus is on ensuring culturally appropriate films for children" (ZIFF Project Proposal 1999, 3). The program has seen a number of changes over the years. Beginning as a life skills development program, it grew into a media culture development program and evolved into a media literacy project encompassing human rights education and research. Some of the highlights of the program include running the Young Journalist Program under UNICEF for eight years.

Since 2007, in collaboration with the Danish Film Institute (DFI) and the Salaam Film and Dialogue Festival of Denmark, ZIFF annually presents an integrated film program involving film viewing and facilitated discussions. ZIFF's outreach screening program is encapsulated in a project called Community Film Screenings funded by the Danish government under the Centre for Culture and Development (CKU / DCCD) project of DANIDA, Denmark's national agency for development cooperation. Describing the program in 2015, the project report says: "While the purpose of the project is to inculcate the culture of engaging with art, and the films we choose also address social-political, environmental or social-justice issues, our goal is to partner with communities that are also affected by these issues and afford social development. This is a strategic partnership which will enhance audience and viewers' experience and engagement. The inclusion of films on the theme of women and gender and the focus on physical and sexual abuse of children and women has resonance in the communities" (ZIFF-CKU Report 2015).

The whole purpose of the Children Film Panorama is to provide a safe and interesting environment for schoolchildren to learn through watching films. Each year we invite about two thousand children to the festival, where they are divided into age groups for film viewing and discussion. These showings are moderated by trained film facilitators, the point being to enhance the educational capacity of the films and the setting. Importantly, human rights literacy is thus undertaken outside environments that are laden with strict cultural values. This is because, as Du Preez and Roux emphasize in their study of positive discipline in multicultural schools, "drawing from cultural values is not only unlikely to solve the problem of discipline, but also undermines the efforts to" effect change (Du Preez and Roux 2008, 14). It should be noted, however, that the purpose of human rights is to protect individual interests, especially those of the powerless, and not to undermine the diversity of cultures.

In the early years, in partnership with UNICEF's Dar es Salaam office, the Children Panorama used the problem-solving method known as SARA (Scanning, Analysis, Response, Assessment). The SARA model is a problem-solving approach to recurring problems. The method presents common situations to stimulate problem solving, emphasizing the capacity to solve a problem in context rather than applying ready-made answers to every recurrence of a problem. From a pedagogical perspective, ZIFF views human rights literacy as a matter of validating procedural activities that influence behavior without compromising current educational values. This way the program quietly contests positions that are held by those with strict religious or cultural views. Though a secular state, Zanzibar's value system is essentially based on Muslim and Bantu cultural values. Sometimes these value systems contradict each other, but in the discussions after watching the films, human rights values are brought forward to counter some cultural beliefs, especially when a specific narrative is seen potentially to jeopardize the realization of peace, political unity, or multicultural ideals.

Using the workshop camp model, up to thirty-five young people would be invited to camps during holidays (coinciding with the festival periods). Here they would explore different themes, all of them carefully selected to help them become assertive citizens. Obviously the camp model changes and adapts, but what is most recurring is the fact that through the mixed-gender camp model, the youth get to understand the influence of gender roles and have time and space to interact and think. The camps effectively provide an opportunity to practice becoming better persons in a supportive environment.

From January 2016 the project took on an enhanced position when the whole of the Village Panorama Community Screenings Project under CKU focused on school screenings. This was a result of the banning of all public gatherings in Zanzibar after the annulled Zanzibar general election in October 2015. The impact of the political situation in the country became obvious when the community screenings were stopped in midstream on October 14, 2015, only ten days before the elections. The Zanzibar Censor Board was allegedly following up on complaints that the film we were screening in the community at that time—*An African Election* (2011, Jarreth Metz, UK / Ghana)—was biased.[1] According to the Internet Movie Database (IMDb), "*An African Election* is a political documentary that exposes the never-before-seen, nitty-gritty of political electioneering in Africa. It captures the intrigues of political campaigns; the almost carnival like atmosphere that is laced with fear of the unknown and the danger that lurks behind-the-scenes (http://www.imdb.com/title/tt1674131/)." The screenings were organized by the European Centre for Electoral Support (ECES) with the aim of utilizing film to educate audiences on the role of the Electoral Commission. Discussions were held both in open-air village settings and in special film screening classes in selected Zanzibar secondary schools. Media education is not part of the curriculum in Zanzibar (as in most Tanzanian schools), and normally students would not take part in such gatherings within a school setting. It was providential that the whole 2015 Zanzibar election debacle was embroiled under the Electoral Commissioners' powers (the Jecha Affair)![2] In the film the crisis was solved through the Ghana Electoral Commissioner's wisdom and the political will of the parties involved, which could have been a valuable lesson to Zanzibar.

Programming: January to June 2016

As a result of the orders banning public events in Zanzibar, ZIFF began the year looking for new ways to continue the human rights project, with an emphasis on implementing film screenings in schools. We first had to get in touch with the education authorities, and in collaboration with the ministry and the schools we began the process of selecting schools to be involved in the program. Ten secondary schools were selected (seven on Unguja Island and three on Pemba

Island) for the research part of the project. These were schools that had the most regular screening schedules and therefore afforded more potential to gather more conclusive data.

We began the School Screenings program on January 13, and they went on until June 9, 2016. The project became very interactive and motivating for both students and teachers. Many schoolchildren had not been able to attend the evening screenings held in their villages due to local customs and other social reasons, but with screenings taking place during class times, they recognized the importance of the films and felt the impact of the screenings on their education and social life. In general, twenty-five Zanzibar schools as well as five villages on Unguja and two on Pemba have access to films on a weekly basis.

We showed films in schools in Bwejuu, Mahonda, Paje, Mikindani, Dunga, Kitogani, and Regezamwendo (Unguja) as well as Gando, Minungwini, and Vitongoji (Pemba). The choice of films was satisfactory, attracting larger audiences than did earlier village screenings. The program reached 2,183 students and 86 teachers on both Unguja and Pemba between January and March 2016; between April and June, it reached 2,475 students and 125 teachers on both Unguja and Pemba. Many of the films shown reflected the normal life of the communities. The following films were selected:

- *Jaya* (2014, Puja Maewal, India, 30 min.—street children). A teenager survives gruesome gang life on the unforgiving streets of Mumbai by posing as a boy. When she meets a wealthy businessman who might be the father who abandoned her, she sets out to reclaim her identity. (We tackle here children's rights to a name, a nationality, family relations, and education, and the child's right to be protected from economic exploitation.) (The UN Convention on the Rights of the Child.)
- *Yesterday* (2004, Darrell Roodt, South Africa, 90 min.—HIV / AIDS). After falling ill, Yesterday learns that she is HIV positive. With her husband in denial and a young daughter to tend to, Yesterday's one goal is to live long enough to see her go to school. (We focus on a child's right to education as well as care and protection.)
- *Faraja* (2014, Nasir Mohamed Al Qassmi and Yusuf Kisokky, Tanzania, 22 min.—early marriage). Sixteen-year-old Faraja arrives in Zanzibar for a holiday, but unbeknownst to her, a suitor has been arranged for her by her extended family. (We focus on a child's right to consensual marriage.)
- *Soko Sonko* (2013, Ekwa Msangi, Kenya / Tanzania, 10 min.—family). When her mother falls sick, Kibibi's father, Ed, is tasked with taking her to the market to get her hair braided before school begins. *Soko Sonko* is a hilarious, fish-out-of-water roller-coaster of

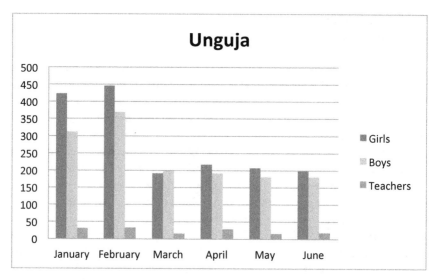

Figure 7.1. Attendance at screenings held in secondary schools in Unguja, January to June 2016.

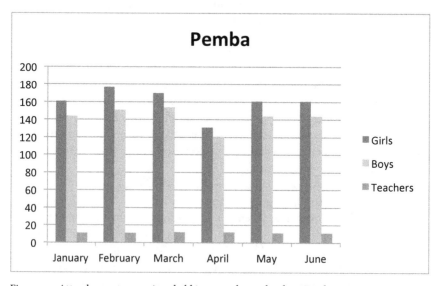

Figure 7.2. Attendance at screenings held in secondary schools in Pemba, January to June 2016.

a journey, about a well-intended dad who braves the fires and goes where no man has gone before . . . because only women have been there! (We focus here on the child's right to parental care.)

- *Storm* (2009, Giacomo Campeotto, Denmark, 88 min.—being children). Freddy saves a dog from its volatile owner and hides it in his room. When Freddy's dad discovers the dog, he insists on handing it

Table 7.1. Attendance at village screenings in Unguja, July 2016.

Shehia	Region	Men	Women	Children	Total
Paje	South Unguja	160	185	251	596
Kizimkazi	South Unguja	230	304	358	892
Kitogani	South Unguja	132	190	230	552
Bwejuu	South Unguja	150	200	340	690
Dunga	Centre Unguja	160	189	268	617
Mahonda	North Unguja	289	358	380	1,027
Dole	West Unguja	560	645	832	2,037
Makunduchi	South Unguja	610	750	680	2,040
Total		**2291**	**2821**	**3339**	**8,451**

Table 7.2. Attendance at village screenings in Pemba, July 2016.

Shehia	Region	Men	Women	Children	Total
Gando	South Pemba	350	487	660	1,497
Wesha	Chakechake	380	410	549	1,339
Vitongoji	Chakechake	254	312	421	987
Total		**984**	**1209**	**1630**	**3,823**

back to the owner. A terrified Freddy convinces his father they must buy the dog. (We focus on a child's right to play and recreation.)

Only *Faraja* is in Kiswahili and set on Zanzibar. We therefore chose to study the reception of this film in particular and how it afforded opportunities to develop film literacy. I present the results of this study a little further on.

On the opposite page are audience figures collected during the project activities (January to June 2016). The figures reveal the extent to which the project reached the target audience and points to growing interest in the project. The number of young people reached is a testament to the interest that film is capable of generating within the general community. There is reason to believe that the type of project in question could have a significant impact on the relevant communities. Though the screenings were held within the class / school context, these were special screenings outside the class system, and students could have opted out. Further, since the schools were in the same villages, the screenings became of community interest when the schoolchildren took the film discussions into the community.

Above are some of the data collected during the project activities in village settings in July 2016. The number of participants in village screenings has grown steadily over the years.

Data Collection and Main Findings

The project used trained facilitators led by Robert Manondolo, a professional high school teacher who has also worked with the festival's Children Panorama for over ten years. He was ably assisted by Jaffeth Mihayo Nzoka and Riziki Mohamed Juma, also professional teachers with experience in film facilitation and Aisha Hussein Mussa, a ZIFF facilitator. Before the project began, twelve facilitators were trained in order for ZIFF to have a pool of staff knowledgeable in film facilitation and discussion.[3]

Evening film shows on Zanzibar have always attracted more women than men. This was again reflected in this project. When we showed the five films in the villages of Paje, Bwejuu, and Dunga on Unguja in August 2016, attendance by adult women was always higher than that of men by at least fifty people.[4] This difference was noticed across all districts of the project in other months. Religion-wise, the vast majority were Muslims as Zanzibar is a predominantly Muslim country (97 percent or more), but there were also some Christians.[5] Most of the spectators were between the ages of twelve and thirty-five.

Our target group (the youth) still dominates, and there is a growing interest among young women. Yet in this group the young men outnumber the women, but not by a whole lot, and our target is to ensure that the number of young women spectators is maintained or increases. This goal is reflected in the selection of the films, which takes the interests of young women spectators into account.

The Community Film Screenings project was initiated in consultation with community members, and therefore we have had the luck and advantage of basically serving a community need. The need was to provide the people, and the youth in particular, with some entertainment to reduce what one sheha, a local government official similar to a ward leader, called "too much free time" in the evenings. The unemployed youth loiter in the streets during the day, and in the evening they are joined by more school-going youth who simply hang around causing mischief.

Interestingly, the response of the communities was very quick and over-whelming in 2015 when ZIFF partnered with the European Centre for Electoral Support (ECES) to undertake election awareness training.[6] We had been able to organize community meetings during the day, showing a film and conducting discussions about the film itself, the elections, and the theme of peace. We had twelve screenings in six days with over 45 participants during the day and 150 to 300 spectators during the evenings. The experience that ZIFF brought to the Zanzibar general elections did therefore enhance the social environment of the country in the political arena.

The focus in the program as regards facilitation of the discussions was more toward eliciting participation, enhancing structured communication, and improving analytical skills. The facilitator would normally attempt to gauge the students' understanding of the issues and conditions evoked in the narrative by asking the students to describe the world of the narrative on the basis of their own experiences. Normally they would be required to indicate how they understood the events and conditions that generate the issues, as well as the factors that perpetuate the problem.

To help bring home the question, the discussions would move toward exploring with the class what is known about the problem in its thematic relevance. This would be followed by questions relating to how the problem is currently being addressed and how successful that has been. Developing the subject matter into a general theme would help make the problem socially specific, which would then lead to brainstorming about new ways of solving the problem. Often the students would be made to look at how the community in the film attempted to solve the problem as well as identify alternative intervention methods.

The discussions would often lead to comparing the discursive environment of the school and the home or even the community, with students decrying the fact that what they are taught at school is never replicated or even taken into account in the home or community. The differences and contradictions that they identify and then have to live with often generate considerable confusion.

Another formal mode of research was convening "evaluation" workshops at the ZIFF offices. At the end of each project, an evaluation meeting in the form of a focus group was held to give the facilitators and researchers an occasion to work together. It was also an opportunity for the researchers to bring a wide and diverse group of audience members together to discuss the project and its outcomes. In late 2015 we held two special evaluation workshops. The first workshop involved shehas (who were all men) and a few lead villagers (mostly women), and the second one included regional and district cultural officers from the whole of Zanzibar.

From the shehas we wanted to learn about the impact that the screenings were having on the community and what the key problems or issues were, in terms of how the project was organized and implemented. These administrative discussions invariably led to discussions of the films, and then the leaders went on to proffer their views. Most of the shehas had seen all the films in the program, and they became useful barometers for understanding the popularity of the program and the films. Needless to say, this is because word of mouth is the most effective reporting system in the village setting, and the shehas were always the first port of call for villagers if there were any problems in the project. Through the shehas we had also expected to get reactions from religious persons in the village, those who would have reacted to the ways in which the evening screenings were conducted, should they have had an impact on the spiritual welfare of the community.

A report appearing in one of the local daily newspapers, *Zanzibar Leo* (February 22, 2016), quoted the sheha of Dunga, Mr. Abeid Hassan Abdullah, as saying that the project had helped contain unruly youths in the evenings. "The youth's manners had deteriorated as they had no respect for elders." He felt that after discussions were prompted about how young men treated girls in the villages, the boys were cowed, especially when some of them were booed for their comments after the screenings.

Ms. Hadiya Makame, leader of a village women's civic organization, discussed what she called "rushwa ya muhali" or "relational corruption," meaning relatives find it difficult to report or take legal action against family members who have committed heinous acts. "This is a crime since it affects lives of young people in our communities and it is a form of corruption," she stated. This was discussed in relation to *Faraja* as well when it was noted that some family members might not in fact have supported the marriage but would have felt powerless to stop the family, as families are expected to come together in such times.

In the second mode of evaluation, we would invite students, teachers, she-has, and community members to a formal evaluation workshop held at the ZIFF offices in Stonetown, Zanzibar. Such a meeting was held on Monday, September 26, 2016. In the discussion we highlighted facilitator-participant responses regarding the human rights values raised in the films, *Faraja* being the key text. The group had twelve men and eight women, of whom six were girls and five were boys under eighteen years.

The participants revealed many personal views regarding values that they felt were cultural or religious and how these "interfered" with human rights (Aisha Hussein Mussa, ZIFF facilitator). They noted that when they watched films in the school context, the human rights were very clear, but outside the school they were confronted with a different set of values that left them confused. They recognized, however, that the communities were also against some anti–human rights practices, but noted that there are few occasions for airing the different positions, making it difficult for discussions to take place. "It is our human right to speak, but we feel scared to speak when adults are looking at us," said Fatuma Khatibu Masoud, a student from Wesha, Pemba, adding, "It is even more difficult for us women because we are not even allowed to speak in front of men." Rehema Khamisi Maabadi from Mahonda Secondary School commented as follows: "We should be able to discuss human rights even before we get to school. When we get to school, it is too late because we already believe what has been forced into our minds at home. . . . After our studies we need to become ambassadors to all others who never had this opportunity."

The films also made people think about other rights such as animal rights. The theme of caring for animals in the film *Storm* from Denmark is novel to an Islam-based culture, where the dog is not much appreciated. To see young people and especially children talk about loving animals and not wanting to hurt them was very heartwarming. The positive outcome from exposure to new cultures was evident.

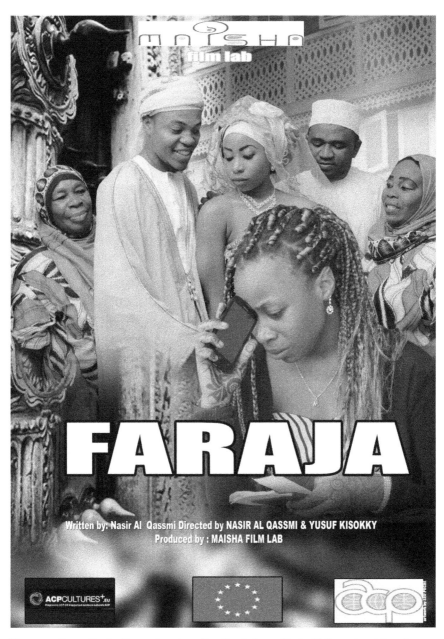

Figure 7.3. Poster for the Tanzanian short film *Faraja* (2014, Nasir Al Qassmi and Yusuf Kisokky).

Faraja and the Rights of Girls and Women

Faraja tells the story of Faraja, a girl of sixteen who comes to Zanzibar to spend time with her father. Her father is domiciled on the island, and she is visiting on holiday, presumably from Europe. Her father rents a house for them for the period of her visit, or so she assumes.

Soon we notice the reverse cultural shock that Africans in the diaspora contend with on returning to the continent after a long stay overseas. Some seemingly innocuous cultural precepts are often overlooked by the returnees, such as the age constructs and even some social taboos. In Swahili culture, salutations from the young to an elder are, for example, highly valued. Likewise, respect is a bastion of one's humanity, next in importance to humility. The film is steeped in Swahili culture—not least in the very interesting relations between Faraja and her aunt, and eventually the marriage proposal. Soon we realize that the family has plans to marry her off. This is presented very casually, something that irks Faraja to no end. The whole atmosphere changes when Faraja completely rejects the betrothal to a cousin of hers, Makame.

Even as Faraja asserts her right to choose her husband, pleading that she is not ready for marriage, she finds herself technically imprisoned in Zanzibar because she would need a passport to travel out of the country. She eventually acquiesces, hoping to make her relatives happy with the wedding, and then she plans to go overseas again.

The central part of the film shows how strong Faraja is when she rebuffs any attempt to consummate the marriage. In the meantime the hapless Makame, the groom, whom we take to be an unhappy accomplice in this spectacle, is forced to endure endless dramas with his defiant wife. He remains patient, hoping Faraja will "come to her senses." Faraja runs away and reports to the police that her husband wants to rape her. The police laugh at her; one of them says he has never heard of a husband raping his wife. Faraja remains defiant even as she returns to the marriage home, plotting how to run away all along. The opportunity comes one day when her father dozes off while resting, and Faraja is able to find her passport and return ticket. She flees to the airport, and only when she is about to fly away does she call her father.

Faraja is a very important text to use for the purposes of human rights education. Although the film's production values are not the best, they suffice and probably surpass the needs and requirements of the exercise. Many a time I am reminded that in African cinema circles, there is always potential "oversophistication" in the sense that we demand film production values that are beyond the needs and capacities of the producers. Where film training is rudimentary, facilities grossly inadequate, and resources absolutely finite, it is in the realm of stupidity to demand film production values that only the more financially, commercially, and technically endowed societies command. As long as our audiences watch the films, enjoy them, and buy them, they are king, as the saying goes. Production values in African films will remain "aspirational" until the resources for training African filmmakers are improved and the spell of poverty that hangs over these communities is lifted. Therefore, when the school audiences in Zanzibar proclaim that *Faraja* is a well-made film technically and aesthetically, I don't wish to argue with them. The structure of the film has a staccato quality and is generally episodic, and often this is taken to be a weakness; but the episodic structure is something that African narratives are often permeated with, and frequently this is not taken into account when analyzing the narrative structures of African filmic works. A study of Nollywood and even Bongo movies (the popular film industry in Tanzania) reveals the predominance of the episodic narrative structure that requires more respect and appreciation.

Here, however, I would rather like to focus the attention on the key rights of girls and women, which include the right to consensual marriage, freedom from violence, the right to education, the right to employment, the woman's reproductive rights, and even freedom of movement, rights that are curtailed when she is forced into a marriage she does not want or is too young to enter into. The (Tanzania) Marriage Act, which was adopted in 1971, essentially fails to protect girls from early and forced marriage. The Marriage Act is clearly discriminatory because it permits girls aged fifteen years to marry "with parental consent" and children aged fourteen years to marry "if a court of law is satisfied that special circumstances exist." According to the Tanzania Media Women's Association (TAMWA), "Child, early, and forced marriage violates the human rights of girls and women, including the right to education, freedom from violence, reproductive rights, employment, freedom of movement, the right to consensual marriage, and hinders the attainment of the Millennium Development Goals (MDGs)" (2014).[7]

Underage brides do not normally give their consent, and most often when they do, it is because they are coerced to do so by the adults in their lives. When the law says people can vote after attaining the adult age of eighteen in Tanzania, it is on the understanding that only then can they be regarded as capable of making decisions outside other legal or institutional support mechanisms. Often, and this was the case in *Faraja*, forced marriage is also accompanied by arranged marriage. These are two different conditions. Where the couple is old enough to consent to having a partner arranged for them, it should not be a problem. In a forced marriage, coercion of some sort is applied.

While child marriage has roots within many traditional African cultures, in Zanzibar it is also comingled with edicts under Islam. In India (and sometimes Zanzibar), underage marriage is practiced to ensure that the strong "caste" system is carried on and that people do not marry outside of their social groups. It is also argued that marrying the children when young makes them susceptible to parental influences. It is calculated that on average, four out of ten girls are married before the age of eighteen in Tanzania. It is further estimated that 37 percent of women twenty to twenty-four years old in 2000–2011 were married or in a union by the age of eighteen in Tanzania. (TAMWA 2014)

As a human rights text, *Faraja* presents us with a very interesting multicultural dimension. We note that most culturalist perspectives are ostensibly articulated with an eye to preserving traditions and protecting them from being derided and undermined by foreign, especially Western, influences. These perspectives often begin by aligning human rights with Western cultural values, arguing that human rights are a Western cultural construct. When religion is brought into the mix, we find the construct too difficult to resolve. For example, in Pakistan attempts to ban early marriage have failed miserably. As recent as January 2016, another attempt at unraveling this social conundrum failed there (Tharoor 2016). The discussions continuously underline the fact that these rights are also for individuals who exist within those non-Western cultures.

In the case of *Faraja*, the formal data collection was done in the form of aided discussions by the workshop facilitators. We chose dialogue as our principal evaluation method, in contrast to conventional questionnaires and surveys, because of the spontaneous nature of dialogue as well as its capacity as a means of communication in communities. Another factor was the rationale identified by Du Preez and Roux: "[dialogue] can generate more naturally occurring data" (2008, 19). Indeed, the students wanted to speak rather than write, saying that writing was an inhibiting form of communication. The researcher had prepared a few lead questions that the facilitators could use to trigger the discussion. The plenary discussions were also preferred because we wanted to use them as formal learning structures enabling students to engage with the responses of others and to continue conversations beyond the class.

Key questions included the following: What conditions described or presented in this film exist in this school, in this class, or in your community? If you recognize the environment of the film, how does the situation speak to you? Often the questions would elicit responses, and this would lead to students describing what they felt while viewing the film. As soon as the students began responding, the facilitator would link the response to the issue of human rights. This would immediately entice more speakers into joining the exchange, because the problem of human rights elicits immediate reactions from students who effectively recognize the breached rights in *Faraja*. Some of the responses were recorded, but most of the time only still images of the respondents were recorded; the facilitator did, however, take notes for the purposes of the daily report, as required by the program.

Although the discussions undertaken in the class did not typically lead to an exchange about the legal or religious precepts related to early marriages, it was noted that many people adopted a very firm stance against a ban on early marriages when they adhere to values that are underpinned by religion and not those of tradition. This is an important cautionary observation when conducting discussions with the young or even the community more generally. This reveals the ominous power of religion in comparison to traditions, which can easily be adjusted.

According to the project manager, Robert Manondolo, the class discussions described above had spectacular outcomes in four secondary schools on both islands. These schools were Mahonda and Makunduchi secondary schools on Unguja, and Wesha and a Vitongoji secondary school on Pemba. He relates an incident where two girls who had watched *Faraja* with an obtuse seriousness proffered no comment after the discussions. When Robert asked the class if they recognized the issues raised as possibly happening in their school, they all shouted yes. The eventual discussion was very heated, with many of the students speaking against the father, who was often seen as the greater villain of the story (he was sometimes called the devil). Just as they were about to bring the discussions to a close, one of the teacher facilitators, Mwalimu (which means teacher) Jaffeth Mihayo Nzoka, asked one of the two girls if they recognized the acts described in the story. One of the girls stood up and said, "Yes, because I am pregnant." A hush fell over the class, and the girl proceeded to cry, which led to her and her friend being taken to the school counselor. It was later learned that one of the girls had been abused by a relative, and she felt too powerless to report him.

In another incident two schoolgirls were found to be pregnant, their lovers having offered to marry them. However, the parents of the two girls both declined the marriage offers and allowed their children to give birth and then continue with their studies despite the wagging tongues in the community. The teachers noted that the students spoke out about their situation after watching *Faraja*, and the students remarked on the strength they found in each other when they realized that as children they had reproductive rights. The girls also said that the support of their families was what made the bigger difference.

Bi Asha Khatibu, a dancer and singer who was for many years a facilitator of the early Children Panorama workshops (1999–2004), recalls the enabling environment that the Panorama camps afforded the children, especially girls who would find their voices in the workshops. Normally these children would not speak in front of large audiences or even at home when it came to discussing social matters. But they felt comfortable in the workshops, which allowed them to air their voices since the environment was conducive to discussion. "It was heartening to see the most vocal speakers were actually girls," Asha Khatibu noted, adding, "It makes my day when I meet these former students of mine who remind me of the time they spent with me in the Panorama camps and how much impact those few days had on their lives."

Commenting on the impact of the film in the children's lives, Farida Nyamachumbe, also a facilitator of the Children Panorama workshops (2000–2010), said that after seeing films on the themes of human rights, children tend to identify similar situations that reflect violations of human rights in their schools or communities. She feels that students now easily recognize human rights and are inclined to accept human rights values because they see them in films, "and as you know, seeing is believing," she concludes.

The last word should be left to Fatuma Khamis Masoud (then aged sixteen), who, at the end of the focus group discussions of *Faraja* on September 26, 2016, issued the following verdict: "Ikitokea kwangu mimi sitakubali kuolewa. Na sitafanya kama alivyofanya Faraja; Nitatumia akili yangu kujitoa kwenye balaa hilo!"—"If it happens to me, I won't agree to being married. And I will not do what Faraja did; I'll use my intelligence to avoid the catastrophe!"

MARTIN MHANDO is Associate Professor of Media Studies and a research fellow with Murdoch University, Western Australia. He was director of the Zanzibar International Film Festival (ZIFF) from 2006 to 2016. He is also coeditor of the *Journal of African Cinemas* and a filmmaker with international awards for *Maangamizi, Mama Tumaini,* and *Liyarn Ngarn,* among others.

Notes

1. On October 15 in an email to the head of ECES, Fabio Bargiac, soon after the banning orders, the ZIFF CEO wrote, "This note is to inform you that following advice from the Secretary of the Zanzibar Censor Board that we stop the public showing of the film *An African Election*, we have now suspended all the public events surrounding the visibility of the Sinema ya Safari ya Amani Project. A letter to that purpose is expected from the Censor Board tomorrow, which we shall transmit to you forthwith. Since the Board has indicated that we should be able to continue with the public showings after the elections we propose that we continue developing the post-elections activities of the Project."

2. Zanzibar was embroiled in a political crisis in 2015 after the general elections were annulled by the Zanzibar Electoral Commissioner, Mr. Jecha Salim Jecha.

3. During the period in question, we collaborated closely with other organizations in undertaking film outreach activities. These include Culture and Development East Africa (CDEA), Goethe Institute, GIZ, Iranian Cultural Centre Dar es Salaam, Barefoot Women, Zanzibar, ECES, World Catholic Association for Communication (SIGNIS), the Zanzibar Department of Culture, the Ministry of Education and Vocational Training, Zanzibar Government, and Jicho Communicative Ltd.

4. The reason for more women than men attending the screenings, contrary to expectations, is attributed to the participation of children at the screenings. Women are more likely to attend to ensure that their children are safe at these events (especially girls). However, many men do go to the mosque for Isha (the last prayers for the day at about eight thirty), and because that would mean walking out to go pray in the middle of the screening, men opt not to attend the screenings at all. In general, not many women go to pray in the mosque.

5. Zanzibar is an autonomous part of the United Republic of Tanzania that was formed in 1964 between Zanzibar and Tanganyika to form the country popularly known as Tanzania.

6. During the 2015 Tanzania general elections, the European Union funded the European Centre for Electoral Support to undertake electoral awareness campaigns in Zanzibar, Tanzania.

7. The Tanzania Media Women's Association is the premiere women's rights lobby in Tanzania.

Filmography

An African Election, 2011, Jarreth Metz, UK / Ghana.
Faraja, 2014, Nasir Al Qassmi and Yusuf Kisokky, Tanzania.
Jaya, 2014, Puja Maewal, India.
Soko Sonko, 2013, Ekwa Msangi, Kenya / Tanzania.
Storm, 2009, Giacomo Campeotto, Denmark.
Yesterday, 2004, Darrell Roodt, South Africa.

References

Du Preez, Petro, and Cornelia Roux. 2008. "Participative Intervention Research: The Development of Professional Programmes for In-Service Teachers." *Education as Change* 12 (2): 77–90. doi:10.1080/16823200809487208.

Federov, Alexander. 2015. "Hermeneutic Analysis of the Cultural Context of the Functioning of Media in Society and Media Texts on Media Literacy Education Classes." *Journal of International Network Center for Fundamental and Applied Research* 6: 214–24. doi:10.13187/jincfar.2015.6.214.

Simmonds, Shan. 2014. "Curriculum-Making in South Africa: Promoting Gender Equality and Empowering Women?" *Gender and Education* 26 (6): 636–52. doi:10.1080/0954025 3.2014.946474.

Tanzania Media Women's Association (TAMWA). 2014. Accessed September 28, 2016. https://www.hrw.org/news/2014/09/02 /tanzania-include-specific-provisions-relating-marriage-new-constitution.

Tharoor, Ishaan. 2016. "Bill Banning Child Marriage Fails in Pakistan after It's Deemed 'Un-Islamic.'" *Washington Post*, January 15, 2016. Accessed August 3, 2018. https:// www.washingtonpost.com/news/worldviews/wp/2016/01/15/bill-banning-child -marriage-fails-in-pakistan-after-its-deemed-un-islamic/?noredirect=on&utm _term=.7a67098067c9.

The UN Convention on the Rights of the Child. Accessed September 29, 2016. http:// unchildrights.blogspot.com/2009/03/summary-childrens-rights-convention.html.

ZIFF-CKU Report. 2015. Unpublished report, ZIFF, 2016, Annual Progress Report, January 27, 2016, ZIFF Archives.

ZIFF Project Proposal. 1999. Unpublished document, ZIFF 1999, ZIFF Archives.

Interviews

Aisha Hussein Mussa (Facilitator, ZIFF),September 26, 2016.
Fatuma Khatibu Masoud (Student), September 26, 2016.
Rehema Khamis Maabadi (Student), September 26, 2016.
Robert Manondolo (Coordinator, ZIFF), September 26, 2016.
Bi Asha Khatibu (Coordinator, ZIFF), September 27, 2016.
Farida Nyamachumbe (Coordinator, ZIFF), June 4, 2016.

PART II
CASES

8 Ousmane Sembène's *Moolaadé*

Peoples' Rights vs. Human Rights

Samba Gadjigo

For close to seventeen years, from 1989 to 2006, I crisscrossed the world with Ousmane Sembène. Most of the time, I took these trips to provide support when he was getting ready to produce a film or going from country to country to promote a new work at festivals, or when we had to respond to invitations from academic institutions or art associations. But when I left my home for the airport in June 2002, it was to embark on a far more intense experience with Sembène. I would be assisting him, and documenting his work, as he shot what was to become his masterpiece, *Moolaadé*. I took a Delta flight from New York to Dakar, and then, the next day, Air Burkina to Ouagadougou, the capital city of Burkina Faso, which I had visited many times to attend FESPACO, the Pan-African film festival. After a night in Ouaga, I was off to an entirely new place: Bobo Dioulasso, in Burkina's southwest.

Moolaadé was Sembène's last film before he died in his Dakar home, Galle Ceddo (house of the rebel) on June 9, 2007, and my camera would capture something more than an "academic" experience. This was an emotional process, for I witnessed and recorded an almost blind, physically weakened eighty-year-old radical storyteller and a crew of remarkably committed filmmakers as they created a defining work of art. After we arrived in Bobo, we headed by car for the region of Banfora, at the northern border with Côte d'Ivoire, east of Mali, to end up in Djerrisso, a small village that was the set of *Moolaadé*. The remote village was verdant and picturesque and had an unforgettable mud mosque at its center. It took Sembène months and months of scouting in Senegal, Mali, Guinea, and Burkina before, finally satisfied, he declared that there would be "no more searching." According to Clarence Delgado, his assistant for close to twenty years, "Sembène was definitely sure that this was the location he was looking for." He was fascinated by both the natural beauty and the history of the village. When I later asked him why Djerrisso, he simply responded, "I was just looking for a setting that would fuel my creative imagination." He wanted to shoot in June, the rainy season, and this region in Burkina is unique in that it rains only at night— an invaluable asset for a filmmaker who shot largely without artificial light, and for whom each hour of sunlight was a necessity and a treasure. Moreover, at that time of the year, the whole land is pregnant with promises of future harvests, the landscape being like a green carpet: "A green, beautiful Africa," said Sembène, "an Africa full of potentials; an Africa that lives and struggles, unlike the miserable Africa we see every day now on foreign television screens" (Gadjigo 2004, 24).

Sembène had traveled from Senegal to settle with his cast and crew of about eighty in this village, in the heart of West Africa: no electricity, no running water, heat of one hundred degrees Fahrenheit, and swarms of mosquitoes, even during the day. My first morning I awoke to the sounds of ordinary daily life, with contemporary African music broadcast here and there by battery-powered short-wave radios. Sembène was already awake, as he generally stayed up late, working, and woke up first. During the eleven weeks of the shoot, he acted like a young warrior: he was on the set from eight in the morning to eight in the evening, using all means necessary to "create images."

When one day, under pressure, he collapsed on the set, he ignored everyone's advice to take a break, insisting on continuing the shoot. "I will have all the time to rest after I die," he told me with finality. Until the end of the shoot, every night, I would see Sembène being attended to by a nurse. She would hook him up to intravenous tubes. And yet, at the first cock's crow, he left his tubes to go to work. As an artist Sembène saw it as his responsibility to reach out to the rest of humankind, or as he put it: "Se déchirer, en allant vers l'autre" ("To tear oneself apart in a move to reach the other") (Boughedir 1972, 9). He was aware of working for a cause that was bigger than himself. Indeed, as Michael Atkinson best put it in 1993: "Ousmane Sembène . . . represents the dying heritage of political films still possessed of a virginal faith in social change, a faith not in film for profit's sake or even film's sake, but for *man's sake*" (Atkinson 1993, 69, emphasis added). This political cinema for "man's sake" or a militant cinema for the defense of humanity's dignity and fundamental rights is also what most impressed Roger Ebert, who wrote in a moving eulogy: "Sembène's death at 84, on June 9, 2007, brought to a close an extraordinary life, one that parallels in some ways Nelson Mandela's" (Ebert 2007).

Sembène was a grade-school dropout, a manual laborer and dockworker who became a radical Marxist and communist, a political and union activist. He turned to literature in 1956 and to filmmaking in 1962. He wrote a handful of poems and ten books of fiction, and he directed thirteen films, including nine features. It is this output, with a focus on *Moolaadé*, that I will discuss, by highlighting two important themes in Sembène's work. The first has to do with Sembène's exploration of the potential of rebellion against tyranny and oppression as a lever for positive change, and the second concerns the ways in which *Moolaadé* and Sembène's work in general challenge, and offer an alternative to currently dominant discourses on human rights theory.

To that end, I will first offer a brief summary of the dominant discourse on human rights, embodied in the French 1789 "Déclaration des droits de l'homme et du citoyen" (Declaration on the Rights of Man and the Citizen), the United Nations 1948 "Universal Declaration of Human Rights," and, finally, "La Charte africaine des droits de l'homme et des peuples," adopted in Banjul, Gambia, in 1981. Second, I will review the life experiences that inform Sembène's political and artistic project. Finally, through a thorough study of *Moolaadé*, I will argue that Sembène's humanism simultaneously integrates dominant Eurocentric and capitalistic approaches aimed at protecting individual human rights while unequivocally advocating for a new world order: a "people's" rebellion against internal and external tyranny and oppression. The latter was the only way to restore dignity and economic, political, cultural, and human rights to the African people.

Human Rights . . . if You Behave

The foundational text of the Western discourse on human rights is the 1776 American Declaration of Independence of the thirteen colonies from England. Written by Thomas Jefferson, the document was signed by John Adams, Benjamin Franklin, John Hancock, and Jefferson himself. The most quoted section of the declaration reads: "We hold these truths to be self-evident: that all men are created equal; that they are endowed by their creator with certain unalienable rights; that among these are life, liberty, and the pursuit of happiness." It was in order to protect these natural, God-given rights to life, liberty, and the pursuit of happiness that the American people took to arms, rebelling against the oppression and tyranny of King George and the British monarchy.

Less than two decades later, in 1789, the Marquis de Lafayette wrote the Declaration of the Rights of Man and the Citizen. Approved by the French National Assembly on August 26, 1789, the document was undoubtedly influenced by eighteenth-century French philosophers (Rousseau and Voltaire, among others) and written with the help of Thomas Jefferson. Whereas the American Revolution rejected tyranny and oppression from outside domination, the French revolution was against its own hitherto-believed-to-be divinely ordained monarchy, the foundation of the feudal social structure of French society under the Ancien Régime. Like the American Declaration of Independence, the French Declaration of the Rights of Man and the Citizen also insisted on the God-given natural, unalienable, and sacred rights of humanity (liberty, equality, and the right to property), but added the rights of the citizen (human-made laws). As a bourgeois revolution, the French declaration insisted on the protection of the individual's rights to property. Also like the American Declaration of Independence, the French "droits de l'homme" reflects John Locke's view that "mankind . . . being all equal and independent, no one ought to harm another in his life, health, liberty, or possessions" (1689). Let's also insist here on the fact that the protection of individual rights was the core of both the American Bill of Rights (mostly the First Amendment, ratified in 1791) and the French declaration on the protection of human rights (freedoms of religion and expression).

After the horrors and devastation of World War II, many European nations were in ruins. Millions of people were dead, and capitalist economies of Western Europe needed peace for the purposes of their reconstruction and for the survival and expansion of the world economic, political, and cultural order. What was at stake was nothing less than the survival of a Western hegemony. It is mainly in that spirit that the United Nations, created in 1945, prepared and issued in 1948 the Universal Declaration of Human Rights. Like the French and the American declarations, here again the emphasis is on the rights of the individual, the Western Man, considered universal, regardless of geography, political conditions, or culture. Moreover, as stated in its preamble, the main objective is to maintain world justice, peace, and order: "Whereas it is essential, if man is not to be compelled to have recourse, as a last resort, to rebellion against tyranny and oppression, that human rights should be protected by the rule of law." Further, in September 1981 this UN Universal Declaration would also insist on equal rights for men and women in its convention on the elimination of all forms of discrimination against women.

To summarize, then, in the dominant, Western conception of human rights, the notion of rights is applied to the protection of the individual citizen's rights so he or she does not resort "to rebellion against tyranny and oppression." The main purpose of the rule of law is to maintain social, political, economic, and cultural order—in other words, to avoid a revolution that would disturb the current world order and usher in radical social change.

The Formation of a Radical Artist

"I came to writing like a blind person who suddenly discovers light," Ousmane Sembène once said (Boughedir 1972, 9). Sembène's extraordinary life experiences shaped his trajectory from an ordinary child to a world-renowned radical Marxist writer-filmmaker and one of contemporary Africa's most recognized proponents of human rights. Born in 1923 in Casamance, Senegal, during the heyday of French colonial rule, Sembène was the son of an ordinary, illiterate fisherman. An unruly child expelled from school at the age of thirteen, Sembène also started life as a fisherman. He moved to Dakar (then the headquarters of French West Africa) in 1938, where he entered the world of labor, first as a mason and then as a mechanic, and where he was, for years, exploited by a paternal uncle. Manual laborer by day, at night he roamed the segregated Dakar movie theaters and voraciously read cowboy comic books.

In September 1940, Sembène was exposed to the horrors of World War II when the naval Allied forces, trying to dislodge the pro-German Vichy forces under Marshal Pétain, bombed Dakar, with the bulk of the damage in his neighborhood. For a few months, a young and disoriented Sembène sought solace in a famous Layene religious brotherhood, celebrated in part for its anticolonial teachings. Sembène was drafted into the French colonial infantry unit in February 1944 and stationed in Niger for eighteen months, being charged with driving troops to the North African front in Morocco. He returned to Dakar in 1946, the only soldier of his contingent without an honorable discharge, having once again been punished for his rebellious nature. As Maurice Ousseynou Fall, his childhood friend, remarked, "Ousmane came back from the war a changed man; he harbored a visceral anger against everything and stopped attending religious gatherings" (Gadjigo 1996b). For Sembène, God was dead.

Returning to his old job as a mason, Sembène witnessed the first massive, fourteen-day strike against the French colonials by native Senegalese administration workers who were fighting for humane treatment, including a living wage. The same year, with the birth of Rassemblement Démocratique Africain (RDA/African Democratic Assembly), the first indigenous, Pan-Africanist political party, created in Bamako (October18–21, 1946), Sembène began attending political rallies and listening to speeches by radical Marxist politicians, including communist historian Jean Suret-Canale. He witnessed the now-legendary 1947 West African railroad workers' strike that for months (October 10, 1947, to March 19, 1948) hobbled the entire French colonial commercial interest in its colonies. Sembène kept an indelible memory of charismatic union organizers including Ibrahima Sarr and Aynina Fall, both at the forefront of the West African railroad workers union. Sembène was born to a new religion (political action), but as he later confided to Férid Boughedir, "Je ne comprenais pas toujours ce que les ora-teurs disaient à ces reunions mais je sentais une certaine méfiance à l'égard des politiciens" ("I did not always fully understand what the speakers were saying, but I developed a certain distrust for the politicians") (Boughedir 1972, 9).

Determined to expand his experiences of the world, and mostly his under-standing of it, Sembène spoke of "finding a job and continuing my education" (Gad-jigo 1996b). He sailed for France in 1947, settling in Marseilles, the "Red City," a place of refuge for members of the French Resistance movement, progressive artists, intellectuals, unions, and political and cultural organizations that fought against the German occupation. Sembène also found himself in the midst of Marseilles' West and North African immigrant ghettos, places thick with what Frantz Fanon called "the wretched of the Earth," the lumpenproletariat of the city. For twelve years, from 1948 to 1960, Sembène worked at the Marseilles harbor as a dockworker, originally unloading and carrying on his back sacks of raw materials, generally sourced from colonies around the world to clothe, feed, and rebuild Europe.

Sembène became one of the first black workers to join the then all-powerful dockworkers' section of the communist trade union CGT (Confédération Générale du Travail). That affiliation, with a social organization that was designed to defend the interests, dignity, and humanity of the working class, naturally led Sembène to become a card-carrying member first of the French Communist Party (1951 to

1960) and then of the MRAP (Mouvement contre le racisme et pour l'amitié entre les peuples / Movement against Racism and for Friendship between Peoples), a Jewish organization that grew out of the Resistance movement during World War II, as well as other communist youth organizations.

At the Vieux Port, Sembène participated in strikes and rallies against the colonial war in Indochina, in support of the Algerian war of independence, and against the Korean War. As a member of the Young Communist League, Sembène was involved in rallies against the trial and execution in New York (1953) of Julius and Ethel Rosenberg, a Jewish couple accused of passing US nuclear secrets to the Soviet Union. According to his comrades in the French Communist Party, Sembène attended numerous rallies against the trial and execution in the electric chair in 1951 of Willie McGee, an African American accused of raping a white woman in Mississippi. Soon Sembène's activism also included the defense of migrant African workers in France; the acceptance, in 1957, of the position of president of the African Workers' Union; and, importantly, participation in radical African independence movements. Those included the Parti Africain de l'Indépendance (PAI), a communist, Pan-Africanist organization created by the Senegalese pharmacist Majhemout Diop in 1957, and the Parti Africain pour l'Indépendance de la Guinée et du Cap-Vert (PAIGC), founded by Amílcar Cabral, an agricultural engineer and anticolonial theorist from Guinea-Bissau who went on to become one of Africa's key anticolonial theorists.

After an accident that broke his backbone in 1951 and a six-month period of recovery, and with the help of the CGT leadership, Sembène was assigned a clerical job that allowed him the leisure to attend French communist schools. He discovered and studied Marxism-Leninism, read the classics of communist literature, and traveled regularly, with the support of the CGT, to the Soviet Union, China, and Vietnam. He also discovered progressive black American writers, including Richard Wright and Claude McKay, and the Turkish communist poet Nazine Hikmet. By the early 1950s, Marxism provided Sembène with a conceptual tool with which to understand the world. The belief that was to steer his entire career had emerged: the only way to restore dignity to the wretched of the earth is through a worker-led revolution, one that would usher in a new world order. Bernard Worms, an old communist friend of Sembène's, told me: "Nous étions convaincus qu'une révolution était possible et nécessaire pour changer le monde et donner le pouvoir aux travailleurs" ("We were convinced that a revolution was possible and necessary in order to change the world and give the power to the workers" (Gadjigo 1996a). More to our point, in reading the classics of communist literature, including writers from the Third World such as Jacques Roumain of Haiti, Sembène embraced the essential role that cultural and artistic expression must play in this political project.

However, Ousmane Sembène was very disappointed by the literature of the Négritude movement, which set out to reclaim black identity and whose most vocal representative in Senegal was the poet and politician Léopold Sédar Senghor. Sembène considered it elitist: "Nowhere did I find in those writings *my* Africa. The Africa of peasants, of workers. That's when I decided to become a writer, to be the voice of the voiceless. Until then I had never written anything more than letters. I came to writing like a blind person who all of a sudden discovers light" (Sembène 1972). Sembène's first poem, "Liberté," published in 1956, constitutes a genuine manifesto, describing his stance on art and the role of the contemporary artist in understanding and promoting positive change for the millions of "voiceless Africans":

> Je voudrais n'être poète que pour toi,
> Ton griot,
> Jouer de la Kora pour te réveiller.
> (I would like to be a poet only for you,
> Your griot,
> To play the kora in order to wake you up.)
> Nous taillerons dans la brutalité,
> La servilité
> Une Nation
> Hommage à l'Afrique libre.
> (With brutality
> Servility
> We will carve out a nation
> I pay tribute to a free Africa.)

For Sembène, as a Marxist and communist, therefore, the African artist, like the griot, should serve both to raise consciousness among the people ("wake you up") and to promote freedom and nation building.

Humanist Cinema for African Audiences

After the screening of *Moolaadé* in New York in 2004, A. O. Scott wrote: "To skip *Moolaadé* would be to miss an opportunity to experience the embracing, affirming, world-changing potential of humanist cinema at its finest. . . . The movie encompasses horror and heartbreak without sacrificing its basic, tough-minded optimism. It also dramatizes, with a kind of clarity I have rarely seen on film, how a society can change from within, how even well-intentioned authority can become cruel and corrupt, and above all, how a single, stubborn act of reflexive resistance can alter the shape of the world" (Scott 2004). Indeed, *Moolaadé* is a "humanist" film. It integrates individual rights and liberties, as defined by the dominant Western human rights discourse, and the power of collective social, political, economic, and cultural action. But it is also about positive change through rebellion and violence. As David Murphy convincingly argued, Sembène's stories, in both literature and film, are an "attempt to carve out a space

for a discourse of resistance around which to crystallize the scattered and fragmented acts of rebellion" (Murphy 2000, 218).

As in most of Sembène's work, the central theme of *Moolaadé* was inspired
by a real-life story. On July 31, 1997, the women of Malicounda Bambara, a
small Bambara-speaking village in the Mbour region (Senegal), made a public
announcement declaring they were putting an end to female genital cutting. This
declaration resulted from work done in Senegal, and in Africa more generally, by
numerous international nongovernmental human rights organizations, beginning in the 1970s. In the case of Malicounda, the women's decision to make a
public statement was said to be the result of their participation in a community
empowerment program initiated by Tostan, a Dakar-based international program that covers issues related to human rights, health, and hygiene. In many
ways *Moolaadé* builds on an earlier film by Sembène, for in 2000, he directed
an eleven-minute short fiction titled *L'Héroïsme au quotidien* (*Daily Heroism*).
The film focused on women's empowerment and was commissioned by the New
York–based Human Rights Watch. It was set in another small Bambara village
called Ngarigne Bambara, in the same Mbour region.

Sembène describes *Moolaadé* as follows:

> *Moolaadé* takes place in a rural setting, in a small village that is symbolic of
> a green Africa. This Africa, all the while living its own life, is linked to oth-
> ers. Thus, we have some external elements whose arrival allows the African to
> know herself or himself better. In *Moolaadé* two values are in conflict. One
> is traditional: female excision. It goes back a long time. Before Jesus Christ,
> before Mohammed, back to the time of Herodotus. It's a tradition. It has been
> made a value in order, in my opinion, to subjugate women. The other value, as
> ancient as human existence, is the right to grant protection to the most vulner-
> able. When these two values meet, cross each other, multiply, run up against
> each other, there is the symbol of our society: elements of modernity, elements
> which belong to our cultural substratum. Added to them are the elements that
> belong to our cultural superstructure, namely religious. (Gadjigo 2004)

Moolaadé is a story about contradiction, crisis, and change. The film's tension
arises from two conflicting values, both central to the human rights narrative:
female genital cutting, or "bolo koli," and "moolaadé." "Bolo," in the Jula language, literally means a hand, and "koli" means "to wash." Here this washing,
or cleansing, suggests that female genital cutting (the removal of the young girl's
clitoris) is seen as a cleansing act, a rite of passage in the process of any woman's
socialization. The second value is "moolaadé" (in the Fulani language), or "kalfa"
(in Jula), the duty to grant asylum and protection to the most vulnerable, to those
running from persecution, oppression, or tyranny. Here again Sembène tackles
the issue of "asylum," and by extension that of refugees. These are current and relevant issues in the context of human rights thinking, particularly since the creation in 1950 of the United Nation's High Commissioner for Refugees (UNHCR)

and the adoption in 1969 of the African Convention on Refugees by the Organization of African Unity. The cutting of the clitoris raises the issue of protecting women's right to control their own bodies, and with *Moolaadé*, Sembène introduces a new dimension to human rights thinking, one absent from the dominant, individual-centered human rights discourse of the West: the duties of the citizen towards the community. As Keba Mbaye, a Senegalese lawyer, indicated: "Selon la conception africaine, le sujet privilégié du droit est la communauté, même si l'individu garde sa liberté et les spécificités de ses droits" ("According to the African conception, the community is the main bearer of rights, although the individual keeps his/her freedom and the specificities of his/her rights") (Mbaye 1992, 187). In the same vein, it is useful to note that the African charter adopted in Banjul, Gambia, in 1981 is referred to as follows: "La charte africaine des droits de l'homme et des peuples" (Charter on the Rights of Man and Peoples). This shift away from the individual, with a concomitant insistence on the family, the community, and the whole continent (Pan-Africanism), is a very important element of *Moolaadé* and, indeed, of the African charter.

Above all, Sembène's last film is about tyranny and oppression on the one hand and collective resistance, rebellion, and change on the other. The internal tyranny and oppression rely on a feudal and patriarchal order but also on a global world order in the form of external economic, political, and cultural constraints. *Moolaadé* recreates, in microscopic detail, elements of an oppressive social reality. Like the Senegalese village of Malicounda that inspired the film's story, Djerrisso is a small Jula (Bambara) village, located in southern Burkina Faso, in the heart of what was once the Mandé empire, created by Soundjata Keita in the thirteenth century. It sits near the borders of eastern Mali and the northern part of Côte d'Ivoire. The film opens at dusk, revealing a breathtakingly beautiful lush green village, symbolic of a renewed Africa. The soundtrack includes a praise song to women by the Cuban-educated Malian musician Boncana Maïga. "Mbe musolu fola, mbe dugu musolu fola" ("I salute women; I salute the women of this village"), "ni den musa ma soro, aw ya bila karan na" ("when a young girl is born, give her an education"), "a sebenin te, a sebenite, musowla bolokoli ma seben" ("it is not ordained, women's circumcision is not in the scriptures"). A crowd of delighted, cheerful children run after a bicycle-pulled cart that has made the journey from the city to the village square. It is loaded with consumer goods: dry bread, imported clothes, batteries, and a motley array of plastic junk. The merchant is named Mercenaire.

In the next sequence, cinematographer Dominique Gentil (who worked regularly with Sembène, as well as with renowned French directors Chris Marker, Jacques Perrin, and Yann Arthus-Bertrand) has the camera hover over Ciré Bathily's compound. Organized around a granary, the compound reflects self-sufficiency, with its customary morning activities: women bringing in water, preparing food, sweeping the yard, pounding millet, and processing cotton. Children take out their livestock. Ciré Bathily, with his three wives—the senior wife, Hadjatou, and Collé Gallo Ardo Sy and Alima as the second and third wives— is part of the village's ruling aristocracy, along with the village chief (Dougou-tigui Doukouré), the kemo (council of elders), and the griot, whose stories and praises give legitimacy to Djerrisso's feudal, patriarchal, and patrilineal political order. The political alliance between the Doukouré and the Bathily clans is here sealed by the engagement and promise of marriage between Ciré and Collé's only daughter, Amsatou, to Dougoutigui Doukouré's heir and son, Ibrahima Douk-ouré, a migrant who lives and works in France. As we will see, the esoteric talking drum, the only "traditional" medium in the village, can be deciphered only by men. In this social structure dictated by "divine order" and immutable tradition or "laada," men rule over their children, older brothers over their younger broth-ers, husbands over wives, senior wives over younger wives, and so on. In sum, the whole social system rests on a rigid, tyrannically oppressive feudal social order, with women at the bottom of the pyramid.

At the center of the village square, two imposing and powerful structures have been erected. One is a mosque, symbolic of what Sembène, in Marxist terms, liked to refer to as the village's superstructure, on account of the manifestation of a religious outlook. The other structure, an anthill, calls for a bit of contextu-alization. As Kémo Ansumana (member of the village council and custodian of collective memory and traditions) explains in one of the most lyrical tirades in the history of African cinema, the value of moolaadé, the granting of protection to the weak and the oppressed, goes back to times immemorial and had only once been violated in Djerrisso, resulting in a revolution. Indeed, "before Islam, well before Islam, there was an uncontested king named Dethie Yerim Diak who ruled over the whole land with an iron fist. But one day, he broke the rule of Moolaadé and as a result, his subjects rebelled, killed him, and buried his body in the center of the village" (in the anthill). Years later, his subjects were converted to Islam, and next to his grave, symbolic of moolaadé, a mosque was erected. Like "kuru kan fuga," the "declaration of the founding of the Mali Empire" by Soundjata in the thirteenth century, Sembène is suggesting that the first declaration on the principles of human rights may well have come from Africa, well before the sign-ing of the American Constitution and the French Declaration of the Rights of Man and of the Citizen. The principles, it would seem, are well rooted in Africa's founding cultural values. In tension, paradoxically, with these values, is another of the village's inviolable codes of practice, one that the men and village elders see as mandated by Islam, by the Koran, which is symbolized in the mosque and the Koranic school in the village square. The practice in question is that of women's excision (bolo koli in Jula or salinde in Soninke).

As the film begins, the hegemony of this seemingly immutable economic, political, social, and cultural order is unchallenged. The values of both moolaadé and the salinde (excision) remain uncontested, thus preserving the political and social status quo. However, Mercenaire's entrance in the village at dusk to youthful cheers of welcome is a whole symbol in itself. Djerrisso may still seem frozen in time with its rigid political social and cultural status quo, but it actually no longer lives in a state of autarky. With his dry bread from the city; his alkaline batteries from France; his chic, fashionable clothes; his plastic junk; and, yes, his condoms and endless womanizing, Mercenaire represents all of the looming threat of the destructive forces of the so-called free market "global economy," what he himself refers to as "mondialisation" (globalization). He is the incarnation, in short, of a whole set of new values.

A former soldier of the United Nations peacekeeping forces in Africa and the Middle East, Mercenaire was jailed for five years, expelled from the UN body, and nicknamed "mercenaire" for having fought internal corruption of his higher-ups. Amsatou said she heard from the radio that a mercenary is a "soldier who kills women, children and makes political coups." But with Mercenaire and his shop, Sembène echoes a theme that is absent from the Western discourse on human rights but central to the African Charter on Human Rights and the Rights of the People. In the early 1980s, the Structural Adjustment Programs imposed on Africa by the International Monetary Fund, just some twenty years after colonial rule, seemed to many to reflect a new round of economic, political, social, and cultural neocolonialism. To political theorists, activists, artists, and political figures, these Western policies encroached upon African sovereignty and threatened the freedoms and cultures of the continent. Indeed, the 1981 Banjul Charter on the Rights of Man and Peoples also included the "defense of economic, social, and political rights."

It is symptomatic that Mercenaire's shop is established opposite the village square, facing the mosque and the Koranic school. And it draws bigger crowds. His overpriced stale bread is cheaper than the local production of millet, his imported clothes more appealing than the local cotton, and, of course, his mass-produced plastic kettles and utensils are damaging inasmuch as they cause real threats to the environment. Mercenaire forces the village—a "little Africa"—into a global consumer-based market economy in which money has become a fetish. This allows Sembène to signal the critical issue of Africa's debt and dependency on the outside First World, represented in *Moolaadé* by France, "where money is printed." Dougoutigui gets from Mercenaire his supply of bread and radio batteries as a loan to be "repaid" by his son Ibrahima Doukouré, who is returning from France. In preparation for Ibrahima Doukouré's imminent marriage to Amsatou, all the future bride's household items are also taken from Mercenaire on credit, again to be repaid by the future groom. The yoke and modern enslavement that this debt and economic dependency represent is in fact an ultimate violation of the Mandé peoples' sense of dignity and freedom. Indeed, in the Jula language, a debt contract is referred to as "juru," meaning a "rope" or, more precisely, a "noose" around one's neck. Money and the consumer economy have become so fetishized that when Ibrahima Doukouré arrives in the village in a van loaded with new consumer goods, the pockets of his two-piece suit loaded with crisp currency, he is welcomed like a prodigal deity, lauded by the griot, and admired as a hero by the village folk.

Ibrahima Doukouré's character allows Sembène to revisit the issue of African migration to Europe, a human rights theme that was already central to his earliest works including *Le Docker noir* (*Black Docker*, first novel, 1956), *La noire de . . .* (*Black Girl*, short story and feature film, 1966), *Lettres de France*, (Letters from France, short story, 1964), *Mandabi* (*The Money Order*, novella and feature film, 1966 and 1968, respectively), and *Guelwaar* (feature film written and directed by Sembène, 1993). Let's also note that the two outsiders, Mercenaire and Ibrahima Doukouré, do not carry with them just the material symbols of a globalizing economic order. As powerful as or even more powerful than those economic symbols are the new voices carried by the alkaline batteries and the battery-powered radios sold by Mercenaire, and the new television set brought into the village by Ibrahima Doukouré. In Djerrisso the esoteric messages of the talking drum can be deciphered only by Ciré Bathily and the menfolk. But the radio, both local, in national languages, and through Radio France Internationale, in French, offers voices to be reckoned with: new voices carrying the seeds of a new consciousness that will trigger rebellion and change. As suggested by Sembène's earlier summary of the film, up to now the feudal and patriarchal social, political, and economic status quo in Djerrisso rested on the equilibrium of, or parallel coexistence between, the two values of moolaadé and salinde (or female genital cutting).

During the early morning, after Mercenaire's arrival in the village, four young girls dramatically enter Ciré Bathily's compound, still dressed in the ceremonial attire worn by to-be-circumcised girls. They theatrically throw themselves on the ground and kneel at Collé Ardo Sy's heels, a gesture that symbolizes a request for protection, asylum, or moolaadé. These four girls, along with two others (offscreen) ran away from the excision ceremony, an act never heard of before in Djerrisso. The two other girls, we will learn later, fled to the city (a locus of detribalization and loss of feudal values) to escape the initiation ceremony. Like all other women of her generation and generations before, Collé has undergone the ritual cutting; like all other women she lives with the physical and psychological trauma of this operation: excruciating scars on her body, torture during sexual intercourse, and life-threatening childbirth for both mother and child. She has only one surviving child, having lost two at delivery. She owes her life, and her daughter Amsatou's, to a woman doctor who delivered Amsatou by cesarean, leaving her with a horrible scar on her belly. All women in Djerrisso have lived this oppression through the shattering of their flesh, in a general culture of silence.

One wonders: why did the four girls run to Collé for protection? As David Murphy suggests, Sembène's stories, in both literature and film, are an "attempt to carve out a space for a discourse of resistance around which to crystallize the scattered and fragmented acts of rebellion" (2000, 218). For the women of Djerrisso, this "space" is depicted as the site of the village well, which is an exclusive space for women, "A Room of Their Own," a source of water and life, where women share news about their lives and life around them. The girls come to Collé because like all females in the village, they have learned at the well a well-kept secret: seven years ago, Collé refused to have her daughter Amsatou cut, leaving her whole but also a bilakoro, a woman with a clitoris, impure with reference to marriage, an outcast, a pariah. Only one man in the village knows of the secret: Ciré himself, who has kept silent to preserve his dignity and standing among the menfolk of the village. Collé's refusal to submit Amsatou to the cutting was inspired by her own traumatic experiences, but also by the human rights programs on the radio, programs to which she and other women have become addicted. Not only did Collé acquire this new knowledge about women's health and empowerment, but she also heard from an imam that "bolo koli," or so-called purification, is not in the scriptures (bolo koli ma seben); it is not mandated by Islam. Thus, the esoteric messages of the talking drum are countered here by the broadcasting of the short-wave radio, restoring the right to information for all, and thus empowering Collé and the village women with new knowledge.

When it becomes public that Collé (called "fato," mad woman) refused to have her daughter Amsatou cut and granted moolaadé to the runway girls, by virtue of the inviolability of the rights of the weak to seek protection (and the equally inviolable duty of everyone to grant it), the balance of moolaadé and salinde that thus far maintained the status quo in the village is broken. Indeed, the very existence and preservation of Djerrisso is in jeopardy because no man would marry a bilakoro, an uncircumcised woman. Ibrahima Doukouré's engagement to Amsatou is broken by his father, Dougoutigui, the village chief. As mentioned earlier, that marriage between Ibrahima and Amsatou was also a feudal political alliance between the two most powerful families of the local aristocracy.

Since no one can forcefully snatch the girls from Collé's protection, only one solution is now offered by "laada" (tradition) to restore order and stability: the power vested in Ciré to force Collé to utter one "redemptive word" that would neutralize the spirit of moolaadé, put an end to the standoff, and restore the feudal law and order.

Pressured by Amath Bathily and other menfolk, Ciré Bathily (who has "never beaten a woman before, not even his daughter") is encouraged to engage in the public flogging of Collé, his "favorite wife," in the most violent and heartbreaking scene of the film. With a whip handed him by Amath, Ciré mercilessly pounds Collé in a divided public square with, on one side, the menfolk and the "Salindana" (the bloodthirsty red-dressed women who perform the cutting) cheering a tearful Ciré: "Tame her! Tame her!" On the other side are all the women of Djerrisso, in

Figure 8.1. The Salindana—the women who cut young girls to "purify" them. Framegrab from *Moolaadé* (2004, Ousmane Sembène, Senegal / Burkina Faso / Morocco / Tunisia / Cameroon / France).

solidarity, supporting Collé and encouraging her, in a chorus, not to say the word: "Don't say it! Don't fall!" As time stops and all ears hang on Collé's lips—Will she say it? Can she hold back and not utter the word?—Mercenaire, "the outsider," who can "no longer bear all this violence," dramatically and unexpectedly enters the scene and snatches the whip from an exhausted, humiliated, and panting Ciré Bathily, who could not break Collé's heroic and "stubborn act of reflexive resistance" (Scott 2004) and bring her to say the redemptive word. As Collé is escorted back to her compound by the women who rally behind her, and Ciré is literally carried back to the compound by his son, the menfolk, mostly Dougoutigui and the griot, are stunned: a woman had never stood up to a man before, as far as anyone could remember. They start asking each other if "they ever laid an uncircumcised woman before," suggesting a new era is about to open for Djerrisso.

As is characteristic of most of Sembène's works, soon Collé's "isolated act of resistance" energizes and triggers a life-changing collective resistance in the village. Indeed, for the women, this moment is a psychological milestone; as they "felt in their bodies and minds" the blows of the whip tearing Collé's flesh, so too they know Collé was resisting for them all and showing the way to dignity. As Albert Camus aptly put it, "Se révolter, c'est dire non mais c'est aussi dire oui; l'esclave qui se révolte dit non à l'oppression et dit oui à la liberté et la justice" ("To rebel is to say no but it is also to say yes. A slave who rebels says no to oppression and yes to freedom and justice") (Camus 1951).

Then we learn that the two girls who were thought to have fled in fact died after throwing themselves in the village well. At this point, violence becomes rampant: Mercenaire is driven away from the village at night and assassinated by the menfolk, his goods and money stolen; Jaatu, one of the runaway girls, meets a horrific death during excision, after she was stolen by her own mother (Salba) and delivered to the Salindana during Collé's beating. All that violence and their newfound solidarity embolden the women, who collectively stand up to the men in the village square and make their own "Djerrisso declaration." Holding a newborn baby girl raised above her head, Salba faces the men seated in the village square and leads a chorus, with the other women chanting: "This one will not be cut; no girl will ever get cut again!" Collé, with a cutlass in her hand and supported by Hadjatou, Ciré's senior wife, forces the Salindana to throw their knives on a spread sheet, thus symbolically disarming them.

In a powerful closing scene, Collé Ardo Gallo Sy, a defiant woman warrior escorted by Sanata, an equally defiant griot woman who sings her praises, and supported by all the women, rises up and confronts the menfolk seated in a semicircle. Throwing the Salindana's red-covered knives used to mutilate the women on a cloth on the ground, she argues that "female genital cutting was never recommended by Islam" and defies any man to dare ever again to put his hands on her: "I will drown this village in blood," she declares, to the victory chant of "Wassa, wassa!" ("Free at last, free at last!").

After this uprising by the women, it seems like nothing will be the same again in Djerrisso. Admiring and proud of his beloved and brave wife, Collé, Ciré withdraws from the circle of men and calls on his son Balla to do the same, because "it takes more than a pair of balls to make a man." As Amsatou, Ibrahima Doukouré's former bilakoro bride-to-be, detaches herself from the crowd of women to march toward the center of the square, another rebellion takes place. This time it is Ibrahima Doukouré who defies his father's threat to disinherit and curse him if he marries a woman who is a bilakoro. After receiving from his father a blow with his umbrella, Ibrahima gives a last blow to the patriarchal and patrilineal system: "Father, it is easy to beat a son; I am your son; you can beat me but know this: the era of kings and chiefs is over, forever!" As a now humiliated and powerless father and village chief throws the handle of his broken umbrella on the ground, Ibrahima joins Amsatou in the center of the square as she also declares, "I am and shall remain a bilakoro."

The message is clear: for Sembène, the current and dominant Western discourse on human rights, with its focus on individual rights, only serves the purpose of maintaining the current world economic, social, political, and cultural order. The only way to change and restore human rights and dignity is for the African people, like the women of Djerrisso and Malicounda, to fight for a fundamental revolutionary change in the current local and global world order.

Moolaadé is a film about a struggle for human rights and dignity, with female genital cutting as its structuring theme. For centuries and from generation to generation, the women of Djerrisso had silently submitted to the cutting of their

Figure 8.2. The Salindana surrender their knives. Framegrab from *Moolaadé* (2004, Ousmane Sembène, Senegal / Burkina Faso / Morocco / Tunisia / Cameroon / France).

genitalia, as if by an order from God. The entire social, political, and cultural order condoned and benefited from the suffering of the women, aided by their own ignorance. Female genital cutting with its varied forms is practiced in more than thirty-eight countries in Africa and around the world. For the millions of women affected, the suffering is endless: excruciating pain during the cutting and the "healing"; possible death by infection; insurmountable health problems during adulthood, pregnancy, and childbirth; and an unnamable ordeal during sexual intercourse.

However, Sembène's goal as an artist was not just to use his camera to record the suffering of these silent women or the hierarchical, oppressive feudal system coupled with the nascent "globalizing" capitalist world order. Instead, he used the resources of a cinematographic language to communicate with his people in all its diversity, throughout the continent. Sembène's is a militant cinema for humanity's sake, a cinema that unveils the current world order based on domination, oppression, injustice, and exploitation. More importantly, the power and timelessness of Sembène's cinema rest on his ability to imagine the alternative possibility of a fundamental change through violence and mass action to end tyranny, oppression, and economic, political, and cultural exploitation. Contrary to the dominant, Western human rights rhetoric of individual rights, Sembène's human rights agenda rests on the use of collective revolution through violence and the establishment of a socialist society of freedom, justice, and equality for all.

Despite all the challenges on the set, it was that light of hope that I saw shining on Sembène's face when, two years later, at the Centre Cinématographique Marocain, in Rabat, we completed the edit of *Moolaadé*. The night the film won the

Prix Un Certain Regard, at the 2004 Cannes Film Festival, eighty-four-year-old Sembène received a standing ovation. On our way back to our hotel that night, Sembène was jubilant and full of energy. But he was already thinking about the struggle ahead: how to get *Moolaadé's* message of change and freedom to the peoples of Africa and the rest of the world. Over dinner that night, far away from the official ceremonies and crowds, we celebrated his achievement, but more importantly, we talked a lot about dubbing *Moolaadé* into all the major African languages and about translating its message of radical change into action.

SAMBA GADJIGO is Professor of French and African literatures at Mount Holyoke College. He is author of *Ousmane Sembène, Une conscience africaine*, writer and director of *The Making of Moolaadé*, and codirector of *Sembène!*

Filmography

Guelwaar, 1993, Ousmane Sembène, France / Germany / Senegal / USA.
L'Héroïsme au quotidien, 2000, Ousmane Sembène, USA.
Mandabi (*The Money Order*), 1968, France / Senegal.
Moolaadé, 2004, Ousmane Sembène, Senegal / Burkina Faso / Morocco / Tunisia / Cameroon / France.
La noire de . . . (*Black Girl*), 1966, Ousmane Sembène, Senegal / France.

References

Atkinson, Michael. 1993. "Ousmane Sembène: We Are No Longer in the Era of Prophets." *Film Comment* 29 (4): 63–69.
Boughedir, Férid. 1972. "Entretien avec Ousmane Sembène." *Jeune Afrique*, December 25.
Camus, Albert. 1951. *L'homme révolté*. Paris: Gallimard.
La Charte Africaine des Droits de l'Homme et des Peuples. Accessed January 24, 2017. http://www.achpr.org/files/instruments/achpr/achpr_instr_charter_fra.pdf.
Déclaration des droits de l'homme et du citoyen. Accessed January 24, 2017. www.assemblee-nationale.fr/histoire/dudh/1789.asp.
Declaration of Independence. Accessed January 24, 2017. http://www.dictionary.com/browse/declaration-of-independence.
Ebert, Roger. 2007. *Moolaade*. Accessed January 24, 2017. http://www.rogerebert.com/reviews/great-movie-moolaade-2007.
Gadjigo, Samba. 1996a. Interview with Bernard Worms. Marseille.
Gadjigo, Samba. 1996b. Interview with Maurice Fall. Dakar.
Gadjigo, Samba. 2004. "The Problem Is More Mental Than Economic: An Interview with Ousmane Sembène." Rabat.
Locke, John. 1689. *The Second Treatise of Civil Government*. Online Library of Liberty. Accessed January 24, 2017. http://oll.libertyfund.org/quotes/497.

Mbaye, Keba. 1992. *Les droits de l'homme en Afrique*. Paris: Éditions Pedone.

Murphy, David. 2000. *Sembene: Imagining Alternatives in Film and Fiction*. Oxford and Trenton, NY: James Curry.

Scott, A. O. 2004. "Heroism and Defiance in an African Village." *New York Times*, October 13. Accessed January 24, 2017. http://www.nytimes.com/2004/10/13/movies/13mool.html.

Sembène, Ousmane. 1956. "Liberté." *Action Poétique* ("Les peuples opprimés") 5: 29–32.

Sembène, Ousmane. 1972. *Archives Sonores de la Littérature Africaine*, presented by Jacques Howlett. Paris: Clef.

Universal Declaration of Human Rights. Accessed January 24, 2017. http://www.un.org/en/universal-declaration-human-rights/.

9   Haile Gerima's *Harvest: 3000 Years* in the Context of an Evolving Language of Human Rights

Ashish Rajadhyaksha

RETURNING IN 2016 to Haile Gerima's well-known *Harvest: 3000 Years* (*Mirt Sost Shi Amit* in the original Amharic) forty years after it was made has a distinctly millennial quality to it: as though returning in a time machine from the future to the past, in the eternal hope of unlocking hidden reserves. Among the many things that confront us as we do so, historically, politically, and technologically, is the astonishing challenge posed by the repositories of celluloid as they now lie in archival vaults, in various conditions of decay, and with them, the twentieth century that they captured and recorded.

This is a paper about returning to celluloid film, and it thus tracks the process of return to a curious historical, technological, and political amalgam of material. This is of course a return to film, itself in danger of being lost, mired in an unresolved conundrum that celluloid continues to present to the twenty-first century. Contrary to how it was perceived in the time of industrial capitalism, celluloid has proved in hindsight to be the very antithesis of a commodity capable of infinite reproduction. Invented together with air travel and electricity, it has found itself unexpectedly abandoned at what many have considered the very height of its creativity, when the world transitioned from industrial to informational technology. Today every one of the marks and scratches on celluloid that need to be erased with artisanal care testify to the fact that—with crumbling files and musty archives—celluloid is of the past. This is a past that celluloid film both witnessed and recorded firsthand, creating a record of its times far more complex than its makers often realized, because celluloid is also *of* its time. It both captures an era and incarnates it.

Such a return to celluloid film is thus imbued with new and rather special concerns as well as hopes. There is, for example, a parallel context of an evolving language of human rights that has brought special significance to a time when film encountered a growing and transforming global human rights movement in ways that neither filmmakers nor advocates of rights had anticipated. Celluloid both captures and literally bears witness to an epoch in which, in most parts of the non-Western, formerly "Third" world, new nation-states were attempting sustainable political coalitions shored up by ethical self-justifications. In providing an ethical armature for their nationalisms, these states often turned to primordial values, and thus found themselves challenged by the technological apparatus of a new and globalizing modernity. These nations were therefore challenged by the cinema; and in mounting this challenge, the cinema has often captured, with an uncanny accuracy, major national struggles to make popular sense of an ethical, rights-based structure of governance, one embedded in fraught local conditions that were themselves caught up in diverse Cold War and neoimperial aggressions. Celluloid has thus borne witness to these times almost as documentary evidence might, in complex ways that its original users would surely not have anticipated. At least in the film under discussion, the filmmakers are still with us, even though they might at times appear a little like prehistoric cave-painters.

Gerima was born in 1946 in Gondar, Ethiopia, one of ten children. "It's a small town, Gondar," he says. "Like most Ethiopian families, we had one foot in town and the other foot in rural, peasant society." Sometime in the mid-1960s, however, he went to Chicago to study theater, to the Goodman School of Drama at DePaul University. Realizing, he later said, that there was nothing he could learn about theater at DePaul that he couldn't already access at home, he moved, first to UCLA and then into film. He did this because "in film you have individualized power . . . the power of the director's vision": "film gave me the possibility of controlling my own story" (Jackson 2010, 25–6). Here he would become a key member of what would come to be known as the L.A. Rebellion, making *Harvest* and several other films. The race politics of Los Angeles in the 1970s–80s thus provide one key context for these films; indeed, the films are also profound explorations of questions of race.

Set in Ethiopia, *Harvest* itself is a three-layered story. At one level it is about the daily life of a family of peasants: a father, a daughter named Beletech, and a son, Berehun. Much of the film works with a hard documentary realism, showing daily life and work. Some of it moves toward tragedy, such as in the episode of Beletech's death trying to save the family's cow in a flood. Another level is defined in a Brechtian sense, by a character who plays against this realism: a madman-visionary and former landlord named Kebebe, who declaims the poverty, rails against the oppression, and speaks directly to the film's baddie, a feudal landowner who struts about in full colonial suit, surrounded by slaves. Kebebe's performance holds the film together, as he sings, speaks, drinks, teaches the son Berehun political theory, eventually kills the landlord, and dies himself, hunted down and killed by the villagers. The film itself is a kind of multilayered montage, as are the circumstances under which it was made and on which it throws light. What I present below, in the spirit of the film itself, is a similar montage of concerns that emerge as we turn back from the present, to look at our crisscrossing of cinematic discourses in a rights framework.

1976: Return to Ethiopia

In 1976 Haile Gerima returned to his native Ethiopia to shoot *Harvest*, his first feature and the first full-length film in the language of Amharic. The film was shot in 16mm. Until recently it was entirely unavailable, but it has now been restored by the Cineteca di Bologna, supported by Martin Scorsese's World Cinema Foundation. Some say that the lack of availability was partly Gerima's own fault: again, very much in line with his times, he has retained rights to all his work, which he has, since *Sankofa* (1993, Burkina Faso / Germany / Ghana / US / UK), personally released through a grassroots distribution outfit, Mypheduh Films company, which he still runs with his wife.

There is another, rather older aspect to the ageing. The Amharic language is the second largest Semitic language after Arabic, equally old but also linked to it, via what is widely seen—especially by proponents of the Rastafari ideology—as an unbroken regal chain going back three thousand years. This conception of an unbroken history is central to the film and relates, Teshome Gabriel suggests, to Ethiopian oral storytelling traditions. Since the Ethiopian-American Teshome Gabriel, an important figure in the history of the University of California at Los Angeles' School of Theater, Film and Television, is going to be a central presence in the argument that follows, it will be well to quote him right away in some detail on *Harvest*.

Contending that the way the film "blends imaginatively oral narrative art with revolutionary film form" makes it an exemplary instance of an "aesthetic of liberation of the Third Cinema," Gabriel says that the film,

> like the storyteller's art, allows us to share the quality of the peasants' life—
> their patience and their endurance. On another level the repeated lyrics, "Your
> 3000-year-old dress is not yet torn," warns us not to be complacent about the
> continuation of that existence. The opening sequences in the film establish
> the central code of the culture of poverty, where a family unit consisting of
> a grandmother, father, mother, daughter (who dies in the film) and son (who
> subsequently leaves the family unit) form a family of exploited peasants. Once
> these opening scenes are established they serve as the code to which all sub-
> sequent shots and sequences of shots refer. . . . Just as an oral form, images
> come and go, appear, vanish and reappear, endlessly recalling other images
> and associations. (Gabriel 1982, 90)

For all its millennialism, the film was made in a crucial year in Ethiopia, and also speaks to a rather more urgent history. Just two years earlier, in September 1974, the emperor Haile Selassie the First had lost power to a revolution. He had once previously lost power during World War II to Mussolini, but this was different: this loss was to the controversial "Derg" era of a Soviet-backed Communist regime led by Colonel Mengistu Haile Mariam, and the country would soon witness famine, war with neighboring Somalia, and, central to the nation's human rights history, the notorious Qey Shibir or Red Terror attack on the Ethiopian People's Revolutionary Party (EPRP).

The Mengistu regime was thus still new, and Gerima was sometimes locally viewed as sympathetic to it, something, says Michael W. Thomas (2014, 183), that made the promotion of *Harvest* "problematic" to many since the film could be read as "sympathizing with the 1974 Revolution, and thus as compromised by the Derg's subsequent atrocities."

This period in which the film is set, between the Selassie and Mengistu regimes, is—and this is crucial to my argument—also the era of classic celluloid. It is a politically tumultuous era in the history of a nation, in which a native cinema is being founded at the same time as a modern state: a time that the film not just depicts but literally *represents*. Together with the politics is the birth of an Amharic cinema. This is a cinema that, says Kindeneh Tamene (2014), is largely driven by "nostalgia along the lines of social change." Tamene sees *Harvest* together with Gerima's later BBC documentary *Imperfect Journey* (1994, Ethiopia / Italy / USA) and films like Salem Mekuria's *Deluge* (1995, Ethiopia / USA) and Yemane Demissie's *Tumult* (1996 USA / Ethiopia) as all profoundly marked by their times. If *Harvest* "contests and subverts the reigning feudal narratives and also anticipates the still unfinished struggle against the post-feudal era," *Tumult* "revisits the 1960s failed attempts by students, in alliance with segments of the military, to topple Haile Selassie's regime" and "eloquently provides a solid foundation for better understanding of the continuing struggles in contemporary Ethiopia," while *Deluge* "revisits from a more personal point of view a more recent moment in 1970s and 1980s Ethiopia under the reign of Mengistu Haile Mariam."

All of these works, says Tamene, are part of "a project to revision the foundational narrative of a 3000 year Solomonic Ethiopia in light of the experience with feudalism and a failed revolution and their legacies." Necessarily the different parts of that complex history intersect. When the military government fell, in 1991, to the Ethiopian People's Republic Democratic Front (EPRDF), for a decade there was almost no film production, writes Tamene. This would change with the demise of celluloid itself. In 1999 the Ethiopian Film Corporation was dissolved and was replaced by the Ethiopian Film Production Association (AFPA). Celluloid was replaced by video, and, led by the Nigerian "Nollywood" video revolution, Amharic cinema too reinvented itself, in the era of the low-cost CD.

The L.A. Rebellion

Celluloid film possesses, in its very apparatus, the ability to make unusual global connections, sometimes intentional, other times in spite of its authors. *Harvest* made common cause with another history that was brewing in faraway Los Angeles. Gerima's film, made while he was at UCLA, also launched what came to be known as the L.A. Rebellion, an upsurge of revolutionary black filmmaking in the 1970s and '80s. The UCLA Film School, undergoing major change that has been attributed mainly to its first black faculty member, Elyseo Taylor, was responding to racial tensions in a Los Angeles that was still recovering from the aftereffects of the Watts Rebellion of 1965, the worst race riots Los Angeles had seen until Rodney King in 1992. Taylor's appointment at UCLA coexisted with his work in community centers at Watts including the Mafundi Institute and Watts Happening café; and UCLA's Media Urban Crisis (MUC) program was designed "to train Black, Chicano, Asian, and Native American students . . . to use mass communication technologies to document their own communities" (Field et al. 2015, 9). Especially significant here was the aesthetic and political context defined by the "Film and Social Change" course that Taylor first taught, but which would be better known by the version created by Taylor's eminent successor, Teshome Gabriel.

We have encountered Gabriel already and will have more to say about him in a moment. Here it is important to note that Gerima moved to UCLA following the influence of Gabriel, whom he had met in 1967 while still studying at the Goodman School of Drama in Chicago. Charles Burnett had already joined UCLA in 1967, Larry Clark would come in 1970, Walter Gordon (who changed his name to become the filmmaker Jamaa Fanaka) in 1971. These would become the core members of what would come to be known as the L.A. Rebellion. Their films were on the one hand set profoundly in Los Angeles and more generally in the racially divided America of the post–Watts Rebellion era. At the same time, they sought identification with Africa in particular and the Third World more generally. In making both claims regarding affiliation, they were influenced by a framework of Third Cinema originally founded by Gabriel. Many L.A. Rebellion artists consciously identified themselves as Third World filmmakers, write Field et al. (2015, 24); they employed "guerilla production practices, emphasized collaboration, and worked collectively," "crewing on one another's films [which] created a sense of camaraderie among the Black filmmakers and their friends who shared their perspectives and sensibilities." There was also the conscious effort to "align the diaspora with struggles in Africa (and other peoples engaged in anti-imperialist fights); and . . . to call attention to the cultural impoverishment generated by assimilation. These same concerns are shared across a number of films and find an acute critique in those centered on the lives of the underemployed residents of Watts in South Central Los Angeles" (ibid.). The same year as *Harvest*, Gerima also made *Bush Mama* (USA), set inside Los Angeles and featuring a black woman named Dorothy, married to a former army officer now in jail. This woman achieves what Field et al. call "an awakened political consciousness, understanding her situation in relation to broader global, systemic oppressive mechanisms" (2015, 23).

Viewed today, more than *Harvest* it is *Bush Mama* that hits home, in a time that has America simmering on a racial edge following widespread police violence and killings of unarmed black people. The black neighborhoods of Los Angeles in the film are disturbingly current, and the edgy street photography—together with the raw acting often by nonprofessional actors—provides a very contemporary testament to the condition of civil rights in the United States.

In one sense *Bush Mama*, seen today, needs no Third World detour to establish its credentials. It is therefore of significance to note that at the time it was made, the film's political claim lay not in capturing the immediate situation that Gerima and the L.A. Rebellion were in (i.e., a racially divided Los Angeles), but in two other things it did. First, in the way *Bush Mama* demonstrated Dorothy's "politicization"—also known in those days as "consciousness raising"—and second, in the way it established such politicization by aligning her condition with "anti-imperialist struggles in places like Angola" (Field et al. 2015, 24). The second detour was a necessary counterpoint to the first in credentialing the radicalism of the L.A. Rebellion.

Although Gerima was going "home" to make his film, he was also returning to Ethiopia in the way Dorothy returns to Angola in *Bush Mama*: in a symbolic sense, to an Africa that represented Los Angeles' alterity. In one sense this was a personal, even autobiographical work, which "shows you the actual footprints of my youth, of where I grew up with my father and the rest of my family." A decade later, with *Teza* (2008), he would go further in outlining "the landscapes of my childhood," set in "a place called Menzero, which is also where my family is from" (Jackson 2010, 25). In another sense, however, he was equally conscious of the symbolic aspect of an American filmmaker extending black solidarity, through his cinematic gesture, with Africa and the Third World more generally. Consolidating two somewhat disparate claims into a single whole, *Harvest* has been seen as (to quote a publicity brochure when it was shown at the Tate Gallery in 2015) "an epic picture of peasant life in contemporary Ethiopia and a milestone in African cinema" that succeeds in being a "distinct new Black cinema sensitive both to the liberation movement in Africa and the political climate in America."

Realism and Documentary Testimony

Such a coalescence of two somewhat distinct ethical claims—one to do with peasant life in Ethiopia and a second to do with black cinema in the United States—is itself in hindsight a key feature of a great deal of celluloid in what we might call conditions of underdevelopment. Such film throws into sharp relief a very specific function of cinematic realism as a space for ethical consolidation because its key purpose, together with producing new and radical content for viewing, is the production of a standpoint from where to view. As Indian theorist Madhava Prasad contends, "This form of realism . . . bestows an immanent unity (as opposed to a unity that derives from a transcendental plane) on its content. Coming into its own with the consolidation of the modern state, it is distinguished by a transformation of the field of perception such that the spectator's gaze is attracted by the unfolding of a sequence of events focused around a central character, and whose meaning is constructed through the diegesis, under the aegis of legality" (1998, 62–3).

Perhaps the difference between the Ethiopia of 1936–41 that was under Italian occupation and Mengistu's Ethiopia of 1974 (although both challenged the Selassie reign) was the fact that the latter was, in some large sense, nationalism proper, whereas the former, arguably, was not. *Harvest* itself records a rather eloquent sequence on this: at a bar, shortly after Kebebe has promised not to lose hope and has sung a wonderful slow song about wealth and poverty, the men are drunkenly reminiscing about what was presumably their experience in World War II: one of them had a bullet in his leg, but "the Italian bumburdina were surrounded, the brave Tigre fighter Gebrehuisot had won through—but when the Italians were destroyed the English rewarded us for this." Another man says that "that was the mistake you made that day."

Such nationalism typically supported, in the heyday of celluloid, the production of a very specific realism: one that was at once millennial—and thus the three thousand years and the myth of the regnal continuities of the Selassie regime—and modern. It was, says Prasad, less a historical production than it was the production of a new kind of spectator's gaze. Although the realism was commonly focused on a "central character" (here it would be our preening landlord), more importantly, it was a realism constructed under the aegis of a new legality. This gaze was accorded supreme authority since this spectator literally saw like a state, conquering madmen, magicians, and landlords alike in its eventual triumphal transformation of these beings into an immanent unity.

Such realism, specific to emerging conditions of nationalism, was bestowed with the authority that the nation could ethically muster, which may not often have been very much. But that authority, such as it was, was in its truth-telling ability directly equated with its status as legally sanctioned documentary *testimony*. As we turn to the cinema's status as providing something of an eyewitness account of past history, we also turn to the role, hardly discussed, that it has played in the former Third World: of providing unconventional testimonies for legal purposes, and thus of according a new status to oral history. Africa has itself been long committed to both. Recent manifestations include the work of the ACHPR (African Commission on Human and Peoples' Rights) in its investigations into the Boko Haram and in the making of films like *A Question of Justice: The Rights of Indigenous People in Africa* (2011, Mette Sejsbo, Denmark; supported by the WGIP [Working Group on Indigenous Populations / Communities]).

All films are, at some level, documentaries, for all films capture reality, sometimes in ways more complex than what might have been encompassed by the conscious perception of those initially involved in capturing that reality, such as its film director, cinematographer, and sound recordist. Few celluloid filmmakers might be said to have been aware of the role that posterity would accord them, and only a few films in history have anticipated, in any conscious way, the possibility that they represented their era or recorded rather more material than what they put to narrative use. What they actually captured has often taken years to decipher, and this has usually happened only in another historical era: when that moment of nationalism had passed, the dust had settled, and you could actually figure out what the camera had seen and caught on screen.

As we return to celluloid, made in and about difficult and dangerous times, inscribing these times in unpredictable ways upon the record, perhaps we need to think about realisms, in the plural. Or at least two kinds of realism that might work in different, and occasionally even contradictory, ways. One, the kind Prasad tries to outline, is a more conventional realism, a representational idiom intended to produce *verisimilitude*, believability, eventually the authority of the state: reality *is* because the state says so. This is a weaker realism: it assumes the cinema's power of believability and its possible hold over the citizen-spectator.

The more complex realism is one that the Third Cinema has privileged: the inscription of the recorded data on the material of recording, namely celluloid film, as itself constituting the historical record. Such a record exists, Third Cinema filmmakers repeatedly insist, as much within the cinema itself as *outside* the screening paraphernalia of celluloid: in the social conditions of its making and showing. The latter is also a context of cultural or "transcinema" production contexts, where celluloid shares space alongside a number of competing technologies of representation, so much so that it can no longer take its own preeminent position within this broader cluster of "productions" for granted.

The "Cinema-Effect" and the Narrative Contract in *Harvest*

How does *Harvest* produce a spectatorial standpoint? As Thomas shows, the audience of the film is introduced to three different groups or figures of Ethiopian society: "firstly, the peasant workers; secondly, the landlord; and, thirdly, the madman who is a veteran patriot who fought against the Italians and claims his land was taken from him (through legal chicanery in his absence) by the landlord" (Thomas 2014, 186). The peasant family represents the suffering endured by the Ethiopian people under the ruling, landed elites, while the madman, Kebebe, is the diametrically opposed visionary and revolutionary.

Another aspect of the film arises from Thomas' observation: the way each of these entities is inscribed into the film record in a rather distinct way. In the scenes that show the family, the father, son, and daughter, the realism is documentary: the actors are not trained ones, and the reality is as close to the actual reality of the village as Gerima could make it. Such a reality parallels and works

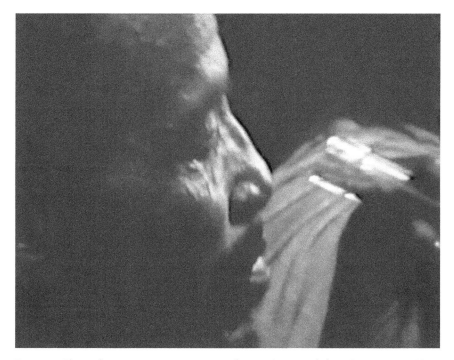

Figure 9.1. The madman-visionary-eyewitness to history. Framegrab from *Harvest: 3,000 Years* (1976, Haile Gerima, Ethiopia).

closely with the film's anthropological ambition to capture oral traditions and practices in song and word. This register of realism is contrasted with at least three other "reality-effects." A second layer is purely fictional: that of the landlord in his suit, on his armchair, strutting about. His house, in its fiction, may well have been a movie set. A third layer, also fictional, develops a rather different register of truth, since it is shot in actual public spaces (the Addis Ababa sequences are especially telling). This is the realism of Kebebe. It is fictional to the extent that Kebebe is fictional: Kebebe, like Dorothy in *Bush Mama*, is an actor reading lines. But, like Dorothy's Los Angeles, Kebebe's realism is linked to the first reality-effect, to the extent that the spaces, the bars, and the fields are all documentary in nature and thus qualify for the status of documentary evidence. And then there is a fourth, largely commentative register of reality: of the horizon, the landscape, the Italian trucks that both Kebebe and Berehun stare at in the distance.

This constellation of multiple registers of realism has two significant consequences. One, each register is grounded discursively within its own rather distinct tradition of truth-effect and thus its own claim, as much within Ethiopia as within a larger history of cinematic representation. This is the history that will allow a Los Angeles–based filmmaker to return to his native land. And two, such a constellation, although captured *par excellence* by the cinema, is not limited to it: it is a kind of "cinema-effect," templated on celluloid film but duplicated by the entire domain of modern symbolic representation, especially and above all the representational paraphernalia of the modern state. Such a production of the "cinema-effect"—a social form of representation, objectivity, and symbolic address—needs to be seen as integral to an expanded conception of cinematic narrative in times such as Ethiopia in 1976.

The further introduction of *narrative* into this particular fray is not least because the cinema's specific claim to distinguish itself from, say, fairground effects lies precisely in its promise of achieving diegetic coherence. Gerima says as much when he contends that the cinema gives you "control" to tell your "own stories" (Jackson 2010, 27). He is evidently speaking of a somewhat special role of narrative here: a specifically cinematic interpretation of the interpellative double-take, where narrative constitutes itself through locating its subject simultaneously within its ambit but also outside it, watching what the narrative is, literally, making of its subject. The question of whom the narrative names as the viewer is, in turn, one that draws on various sources, for the "cinema-effect" makes available a capacity to simulate what we may now describe as its direct ancestor within realism.

As we move the interpellative "double-take," then, into a second register, that of transforming the representational aspect of authenticity into a process of its authentication, *Harvest* casts its net wide. Its legacies are clearly most commonly and ubiquitously fabricated on the critical prior template of the authenticity production machine of the nation. In the film they tend to reenact the state's mechanisms of self-authorization: perhaps this is the reason why Gerima was seen as supportive of the new Derg regime. Inevitably, *Harvest*'s authenticity effect is forged on its best-known model, provided by the paradigm of *national* belonging and the value placed on such belonging, even in counterfeit forms.

It is into the space of *negotiating identity*—transacting between narrative and institutionalized practices—that Indian theorist Sudipta Kaviraj inserts what he calls an "agenda of historical semantics" (1995, 92). Suggesting that we may be better able to understand political and social organization as primarily a narrative practice, Kaviraj unambiguously defines narrative as something charged with the purpose of initiating its audience into the rites of membership of a culturally determinate collective, a "narrative community." "In some ways," he proposes, "it is better not to treat democracy as a governmental form. . . . A better strategy . . . is to treat it, more problematically, as a 'language,' as a way of conceiving, and in more propitious circumstances, of making, the world" (ibid.). This language in turn institutionalizes something that could be more appropriately seen as *not* universal, but local and particular—and here we are introducing the demands made by group-differentiated cultural formations for legal visibility, which Kaviraj calls a narrative contract.

> The telling of a story brings into immediate play some strong conventions invoking a narrative community. Ordinarily these are coincident in terms of their frontiers with social communities of some form: societies, particular groups, sometimes movements aspiring to give themselves a more demarcated and stabler social form. To some extent, all such communities, from the stable to the emergent, use narrative as a technique of staying together, redrawing their boundaries or reinforcing them. Participating in a movement quite clearly involves accepting something like contractual obligations and, I suspect, some of this affiliation of individuals to movements counteracting a monadic individualism is accomplished by narrative contracts.
>
> Narrative therefore does not aspire to be a universal form of discourse. It draws lines, it distributes people, unlike rational theoretical discourse which attempts to unite them in an abstract universe of ideal consensus. Narratives are not for all to hear, for all to participate in to an equal degree. It has a self in which it originates, a self which tells the story. But that self obviously is not soliloquizing or telling the story to itself. It implies an audience, a larger self to which it is directed, and we can extend that idea to say that the transaction of a narrative creates a kind of narrative contract. (Kaviraj 2010, 201)

What is the purpose of such a definition of 'narrative'? What is it supposed to do? If it is a contract, what is its legal status? Kaviraj's definition of narrative is in some ways the opposite of what the term usually means in literary theory. While this definition would follow Roland Barthes' earlier use of the phrase to emphasize the transactional nature of narrative as a "medium of exchange, an agent, a currency, a gold standard" (Barthes 1974, 89), it also departs significantly from that conception in its insistence, contrary to the way narrative aspirations are usually understood, on *nonuniversality*. It privileges instead its here-and-now capacity to create divides between those who are "in the narrative" and those who are outside it, looking in.

To Madhava Prasad (1998, 60–1), what such a narrative definition does is something rather complicated, especially in conditions where there is an absence of a rationalizing authority on the level of narrative discourse. Such an absence can, he says, sometimes signal the rise of a contiguous space "outside of and above the text." Occupying the space of a missing element in the narrative, leading to the "strategic suspension of rational mediation" that so marks the realisms of a peripheral modernity, is the figure of the "citizen," which, in its "in-betweenness," performed [a] double function. . . . The citizen as the mediating figure between state and individual is an elusive mechanism of social organization in conditions of underdevelopment."

[In the realist aesthetic] the spectator has the opportunity, the *right*, to repeat the production process—the processing of raw material to generate meaning—that has already been accomplished by the producer / artist. Even if all the spectators arrive at the *same* meaning, they must be assumed to have done so individually, through their own labour of interpretation. (Recent film theory thus makes a virtue out of a necessity when it claims as its own discovery the fact that spectators are active producers of meaning rather than passive recipients of it. This productive labour of the spectator is assumed by the realist text and does not constitute either a sign or a guarantee of resistance). (Prasad 1998, 21)

Teshome Gabriel, or, Another Third World Is Possible

In this particular instance, the filmmaker Gerima at least had a very serious interpreter to deal with: several of the L.A. Rebellion films were being made under the direct theoretical influence of Teshome Gabriel and his celebrated course at UCLA that would culminate in the book *Third Cinema in the Third World: The Aesthetics of Liberation* (1982). Gabriel's theory is, in a major sense, the presiding framework for Gerima's cinema.

In a very short book that confidently traverses from Africa to Asia to Latin America, from China to Cuba and from Jean Rouch to Tomás Gutiérrez Alea, with astonishing brevity and confidence, Gabriel provided a genealogy of not only the Third Cinema but the Third World itself. He draws directly on Frantz Fanon, the inspirational guide for the Third Cinema, who had traced "three stages in the development of ideological consciousness in the direction of cultural decolonization in the Third World: (a) the unqualified assimilation phase where the inspiration comes from without and hence results in an uncritical imitation of the colonialist culture; (b) the return to the source or the remembrance phase, a stage which marks the nostalgic lapse to childhood, to the heroic past, where legends and folklore abound; and (c) the fighting or combative phase, a stage that signifies maturation and where emancipatory self-determination becomes an act of violence" (Gabriel 1982, 7).

To Gabriel, both (b) and (c) were rooted in "indigenous culture." His idea of a "Third World film style" now grew from three stages too. These were "(a) a dependency on the Hollywood model of conventional cinema, submitting both to the concepts and propositions of commercial cinema; (b) national cinemas that promote the decolonization process but without at the same time decolonizing conventional film language; and (c) the emergence of decolonization of culture and liberation—here the entire spectrum of conventional production apparatuses of cinema undergoes a radical alteration. Corresponding to Frantz Fanon's third phase, the call in this last stage of the evolution of cinema is for a 'guerrilla cinema'" (Gabriel 1982, 7).

Gabriel shows how national governments across the Third World have sought to "appropriate the medium of the cinema for propaganda favorable to their own needs," which have typically been met with "various complex obstacles" including, crucially, the "absence of a critically sensitive audience." The main point, and perhaps the main obstacle, has been the fact that in their very nature, Third World filmmakers argue that "regardless of how 'innocent' the content of a film may seem, the film must necessarily reflect a certain class point of view. Therefore, they advocate a cinema which corresponds to the cultural tastes and political needs of the society it represents. The overriding concern of these filmmakers is not in aestheticizing ideology but in politicizing cinema" (Gabriel 1982, 2). Having made his central premise thus, Gabriel then goes further: he proposes an across-the-board aesthetic grammar of filmmaking that he wanted this kind of film to use: long takes, cross-cutting, panning and close-ups, the use of silence, and so on. To him the final task of this cinema was, above all, "oriented toward a peaceful co-existence with folk culture," an oral tradition reasserting itself in a new medium.

This formulation has been attacked, perhaps correctly, for its excessive determinism (and its fascination with Venn diagrams) together with an overly literal, even programmatic, implementation of the theories of Frantz Fanon in the cinema. And yet, as we look back to cinematic practices that have become ubiquitous in several Third World cinemas—a compulsive return to a past, a replaying of the dark days, of war, hunger, and feudal oppression against which the utopias of the future are to be measured, a mire from which the spectator can apparently be liberated only through a trauma-inducing reliving of the past in the present—it appears that Gabriel's three phases may well have more use to them than has been realized. In this section I stay within the spirit of Gabriel's desire to take the debate beyond Africa. I shall, however, rewrite Gabriel's neat categories and present, instead, a messier and more provisional version of his phases. I do so in the belief that what Gabriel can best do but does not actually achieve himself is to throw new light on the possibility of bringing a rights-based language to bear on radical "Third Cinema" aesthetics.

In conclusion, as I revisit the concerns outlined at the beginning of this text around returning to a celluloid artifact made in the last century, let me propose a small set of modifications to Gabriel's periodization. These modifications are of course made today, in an especially fraught period. On the one hand, the crises of nationalism have forced us to return to earlier histories and to alternative legacies that may still be rescued in today's times. On the other, the relevance of the Third Cinema as a political category may well be over, and no straight link may be made any longer that could bring together the United States with Asia, Africa, and Latin America. In this situation, as we return to this film, to celluloid's eyewitness recording of nationalist struggles, I propose a replacement of Gabriel's formulations with a rather more broad-stroke periodization that maps onto his but changes it somewhat as well.

I suggest, then, a first phase that corresponds with his "unqualified assimilation" but emphasizes not so much the politically tainted assimilationism against which political consciousness-raising supposedly happens, but rather the way this conflict produces an *imperial-modern*. This kind of assimilation typically happened in many metropolitan regions where film industries produced their original golden era of celluloid. Although such a metropolitan-colonial modernity may not be found easily in Africa, it does find shape, as Okwui Enwezor showed with Nigerian "highlife" in 2002 at the Century City exhibition at the Tate Modern, in places like the Mbari Club in Lagos, at once local and international, as it does more familiarly in ex-colonial cities such as Hong Kong, Mumbai, Shanghai, and Jakarta. In all these cities, the cinema, together with music and the plastic arts, creates a "golden era" of glamorous colonial modernity; it is this era that is typically interrupted by war and the onset of a long, more troubled second phase with the arrival of postwar independence in much of what would rapidly grow into the Third World.

What we get, in films like *Harvest*, is Gabriel's second "remembrance" phase, but it is rather less benevolent than Gabriel might have wanted. It is an ineffable legacy of times past, but it also inaugurates a more current and often nastier onset of high *state-nationalism*, when newly independent nations attempt, through a combination of coercion (censorship) and persuasion (subsidies), to discipline their cinemas into playing properly national roles: at times to follow their auteurs and make "better" films, at other times to follow a more rigid state *diktat*.

This indeed may have happened in Ethiopia itself, as Gerima, Mekuria, and Demissie, among others, sought to provide, in Tamene's (2014) words, a proto-state project to "revision the foundational narrative of a 3000 year Solomonic Ethiopia in light of the experience with feudalism and a failed revolution and their legacies." On the other hand, the Selassie period remains also of foundational significance for its ability to produce a new metropolitan counternarrative for imperialism itself, in its regal figure as a staging ground for alternative black nationalisms. This is surely the most complicated aspect of *Harvest* and also its most controversial face, both in Ethiopia for its revolutionary ambiguity and in Los Angeles.

And then there is Gabriel's third, "combative" phase, which we must replace now with the era of the "new" cinemas, often as a result of both new developmental initiatives and new markets usually presaging the arrival of *reformasi*, the end of military or other state-dominated rule, and the arrival of democratization, eventually signaling the onset of globalization: our "present" from which we return to this vexed history.

In returning to this history, we also return to the era of celluloid. We return to the fraught political conditions under which the film spectator, existing somewhere "outside of and above the text," occupied the space of a missing element in the narrative. Such a spectator, we have seen with Prasad, exists in several narratives that marked the realisms of peripheral modernity, in "strategic suspension of rational mediation." Such a figure, in his or her "in-betweenness, performed [a] double function" that he says stood as a "mediating figure between state and individual," thus becoming an "elusive mechanism of social organization in conditions of underdevelopment" (Prasad 1998, 60–1).

I therefore propose here a rights-based trajectory that moves parallel to this elusive "citizen" that such a spectator embodies, and I further suggest that there might be a link to be made between such a trajectory and Gabriel's three phases of historical evolution. And finally, I propose that the true significance of Gabriel's injection of a Third Cinema so centrally into the emerging language of a Third World aesthetic lies in the way the category of citizen is transformed. Armed with a new language of human rights, this citizen now embodies several contradictions endemic to Third World nationalisms after World War II, and it is film, in its celluloid phase, that alone appears starkly to illuminate this.

The first of Gabriel's phases, the "assimilationist" phase, might thus be seen as one where modern nation-states are to be made more aware of human rights as a category, and efforts are made to set up institutions as well as ethical-narrative structures that might define a framework of complementarity between the state and civil society. Civil society would not stand outside the state but would make the state more responsive, especially in terms of recognizing its constitutional obligations toward its citizens.

This is, if you like, the stage defined in *Bush Mama* by Dorothy's "conscientization" and in *Harvest* by the failure of the people of the Ethiopian village, barring the boy Berehun, to recognize the radicalism of Kebebe's gesture in killing the landlord. It is a phase in which places like feudal Ethiopia appear to be in need of a vibrant civil society to make the state accountable—and sometimes appear incapable of doing so. While such incapacity might be more easily ascribed to "backward" conditions, it becomes a much greater problem when its exact manifestations are realized in supposedly more advanced Los Angeles, when the state, far from accepting the self-organizing capability of its citizens, seeks to coerce them into submission—as Dorothy is coerced into considering an abortion. The assimilationist phase must now, in all its complexity, be understood as one in which the state and its policies are allowed to determine how far the self-organizing powers of the citizens will reach. In other words, how the state's constitutional framework, which is meant to guarantee certain basic freedoms, might be effectively and progressively realized.

Gabriel's second phase, that of state-nationalism, diverges dramatically across countries, depending as it does entirely on the political capability of new states to discipline (and, where necessary, to take over) their cinemas. Such a

Figure 9.2. The colonial landlord. Framegrab from *Harvest: 3,000 Years* (1976, Haile Gerima, Ethiopia).

phase coincides with the onset of state totalitarianism, when it is asserted that these new institutions of civil society that ensure citizen rights, especially of a civil and political kind, can only exist autonomously from the state. Such autonomy is very rarely granted, even in "developed" states, not only because of political resistance but because of the conceptual difficulty in identifying any agency other than the state that could guarantee essential freedoms to the individual.

Let me make a brief detour here and take a contrary example, that of China: partly because it features so centrally in Gabriel's thinking, and partly because China remains, in today's times, twinned to Africa as both its Big Asian Other and an example of everything Africa seemingly is not. China, politically, saw its equivalent of Gabriel's second phase in perhaps the most extreme instance of state takeover of the cinema seen anywhere, during its nationalization (*guoyouhua*, 1949–52) era, when the Chinese Communist Party (CCP) confiscated what remained of the Kuomintang's film facilities and turned them into state-run studios. This was followed by an even more intense phase of "socialist realism" between 1953 and 1965 when the CCP "deployed film as an effective weapon of propaganda and expanded its film operations, setting up new studios in key geographic locations, sending projection teams to remote areas, and training new personnel in workshops and film schools," even as "filmmakers did their best to cultivate national styles and explore acceptable genres . . . without offending the CCP leadership" (Zhang 2004, 189–90).

Gabriel himself proposes that the central aspect of this crisis was the "ideological clash between Madame (Chiang Ching) and Chairman Mao Tse-tung and Liu Shao-ch'i [Liu Shaogi] (the then chairman of the People's Republic) on the point of the artist's role in society" (Gabriel 1982, 68). Liu Shao-ch'i's reliance on professionals in the arts was opposed to Madame Mao's and Mao Tsetung's preference for the artistic works of amateurs, and this, to Gabriel, was crucial to the way film in the Cultural Revolution of 1966 emerged as a political imperative.

However it is understood, the cinema of this time was, as Vietnamese scholar Ngo Phuong Lan remembers, "an indispensable part of the people's life and struggle," where "every film produced was warmly welcomed by spectators after days of impatient waiting" (2002, 685). It is, adds Wang Hui, impossible to understand the Chinese sixties if they are divorced from a deep suspicion of, and the active damage done to, the socialist state and party orders. But it is also impossible to understand the end of the Chinese sixties "if it is divorced from the reconstruction and reconsolidation of these orders" (2006, 685). The consequences of this duality are felt only later, as we deal with a highly conflicted legacy in the third phase (of "combativeness"), when it appears impossible to enter the future without first detouring through the past and resolving or at least making peace with those conflicts. This then is the true meaning of Gabriel's "remembrance."

The historical contemporary becomes visible only through a curious optics. The past becomes a foreshortened past: it is a "shortened," accelerated twentieth century. And the conflicts over the past involve not arcane matters that concern only historians, but extremely contemporary battles over historical depoliticization. The space of the political becomes "something that was . . . internal to but seemingly external to the sphere of economic activity." The claim is now made for a "de-nationalization" of economic liberalization. Such denationalized globalization is often "simply the process of identification with a different national hegemonic form," and Wang Hui insists on unearthing within it nothing less than a "fierce conflict between two different national power blocs, two political systems, two ideologies" (Wang Hui 2006, 697–8).

Such dissensions over the past are of course the very essence of a slew of new-generation filmmakers, many of whom work precisely from globalized centers such as the UCLA Film School, who make films about the past but from a vantage point that is outside of perhaps the most influential version of Africa's third phase, that which typically follows the horrors of nationalism.

Whether intentionally and with high political purpose, or unbeknownst to them, cinemas have played, let us agree, a role of some complexity across the

Third World. They have fought wars over territory that have been layered by precolonial and colonial conquests all the way to the militarization of warlike communities, and, after independence, they have engaged in diverse political conflicts. Typically, it is the cinema that provides the arena for narrative battles to take place, and it is the cinema that has produced many of their militant protagonists.

All these wars now become startlingly current as the historical present seeks to establish institutions capable of free speech that are almost completely autonomous from the state— such as media and educational institutions—even as international civil society attempts to turn the global gaze on renegade nations incapable of undergoing democratic reforms. Even as human rights movements go beyond merely legal remedies and turn to diverse strategies, the discourse encompasses movements focused on women's rights, caste and race equality, and regional, minority, and environmental issues. Many of these movements are resolutely global in nature, more concerned, contrary to their earlier role of building a vibrant, independent, and separate movement, with shielding local radical movements and struggles to protect their "right to protest" and to extend legal and constitutional safeguards to the activists and leaders of these movements.

Such a role of reprocessing also provides celluloid film's history with a historically new purpose, as cinema is revealed in hindsight as playing a rights-based role it had never consciously claimed for itself. The cinematic image is itself as though recredentialed for having been an eyewitness to what we today see as history being made. But there is yet more. Adapting Roland Barthes's description of photography's ability to capture a future anterior, a "this will happen / this happened" moment in history, I suggest that *Harvest*'s cinematic images become especially powerful with the two-eyed view of the past: when it inserts into history the spectatorial condition of engaging what has happened as though it will now happen (Barthes 1981, 96).

The filmic aura of Gabriel's "remembrance" thence develops numerous variants: that which is captured on film, captured but erased and then resurrected; that which becomes evidence of what past spectators once saw; that which present-day spectators remember of the past as they revisualize it on screen; and that which may have happened or is believed to have happened.

Harvest is, in conclusion, thus profoundly about its time in a way that Gerima himself may not have envisaged. For it is about a present thrice represented. Once, by a historical present framing a distant and primitive past from which we have all emerged. A second time, by a nation-state still coming to grips with its history. And, third, by an African diaspora in the United States mobilizing Africa's past for numerous reasons that are now its own. All of these histories feature in the film's memorable end. Told with the slow movement of a leisurely Amhara storyteller, much of it includes extensive recitation and occasional action, before its climax in which Kebebe finally kills the landlord. In the end we have freeze-frames of Berehun, hanging to the back of a truck, as voice-overs say: "I am your servant. I am your shoeshiner—shoemaker—your coolie. Your messenger—janitor—servant. I am your nurse—labourer—maid. I am your blacksmith—steelworker—foundryman. I am your guard—your protector—your soldier—protecting your boundaries. Your baker—your feeder. I am the weaver—maker of your clothes. I make your comfort possible. I am your builder—I am your farmer—who brings in your harvest. With our labour—with our backs—with our sweat."

ASHISH RAJADHYAKSHA is a film historian and curator. He is author of *Indian Cinema in the Time of Celluloid: From Bollywood to the Emergency* and coauthor (with Paul Willemen) of the *Encyclopaedia of Indian Cinema.*

Filmography

Bush Mama, 1976, Haile Gerima, USA.
Deluge (*Ye Wonz Maibel*), 1995, Salem Mekuria, Ethiopia / USA.
Harvest: 3000 Years (*Mirt Sost Shi Amit*), 1976, Haile Gerima, Ethiopia.
Imperfect Journey, 1994, Haile Gerima, Ethiopia / Italy / USA.
A Question of Justice: The Rights of Indigenous People in Africa, 2011, Mette Sejsbo, Denmark.
Sankofa, 1993, Haile Gerima, Burkina Faso / Germany / Ghana / US / UK.
Teza, 2008, Haile Gerima, Ethiopia / Germany / France.
Tumult (*Gir-gir*), 1996, Yemane Demissie, USA / Ethiopia.

References

Barthes, Roland. 1974. *S/Z: An Essay.* Translated by Richard Miller. New York: Hill and Wang.
———. 1981. *Camera Lucida: Reflections on Photography.* Translated by Richard Howard. New York: Hill and Wang.
Field, Allyson Nadia, Jan-Christopher Horak, Shannon Kelley, and Jacqueline Stewart, eds. 2015. *L.A. Rebellion: Creating a New Black Cinema.* Oakland, CA: University of California Press.
Gabriel, Teshome H. 1982. *Third Cinema in the Third World: The Aesthetic of Liberation.* Ann Arbor: UMI Research Press.
Jackson, J. L. 2010. "Decolonizing the Filmic Mind: An Interview with Haile Gerima." *CALLALOO: A Journal of African Diaspora Arts and Letters* 33 (1): 25–36.
Kaviraj, Sudipta. 1995. "Democracy and Development in India." In *Democracy and Development: Proceedings of the IEA Conference Held in Barcelona, Spain*, edited by Amiya Kumar Bagchi, 92–130. London: Palgrave-Macmillan / International Economic Association.
Kaviraj, Sudipta. 2010. *The Imaginary Institution of India: Politics and Ideas.* New York: Columbia University Press.

Ngo Phuong Lan. 2002. "A Time to Die, a Time to Live." In *Being & Becoming, the Cinemas of Asia*, edited by Aruna Vasudev, Latika Padgaonkar, and Rashmi Doraiswamy, 486–8. New Delhi: Macmillan.

Prasad, M. Madhava. 1998. *Ideology of the Hindi Film: A Historical Construction*. Delhi and New York: Oxford University Press.

Tamene, Kindeneh. 2014. "A Brief Overview of Ethiopian Film History: From Early Cinema to the Contemporary." Addis Ababa University, June 6. Accessed October 10, 2016. https://www. academia.edu/7281313/A_Brief_Overview_Of_Ethiopian_Film_History.

Thomas, Michael W. 2014. "*Harvest 3000 Years / Mïrt sost shi amät* (Haile Gerima, 1976): A Revolutionary Ethiopian Film." In *Africa's Lost Classics: New Histories of African Cinema*, edited by Lizelle Bisschoff and David Murphy, 182–90. London: Legenda: Moving Image 5, Modern Humanities Research Association and Maney Publishing

Vasudev, Aruna, Latika Padgaonkar, and Rashmi Doraiswamy, eds. 2002. *Being & Becoming, the Cinemas of Asia*. New Delhi: Macmillan. Wang Hui. 2006. "Depoliticized Politics, Multiple Components of Hegemony, and the Eclipse of the Sixties." Translated by Christopher Connery. *Inter-Asia Cultural Studies* 7 (4): 683–700.

Zhang Yingjin. 2004. *Chinese National Cinema*. London: Routledge.

10 Abducted Twice?

Difret (*2015*) *and* Schoolgirl Killer (*1999*)

Tim Bergfelder

As part of their foreign affairs series *Under the Sun*, British public broadcaster BBC2 screened the film *Schoolgirl Killer* on terrestrial television in June 1999, directed by documentarist, journalist, and author Charlotte Metcalf. The fifty-minute film depicts the true story of Aberash Bekele, a sixteen-year-old schoolgirl from the Ethiopian countryside on trial for murdering a man who had forcibly abducted and raped her (aged fourteen at the time). In an extraordinary turn of events, Bekele was acquitted by the court, an outcome that signaled a profound challenge to traditional values and gender relations in Ethiopia. Sixteen years later, the same story formed the basis for the feature-length drama *Difret* (2015). An independent American-Ethiopian coproduction, the film gained publicity through the patronage of Hollywood star and philanthropist Angelina Jolie, who acted as executive producer and whose promotion facilitated the film's screening at the 2014 Sundance festival, where it won an audience award.

Difret was successfully distributed theatrically in the United States, Europe, South Africa, Australia, and some parts of the Middle East; it received further prizes and awards at various festivals, and it reached a wider public through its DVD release. Yet at the same time in Ethiopia—the country in which the film's story is set—*Difret* became mired in controversy and legal actions, its makers accused by Metcalf and Bekele for disowning the latter of her own story. Repeated injunctions and local screening bans disrupted the distribution and circulation of *Difret* in Ethiopia. Although the legal differences between Bekele and the makers of *Difret* were eventually resolved in out-of-court settlements, the story of the two films raises a number of interrelated but also sometimes conflicting questions concerning the legitimacy and ethics of certain forms of representation, a subject's rights to one's story, and the efficacy of human rights advocacy and human rights–focused film production. By tracing the production genesis, modes of representation and address, sociocultural contexts, and reception of the two films, this chapter aims to offer some insights into the practices of human rights filmmaking in and about Africa.

Charlotte Metcalf's choice to tell Bekele's story was not a random decision. Her experiences in and of Africa date back several decades, and her filmmaking (ranging from short films to longer exposés) has repeatedly been located at the intersection of current affairs reportage, news journalism, and human rights advocacy. During her career, Metcalf has traveled to and filmed in countries including Eritrea, Ethiopia, Ghana, Kenya, Nigeria, Uganda, Zambia, and Zimbabwe, her work being commissioned by broadcasters such as the BBC and Channel 4, but also often emerging out of collaborations with NGOs and charities. Metcalf had been to Ethiopia before making *Schoolgirl Killer* in the aftermath of Mengistu Haile Mariam's Derg regime (1974–87), when she talked to and filmed ordinary victims and witnesses of the "Red Terror" but also managed to interview members of the political and religious establishment, such as the then–prime minister Meles Zenawi and the former patriarch of the Ethiopian Orthodox Church, Abune Paulos (Metcalf 2003). Reflecting on the ethical implications and legacy of her work in her autobiographical book *Walking Away, a Filmmaker's African Journal*, Metcalf has stated that

> after early doubts and disappointments, I have recovered my belief that the right films, properly used, can be of value. . . . If I have changed people's minds or raised a little money for a good cause then my job has been worth doing. But that growing confidence in the efficacy of film leaves no room for complacency. I am neither an aid worker nor an activist. I am a filmmaker and my usefulness can be legitimately questioned. Sometimes I am accused of interfering in people's ways of life, of "judging" them. Sometimes I have to remind myself that, seen through African eyes, mine is the alien culture and of course my Western liberal values have coloured my views occasionally. (Metcalf 2003, n.p.)

In the mid- to late 1990s, the state of women's rights in contemporary African societies became the focus of Metcalf's work. *The Cutting Edge* (1996) and *Welcome to Womanhood* (1998) were produced by the BBC in collaboration with TVE (Television Trust for the Environment), a charity founded by the United Nations Environment Programme, WWF-UK, and Central Television in 1984. The former film was part of a series, under the umbrella title *Not the Numbers Game*, that featured contributions by women filmmakers from various countries (Bosnia, Cambodia, India, Indonesia, and Peru). Metcalf's film centered on the practice of female genital mutilation among the Sabiny people in a remote part of eastern Uganda and on the local female activists trying to eradicate the practice, supported by a program funded by UNFPA (the United Nations Population Fund). The second film followed Nigerian-born journalist Donu Kogbara returning to Uganda two years later to report on how successful the progress of the activists has been.

Metcalf's *Young Wives' Tales* (1998) was again produced by TVE as part of another multipart collective release, *A Question of Rights*, which also included short films depicting the state of women's reproductive rights in Latvia, Jamaica, and Fiji. Metcalf's contribution addressed the traditional practice of child brides in Ethiopia and its harrowing psychological, social, and physical consequences by highlighting the plight of an eleven-year-old girl about to be married in the Ethiopian Highland town of Bahir Dar. An edited version of the film was featured on Channel 4 News, and on its own the film was the runner-up for the UNICEF award at the One World Media Awards (Metcalf 2003).

It was during the filming of *Young Wives' Tales* that Metcalf first encountered the Ethiopian Women Lawyers' Organization (EWLA), founded in 1995 by Meaza Ashenafi, a former Ethiopian High Court judge, though Metcalf's initial contact was another lawyer, Original Georgis, who drew the filmmaker's attention to the case of Aberash Bekele. As Metcalf recounts in *Walking Away*: "I was in Addis Ababa interviewing Original about child brides. She was talking to me in front of a board on which were pinned photographs of little girls who had been forced into arranged marriages, but I was only half listening. I had been drawn to one photograph, of an extraordinarily beautiful face in which a pair of intense eyes were staring at me defiantly" (Metcalf 2003, n.p.). The individual thus described, Aberash Bekele, was already something of a national cause célèbre before Metcalf came onto the scene, her case illustrating the deep chasm in Ethiopia between official law and the law as being practiced in the context of regional community traditions.

The bare facts of Bekele's ordeal seem to speak for themselves. Aged fourteen and the daughter of subsistence farmers in the Arsi region of the southern Ethiopian province of Oromia, she was kidnapped by a group of horsemen from a neighboring village while walking back from school. Her main abductor took her to his hut, where he beat and raped her, part of his design to make her submit into marriage. The following day, Bekele managed to steal a gun from one of her tormentors and attempted to escape. In the ensuing commotion, she shot and killed her supposed husband, and the arriving police only just saved her from being killed by an angry mob.

In order to understand the specific sociocultural background of this incident, it is necessary to delve deeper into the Ethiopian context. As anthropologist Helen Pankhurst has noted, the practice of *t'ilf* (or *telefa*), referring to marriage by abduction, is one of six common types of marriage in traditional Ethiopian culture, alongside ceremonial, religious, and civil marriage, as well as marriage preceded by provision of labor and paid labor marriage (Pankhurst 1992, 102–3). Pankhurst acknowledges that in reality, "the categories are far from rigid and conceptually not very satisfactory. . . . They obscure distinctions between, differences within, and similarities across categories" (Pankhurst 1992, 103). According to Pankhurst, a clear definition of domestic relations in Ethiopia is impeded further by a high incidence, at least among some ethnic groups, of polygyny, extramarital affairs, and serial marriage (repeated divorce and remarriage). Indeed, conceptual haziness also extends to what *t'ilf* or *telefa* can encompass in everyday experience:

> The *t'ilf* marriage can be either premeditated or impulsive and can include various degrees of cooperation on the part of either the parents and/or the bride. Thus, the term, which implies the taking of the bride without her consent, might well be used to describe an elopement. In the case of a real abduction, or when the ritual is enacted despite consent, the bride is captured by the groom and his friends, often on her way to and from the market, from collecting water, or from school. When carried off, the woman will often scream and fight her "attackers," even when the match is to her liking. (Pankhurst 1992, 104)

In contrast to the somewhat fluid and ambiguous status of traditional practices, the official legal situation for Ethiopian women has been comparatively clear for some time. As Lahra Smith has outlined, the first step toward women's legal emancipation in Ethiopian society was initiated by the socialist policies of the Derg in the 1970s: "Women—particularly some peasant and rural women—for the first time assumed prominent roles in local organisations, including the Revolutionary Ethiopian Women's Association (REWA). . . . However, REWA became much like other party- and state-dominated women's associations of the time across Africa in its use as a party tool rather than a radical or transformative vehicle for Ethiopian women's empowerment" (Smith 2013, 173). From the 1990s onward, as Smith documents, a momentum toward greater recognition of women's rights became evident: "The 1995 constitution includes bold and very specific protections for women, making Ethiopia a leader in constitutional provisions for women. Article 25 of the constitution guarantees the right to equality for all. The rather lengthy Article 35 provides various enumerated rights for women, including specifically 'equal rights with men in marriage' and certain 'affirmative measures.' . . . Further constitutional language notes the influence of 'laws, customs, and practices that oppress or cause bodily or mental harm' that are prohibited" (Smith 2013, 174).

However, to this day a notable discrepancy persists between the aspirations and ideals enshrined in the constitution and everyday life. As "Girls Not Brides," an online platform campaigning against childhood marriage worldwide, notes with regard to Ethiopia: "Two in every five girls are married before their 18th birthday and nearly one in five girls marries before the age of 15. . . . The legal age of marriage in Ethiopia is 18 years for both girls and boys, but these laws are not always enforced. Ethiopia's Criminal Code outlines special provisions to punish the perpetrators of early marriage. However, Ethiopia has no functional national or regional system to register births, deaths, marriages, and divorce, making it difficult for authorities to prove a girl is underage" (Child Marriages around the World: Ethiopia).

Setting aside logistical problems and resource issues regarding the ensuring and policing of women's rights, Lahra Smith has warned that the simple imposition of laws that do not engage traditional values at a local level are bound to fail. As she argues, customary practices impacting women, such as domestic violence, forced marriage, bride abduction, and polygamy "are defended by families and communities at the village level, most often based on values of cultural tradition and belief in their importance for health, safety, and the continuation of community norms. Although it would be misguided to say that legal changes are not important . . . the greater challenge is in promoting a process of community dialogue of these various practices, which might see the expansion of conditions for women and girls to have greater physical and emotional security" (Smith 2013, 181–2). In the following pages, I will explore to what extent the complex dynamic between official law and traditional practices in Ethiopia is represented in the two films.

Schoolgirl Killer

Metcalf's film begins with a close-up of Bekele, sitting silently in a car looking outside. As the car passes through rural scenery, overtaking horse-drawn carts, the camera pulls back from Bekele's face; as her initially tense facial expression softens, it is revealed that she holds a teddy bear in her arms. As British television critic Robert Hanks noted when the film first aired on BBC2 in 1999, the film gains its power to startle through the juxtaposition of seemingly contradictory images such as a child's cuddly toy and "a woman's serious, beautiful face," attesting to the fact, which became part of the argument of Bekele's prosecution, that she looked much older than her real age (Hanks 1999). A shot from her perspective sees groups of men standing at the roadside staring back at the car. The voice-over narration begins to outline Bekele's predicament (she is being taken to court), and a mournful piece of classical music underscores her journey to the courthouse. The voice-over ceases momentarily, and a violin continues its melodic lament as the defendant takes her position in the dock, seemingly determined, while the judges position themselves opposite her.

In her book, Metcalf described the Bekele she first met as "luminously beautiful" and "slightly on the stocky side, which saves her from being entirely celestial, and moments of adolescent petulance tend to undermine her natural grace" (2003, n.p.). Metcalf's admiration for Bekele is clearly evident in *Schoolgirl Killer*, which abounds in close-ups of the young woman's face. Scenes of her recounting her ordeal in a shy but remarkably mature, articulate, and nonsentimental way are interspersed with scenes of her playing with other girls her own age in the orphanage in Addis Ababa; she is seen in more carefree surroundings, smiling broadly and appearing more childlike. The contrast to other protagonists becomes clear when Metcalf interviews the parents of the man Bekele has

Figure 10.1. Close-up of Aberash Bekele. Framegrab from *Schoolgirl Killer* (1999, Charlotte Metcalf, UK).

killed. They sit in a darkened hut, the father animated by outrage and anger, the mother more reserved and introverted in her grief. "She is the killer of the son who was so good to me," the father complains. "She stole our means of survival. He abducted her for marriage, not to be killed by her." As the parents conclude their grievances against Bekele, they forlornly hold up a framed photograph of their dead son, their fingers touching each other in a tender gesture. In the next shot we see horsemen with Stetson cowboy hats riding across the "remote and rugged region of Ethiopia's Wild South," as the voice-over informs the audience, the generic connotations being amplified by a suitably Ennio Morricone–style "Western" musical motif.

The film maintains the contrast between the quasi-idyllic space of the orphanage in Addis and the "rugged" countryside with its patriarchal structures. Metcalf interviews the village elders who have attempted to mediate between the various parties in the case, and then moves on to speak to Bekele's parents and elder sister, Mestawet, who has been a victim of marriage by abduction herself, ending her dreams of becoming an Olympic athlete. Mestawet's husband justifies his behavior to Metcalf by arguing with a permanent smirk on his face that he "decided to show her who's boss," and that he was "scared someone else would grab her." Meanwhile, to contrast the husband's comments, the camera shows Mestawet's present life running a local shack selling homemade alcohol to inebriated locals while also bringing up four young children.

Once again the film shifts its perspective and shows Bekele in the company of her "surrogate mother," as the voice-over claims, Meaza Ashenafi, one of the founders of the Ethiopian Women Lawyer's Association (EWLA). Ashenafi states how Bekele's case helped the association's crusade, and that the girl's "symbolic" act of resistance and "revolutionary" defiance made her an ideal candidate to promote the association's goals more broadly. The focus once again shifts to the trial, with more close-ups of Bekele in the dock, while her female defense barrister interrogates eyewitnesses.

The film returns to pick up the story of Mestawet and Aberash's younger sister Mulatu, who faces a similar fate as her two older sisters, and also explores the case of Sawnet, another fourteen-year-old who has just recently been abducted and raped. Meanwhile in Addis, Ashenafi and her colleague Daniel discuss Bekele's safety against the backdrop of the cosmopolitan capital's affluent elite drinking espressos in chic cafés and reading European newspapers. As the camera returns to the "Wild South," a pastiche of Morricone's harmonica motif from *Once Upon a Time in the West* (1968, Sergio Leone, Italy / USA) signals a return to lawlessness and to a climate of revenge and blood feuds, but also includes new instances of defiance, as Sawnet has managed to escape her abductors and is back home with her parents. Shortly before the day of the verdict in Bekele's case, the latter is reunited with her older sister and family. The film ends with Bekele's acquittal and brief scenes of family joy and celebration, but overall there is a bleak outlook. Mulatu states that she has no hope and all she can do is wait to be abducted. Captions inform the viewers that Mestawet left her husband after filming ended with her whereabouts unknown, and that Bekele, even though acquitted, will have to live the rest of her life away from her family, as her safety cannot be guaranteed in her home region.

Although *Schoolgirl Killer* strives to present the complexity of traditional Ethiopian society and values in a balanced manner while at the same time arguing for cultural change, it is first and foremost the story of a remarkable individual, Aberash Bekele. While the other protagonists, such as Bekele's and her abductor's respective families, the family of Sawnet, the village elders, and the metropolitan lawyers, are important contributors, Bekele's unique plight (however symbolic more broadly) is at the heart of the film. As Metcalf later recalled, the airing of *Schoolgirl Killer* in 1999 had immediate beneficial outcomes for some of the protagonists of the film: "When the film was finally broadcast there was an extraordinary reaction. The story captured the public's imagination and I was inundated with letters and offers of help. Some people sent cheques, others asked what they could do. Aberash and Mulatu were found places in a secure, safe boarding school and . . . we set up a trust to pay their school fees" (Metcalf 2003, n.p.).

Whether Metcalf's film had a broader impact beyond the lives of Aberash and Mulatu is open to question, but Bekele's high-profile court case certainly had a measurable influence on public behavior. As Metcalf noted, in the first five years after Bekele's acquittal, no abductions were reported in Arsi province (Metcalf 2015a). It is evident from some of the comments made in *Schoolgirl Killer* that Bekele's defiance helped embolden Ethiopian girls and women. In a radio interview in 2015, Metcalf further speculated that the increased accessibility of mobile phones since the late 1990s has given young women an added level of safety they previously lacked (Metcalf 2015b). Furthermore, since 1999 the campaigns of groups such as EWLA had increasing publicity globally, which brought with it prominence and international recognition to figures such as Meaza Ashenafi, who would play a far greater role in the retelling of Bekele's story in *Difret* than she had played in *Schoolgirl Killer*.

Difret

True to dramatic conventions, *Difret* (the word meaning both "courage" and "violation" in Amharic) opens with the caption "based on a true story." Its first scenes are set in the bustling streets of central Addis. Like *Schoolgirl Killer*, the film begins with a woman in a car, but unlike the lingering facial close-up of Bekele in Metcalf's documentary, the initial images are more fragmentary, homing in on a well-manicured hand with painted fingernails on the driver's wheel, followed by a face framed in the rearview mirror. The film then cuts to an interior space identified by a sign on the wall as belonging to the Andenet Women Lawyers's Association. Enter the woman from the car, confident, casually but fashionably dressed, modern lawyer Meaza Ashenafi (played by Meron Getnet), who helps female victims of domestic violence.

After a short scene in which Meaza assures a client that she will speak to her abusive husband, the film cuts to the countryside, following two carefree young girls on their way to school. One of them, Hirut (as Bekele is called in *Difret*), is commended by her teacher for her work but is too shy to respond. As she makes her way home, she is rounded up by a group of men on horseback who abduct her, leaving her torn school notes behind. Initially subdued, she begins to scream when carried by her attackers into a dark hut. As one of the attackers approaches Hirut to beat and rape her, the film cuts away and finds Meaza Ashenafi tracking down her client's abusive husband. Threatening to have him arrested, which would see him lose his job, she keeps the upper hand in the confrontation, walking away confidently. The film then cuts back to the hut in which Hirut is held, and what follows is a reenactment of Bekele's stealing the gun, killing her rapist, and escaping her abductors.

By juxtaposing and cutting between Meaza and Hirut/Bekele's stories from the start of the film, *Difret* establishes a privileged relationship between the two

Figure 10.2. Hirut (Tizita Hagere) and Meaza Ashenafi (Meron Getnet) in *Difret* (2015, Zeresenay Mehari, Ethiopia / USA). Framegrab.

characters that does not exist in the same way in *Schoolgirl Killer*, where Ashenafi does not appear until a third into the film. Moreover, by opening the film with Ashenafi, *Difret* signals in its very first seconds that she, rather than Hirut, will be the film's central protagonist. The film takes dramatic license in placing Ashenafi at the center of all the relevant action, which resembles the narrative conventions of a standard Hollywood biopic.

Thus, it is feisty and indomitable Meaza who comes to Hirut's rescue and takes her back to Addis; it is Meaza who takes up the struggle against a backward and biased local police and prosecution team, using her influence and connections as a former High Court judge to force the local authorities to give Hirut the chance of a fair trial. Meaza takes Hirut back to her own flat and bonds with her over some home cooking. Meaza is accused by her colleagues in the EWLA of being a maverick and too daring in her support of Hirut, thereby endangering the survival of the association. Meaza makes an impassioned statement in front of a High Court judge. Meaza questions her own confidence momentarily but regains her conviction that the cause is worth fighting for. The day of Hirut's acquittal arrives; after a short celebration, Hirut has to part from her family, and there is a tearful farewell between Hirut and Meaza, who looks on solemnly as Hirut disappears into the crowd. This final shot is followed by a caption that reads: "Between 1995 and 2002 Meaza's organization helped over 30,000 women and children."

In its adherence to classical Hollywood's principle of character-centered causality, *Difret* makes a powerful case against the practice of marriage by abduction, but at the cost of psychological and cultural complexity and by streamlining the events of Bekele's case into a more consumable narrative.

Although *Schoolgirl Killer* portrays Ashenafi as a prominent voice within EWLA and as the association's most articulate spokesperson, Metcalf's film also shows the efforts by a number of other people both related to EWLA and beyond in helping Bekele. Except for one lengthy sequence depicting a community meeting headed by elders in which Hirut's case is decided on, there is little investigation into the motivations or psychology of the rural population, and stereotypes of cowed and subdued women versus cocky and malevolent male villains abound. This is in sharp contrast to a character like Mestawet in the earlier film, who is both a victim of serious injustice and at the same time openly rebelling against her destiny. In *Difret*, Hirut's older sister is alluded to but does not feature in person; the rural women are seemingly all quietly resigned to their fate and submission.

The starkest difference between *Schoolgirl Killer* and *Difret* is in the depiction of the character of Hirut/Bekele. Whereas Bekele was in Metcalf's description "shy but self-possessed" (Metcalf 2003, n.p.) and comes across as such on-screen, Hirut remains for almost the entire duration of *Difret* a traumatized, mute victim with a permanently haunted expression on her face. Instead of telling and owning her own story, she becomes a cause for the brilliant lawyer heroine. The titular "courage" thus seems to apply almost exclusively to Ashenafi. Moreover, whereas Bekele in 1999 was visibly on the cusp of adulthood as far as her appearance was concerned (which contributed to her legal problems), Hirut as portrayed by newcomer Tizita Hagere looks her age, further cementing her status as an innocent and helpless victim and making attempts by the prosecution team to argue for her being of age implausible and suggesting deliberately ill intent. There is also an interesting difference in the way Hirut/Bekele's abduction and escape are portrayed. Whereas Bekele recounts her ordeal in Metcalf's film calmly and makes clear that the killing of her abductor was a rational decision, the cinematic depiction of Hirut's abduction foregrounds both visually and aurally the character's disorientation and psychological distress, suggesting a more instinctive and unconscious explanation for her actions.

Although frequently presented and marketed as an "Ethiopian" film, *Difret* is more accurately described as an international coproduction, with many of its origins in the United States rather than in Ethiopia. The film's first-time director, Zeresenay Berhane Mehari, was born in Ethiopia but received his professional training in the United States, graduating from the University of Southern California's School of Cinematic Arts. Most of the contributing producers, except for Jolie and Australian Jessica Rankin, are from the Ethiopian-American or more broadly Afro-American community, while cinematographer Monika Lenczewska and editor Agnieszka Glinska come from Poland.

Difret's international and diasporic credentials are not atypical as far as the perception of "Ethiopian" film in the West is concerned. As Alessandro Jedlowski has rightly pointed out, scholarly interest in Ethiopian film before the 2000s has often centered on the work of Ethiopian-born director Haile Gerima, who is closely associated with the L.A. Rebellion film movement and has lived in the United States since the 1960s (Jedlowski 2015, 170). However, since Ethiopian film has experienced a boom period in domestic production since the beginning of the new millennium, generating an expanding local film culture replete with stars and popular genres (Jedlowski 2016), public knowledge of Ethiopian cinema in the West still mostly remains associated with art house productions that emerge from the Ethiopian diaspora. Thus, the "first Ethiopian film" to be screened in the official selection at the Cannes film festival, *Lamb* (2015), is mainly financed by French, German, and Norwegian backers, and directed by Yared Zeleke, an Ethiopian film graduate from New York University.

To stress the diasporic origins of films like *Difret* or *Lamb* is not to argue for a policing of who may or may not legitimately author and produce "Ethiopian" films, but to draw attention to the fact that such films are not necessarily directed at a domestic audience or representative of filmmaking practices in Ethiopia. In order to explore further the issue of what kind of audience *Difret* is directed at, it is useful to consider the role and function of Angelina Jolie in the genesis and marketing of the film. Even though Jolie was not directly involved in the creative conception and production, her postproduction association with the project became crucial not only in promoting *Difret*, but also in drawing attention to the human rights issues the film addresses.

Coinciding with her rise to film stardom and critical acclaim for her acting in the late 1990s, Jolie has become in the new millennium one of the key global exemplars of what has been termed "celebrity humanitarianism" (Littler 2008; Chouliaraki 2012, 2013). Noting how Jolie's acting career and celebrity activism (e.g., her role as UNHCR ambassador since 2001, cochairing the Clinton Global Initiative's Educational Partnership for Children of Conflict, her Jolie Legal Fellowship that assists NGOs in Haiti, and numerous targeted campaigns in Latin America, Asia, and Africa) have become interdependent aspects of her public persona, Jo Littler has argued: "'Do-gooding' becomes both a facet of her image and one of a range of Angelina Jolie's 'real-life roles' that can be discussed. The specific type of charity and humanitarian work is significant here too. Its transnationalism indicates a globalized sensibility and a cosmopolitan caring, an effect augmented by Jolie's high-profile Benetton-style adoption of a range of differently shaded children from a variety of different countries. And her engagement with politically sensitive subjects such as refugees, environmentalism and Darfur marks her as a very modern breed of American liberal" (Littler 2008, 238).

Discussing the inherent theatricality of celebrity humanitarianism, Lilie Chouliaraki has compared Jolie with and distinguished her from the performative conventions of earlier styles of celebrity advocacy, in particular that of UNICEF ambassador Audrey Hepburn in the 1980s. Defining the latter's humanitarian persona as centered on strategies of "de-celebritization" and "unconditional altruism," Chouliaraki describes Jolie's performative register as follows: "Jolie's strategies construe a different persona, which rests on: *hyper-celebritization*, an intensification of her celebrity persona . . . , and a process of ethicalization that promotes a utilitarian altruism" (Chouliaraki 2012, 10).

Difret provides a good case study to observe and illustrate the performative strategies that Chouliaraki identifies. In the first instance, the film encourages a slippage between Jolie's screen and public personae and *Difret*'s central character, Meaza. The latter is not dissimilar to the confident, glamorous, and self-assured female protagonists that Jolie has been portraying throughout her acting career, and like Meaza, Jolie is a passionate campaigner for humanitarian causes. Before *Difret*, Jolie had portrayed a humanitarian aid worker in Ethiopia in the 2003 film *Beyond Borders* (Martin Campbell, USA). The latter film ends with Jolie's character becoming an ambassador for UNHCR, another instance of blurring the distinction between Jolie's screen and public personae. In these respects, then, Jolie's professional and philanthropic background creates an intertextual connection to the story *Difret* tells.

Although Jolie was "merely" one of the film's executive producers, she played a prominent part in the marketing of the film to the extent that it was often perceived and referred to by critics as a film "by" Angelina Jolie. This misperception is not surprising given that the theatrical trailer prominently displays only Jolie's name, relegating the director and screenwriter alongside the other producers to the small print. Similarly, the DVD cover prefaces the film title with "Angelina Jolie Presents" and features a quote by Jolie declaring that this is "a movie that could lead to change. Everyone should watch it." Jolie also recorded an introduction to the film that is included as a bonus feature on the DVD. Addressing the audience, Jolie begins by saying that "it is a great honor to introduce to you the remarkable film *Difret*," before continuing in a calm voice and with a serious expression: "When I first saw this film I was moved to tears by the story that they managed to show: the sad and the hopeful, the old and the new, the harmful tradition of *telefa*, and the possibility that culture can change. . . . Films like these are so important to continue to support and to make, as they help us all to push the art of filmmaking forward, and shed light on untold stories, about Ethiopia and beyond. Thank you, and enjoy the film."

What is quite clear about this introduction is that although Jolie elsewhere recommends that "everyone should watch" *Difret*, the audience she addresses is a primarily Western public. Her comments veer between the specific (she mentions *telefa* as if she had known about this practice for a long time) and vague generalizations ("the sad and the hopeful, the old and the new, Ethiopia and beyond"). She states her solidarity with her fellow professional film community around the world ("they help us all to push the art of filmmaking forward") and acknowledges her privileged position in being in a financial position to offer assistance ("films like these are so important to continue to support"). She speaks of the "possibility that culture can change," even though she does not offer any concrete suggestion of how that might happen. More than just speaking as an executive producer, Jolie performs the role of a mediator to or enabler of a cosmopolitan ethics with which a liberal Western audience can identify and connect. The employment of generalizations on the theme of a common humanity is an essential discursive strategy in this respect, as Chouliaraki has noted: "Rather than providing didactic exhortations of the 'you should help the poor' type, such quotes 'impersonate' this disposition: they perform a discourse that, through references to an undefinable 'everybody,' presupposes the altruistic disposition as an already existing virtue not only of the celebrity herself, but also of her publics—hence the 'aspirational' nature of the discourse" (Chouliaraki 2012, 2–3).

Also in line with Chouliaraki's categorization of Jolie's performative register is the latter's recourse to emotions ("When I first saw the film I was moved to tears"). Describing Jolie's acting out the "passionate witness," Chouliaraki has noted that the spontaneous expression of emotion is essential in confirming the celebrity's authenticity, but she casts doubts over this mode's efficacy in truly generating social change: "The confessional style of humanitarianism may not actually work as a force of moralization in the West. Insofar as its communicative structure prioritizes the 'authentic' emotions of the celebrity and our own connectivity towards her, it encourages a narcissistic disposition of voyeuristic altruism rather than one of commitment to the humanitarian cause" (Chouliaraki 2012, 17).

After *Difret* was first shown at Sundance, the film's worthy content and its association with Jolie as executive producer won it a certain amount of goodwill and sympathy, if not necessarily critical acclaim. Dennis Harvey in *Variety* noted that the film presented "an important message in clunky narrative terms" where "everything is spelled out in pedestrian fashion" (Harvey 2014), while Leslie Felperin in the *Guardian* found "the acting . . . a bit ropey and the script . . . a little too on-the-nose at times" (Felperin 2015). Yet, despite some lukewarm reviews (alongside more positive ones), *Difret* achieved one of its key goals in attracting attention to the issue of women's and girls' rights in Ethiopia, perhaps most prominently when the film was featured on CNN on the occasion of President Obama's historic visit to Ethiopia in 2015. However, it was not Bekele who was interviewed by CNN's Christiane Amanpour, but Ashenafi and producer Mehret Mandefro (Amanpour 2015).

Indeed, despite the film's insistence on being based on a true story, the filmmakers had not contacted Bekele before making the film, nor had they asked for her permission, nor was her name mentioned anywhere in the publicity for the film. Nor was there any acknowledgment by the filmmakers of Metcalf's original documentary. Thus when Bekele was granted a last-minute injunction against

Difret being shown in Ethiopia, she was backed up by Metcalf, who in an open letter declared that she was "horrified" about "people squabbling over the story rights." She continued, "This is a true story that I have already told and Aberash and I and all the people involved in the making of the documentary would appreciate some recognition of the fact that we brought this story into the public domain well over a decade ago" (Metcalf 2014).

Metcalf's intervention may have been motivated by a wish for professional or personal recognition; Bekele's own reasons for taking on the filmmakers were somewhat ambiguous. In an interview with US magazine *Time*, Bekele suggested that "I was at a place where my life was still in danger, and I felt like the film coming out would put my life at risk" (Luscombe 2015). Yet in an interview with the British *Daily Mail*, the main complaint appeared to be that Bekele was "angry at the filmmakers for using her story without her consent, and failing, initially, to pay her compensation" (Creighton 2015). It is certain that a financial motive played a part in Bekele's actions. As Bekele revealed in the above *Time* interview, her life since the late 1990s has remained financially precarious. Having worked as a housemaid in Dubai, Bekele has recently returned to Ethiopia, where she had begun working for Harmee, an NGO that tackles violence against women in Bekele's home province of Arsi (Metcalf 2015a). According to the *Ethiopia Observer*, the grounds for the lawsuit to ban the showing of *Difret* were Bekele's claims "that the film, *Difret*, which was taken from her life story gave way too much focus to Meaza Ashenafi, the lawyer who defended her, leading her to take the legal action in an attempt to get her credit back and unspecified amount of compensation" (Fantahun 2014a). After an out-of-court settlement, the ban on *Difret* was lifted. Metcalf later claimed that "Bekele ultimately signed an agreement, which means she feels unable to complain or take further action," but Metcalf quotes her saying that the experience of *Difret* left her "doubly abducted" (Metcalf 2015a).

Bekele's out-of-court settlement was not the end to *Difret*'s legal troubles in Ethiopia. New objections to the film were raised by the family of the late Etagegnehu Lemessa, Bekele's defense barrister in the original trial, who felt that *Difret* "distorted" their late relative's contribution to the case (Fantahun 2014b). Indeed, although the character does appear in *Difret*, Lemessa plays a decidedly secondary role to Ashenafi. By this time, Angelina Jolie may well have had an acute sense of déjà vu, as many of the controversies over *Difret* (victims feeling misrepresented, claims of "stolen" stories) echoed those she had experienced following her 2011 directorial debut about the Bosnian conflict, *In the Land of Blood and Honey* (Child 2011).

In an interview with an Italian journalist a few months after the injunctions in Ethiopia, director Mehari said that he first heard of the case of "Hirut Assefa" (still using the fictional name after the court cases and not mentioning

Bekele's once) through Ashenafi, whom he had met through the latter's brother back in 2005 (de Franceschi 2015). At no point does Mehari acknowledge the existence of Metcalf's documentary. Towards the end of the interview, Mehari directly addresses the legal issues the film encountered in Ethiopia with counterclaims that contradict both Bekele's and Metcalf's accounts: "The legal challenges the film has encountered stems [*sic*] from an organized effort to discredit Meaza's work and legacy on the case we chronicle in the film. Human rights lawyers are often not popular in the countries where they challenge the customs and traditions and Ethiopia is no different. The film was initially banned for allegedly giving 'too much credit' to Meaza, but there was no legal grounding for the claim nor was it valid so the ban was lifted" (de Franceschi 2015).

The controversies surrounding *Difret* are regrettable as Bekele's inspirational story remains a crucial beacon for social change, as the battle over women's and girls' rights in Ethiopia is far from won. Indeed, as Metcalf points out, it is ironic that after a decade when the practice of marriage by abduction almost disappeared, new instances have been reported in recent years (Metcalf 2015a). Meanwhile, the indisputably important work of organizations such as EWLA has been facing increasing pressures and restrictions from the Ethiopian government. As Smith notes: "Unfortunately EWLA and many other excellent civil society organizations have had to scale back their activities in the wake of the Charities and Societies Proclamation, as well as anti-terrorism and media laws of 2009, all of which are intended to shrink non-state involvement in many of these types of citizen-creation activities" (Smith 2013, 83).

By 2010, it was reported that the then director of EWLA, Mahdere Paulos, had fled Ethiopia in fear of government retaliation (The Woyingi Blogger 2010). Ashenafi, meanwhile, had moved on to other ventures, including serving as women's rights advisor in the Division of Gender and Social Policy Development at the United Nations Economic Commission for Africa, and launching a bank "intended to contribute to women's economic empowerment and inclusive financial services" (Mohammed 2013).

Conclusion

Bekele's story and how it was transformed twice on the screen, first in a documentary and then in a mainstream drama, offers a number of insights into the way human rights issues can be raised and promoted through the medium of film. Neither film should be regarded as an "authentic" representation of a particular individual's story. Both are filmed from the perspective of outsiders and are addressed to a Western audience, and although my chapter title alludes to the original quote from Bekele that the experience of *Difret* left her "doubly abducted," one could legitimately ask whether *Schoolgirl Killer* too in its own (and arguably more complex) way instrumentalizes Bekele's story for its own ends. As I argued in my discussion of *Schoolgirl Killer*, Metcalf's film aims to portray Bekele as a new kind of heroine who is defined as much by her oppression as by her will to freedom and self-determination. Mehari's film ultimately aims to raise awareness of the activities of the EWLA and Ashenafi's legacy more specifically, and adopts the biopic template and recourse to celebrity advocacy to make the film more palatable to its mainly Western audiences. Both films use stereotypes and generic conventions. But in the process of defining and redefining historical facts as ethical models and templates for the future, questions over the ownership of one's or a nation's story emerge and sometimes disrupt originally good intentions.

TIM BERGFELDER is Professor of Film Studies at the University of Southampton. He is coeditor (with Lisa Shaw and João Luiz Vieira) of *Stars and Stardom in Brazilian Cinema*.

Filmography

Beyond Borders, 2003, Martin Campbell, USA.
The Cutting Edge, 1996, Charlotte Metcalf, UK.
Difret, 2015, Zeresenay Mehari, Ethiopia / USA.
In the Land of Blood and Honey, 2011, Angelina Jolie, USA.
Lamb, 2015, Yared Zeleke, Ethiopia / Germany / France / Norway / Qatar.
Once Upon a Time in the West, 1968, Sergio Leone, Italy / USA.
Schoolgirl Killer, 1999, Charlotte Metcalf, UK.
Welcome to Womanhood, 1998, Charlotte Metcalf, UK.
Young Wives' Tales, 1998, Charlotte Metcalf, UK.

References

Amanpour, Christiane. 2015. "Transcripts: Ethiopian Film Tells Story of Kidnapped Girl." CNN. July 28. Accessed April 11, 2017. http://transcripts.cnn.com/TRANSCRIPTS/1507/28/ampr.01.html.

Child, Ben. 2011. "Angelina Jolie Sued Over *In the Land of Blood and Honey*." *Guardian*, December 6. Accessed March 31, 2017. https://www.theguardian.com/film/2011/dec/06/angelina-jolie-sued-land-blood.

Chouliaraki, Lilie. 2012. "The Theatricality of Humanitarianism: A Critique of Celebrity Advocacy." *Communication and Critical/Cultural Studies* 9 (1): 1–21. doi:10.1080/147914 20.2011.637005.

———. 2013. *The Ironic Spectator: Solidarity in the Age of Post-Humanitarianism.* Cambridge: Polity Press.

Creighton, Sam. 2015. "Angelina Jolie's Film Exploits My Rape Agony." *Daily Mail*, April 24. Accessed March 31, 2017. http://www.dailymail.co.uk/news/article-3054647/Angelina -Jolie-s-film-exploited-rape-agony-says-Ethiopian-girl-wasn-t-told-Hollywood-star -using-story.html.

de Franceschi, Leonardo. 2015. "An Ethiopian Story. A Conversation with Zeresenay Berhane Mehari." *CinemAfrica. Africa e diaspora nel cinema*, January 18. Accessed March 31, 2017. http://www.cinemafrica.org/page.php?article1526.

Fantahun, Arefayné. 2014a. "Ban on *Difret* Film Lifted." *Ethiopia Observer*, September 29. Accessed March 31, 2017. http://www.ethiopiaobserver.com/2014/09/ban-on-difret-film -lifted/.

———. 2014b. "*Difret* Film Banned Again for Distorting Facts." *Ethiopia Observer*, October 31. Accessed March 31, 2017. http://www.ethiopiaobserver.com/2014/10/difret-film-banned -again-for-distorting-facts/.

Felperin, Leslie. 2015. "*Difret* Review." *Guardian*, March 5. Accessed March 31, 2017. https:// www.theguardian.com/film/2015/mar/05/difret-ethiopian-docudrama-rape-case.

Girls Not Brides. 2017. "Child Marriages around the World: Ethiopia." Accessed March 31, 2017. http://www.girlsnotbrides.org/child-marriage/ethiopia/.

Hanks, Robert. 1999. "*Schoolgirl Killer.*" *The Independent*, June 15. Accessed March 31, 2017. http://www.independent.co.uk/arts-entertainment/robert-hanks-television -review-1100456.html.

Harvey, Dennis. 2014. "Sundance Film Review: *Difret.*" *Variety*, January 24. Accessed March 31, 2017. http://variety.com/2014/film/global/sundance-film-review-difret-1201069956/.

Jedlowski, Alessandro. 2015. "Screening Ethiopia: A Preliminary Study of the History and Contemporary Developments of Film Production in Ethiopia." *Journal of African Cinemas* 7 (2): 169–85.

———. 2016. "Avenues of Participation and Strategies of Control: Video Film Production and Social Mobility in Ethiopia and Southern Nigeria." In *Production Studies, the Sequel! Cultural Studies of Global Media Industries*, edited by Miranda Banks, Bridget Conor, and Vicki Mayer, 175–86. New York and London: Routledge.

Littler, Jo. 2008. "I Feel Your Pain: Cosmopolitan Charity and the Public Fashioning of the Celebrity Soul." *Social Semiotics* 18 (2): 237–51. doi:10.1080/10350330802002416.

Luscombe, Belinda. 2015. "11 Questions with Aberash Bekele." *Time*, September 17. Accessed March 31, 2017. http://time.com/4038102/11-questions-with-aberash-bekele/.

Metcalf, Charlotte. 2003. *Walking Away. A Filmmaker's African Journal.* Much Wenlock: Eye Books, unpaginated e-book.

———. 2014. "*Difret* Film—A Decade Ago." *Ethiomedia*. September 16. Accessed March 31, 2017. http://www.ethiomedia.com/aug14/4108.

———. 2015a. "The Rape Victim Who Fought Back and Shamed a Nation." *Newsweek*, January 9. Accessed March 31, 2017. http://www.newsweek.com/2015/01/16/rape-victim -who-fought-back-and-shamed-a-nation-297757.html.

———. 2015b. *Woman's Hour*, BBC Radio 4, March 31. Accessed March 31, 2017. http://www .bbc.co.uk/programmes/b05nv240.

Mohammed, Nassir. 2013. "Meaza Ashenafi Mengistu." *Ethio-Nation*, August 15. Accessed March 31, 2017. http://www.ethionation.com/sites/biography/3511-meaza-ashenafi -mengistu.html.

Pankhurst, Helen. 1992. *Gender, Development and Identity. An Ethiopian Study*. London: Zed Books.

Smith, Lahra. 2013. *Making Citizens in Africa. Ethnicity, Gender, and National Identity in Ethiopia*. Cambridge: Cambridge University Press.

The Woyingi Blogger. 2010. "What happened to the Ethiopian Women Lawyers Association?" *The Woyingi Blog*, October 11. Accessed March 31, 2017. https://woyingi.wordpress.com/2010/10/11/what-happened-to-the-ethiopian-womens-lawyer-association/.

11 *Timbuktu* and "L'homme de haine"

Kenneth W. Harrow

Make my head into a figurehead
and as for me, my heart, do not make me into a father nor a brother
nor a son, but into the father, the brother, the son
nor a husband, but the lover of this unique people.
. . .
make me into the executor of these lofty works
the time has come to gird one's loins like a brave man—

But in doing so, my heart, preserve me from all hatred
do not make me into that man of hatred for whom I feel only hatred
for entrenched as I am in this unique race
you still know my tyrannical love
you know that it is not from hatred of other races
that I demand of myself to become a hoer for this unique race
that what I want
is for universal hunger
for universal thirst

to summon it to generate,
free at last, from its intimate closeness
the succulence of fruit.

> (Aimé Césaire, *Notebook of a Return to the Native Land* [1956] 2001, 37–38)[1]

How do we align ourselves? Is this question political, religious, racial? Is it a human rights question, or one that undermines human rights in their universalist aspirations by emphasizing identity politics? Various configurations of those identifying themselves as "we" have been marked in historical African struggles, at times struggles so vast as to encompass the fundamental questions of human freedom and rights.

The slave trade and the abolitionist cause shifted given notions of the enslaved so that eventually they were viewed in terms of race, although in the ancient and early modern periods it was not race but economic and political status that identified the subordinated[2]: plebian and patrician, serf and lord, peasant and noble. The term "master" might apply to the lord of the domain, to the member of the guild, to the rabbi, abbot, or maître of the medieval university, and so on. Every master had his apprentice, knecht, laborer, or servant—a word that in ancient languages was identical to slave. The root for servant-slave in Hebrew and Arabic is "abd," and in the appropriate forms of the name, one finds examples of "the one who serves the lord" (i.e., Allah or Adonai), such as Abdel and Abdallah, along with ebed or avad [עֶבֶד, عبد]. The slave, seemingly occupying the lowest status, acquires the legitimacy of the master and his rank. Servant warriors, like the generals of Imperial Byzantium or of Mamluk slave-rulers in medieval Egypt—like servants with names Abdallah—all complicate the question of low and high status, as in the Hegelian master-slave relationship where the apparent high status of the ruler is supplanted by the servant's work and consciousness. As servant aligned with race, the slave trade drove the logics of identitarian politics.

Césaire's call, in the opening epigraph from the *Cahier d'un retour au pays natal*, to be "the lover of this unique people," emerged from the soil of the Caribbean plantation that fostered gross categories of black, white, and mixed-race peoples (Young 1994), with refined subcategories—quadroons, octoroons, and so on—and further extensions of such racial delineations to all other peoples of the earth. Racial alignments shifted with the rise of empires and colonialism. Whereas racialism was in ascendancy through the eighteenth and nineteenth centuries, by the twentieth century it began to compete with emerging national identities as the basis for defining personhood. Nation-states and their wars for imperial domination supplanted the fight over slavery, which legally ended in the mid-nineteenth century. After the end of the Cold War, with the rise of globalization, dated religious conflicts, thought to belong to the mists of time, recurred. Wars between Christian and Muslim returned, as seen in the Lebanese civil wars. After the George W. Bush years, with the rising militancy of the jihadist movement, newly resurrected divisions within the Muslim community also resurfaced: contemporary Shiite and Sunni struggles for Middle Eastern regional control pitting Saudis against Iranians, have driven national or racial identities to the background. Cultural and religious alignments have become increasingly conflated.

As Daesh appeals resonate with North African and Middle Eastern youths, born with European nationality, the jihadist flag has given rise to anti-Western coalitions, the offspring of numerous wars in the Middle East. Since the Arab Spring, the conflict has diffused south to Kenya, Mali, Niger, and Burkina Faso. Wars in the Sudan, Chad, and the Central African Republic gave the religious alignment of the combatants the cast of universal difference, as race had once been in the eighteenth to twentieth centuries, when Césaire spoke of his tyrannical love for his people.

After World War II, universal rights were seen as the consequence of the just struggle for freedom. In Césaire's formulation—"ce que je veux / c'est pour la faim universelle / pour la soif universelle" (50) ("what I want / is for universal hunger / for universal thirst" [38]). In his *Discours sur le colonialisme,* he joined together the logics of antislavery and anticolonial struggles, projecting a future that would see the eventual end of slavery, colonialism, racism, and fascism. Negritude embraced this agenda. Cinema in Africa emerged at a time when anticolonialism, antiracism, and socialist Third Worldism were dominant. African cinema opened its salvos in the long wars for freedom by seeing alignments in terms of the righteousness of revolutionary struggle. In Ousmane Sembène's *Ceddo* (1977, Senegal), for instance, the righteous were the indigenous, "animist" ceddo warriors, overcome by the invading, allogeneous Moors and their Islamic, mostly white, mostly Arab, mostly foreign religion.

From the struggle for freedom in Angola, with Sarah Maldoror's *Sambizanga* (1972), to South Africa's *Mapantsula* (1988, Oliver Schmitz), to Sembène's *Emitaï* (1971, Senegal), *Camp de Thiaroye* (1988, Senegal / Algeria / Tunisia), and *Xala* (1975, Senegal), one version or another of this division can be seen in the vast majority of sub-Saharan films of the 1960s–1980s, where the degraded figures of *assimilés* were set against national liberationist heroes or martyrs. When that paradigm began to fade, as in *The Blue Eyes of Yonta* (1992, Flora Gomes, Guinea-Bissau / France / Portugal), for instance, it wasn't because the ideal of revolutionary justice had become eroded, but because of the actual failures of the FLN (the Algerian National Liberation Front) or their militant equivalents to adhere to the revolutionary ideals. Corruption and greed, failures of leadership, failed states and the new autocracy as delineated by Achille Mbembe were seen in the failure to adhere to the revolutionary ideals that had led to independence. The 1980s were a turning point, and by the end of the decade, the truly new face of African cinema was Nollywood's—an African cinema that, for the first time, was resolutely nonideological, nonengagé, neoliberal, and hungry for profits.

This long prelude over alignment is necessary because it is only by viewing this backdrop as a changing horizon that we can begin to assess contemporary films concerned with jihadism, nationalism, and the compromised struggle for freedom. Two films set off the shift in the frame—Issa Serge Coelo's *Daresalam* (2001, France / Burkina Faso / Chad) and Abderrahmane Sissako's *Timbuktu* (2014, France / Mauritania). While still deploying narratives and discourses grounded in the long centuries of struggles over ostensibly universal values of freedom, changes as vast as Hegel's reversals of power in the master-slave relationship have been taking place.

In its early years, the African cinema of Med Hondo, Sembène, and Sarah Maldoror, was basically grounded in Fanonian and Cesairean notions of struggle, freedom, oppression, and cooptation / compromise. Themes included assimilation to the West versus fidelity to the race and the blood, and courage and revolution versus oppression. Wealthy European slave dealers, corrupt capitalists, arrogant colonialists, and greedy neocolonialists defined the cast of characters of most of the films of the first wave of African cinema. Subsequently, a new generation, including Jean-Pierre Bekolo, Jean-Marie Teno, and Fanta Régina Nacro, prepared the ground for Mahamat-Saleh Haroun and Sissako, who turned their gaze toward their own national rulers, even as they challenged the consequences of globalization. In place of the revolution (e.g., *Sambizanga*; *Mortu Nega*, 1988, Flora Gomes, Guinea-Bissau) or disillusionment with the current state of *commandement* or autocracy (e.g., *Finye*, 1982, Souleymane Cissé, Mali), new ways of celebrating the glories of African culture arose, as in Sissako's *La Vie sur terre* (*Life on Earth*, 1998, Mali / Mauritania / France) and *Heremakono: Waiting for Happiness* (2002, France / Mauritania). A kind of neo-Negritude vision presented the soul, music, dance, arts, and humanity of the common people (e.g., *Grigris*, 2013, Mahamat-Saleh Haroun, Chad / France)—with the grace of the griot, the griotte, and her musicality.

Chad and Mali, two arenas for violent struggle, provide the stage for the agonistic encounter between dystopic warfare and local humanist visions of love, artistry, and righteousness. They serve as the backdrop for Coelo's and Sissako's opposing narratives: at the outset *Daresalam* presents the case for the call for revolution and jihad against an oppressive government; and from the outset *Timbuktu* rejects the jihad and its pretentions to serve a higher cause in overthrowing the national government. Both films appeal to the soil, to autochthonous values, and to just solutions to human conflict or deprivation; both hold to a vision of higher ideals, to the opposition to repressive forces; yet both come to quite different representations of historical justice. This was not the case when Sembène set out to give definition to an African notion of commitment.

The engaged African film begins, as with *Xala*, by defining the antagonist as the target of the struggle. In Sembène's "night school," the opposition to oppression needed a language, and the first few words that stuttered out its protocols were needed to define where the enemy's forces were located. Over time, Sembène modified his Manichaean vision, but the conventional figures of oppression and resistance had to be identified. Typically they included French ruling figures, like the French generals in *Camp de Thiaroye* or the officers in *Emitaï*. In *Ceddo* it was another foreign oppressive figure, the repellent Moor imam, set against the beautiful, patriotic princess; the French slave trader was also present in the background. The heroes, too, could be easily identified, as with the leaders of the railroad strike in his novel *Bouts de bois de dieu* (*God's Bits of Wood*, [1960] 1970). In beginning with conflict, with clearly identifiable protagonists and antagonists, the model of similar films, like the American Western, could be generated, as with the establishing shots of *Xala* or with Gaston Kaboré's *Wend Kuuni* (1982, Burkina Faso).

The conventions of classic Hollywood cinema typically entailed, early in the film, the introduction of an obstacle to the protagonist's path, a secondary plot that required resolution before the primary goal could be achieved. Finally, the love interest was at the heart of this resolution and secondary plot, and inevitably the film would bring closure to the central conflict.

Both *Daresalam* and *Timbuktu* begin with easily recognizable contexts that set out the basis for oppression and resistance. In both cases it is the ruling powers that quickly demonstrate their abusive nature, calling for heroic stances to oppose them. It would seem almost irrelevant that in *Daresalam* the call for heroic resistance is answered by the rebel group FRAP (Revolutionary Front of the People's Army), marked as a righteous movement since its members, at least in part, are observant Muslims, in contrast to the evil government that proves itself abusive from the outset. The path to resistance is laid out; the war must follow; the plot functions so as to explain it all and to lead us to the conclusions to be drawn. The ending must bring the inevitable closure.

Timbuktu is practically identical to the classic realist film in following this structure, although the actors' roles are reversed in the two films. The opening oppressive gestures, the imposition of force on ordinary folks, are here carried out by the rebels themselves, a group whose identity is tied to its religious appurtenances rather than ethnic, national, or racial typing. The resistance must be mounted; the love interest must be exposed and ultimately brought to its conclusion; the consequences must be understood at the end so that, in both cases, knowing how to forge a political consciousness becomes possible. The ending may be tragic, but the real sense of its closure lies in the truth the films both ask us to embrace. We can understand, and thus ultimately are able to act so as to oppose the evil forces exposed to us as the film develops its initial narrative threads. The roles of master and slave and their clothing and appearances are all highly legible. We are presented with the choice of resisting them as an obligation, and certainly not as a posture. At the end of Haroun's *Daratt* (2006, Chad / France / Belgium / Austria), Atim fires his gun in the air rather than shoot his father's killer, Nassara. He walks off with the blind grandfather who sent him on the mission. A horizon in the desert provides the setting for opacity, blindness, and patriarchy. The vengeance of the cowboy movie is denied. The endings of *Daresalam* and of *Timbuktu* are not of that nature.

Daresalam practices a feint or sleight of hand by sidestepping the question of how to accomplish the goals of the revolution without falling into what Fanon terms in chapter three of *The Wretched of the Earth* ([1961] 1968) the "pitfalls of the national consciousness" and the demise of the revolution's ideals.[3] The celebratory joy that breaks out spontaneously in *The Battle of Algiers* (1966, Gillo Pontecorvo, Italy / Algeria), when the flag is waved, the crowd dances, and a new day begins for the formerly colonized people, remains untainted in that classic revolutionary film with its ending with the pronouncement that independence was finally won. *Xala* opens with that moment of joyful celebration. However, eventually the protagonist, El Hadj, proves to be corrupt, and at the end he is impotent and ulti-mately suffers a demeaning ritual. In the final scene of his "exorcism," he might be thought to have come through a trial by fire so as to be cured, but the image of his body covered by spittle mostly evokes the humiliation of the former patriot who had fought for his country's freedom and failed to live up to its ideals. Similar dis-couraging endings might be seen in *Bamako* (2006, Sissako, Mali / USA / France), *The Blue Eyes of Yonta* (1992), or even *O Heroi* (2004, Zézé Gamboa, Angola). In *Un homme qui crie* (*A Screaming Man*, 2010, France / Belgium / Chad), Haroun makes no real effort to deflate the stature of the protagonist "Champion" since he is never really represented as patriotic. In the end his son Abdel dies before his father can save him, bringing the bleakness of the dry season, which is also the literal meaning of *Daratt*. The sons in both Haroun films no longer seem able to succeed to the place of their fathers. And as *A Screaming Man* comes later in Haroun's corpus, four years after *Daratt*, it is striking that its tone has darkened, that the imperatives of war and destruction are not seen as events marking the past but continue to shape the present world of globalization as represented in the Chinese-owned swimming pool in *A Screaming Man*.

With the ending of *Daresalam*, Djimi rejoices at the birth of his child, sym-bolically announcing the coming of a new order before that order has actually appeared on the horizon. This might be said, as well, of Cissé's endings to *Finye* and *Yeelen* (1987, Mali / Burkina Faso / France / West Germany / Japan), with the heavy symbolism of the child carrying the burden of a false closure, or a posta-pocalytic moment. This is also the case of the ending of the Afro-futurist short film *Pumzi* (2009, Wanuri Kahiu, South Africa / Kenya) where the "mother" sacrifices herself in order that new life on earth might become possible. Djimi's celebration follows his decision to quit the rebellion and return home, having learned, a little like Candide, that the best advice he can give at this moment is to cultivate his garden and to try to accept his losses, which include the death of his mother and his best friend, Koni. Koni had defected from the revolution-ary movement FRAP, which he and Djimi had initially joined, and opted to join the government, seeking to effect gradual change and diplomatic dialogue rather than militancy and fighting. With Djimi's decision to return home rather than to rejoin his comrades, and Koni's death announced toward the end, the failures of the revolutionary uprising are cemented.

> the time has come to gird one's loins like a brave man—
> But in doing so, my heart, preserve me from all hatred
> do not make me into that man of hatred for whom I feel only hatred (Césaire
> [1956] 2001, 37)[4]

Timbuktu also ends with deaths that signal the ultimate failure of the insurgent movement—in this case the jihadists'. After the execution of the parents, Kidane and Satima, the portrayal of the children serves to depict the moral failure of the jihadists' venture: we see the disoriented daughter Toya running helplessly over the dunes, as though our sympathies for her could only ever be accomplished by having the jihadists dislodged from the center of African civilization—in this case, the ancient city of Timbuktu.

We can't see the final images of Toya running lost over the dunes without feeling both sadness for her and extreme anger at the brutality of the killing of her parents. The twin affects of sorrow and anger arise from the injustice and from the ambivalence of the circumstances that led to Kidane's condemnation, to the double injustice of fate that led to the encounters between brutal gunmen and the sensitive Tuareg musician. Kidane's speech and musicianship, the attractiveness of his family and of his own appearance, all set him off from the jihadists whose boots first are seen soiling the mosque and whose guns' opening salvos are used to decimate the Dogon statues, disrupting the echoes of music, the beauties of Timbuktu's life, culture, and religion. The message is, unfortunately, as clear as the liberal values that define the Malian world that this film is intended to extol.

The sensitive hand of Sissako in delineating the nuances of an African aesthetic, in *Heremakono* and especially *La Vie sur terre*, are also rehearsed here—his songs of praise, his encomiums for Malian and Mauritanian culture, for the people who live on the borders of the desert and share its particular splendors. We are made to agonize over the pointless destruction carried out by those who excuse their dominion by evoking an empty notion of religion. At times the emptiness is simply because the adherents demonstrate repeatedly their indifference to the religious injunctions they are supposed to be imposing on the population of Timbuktu, but it is more because they are never really presented as though there were a serious case to be made. The quote above of Césaire, which Sissako would normally have been identified with, that he is not a man of hatred, *un homme de haine*, is undermined by the film's classic protagonists and antagonists, obstacles placed on the path of the protagonist, and the closure—especially the closure.

To be sure, as I have argued elsewhere (Cazenave et al., 2016), the jihadists are humanized, and Sissako was criticized for this. They are not depicted as demons, but rather as ordinary people who refrain from acts of butchering, for much of the film. But as the series of commands, acts of resistance, and resulting sympathetic alignment of the audience with the conquered people of Timbuktu become clearer, the delineation of victim-oppressor is accentuated. We move toward the scene of the stoning of the adulterers, with all the inexorableness of the classic Hollywood narrative. And once they are stoned to death, the secondary plot involving Kidane's inadvertent killing of Amadou takes on the appearance of an ineluctable tragedy, where the price to be paid for establishing a proper order at the end will have to be the deaths of the beautiful, loving couple: the ideal figures of an Africa toward which the negritude poet had turned.

As we are instructed to learn the underlying horrors of what the jihadists' movement will entail, we are compelled to join in the poet's enthusiasm and love for what is being destroyed. The poet, as surrogate for Dramane in *La Vie sur terre*, speaks *sotto voce* in the songs, the music that echoes against the walls of Timbuktu. He writes, "you still know my tyrannical love / you know that it is not from hatred of other races" (Césaire [1956] 2001, 38). As Toya's pitiful dashing at the end echoes the flight of the beautiful gazelle that the jihadists try to shoot at the beginning, we are introduced from the outset to a cinema of an "amour tyrannique" that has to stand against those who set out to destroy it. "*La haine tyrannique*," one might say, is developed as each scene generates a sense of understanding how "amour tyrannique" works to present before our eyes the spectacle of magical movements, music, dance, and poiesis. When Zabou, the mad Haitian woman, strides indomitably down the alleyways of the city, impeding the movement of the jihadists' vehicles, we are drawn to her, repelled by them. The invasion of the city at the outset sets up similar oppositions, and the film appears to be simply a working out of the logic based on the binary oppression-resistance.

The ending brings certainty that the culture of Timbuktu was special, yet another example of the poiesis that the people of Mali and Mauritania and the cultures of the region had been able to forge. But this time the threat did not originate with the West, the colonialists, or even the global order, but rather with the guns and dull fanaticism of jihadism.

> make me into the executor of these lofty works
> the time has come to gird one's loins like a brave man— (Césaire [1956] 2001, 37)[5]

To arrive at this ending, Sissako takes, in fact, the opposite narrative trajectory of Coelo. In *Daresalam* the identities of the "peasants" and the "government" are laid out in the initial town hall meeting. There the brutal government official, surrounded by armed guards and speaking in French, proves condescending and arrogant, distant from the "simple" Arabophone villagers. He angrily demands that Chief Ali have all the peasants pay up, despite Ali's reasonable, patient plea that both the tax and repayment of the debt loan exceeded their ability to pay. When the guards begin to belabor the villagers, Koni throws a spear at the commanding officer, hitting him in the stomach. Koni flees, setting up the confrontation with the government.

Meanwhile, Djimi, Koni's closest friend in the village, has come across the rebels of FRAP as he and his mother seek help for a sick baby at a dispensary in another town. The rebels treat them respectfully and give information on the dangers of the road. On their return, they discover the government soldiers have attacked their village. Djimi would seem to have no choice but to join the rebels, especially as the baby has died on their trip back from the dispensary. He reunites with Koni, the brave figure of resistance, and learns to become a soldier for FRAP.

The bare bones of this opening set of scenes are laid out schematically, as though a lesson were being taught. It lacks especially the subtleties and cinematic beauties that grace Sissako's more refined mise-en-scène and narrative. Thus, in *Timbuktu* when the jihadists enter the city and march, armed and booted, into the mosque, their encounter with the imam, just like their confrontation with the woman fishmonger at the market, is met with an admirable and courageous resistance, which they hear without responding like the government soldiers and commanding officer in *Daresalam*. Even the leaders of FRAP in *Daresalam* speak as though reciting wooden revolutionary rhetoric out of a manual; the jihadist leader in *Timbuktu* never resorts to fixed clichés.

The logic of Coelo's simpler, purer narrative, ironically, leads him to an ambiguous ending. Djimi has learned of the moral failings of the rebellion and returns home, bringing a new wife to his family. The film concludes with Djimi's joy when she gives birth to a new child. The ending of *Daresalam* could not be more different from that of *Timbuktu*, which is filled with Toya's inchoate running and despair. We might ask why Sissako, himself like Césaire, who refuses to be "un homme de haine," would have built such a classic, well-made narrative when the signature of his earlier work was always its greater political subtleties.

At almost every point *Daresalam* seems a simpler, more straightforward film than *Timbuktu*, yet it refuses to lead us to the classic moment of truth, which we might see now as haunting Sissako's work. A few examples of the narrative logics demonstrate this. In order to set off the rebellion, Coelo has the issue of oppressive tax collection painstakingly elaborated. Djimi's father celebrates having had a good harvest, yet after paying his taxes, he finds he doesn't have enough left to pay off his share of the national loan, and he asks Chief Ali to wait—as other peasants appear also to have done. The commanding officer, who bought Chief Ali's grain at a low rate and who had treated him with disdain and menacing words, now returns to insist on the full payment. This is followed by the minister of the interior, who returns to Galbal to be greeted with the usual welcome from the "petits gens," the peasants located far from the capital. When the minister begins talking, he raises his arms and speaks to the men of the villages in imitation of De Gaulle: "Je suis content que vous soyez tous présents à cette importante rencontre" ("I am happy that you are all present here at this important meeting"). Like the "commandement" so well described by Achille Mbembe, he speaks the official language of power, government French, denoting the continuities of colonial authority that is now vested in the abusive strictures of the central government. He is an easy target for the audience to despise, and indeed De Gaulle is mocked in almost identical terms in Teno's *Afrique, je te plumerai* (1992, Cameroon / France / Germany). He continues to address the crowd as the "big man," intoning, "Le président de la République vous salue beaucoup" ("The president of the Republic greets you a lot"). Then the gross dimensions of power make their appearance—something we do not see in *Timbuktu* until after Kidane has killed Amadou. The minister tells those refusing to pay their debt to take two steps forward. We expect them to be beaten. But then he orders his soldiers to execute Chief Ali. Brutally and quickly. One man shouts out in Chadian Arabic, "Death won't stop us." Just as Koni had launched his spear at the commanding officer earlier, now the population seems to move into open revolt.

At just this moment, in a cross-cut we see Djimi returning with his mother to bury the baby, while Koni flees from Galbal with soldiers in pursuit. They meet and Djimi joins him. In a dramatic shot, as they take flight, we see Djimi pausing on the ridge as the soldiers are about to appear.

Djimi and Koni disappear, and in a short, jarring sequence we see someone who might be Djimi's mother being abused by the soldiers, evidently raped and left for dead. Here in the early movement of the narrative, we understand how the revolt had to take place, how the evil soldiers and government must come down. But by the end, that no longer seems a real possibility, and when Djimi learns of what happened to his mother, he takes the news with more resignation than revolt, learning to move on, and even shortly thereafter to rejoice when his son is born.

In *Bamako*, when the Ghanaian woman dies in the desert trying to make it to Europe, Sissako does not transform the film into an action film or a melodrama, but he incorporates the account of her death into the testimony at the mock trial. The vivid description serves to awaken an awareness in the population that is listening with rapt attention—and indirectly in us, the spectators of the film— as we learn how this tragic death was a consequence of the horrific policies of the World Bank. Our anger is then translated into the lawyers' summary words, highlighting the injustices and pain in direct rhetoric, something like a harangue in which the meaning and immorality of the public policies of the World Bank and its engines are condemned roundly. In all this, there is not the slightest doubt or subtlety. In this regard *Bamako* is divided against itself in that Chaka's death and the departure of Mele—the key events that mark the lives of the two central characters—leave us with the uncertainty of not knowing why he committed suicide or she had to leave, and whether these events were related or not. What we do have is the unforgettably heartbreaking singing she performs in the club and her sadness in dancing with what might be a client, along with Chaka's tenderness and despair. They function as poetic figures enacting the drama of pain inflicted under all the conditions evoked in the trial, and thus as parallels to the trials of an Africa described by the lawyers orating in high dudgeon over the abuse.

Similarly, in *Heremakono* Sissako creates scenes marked by melancholic tones at the site of those departing for Europe from Nouadhibou. Never once are the broad economic and political conditions offered as explanations. We have to infer the reasons for the deaths, for the mourning over the losses. When Maata, who has adopted Khatra, explains to Michael, who is about to embark on the dangerous sea journey to Europe, that he hates departures, that he would not leave, even when his friend offered to pay his way, we understand something of the logic of Boubacar Boris Diop's novel *Doomi Golo* (*The Hidden Notebooks*, [1983] 2016), or Moussa Traoré's *La Pirogue* (2012, France / Senegal / Germany), that there are those who choose to leave and those who are left behind. And that a trail of death surrounds these journeys from their inception to their sad conclusions. There is no classic exposition offered or needed in Sissako's narratives of suffering or celebration. Rather, the ineffable music and dance, the suggestive tales Maata tells, and above all the intimacy, all suggest, gesture, and gently perform their dances. This quality is there throughout *Timbuktu*, but now subordinated to a clear intention to inform and instruct.

Three scenes that adumbrate the conclusion flesh out this intention: the sequel following the fight between Kidane and Amadou, the dance of the jihadist at Zabou's at the time of the stoning of the adulterous couple, and the concluding deaths of Kidane and Salimata.

Kidane and Amadou's fight ends with the death of Amadou. The long shots that follow constitute one of the most memorable series of shots in all of African cinema. The scene is, in fact, spectacular, leading one to ask how to read spectacle in a Sissako film. The two qualities of Sissako's cinema that have shone in the past, and garnered him considerable praise, have been the ineffably light touch marking his cinematography, and especially the effect generated by intimacy. Both have served his overall project of celebrating Africa's beauty, from the dunes of Mauretania and Mali to the close, warm relations between adult and child, parental figures, teachers and apprentices, or even the kindnesses and gentleness of those less closely tied.

One thinks especially of the magic generated between Khatra and Maata, between the young girl and her singing tutor, the neighboring griotte, in *Heremakono*. By the end the girl's voice has become trained, the melismas mastered, fluttering and moving like the flutes or koras that form the musical backdrop. Typically Sissako avoids melodramatic emotional expressions, tight close-ups, and sensational moments. Spectacle is implicit in the landscape's own beauties, not in the cinematic acrobatics: the dead woman in the desert, with the insects crawling on the sand, bring us close to her tragic fate. We do not close in on her eyes or ears; there is no entry into the graphic and vulgar materiality of the body, as in the amputated ear in *Blue Velvet* (1986, David Lynch, USA), where the camera's intense close-up exposes the ants entering the ear's canal. Nor does Sissako portray a razor slitting an eye, or a gunshot with the bullet in flight (*Tears of the Black Tiger*, 2000, Wisit Sasanatieng, Thailand), the torn flesh of a Tarantino moment.

Yet in *Timbuktu* we approach all these moments, as if the obscenity that the Greeks deemed unfit for representation on-stage could no longer be avoided.

Nothing in the first half of the film crosses the line between off-stage (ob-skena) and on-stage, but the mise-en-scène prepares us for what follows. The fishmonger in the market holds out her hand, taunting the jihadists with her defiance; the man whose clothing offends simply removes his pants, which are deemed too short. The imam repeatedly challenges the jihadists to behave with religious decorum, to observe the humane values he sees as central to Islam. He appears immune, but it is early in the occupation.

Despite the resistance, the invading jihadists will not decamp: the marriage between the Nigerian fighter and the woman he wants will have to go through, despite her tears and the mother's pleas; the adulterous couple, buried up to their heads in the sand, will be stoned to death, and we will have to see the stones launched. If it isn't the direct spectacle, or the gross Hollywoodian displays of violence that mark each killing, if we are misled at the outset into imagining jihadism is not precisely what the West vulgarly wants to label terrorism—because the kidnapped man is given his medicine, because Satima is not raped by her jihadist suitor Abdelkarim, because the mad Haitian Zabou gets away with her gestures of defiance when she marches bare-headed in front of the jihadists' four by four—in the end we understand that all of these scenes were merely narrative ploys intended to heighten the effect of the stoning, and especially of the final killing of Kidane and Satima. As such, then, the subtlety actually heightens the melodrama and the spectacle, signaling something of a shift in Sissako's work in the direction of the classic Hollywood film, whose subplots and foreshadowings have always served a similar function to intensify the effect at the climactic moments.

There are a few key moments that demonstrate this shift—and as such show the radical difference between *Timbuktu* and *La Vie sur terre*, though I would argue it is also true of *Heremakono* as well. In the first scene, Kidane, now armed despite Satima's pleas that he leave the gun behind, confronts Amadou in the river. They struggle, a shot is heard, and for a moment, as both men fall, we are uncertain who has been shot. Then Kidane staggers off, and Amadou stumbles and falls. The camera draws back, and the most spectacular shot in Sissako's canon emerges, as though the action were merely to prepare us for what follows.

Narratively this scene prepares us for the tragedy of his death, where the circumstances and brutality of Islamic justice combine to destroy the beautiful family to which we were introduced at the outset of the film. But in parallel fashion, the scene illustrates the immense distance between Kidane and Amadou, between killer and victim, between the nomadic Tuareg herdsman and the sedentary Songhay fisherman, between the two conventionally understood pillars of Timbuktu's people, the people of the desert and the people of the river, the people who had known power and slave-dealing, the people who had newly acquired power and turned the tables on their former masters, the people associated with the north and lighter-skinned populations, the darker people closer to

Figure 11.1. Kidane wading across the Niger. Framegrab from *Timbuktu* (2014, Abderrahmane Sissako, France / Mauritania).

the sub-Saharan populations—in other words, the two worlds that comprised the conventionally understood universe of the Sahel—who now are split in two. And if it was not caused by Islamism—in fact, both communities are Muslim—or by jihadism, since in fact there were many on both sides of any of the religious divides, it echoed the deeper history brought about during the time of colonialism and especially its aftermath that saw the gradual diminution not to say demise of Tuareg hegemony. Hovering in the backdrop of this shot that reveals the tragic and splendor of the Niger and its inhabitants, the tensions implicit in autochthony and allogeneity over who belongs in the river or by the river, in the city or out of the city, is the conjunction with the arrival of new conquerors, almost none of whom belong. The one exception, who denies being from the region, is the interpreter for the judge, whom Kidane recognizes and identifies.

The convention of crossing a river isn't lost on the viewer. Kidane has crossed a threshold; the old life will have ended; the new will be formed in the wash of what was destroyed and lost. As he crosses, a mere figure lost in the distance and the great spaces of the water, the sound of the horns quietly comes up, evoking loss and misery. He pauses as he reaches the far shore. We can't perceive what he is doing or feeling at that moment; but the pause is pregnant, as it is clear that he has now put himself and his family into the hands of the Islamists and their justice, their power. Although he later commends himself into the hands of Allah, it is the judge sitting before him, whose language he doesn't share, who now controls whether he can see his daughter again and how his life will end. We draw increasingly close to him as he makes his final arguments for the disposition of his life; but in doing so we are engaged increasingly firmly in rejecting the judgment of those who will condemn him. Whatever ambiguity attended the moment of the shot, the responsibility for his and Amadou's acts, and the deeper history that united and divided them, is now resolved, clarified, and drawn into a truth that stands in opposition to the truths handed down by the Islamic court.

Kidane's staggering gait when he rises from the struggle with Amadou resolves itself into his sluggish stride through the water. The shot is in sepia tones, as if the moment were now increasingly entering into the past. The long shot provides the viewer with distance from him and his expression, although that is supplanted by the melancholic musical tones and the sound of birds. The music begins when he is halfway across. His crossing takes slightly more than a minute, during which we are to absorb the weighty import of what has transpired. If Timbuktu fell to these Islamists, whose precise identity and militia affiliations are left uncertain, but whose adherence the wider global audience will easily identify, so too is the sense of dread, sadness, and loss realized in this moment. As in the speeches at the trial in *Bamako*, on the one side stand the lawyers representing truth and justice, on the other, the defenders of a global, dominant, unjust order. The judges in *Bamako* sit high up in their robes and enact the gestures of a justice we know will never be carried out in the present world. So, too, does this scene convey the sense of a larger scheme of justice we are called to embrace, one where this dispute and its consequences might be evaluated fairly, and where the beautiful, tragic Tuareg family and its music, its life, might remain, might have a possibility to survive—where the Africa of the past and the present might not be destroyed.

But it is at the moments of destruction, when the couple are being stoned, when Kidane and Satima are shot, that the cinematic moment encapsulates the affect and the import—in short provides the fullness of the conjuncture, represented here by the encounters set up by the arrival of jihadism. Those conjunctures do not mark the West as overdetermining their meaning: the weapons and how the jihadists arrived, tracking from the north, from the fall of Khaddafi to the Tuareg militia movements, are not detailed. The foreignness of the jihadists and their clear familiarity with European languages and football are intended to convey their nonautochthonous identities; still, their numbers include speakers of Songhai or Tamachek, which the locals all can recognize. The dominant features of this conjuncture are now threaded by Al-Qaeda of the Maghreb, the various groups that have come to inhabit the desert, and the older elements of Timbuktu society and culture that cannot resist the new powers. And the representation that is deployed by Sissako signals his shifting in the direction of a purveyor of messages and truth.

The last scene of the film, to which I have often alluded, focuses on Toya, whose future has now become marked by loss. Although such loss had marked the young boy Khatra in *Heremakono* at the outset, when his forbidden singing and adoption by Maata signaled his origins in Saharoui lands, the future opens for him at the end of the film as he assumes his role as an electrician and a new child of an Africa not lost to emigration blues. In *Timbuktu*, the ending is quite the opposite. Toya's flight is chaotic and without direction. Her face now is seen

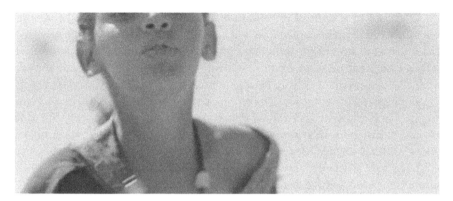

Figure 11.2. Toya fleeing in fear. Framegrab from *Timbuktu* (2014, Abderrahmane Sissako, France / Mauritania).

in medium-close-up, at times cropped by the frame so that we lose sight of parts of her head.

She groans in pain or fear. The scene is cross-cut with shots of Islamic soldiers chasing down the motorcycle rider who had brought Satima, and of the young boy adopted by Kidane, fleeing as well—all these figures running over the dunes like the gazelle being hunted at the beginning. The answer to the question of how we are to understand the conjuncture is completed. In contrast, the last shot of Khatra climbing a dune and making his way forward is open at the end of *Heremakono*.

The question is not which is better, or which works better, but what it means when a film like *Daresalam* avoids the certainties of closure, while *Timbuktu* embraces closure and spectacle, even under the most sympathetic of situations. Can *engagement* become a marker of the new school for African cinema, a neopolitical turn for a neoliberal age? And if so, might that same question be posed for a number of other film developments in Africa, most notably neo-Nollywood and its offshoots elsewhere? Does Sissako's turn represent a revision, or a rapprochement to the very neoliberalism he has been at such pains to critique throughout his career?

If so, we can envisage a trajectory that takes us from his early, poetic realist qualities to this more decided political realist position, especially when couched within the structure of classical realism. The poetry, of course, is always there. The scene of the football match in *Timbuktu*, for instance, is ineffable, as are also the musical components that define *Timbuktu*'s gentle world of love and pleasure, qualities that also appeared in Mele's unforgettable singing in the club in *Bamako*, or the griotte and her apprentice's in *Heremakono*. Poetry was always there in Sissako's vision of the world, but poetry that ends with a well-defined conclusion risks turning into a lecture instead of what works precisely within the realm of what is inexpressibly moving.

The risks of alignment are always marked by exclusions. The risks of non-alignment are equally undeniable. How could the resistance to injustice, the foundation for any notion of human rights, reject the claims of Negritude or of African-centered perspectives on the world? And Timbuktu has been known, after all, as a center not only for Malian music, for the beauties of its mosques, its various expressions of the motions of the gazelle, but also for its Muslim repositories. The battle over who should decide on the contents of those archives is no less violent than the systems of justice that determine social behavior, public appearance, or the relations of love, and what risks being lost in the combat, as Césaire stated all too well, are the qualities of openness that are threatened when one becomes "un homme de haine."

KENNETH W. HARROW is Distinguished Professor of English at Michigan State University. He is author of *Trash! A Study of African Cinema Viewed from Below* (IUP, 2013).

Notes

1. The quote in original French:

> Faites de ma tête une tête de proue
> et de moi-même, mon cœur, ne faites ni un père, ni un frère,
> ni un fils, mais le père, mais le frère, mais le fils,
> ni un mari, mais l'amant de cet unique peuple.
>
> . . .
>
> faites de moi l'exécuteur de ces œuvres hautes
> voici le temps de se ceindre les reins comme un vaillant
> homme—
>
> Mais les faisant, mon cœur, préservez-moi de toute haine
> ne faites point de moi cet homme de haine pour qui je
> n'ai que haine
>
> car pour me cantonner en cette unique race
> vous savez pourtant mon amour tyrannique
> vous savez que ce n'est point par haine des autres races
> que je m'exige bêcheur de cette unique race
> que ce que je veux
> c'est pour la faim universelle
> pour la soif universelle
>
> la sommer libre enfin
> de produire de son intimité close
> la succulence des fruits.
> (Aimé Césaire, *Cahier d'un retour au pays natal* [1956] 2001, 49–50)

2. Historical alignments have shifted over time. Race emerged with the dependence on West African trade by the eighteenth century. See Smedley and Smedley (2005).

3. "HISTORY teaches us clearly that the battle against colonialism does not run straight away along the lines of nationalism. For a very long time the native devotes his energies to ending certain definite abuses: forced labour, corporal punishment, inequality of salaries, limitation of political rights, etc. This fight for democracy against the oppression of mankind will slowly leave the confusion of neo-liberal universalism to emerge, sometimes laboriously, as a claim to nationhood. It so happens that the unpreparedness of the educated classes, the lack of practical links between them and the mass of the people, their laziness, and, let it be said, their cowardice at the decisive moment of the struggle will give rise to tragic mishaps" (Fanon [1961] 1968, 148).

4. Original French:

> voici le temps de se ceindre les reins comme un vaillant
> homme—
> Mais les faisant, mon cœur, préservez-moi de toute haine
> ne faites point de moi cet homme de haine pour qui je
> n'ai que haine (Césaire [1956] 2001, 50)

5. Original French:

> faites de moi l'exécuteur de ces œuvres hautes
> voici le temps de se ceindre les reins comme un vaillant
> homme – (Césaire [1956] 2001, 49–50)

Filmography

Afrique, je te plumerai (*Africa, I Will Fleece You*), 1992, Jean-Marie Teno, Cameroon / France / Germany.
Bamako, 2006, Abderrahmane Sissako, Mali / USA / France.
La battaglia di Algeri (*The Battle of Algiers*), 1966, Gillo Pontecorvo, Italy / Algeria.
Blue Velvet, 1986, David Lynch, USA.
Camp de Thiaroye, 1988, Ousmane Sembène, Senegal / Algeria / Tunisia.
Ceddo, 1977, Ousmane Sembène, Senegal.
Daratt (*Dry Season*), 2006, Mahamat-Saleh Haroun, Chad / France / Belgium / Austria.
Daresalam, 2001, Issa Serge Coelo, France / Burkina Faso / Chad.
Emitaï, 1971, Ousmane Sembène, Senegal.
Finye, 1982, Souleymane Cissé, Mali.
Grigris, 2013, Mahamat-Saleh Haroun, Chad / France.
Heremakono: Waiting for Happiness, 2002, Abderrahmane Sissako, France / Mauritania.
O Heroi, 2004, Zézé Gamboa, Angola.
Un homme qui crie (*A Screaming Man*), 2010, Mahamat-Saleh Haroun, France / Belgium / Chad.
Mapantsula, 1988, Oliver Schmitz, South Africa / UK.
Mortu Nega, 1988, Flora Gomes, Guinea-Bissau.
La Pirogue, 2012, Moussa Traoré, France / Senegal / Germany.
Pumzi, 2009, Wanuri Kahiu, South Africa / Kenya.
Sambizanga, 1972, Sarah Maldoror, Angola / France.
Tears of the Black Tiger, 2000, Wisit Sasanatieng, Thailand.

Timbuktu, 2014, Abderrahmane Sissako, France / Mauritania.
Udju azul di Yonta (*The Blue Eyes of Yonta*), 1992, Flora Gomes, Guinea-Bissau / France / Portugal.
La Vie sur terre (*Life on Earth*), 1998, Abderrahmane Sissako, Mali / Mauritania / France.
Wend Kuuni, 1982, Gaston Kaboré, Burkina Faso.
Xala, 1975, Ousmane Sembène, Senegal.
Yeelen (*Brightness*), 1987, Souleymane Cissé, Mali / Burkina Faso / France / West Germany / Japan.

References

Cazenave, O., P. Taoua, A. Sow, and K. Harrow. 2016. "*Timbuktu*—the Controversy." *African Studies Review* 59 (3): 267–93. doi:10.1017/asr.2016.91.

Césaire, Aimé. (1955) 1972. *Discourse on Colonialism*. Translated by Joan Pinkham from *Discours sur le colonialisme* (Paris: Présence Africaine). New York: Monthly Review Press.

Césaire, Aimé. (1956) 2001. *Notebook of a Return to the Native Land*. Translated by Clayton Eshleman from *Cahier d'un retour au pays natal* (Paris: Présence africaine). Middletown, CT: Wesleyan University Press.

Diop, Boubacar Boris. (1983) 2016. *Doomi Golo: The Hidden Notebooks*. Translated by Vera Wülfing-Leckie and El Hadji Moustapha Diop. East Lansing: Michigan State University Press.

Fanon, Frantz. (1961) 1968. *The Wretched of the Earth*. Translated by Constance Farrington. New York: Grove Press.

Sembène, Ousmane. (1960) 1970. *God's Bits of Wood*. Translated by Francis Price. London: Heinemann.

Smedley, A., and Brian Smedley. 2005. "Race as Biology Is Fiction, Racism as a Social Problem Is Real." *American Psychologist* 60 (1): 16–26.

Young, Robert. 1994. *Colonial Desire: Hybridity in Theory, Culture and Race*. London: Routledge.

12 *Beats of the Antonov*

A Counternarrative of Endurance and Survival

N. Frank Ukadike

LIKE MANY OTHER African nations, Sudan has a long and complicated sociocultural and political history dating back to the precolonial period. Then and now, the country's history is a manifestation of perennial conflicts and violence, such as we see depicted in *Beats of the Antonov* (2014), a documentary film directed by Hajooj Kuka. The film showcases the courage and resilience of villagers living along the Blue Nile and the Nuba Mountains within the state of Kordofan. When in 2011 the country was divided into two—Sudan, an Arab republic in the North, and South Sudan, an ethnically diverse, "black" nation with a mix of Christians and people who believe in African religious traditions—these people found themselves on the "wrong" side of the border. The Sudanese government is doing whatever it can to get rid of the rebel forces in the area, not least by obliterating their base—the villagers—through massive bombardments that have now forced these civilians to gather in mountain hideouts or refugee camps. But still the bombings continue, and so does the fighting back, led by the rebel forces.

The film takes the viewer through the lives of displaced people who have lost family members, homes, farms, and belongings. But instead of a devastated and defeated people, we find a vibrant culture, people who have gained new purpose and energy in the face of conflict. The response to the violence is often singing, dancing, laughter, and marvelous music that comes from the traditions and practices of their culture. This is their chief survival technique. Stylistically and narratively, *Beats of the Antonov* is a unique film that demonstrates Kuka's capability to turn collective injury and suffering into a creative opportunity.

Let me remind the reader that even before Sudan's independence in 1956, the enormous cultural disparity between the North and South of Sudan dismayed the British, who, therefore, opted for separate administrations as the best way to rule the two. This explains why the South (not the predominantly Islamic North) was seen by the British as a fertile ground for Christian missionary work among the black Sudanese. It is easy to understand why, during this time, anti-British sentiments were so intense in the northern region, leading to a series of rebellions against the British and to the disruptions that were to follow. During this period, when the British had begun dismantling their empire after World War II, Sudan was granted independence in 1956 as one country, although for decades it had been ruled as two separate territories. At independence, there already existed a discordant relationship between the North and South, torn by ethnic and religious differences. Even so, power was nevertheless handed over exclusively to the northern leadership in Khartoum, ultimately assuring the eruption of civil war within months.[1]

Since 1956, Sudan has never been at peace with itself—it is always on the verge of civil war. As has been pointed out, the Sudanese people have lived through one of the longest periods of violence in Africa's postcolonial history.[2] The most recent war in Sudan, which officially ended in 2005, was inspired by the tumult following the military coup led by Colonel Omar al-Bashir, which toppled the government, followed by the introduction of full Sharia law nationwide, abolishing many social and political freedoms. Bashir declared himself president and is still, to this day, ruling the country with an iron hand and suppressing opponents. On the other side is the guerilla group, the Sudan People's Liberation Army (SPLA), based in South Sudan. Representing the highly oppressed and marginalized people of African heritage, they launched an oppositional movement against the government, eventually leading to a full-scale civil war. On January 9, 2011, a referendum paved the way for the South to break away from Sudan, a measure intended to bring peace to the people of the South, but when the inhabitants of the Blue Nile and the Nuba Mountains refused to lay down their arms, the Sudanese government would not let them go, preferring instead to launch a new war with these people in the border regions.

Over the years, the conflicts and abuses in the Southern Kordofan and Blue Nile states have continued unabated. Despite two significant peace accords, this region has faced several conflicts, such as the fighting that is going on between the Sudanese Armed Forces (SAF) and the Sudan People's Liberation Movement-North (SPLM-N), a northern affiliate of the Sudan People's Liberation Movement (SPLM) in South Sudan. This conflict has resulted in a massive displacement of tens of thousands of people and in restricted access with respect to humanitarian activity. The attacks have caused unjustified civilian deaths (including those of children), numerous injuries, and the destruction of civilians' property. In the Nuba Mountains and the Blue Nile regions where *Beats of the Antonov* is set, government forces and allied militias have engaged in pogroms, having constantly attacked civilians in villages and other populated areas, through ground offensives and indiscriminate bombings. Government forces are known to have focused on economic targets as well, burning crops, looting foodstuff, and destroying farmlands and livestock; torture and rape have been used as weapons of war.[3]

Filmmaking in Sudan before Hajooj Kuka: A Brief History

Given the perennial conflict and atrocities committed during the decades of war in the region, many documentaries have been made about Sudan, such as *Darfur Now* (2007, USA), directed by Ted Braun, and *Lost Boys of Sudan* (2003, USA), directed by Megan Mylan and Jon Shenk. Coproduced with Steven Markovitz of Big World Productions, *Beats of the Antonov* is a film that interrogates, demystifies, and complicates the "formulaic" narratives that are repeatedly used in the depiction of Africa. It was released at a time when filmmaking in Sudan was considered a thing of the past. A cursory examination of the history of filmmaking in Sudan reveals that cinema was introduced to the country almost at the same time it was invented. Sudan became one of the first countries in Africa and the Middle East to embrace the medium; in fact, one of its citizens, Gadalla Gubara, was a pioneer filmmaker recognized in history books as the first African filmmaker (Ukadike 2003, 41). Gubara produced Africa's first color film, *Song of Khartoum*, in 1955—a contribution to the city symphony genre. In Sudan's early development of its film culture, theaters sprang up in many parts of the country showing American, Italian, and Egyptian comedies, as well as action films and romance melodramas. Over the years, however, due to economic hardship, prevalent conflicts, and uncompromising politics, the film industry in Sudan stagnated.

The origin of film production in Sudan can be traced back to the British colonial authorities, who, in 1912, made a documentary film about King George V's visit to the country. This film was screened in an open-air theater under the auspices of the colonial administration's ideology of producing educational / instructional / propaganda films for the colonies. In the case of Sudan, it should be noted that a joint authority by Britain and Egypt ruled the country from 1899 to independence in 1956. In the 1920s, however, Greek immigrants were the first to establish movie theaters in Khartoum, which showed silent films.

By the 1950s, the film business began to proliferate in Sudan, and the authorities established the Sudan Film Unit for the purpose of producing short newsreels and educational films, many of which were taken all over the country to be shown via mobile cinema trucks. By 1952, this film unit had made its first locally produced short drama, *Homeless Childhood*, which focused on issues related to homeless children. The first feature-length film, produced by Studio Al Rasheed —*Hopes and Dreams*—was directed by Ibrahim Mallassy in 1970. After this endeavor, feature-length filmmaking stalled, and the bourgeoning enterprise was reduced to yielding only a handful of films. As in many African countries, government or private financial support to propel the industry was not forthcoming, as the general belief was that cinema was a luxury and filmmaking a risky business whose future could not be guaranteed.

The death blow to the Sudanese film industry was delivered in 1993 when the minister of culture and information ordered the suspension of the activities of the Sudan Cinema Corporation, which at that time was also the only distributor of films in the country, thereby effectively triggering the demise of what had once been a promising industry. Currently, very few cinematic undertakings are visible in the country, apart from the occasional staging of foreign film festivals. Like many other African countries where movie theaters have been converted into churches and supermarkets, in Sudan the many government-owned theaters are either crumbling, have been demolished, or have been sold off entirely; the prestigious Colosseum Cinema Theater has become Khartoum's riot police headquarters.[4]

The local producers faced insurmountable challenges as the economic situation was not conducive to filmmaking. In addition, they were unable to win back audience loyalty as many of the people could still watch the cheap Indian films that were shown in the few remaining local theaters or could download Nollywood and other films from the internet in the comfort of their living rooms.

Since government parastatals such as the Sudan Film Unit—which in its heyday made a great number of documentaries on diverse social, economic, educational, and informational subjects—no longer exist, the attempt to revamp feature filmmaking has been to no avail. However, one genre of independent filmmaking that is gradually resuscitating itself and bringing the Sudanese cinema back to the limelight is the documentary. In the new millennium, a good number of Sudanese documentary filmmakers have gained international recognition and won prestigious awards. One such example is Taghreed Elsanhouri, who has three films to her credit: *Sudanna al Habib* (2012), *Mother Unknown* (2009), and *All About Darfur* (2005). Despite all odds militating against production, Elsanhouri remains optimistic about the future of cinema in her country. According to her, "a new generation is making that future as [there] . . . are so many stories to tell. [Then again] we also have our limits—bureaucratic and otherwise—but even those limits can be turned into creative opportunities both stylistically and narratively" (Kushkush 2014).

A man of many talents, Hajooj Kuka was born in Sudan but is currently based in Nairobi, Kenya, from where he frequently travels to the Nuba Mountains and Blue Nile in Sudan to do his creative work. Kuka studied electrical engineering at the American University of Beirut and digital design at San Jose State University in California. He is the creative director of 3ayin.com, a website that works with local reporters in hopes of bringing news of the war to the Sudanese people through short documentaries. Formerly a war correspondent in the Nuba Mountains of Sudan, Kuka has also worked at the Middle East Broadcast Network in Virginia and at Shilo Inc. in New York City as a video editor and post production tech / editor. His previous work includes the documentary *Darfur's Skeleton* (2009, Sudan), which explores the conflict in Sudan's troubled region since 2003.[5]

Transcending the Limits of Representation

Beats of the Antonov opens with the image of an aircraft flying through a beautiful blue sky. As it descends upon the village, we hear the villagers shouting, "The plane is coming," as they run to their makeshift shelters. This is followed by a massive bombardment of the refugees. As the plane leaves, the camera shows these people as they come out of their hiding places singing and laughing in the face of the calamity and the environmental destruction the bombardment has just caused. We see their houses burning as the people—men, women, and children—join hands in extinguishing the flames. It appears odd that people who have just survived a deadly bombing raid would emerge from their hideouts smiling, singing, and dancing. But as depicted in the film, these are cultural signifiers in the expression of national consciousness, and, as an ideological tool, they call attention to the celebration of culture as a defiant declaration of diversity, inclusion, and self-determination in the face of extreme oppression.

The Antonov of the film's title originates from the Ukrainian-made Russian planes preferred by President Bashir's government in the decimation of the rebel villages. Instead of adopting the familiar documentary talking-head tactics to narrate Sudan's conflict, the filmmaker opts for a collective participation as a way of synthesizing Sudan's identity crisis, a crisis that was instigated by the ruling oligarchs who want to impose a nationalist ideology of Arabification in Sudan at the expense of its diverse African cultures and populations.

The government's massive bombardment of the civilians in these areas started in June 2011 and was designed to intimidate and terrorize the people. This emphasis on the collective by the filmmaker has proved to be effective in capturing the suffering and resilience as we see the people speak, sing in their own languages, and go about their daily chores. We identify with the people who have lost relatives, homes, farms, and livestock as they improvise ways to continue raising their cattle and cultivating crops needed for their existence. As a counternarrative of endurance and survival, the intensity of the people's plight can be understood only from the director's creative use of cinematic convention in the manner in which he weaves "together the voices of militants, social workers, intellectuals and everyday people to tell the story of the refugees who are struggling to reclaim their humanity in the midst of a complex conflict."[6] As the director explains, "I named the film after the Antonov, a Russian airplane bombing the Nuba Mountains and Blue Nile. 'Beats' refers to the sound of the bombing—people are running and they are scared—but 'beats' also refers to the music that heals the people."[7] How can this be possible?

Well, before deciding to shoot this film, Kuka lived for two years with these people whom Bashir considers his nemesis, fascinated by their resilience as they cling to their cultural identity as a means of defying the status quo. As Ben Small has rightly pointed out, "While the war and persecution provides a context, culture is the star of the show, and Kuka captures the raw passion of these people in abundance."[8] This passion is anchored through their oral traditions as well, and I see this as the other "star" of this documentary.

For the marginalized South Sudanese, their struggle is about liberation and preservation of culture. As in Amílcar Cabral's (1970) philosophy of culture, which states that "the liberation struggle is, above all, a struggle both for the preservation and survival of the cultural values of the people," in the film, music plays a fundamental cultural role in collective mobilization. As noted above, "beat" refers to the music that heals the people. The history of African music is an essential part in understanding *Beats of the Antonov* and the broad scope of the African continent and its people, specifically music's function in maintaining culture and resistance to oppression. A great diversity permeates the African continent, and music acts as a unifying force among the various ethnic groups. African music has contributed to the dissemination of information through its emphasis on family, religion, and storytelling in a manner that has transcended the impact of time into popular artistic conventions, such as in the artistry of film narratives and their methods of signification.

The roles of music and dance are tightly woven together in sub-Saharan Africa, and music intersects with every aspect of life. Music expresses life through the medium of sound: "By helping to mark the important moments in life, music helps to underscore the divine and eternal value of human life by turning it into a universal language through music" (Robotham and Kubik 2016, 46). African music also helps connect peoples in a variety of ways, strengthening the fabric of the community, which in turn reinforces people's commitment to support each other and the community as a whole, as witnessed in *Beats of the Antonov*, an issue we shall return to shortly.

As African society has changed over time in response to the forces of colonization, independence, and globalization, the role of music has changed as well by adapting to the new situations in which the people of Africa find themselves. Although there have been changes in some of the forms of music, including the infusion of instruments, music styles, and genres from the Western world, overall, music remains a prominent aspect of African life today. The music displayed in the film was, according to the director, "made by instruments created from found objects; a radio was used as an amplifier to create an electronic Sudanese sound that was unique. The music moved me so much that I knew the story behind it was key."[9] Throughout the film, Kuka shows the immense dexterity of the Sudanese people with respect to instrument building, as well as in the survival technique of improvisation, a hallmark of their resilience, expressed within the new situations where refugees living in the Blue Nile and Nuba Mountains find themselves. As the impoverished people of the refugee camps cannot afford to buy expensive musical instruments, improvisation serves as a means to not only legitimize their culture, but also showcase their solidarity as they resist oppression.

In order better to understand Africa's relationship to music, one must know the cultural context in which genre formation occurs. In the film, the community joins in musical performance; this belongs to the genre of group music. There is no space here to dwell on the three musical genres of Africa identified by Mario Azevedo, namely, personal music, group music, and listener's music; but I will emphasize that group music as a musical style in Africa is a much more public and less personal experience: "Group music is music performed by a group, for that group" (Azevedo 2005, 254). Unlike the implications of personal music, group music more often than not includes dance as an addition to the artistic experience. Group music events span a broad range, from female dance circles to entire communities taking part in a celebratory festival. The revolutionizing insights of traditional African group music also became extremely popular over time, appropriated and used as vehicles for revolutionary slogans during the struggle for independence, for example, and eventually manifesting themselves in what the larger artistic world now knows as hip-hop.

In *Beats of the Antonov*, people of diverse African ethnicities are seen articulating views about the situation of their country; they reminisce about their doubts and aspirations, "sharing their struggle to keep the fragile thread of their identity from unraveling."[10] Playing the rababa, a stringed instrument made from found objects, one of the film's prominent musicians, Jodah Bujud, explains, "When you play the rababa, people forget their hardships for a moment. They enter a state of happiness." Echoing this sentiment, Sarah Mohamed (also known as Alsarah), a Sudanese American songwriter who went back to Sudan with Kuka "to get a closer look at the music and its role in the story of the people's displacement,"[11] was fascinated by the presence and entrenchment of music as a cultural artifact, particularly the "girls' music," whose immense popularity is attributable to women's inclination to narrate their stories themselves through music.

It is the "girls' music" that becomes much more prominent as the film progresses. It is a genre categorized as belonging to the community of young women in Sudan who design, write, and perform their music in groups, using humor and satire. The lyrics touch on every aspect of the lives in the community; they sing about love, health, war, and so on. One lyric warns about the rebel advances, asking the enemies to get out of their lives, while chanting, "This boot is too big for you, you better be gone, my friend." Speaking about the autonomous nature of this practice, Alsarah states that there is no restriction: "Everyone is allowed to sing. Anyone has the right to drum. You can use a bucket to drum. In the end everyone sings together."[12] Others are eloquent and philosophical about how to

Figure 12.1. Entrenchment of music as a cultural artifact: young women prepare to perform "girls' music." Framegrab from *Beats of the Antonov* (2014, Hajooj Kuka, Sudan / South Africa).

discern the implications of this unending conflict in Sudan. So, while for Insaf Awad, a Sudanese refugee, it is important for people to protect their cultural heritage for posterity, Albaqir Elafeef, of the Sudanese Civil Society, believes that the war is caused by what he calls the northerners' "identity crisis," as their ultimate goal is to get rid of all the African elements in Sudan.

Countering the Government's Policy of Divide and Conquer

Watching *Beats of the Antonov*, as the viewer is drawn into the perspective it offers about the people we see on screen, we do not need to be reminded that this is a film about Sudan telling the Sudanese story. There are no cinematic pyrotechnics, no linear structuring as in conventional narratives; this film is rather more episodic than sequential, and as a cluster of vignettes of life, the structure is interspersed by performances, conversations, and images of instrument building, traditional wrestling, and songwriting sessions—all used to lay bare the appurtenances of traditional living—which the viewer is invited to experience. As the images portraying the struggles are shown, Kuka intersperses this narrative with commentators drawn from all walks of life—intellectuals, militia, ordinary people, and men and women—as they reflect on their society and everything pertaining to Sudanese history, politics, and culture, as well as the current quagmire in which the country is immersed.

Through the voices of the people interviewed, the viewer learns much about the conflicting identity crises that have torn the country apart, the sense of belonging or not belonging to Arab or African traditions, or the implications of identifying with one or the other side. In Sudan, the government's policy of divide and conquer is apparent because of the way it classifies the Sudanese people along racial and ethnic lines, "breaking them up into Arabs and Blacks, then further breaking the Arabs into first and second class Arabs," as stated in the film by Ibrahim Khatir, an SPLA officer fighting with the rebel forces in the Nuba Mountains. He tells us that the National Ruling Congress promotes Arab identity as first-class citizenry while black African languages and traditions are relegated to a lower rank. It is interesting that, in the film, the citizens of the Blue Nile and the Nuba Mountains continue to glorify and allude to the duality of their traditions—singing and dancing to the beats of their music that conveys both their African and Sudanese heritage.

Khatir even goes further, expanding on the contradictions inherent in the duality of the Sudanese heritage (African and Arab), the Sudanese people's complex relationship with their roots (language and cultures), and the falsehood of one group claiming ethnic superiority over the others (religious / cultural hegemony). As he analyzes this complex structural formation, he describes himself as a commander of the political training division of the SPLA, one who is from an Arab ethnic group called Myseria. As he continues to talk, the camera cuts to a group of officers smiling and exchanging handshakes, exposing a tall, lanky older man in military uniform who walks into the celluloid frame greeting the others being addressed by Khatir. He is Brigadier Habob, who, like officer Khatir, is a Sudanese. Yet he comes from another Arab ethnic group: Shawiga. Khatir notes there are many others like Brigadier Habob and himself in the army fighting with the rebels despite their Arab heritage, and this clearly subverts the "divide and rule" policy of Bashir's government. It is important to point out that Khatir and Brigadier Habob both have physically African and Arab features in the same manner that Albaqir Elafeef has pointed out that "inside every Northerner there is a tiny Arab." It is then ironic, as explained in the film by a woman in the refugee camp and by Yuris Elahaimar, an SPLA member, that the Sudanese president Omar al-Bashir, who has since been indicted by the International Criminal Court for war crimes and crimes against humanity, would refer to the black African Sudanese people as "Black Sacks" when he himself is a black man. To understand the intricacies of ethnic formation and how this conflict started in Sudan, I will now provide a brief historical overview.

The devastating civil war in Sudan results from ethnic and religious conflicts. Today, more than 70 percent of the Sudanese people are of Arab descent; the rest have other, diverse ethnicities. The desire for an Arab presence in Sudan is traceable to the seventh century when the Arab-Muslim armies made several attempts to invade Sudan but were unsuccessful. Over time, their tactics shifted to establishing friendly trade relations with the Nubian people of Sudan, such relations being seen at that time as more effective than the pursuit of brute force, given the goal of conquering the country. By the fifteenth century, this relationship had paved the way for the Arab merchants and missionaries to begin to settle in Sudan, which, in turn, ushered in intermarriages between the Arabs and Nubian people and the introduction of Arab Muslim culture to the Sudanese context, including Christians and believers in the traditional African religions.

However, Sudan possessed rich mineral and human resources—primarily gold and slaves—which in 1820 compelled the viceroy of Egypt under the Ottoman Empire, Muhammad Ali, to send his army to conquer Sudan. By 1821, the Sudanese leadership had crumbled and was subjugated, brought under the conquering empire of Muhammad Ali. Interestingly, by the mid-1800s, after the decline of the Ottoman Empire, the British were poised to play an active role in Sudan's politics. They convinced the governor general to begin the process of abolishing slavery in Sudan, a controversial move that sparked tensions between the government and the Sudanese people who depended on the slave trade economically. By 1882, Sudan was under joint British-Egyptian rule—setting off another kind of identity crisis for the people, especially for the South Sudanese minority.[13] This question of identity, and how it plays out so well in the film, is succinctly summarized in the following way: "While *Beats of the Antonov* is a story set in a time and place of conflict, it is also a story of a people coming to terms with their culture and identity, confronting the reality that identity was at the heart of the conflict. The tension between the so-called Arab north and the African south still plays out in areas of North Sudan as the Khartoum government continues its efforts to impose not only its rule, but its culture" (MSPIFF festival flyer).

An interesting thing about Kuka's approach to filmmaking is that he never gravitates toward any particular side of the conflict or the pervasive cultural divide inherent in Bashir's government. He "presents all sides—from those Sudanese eager to embrace both an African and Arab identity, to those willing to erase their Africanness and therefore their blackness" (Blay 2015), hoping to fit into the Arab identity. Hence, in the film we see a young woman playfully noting how she lightens her skin in order to look "more Arab." Although this may seem pathetic, it does mirror everyday reality in Sudan, where lightening of one's skin can be seen as a tool of oppression and to reflect the Sudanese cultural and ideological politics, as well as the oppression imposed on the Sudanese people who are not of Arab descent. In this sense, the revelation that follows shows the contradiction involved in oscillating between two traditions: Arab and African. In this scene, when the young woman who uses skin lightening cream is asked if she would allow her baby's skin to be lightened, her answer is an emphatic *no*. Why? Because, according to her, she wants her baby to be who she really is. In another context that is related to the Sudan situation here described, Godfried Asante has noted that "while most critics of skin bleaching . . . tend to pathologize black users as wanting to be 'white,'" they have "indicated that these women do not necessarily want to be like a 'white person' [or Arab person, for that matter] but rather *less dark*" (Asante 2016, 89, emphasis mine).

A great many such people have, unfortunately, been taught to believe that the lighter one is, the higher the probability of being accepted. This practice is also an ugly reminder of similar situations in black Africa and the African world in general with respect to the prevailing cultural erasure of one's African heritage, which Frantz Fanon long ago suggested "produces complete alienation from the self" (Fanon 1967, 109). Sadly, this practice and perspective are still in effect today, such as the process of changing one's features to look less black. This can also be seen in many black women's choice to wear fake or quite straightened hair over their God-given natural afro. Some black leaders might call this a misplaced practice and priority that is comparable to skin lightening, now at the zenith of its popularity and, unfortunately, an apparently unstoppable trend in Africa and much of the black world. Most analysts are likely to agree that these practices are rapidly obliterating or diminishing such people's pride in being black and beautiful. It also seems beyond ironic and economically wasteful that the importation of this "beauty" paraphernalia is generally from China and India, as it is only recently that a few of these products have been manufactured in Africa. Moreover, consider how sad and perhaps ridiculous it is for a two-year-old black child already to be wearing fake elongated (straight) hair, the so-called attachments that Robert Mugabe described as "dead people's hair." A good many black people still cherish and admire the intricate patterning of real, traditional hair braids, and if you look carefully at the women in *Beats of the Antonov*, you will find one seeming black goddess who does not cover her wonderfully braided hair.

One of the outstanding features of *Beats of the Antonov* is that the director allows the villagers to tell their own stories through their words, songs, dances, and rhythms. There is no omniscient voice-over or voice-of-God narration, but rather an articulation to the camera when necessary, not provoked or cued to reflect a certain ideological stance or perspective. Here we find the appropriation of an integral arm of Africa's oral tradition, one invoking a cultural hermeneutic, immersed in sound, music, rhythm, and dance, thus functioning as a defiant support of diversity in the face of oppression. Ultimately, it is a matter of making the Arabification of Sudan appear as the nonsense it is. The film uses a multiplicity of voices to nullify the ideology in question, and the range of expressions—through the voices we hear, the languages that are spoken, and the rhythms of the music—demonstrate the idiocy of even thinking about imposing one majority culture on the people through the barrel of a gun. As Patrick Mullen aptly stated in his review in *Point of View* magazine, "The music itself is beautiful, though—the film has a great soundtrack—and the delight one receives in hearing the music lets the tunes subtly note the richness that the diversity of cultures brings to the world" (2014).

In the context of African cinema, few narrative and documentary films have as effectively as *Beats of the Antonov* promoted collective participation in exploring war and suffering. Its creative originality draws on the quintessential narrative code embedded in oral tradition (music, dance, and rhythm) in a manner reminiscent of Moussa Kemoko Diakité's *Naitou l'orpheline* (1982, Guinea) for its impactful use of music. Considered within the cultural context of artistic authenticity, *Beats of the Antonov* and *Naitou* are exemplary. They both explore with conviction the role of African cultural traditions as a creative foundation of cinematic narrative, which is why, in all their manifestations, it could be argued that their techniques owe no allegiance to any one stylistic trend. *Naitou* has no dialogue, only music and dance performed by the Ballet Africain de Guinée, which provides many of the multifarious African art forms employed in the film in the same manner that the traditional music used in *Beats of the Antonov* beautifully and creatively conveys a kind of national identity that is about the soul of Sudan.

Community Aesthetics / Aesthetics of Resistance

Beats of the Antonov's use of certain cinematic and narrative strategies make it stand out from other documentaries. Bill Nichols's observation regarding the dichotomous relationship between fiction and documentary film is germane to *Beats of the Antonov*. He notes that "if narratives invite our engagement with the construction of a story, set in an imaginary world, documentary invites our engagement with the construction of an argument, directed toward the historical world" (Nichols 1991, 118).

One striking element of this film is its use of multiple storylines (episodes) that often evoke a sense of pathos in the viewers, allowing them to relate to the storyline on a personal level. The way the sound is used in each episode is also exceptional. *Beats of the Antonov* impeccably incorporates the raw sounds of war and pairs them with a cinematic score to create something similar to a scene one would see in a Hollywood movie. For, as in the use of cinematic convention to draw the viewer into a chase, the chosen scores reflect the mood of the individual images on the screen as well as the mood of the scene as a whole. Thus, via such stylistic elements as music, camera movements, mise-en-scène, lighting, and color, the viewer develops an emotional relationship with the refugees' actions and goals. In addition, the film works with an assortment of other cinematic conventions. At times it actually seems like a western with wide-angle shots exposing a large landscape where the action is taking place. As in westerns, this landscape can be both beautiful and deadly. Yet the director also pays meticulous attention to detail, such as the huge crater made by the bombing runs of the Antonov planes, and the camera lingers on the destruction: the burning houses and dead cows that have just been hit by bombs. Perhaps the most difficult image for me to digest is when a gyrating camera, a typical documentary convention, is used to follow the rebels as they engage the enemy. The camera is right there with them, and, typical of war reporting, this hand-held camera maneuvers jerkily, observing as it ducks and dives between volleys of gunfire from an invisible enemy, as in Joris Ivens's film about the Spanish Civil War, *The Spanish Earth* (1937, USA).

The scene with the badly wounded soldier being dragged out of the line of firing, which we see at the end of the skirmish, parallels the images of cows that have been decapitated as a result of the raid, thus reminding the viewer of the atrocities resulting from the violation of human rights and the enormous sacrifices being made in the interest of freedom. The face of an old woman telling us about how much has been lost over the last two years, as a result of living with daily threats from the planes, will also remain indelibly imprinted in the minds of most viewers. As the camera comes in for a close-up of her face, she talks about how the planes killed one of her children as well as her goats.

For quite a few years, the world has been hearing about horrible tales of atrocities being committed against innocent civilians by both sides of the conflict, and yet foreign-produced military supplies continue to flow to the opposing sides. South Sudan is now considered to have "one of the most armed populations of any state in the world. The proliferation of arms there has directly contributed to the violence and instability that have plagued the country for years. Despite overwhelming evidence of the tremendous harm they cause to civilians and public infrastructure," as we have seen in *Beats of the Antonov*, "weapon acquisitions and transfers continue unabated in South Sudan" (Broga 2016). This serves as a clear indicator that if the armed conflicts in several Sudanese states continue, the impact on civilians will be devastating. The wars in Southern Kordofan and Blue Nile states, as well as Darfur, "have been characterized by unnecessary and avoidable civilian deaths and injuries, sexual violence against women and girls, unlawful destruction of civilian property, and have forced hundreds of thousands of civilians to flee their homes" (https://www.hrw.org/africa/sudan).

Let us recall that African cinema has always been concerned with wide-ranging issues, from the decolonization of history and liberation to Africa's resistance against oppression, internal or external. Indeed, during the first decade of African film practice, this concern specifically manifested itself in anticolonialist projects. After independence, however, when African elites proved to be even more abundant than the colonial administrators they replaced, cinema placed all contemporary issues on its agenda.

In confronting the adversity caused by a terrible war of attrition, in *Beats of the Antonov*, Hajooj Kuka has undoubtedly crafted a compelling story of agency, endurance, survival, and resilience. This resilience coalesces into a great accomplishment, a formidable task, and the creation of a cinema of contestation between the filmmaker, the audience, and the political leadership. *Beats of the Antonov* jolts the conscience of its audience as it educates, as it gives a clear assessment of the oppression and resistance situated within an overall context of a broad social, cultural, and political framework. I have argued elsewhere (Uka-dike 1994) that in oppositional structures, experimentation with technique con-forms with one's search for new organizing principles in the depiction of a new situation, such as the conflict in the Blue Nile and Nuba Mountains. When the filmic criteria work, they strengthen the rapport between the filmmaker and the spectator—a rapport, as cultural producers and critics in the developing world have argued, that is necessary for the development of further cinematic codes embedded in internal structures. This process is essentially one of rejuvenating community aesthetics.

If we were to look at the film from this perspective, as seems best, Kuka has reached that milestone in channeling the film medium toward a meaningful goal. This brings us to another key characteristic of *Beats of the Antonov* that sep-arates it from some traditional narratives: its rhetorical form or episodic mode. Rhetorical form, in this case, refers to the way that the film seeks to galvanize its audience. Or, as David Bordwell and Kristin Thompson write in *Film Art*, the rhetorical form presents an argument and lays out evidence to support it, and the "goal in such a film is to persuade the audience to adopt an opinion about the subject matter and perhaps to act on that opinion. This type of film goes beyond the categorical type in that it tries to make an explicit argument" (2009, 359).

In *Beats of the Antonov*, this argument emerges through the episodic treat-ment and collage of images strung together through masterful editing. The type of editing used here is akin to the Russian montage that juxtaposes ele-ments or disparate shots / images that have no narrative or causal relationship but whose meanings derive from the method of putting the images or the jux-taposed situations together for impact. In the case of the episodic mode, the storytelling technique and the film form pivot "consistently around explicit meaning and ideological implications" (ibid.) of the argument. *Beats of the Antonov* is a film that makes a special appeal for the preservation of an authentic life and culture. It challenges the viewer to help disseminate this vital informa-tion and solidifies the argument that the Sudan and the support for self-deter-mination shown in this film differ from the image of the country that is usually offered up by the Western news media and television broadcasts. The film makes no attempt to disguise its formal structure, nor the inherent subjectivity that comes with the region.

It has been well documented that "the government has barred humanitarian agencies from working in rebel-held areas of Southern Kordofan and Blue Nile, and that it has failed to agree to terms for humanitarian access with the rebel group (SPLM-N)" (https://www.hrw.org/africa/sudan). Hence, instead, the film concludes with a powerful scene of children playing happily with the clay toys they have made in the refugee camp. These kids represent symbols of optimism and hope, but as the camera in the next wide-angle shot points to a huge, deso-late environment littered with white shacks (tents provided by the UN agency,

Figure 12.2. A woman carrying firewood walks to the UN refugee camp where she lives in one of the white tents. Framegrab from *Beats of the Antonov* (2014, Hajooj Kuka, Sudan / South Africa).

UNHCR), the audience, like the kids, clearly grasp that growing up in this place is a baptismal rite of passage as one emerges from hell to a state of peace, tolerance, and acceptance of others. This is an ironic juxtaposition of opposites (children in a playful mood and the desolate camp) that repurposes the film's argument into a succinct, actionable goal that reflects the subjective ideology shared by the filmmakers and their subjects. Rather than employing a traditional documentary story structure that is indicative of an omniscient voice-over, this alternative structure is based on a well-developed argument, perceptible analysis, sustained commentary, vivid scenes, and strong episodic vignettes that provoke striking dramatic tension.

Beats of the Antonov as Ideological Warfare

Ultimately, *Beats of the Antonov* channels its unconventional and episodic rendering to challenge the misplaced sense of trust that Africans seem to have in even the largest media conglomerates. One of the goals of *Beats of the Antonov* is thus to change the views and ideologies of the spectator. French Marxist philosopher and structuralist Louis Althusser (1969) defined ideology as "a representation of the imaginary relation of individuals to the real conditions of their existence" (233). To Althusser, ideology was a "system possessing its own logic and rigor of representation (images, myths, ideas or concepts as the case may be) existing and having a historical role within a given society" (ibid.). The key facet of ideology in Althusserian theory is its potential to be false, "false ideas or false consciousness—which can be contrasted with true or scientific knowledge"

(Stam, Burgoyne, and Flitterman-Lewis 1992, 21). *Beats of the Antonov* presupposes that its audience has been made victim to a harmful and fictive ideology championed by the repressive Bashir government and the foreign arms suppliers that profit at the expense of the marginalized citizens, their families, and the environment. Althusser's approach is useful as one analyzes Kuka's film because it treats "ideology not as a form of false consciousness deriving from the partial and distorted perspectives generated by distinct class positions, but rather, as Richard Allen puts it, as an 'objective feature of the social order which structures experience itself'" (ibid., 22).

Kuka tells his story without resorting to reductionist conventions. He saw the need to be innovative, carefully appropriating and subverting cinematic codes and portraying the characters and "narrative" actions as taking place in unpredictable cultural and natural surroundings. In the end it was time to make a passionate plea: "Watch this film with an open heart. Despite years of adversity, the Sudanese people have retained—and even developed further—a signature strength and resilience and even joy. That is who we are, and that's the main message of my film."[14]

N. FRANK UKADIKE is Associate Professor in the Department of Communication and the Program in Africana Studies at Tulane University in New Orleans. He is editor of *Critical Approaches to African Cinema Discourse.*

Notes

I wish to acknowledge the generosity of the coproducer of *Beats of the Antonov*, Steven Markovitz of Big World Productions, for making the film available to me for this study.

1. Sources for this historical overview include the following: Central Intelligence Agency, "The World Factbook: Sudan," accessed February 18, 2016, www.cia.gov/library /publications/the-world-factbook/geos/su.html; *Encyclopaedia Britannica Online*, s.v. "Sudan," accessed February 18, 2016, www.britannica.com/EBchecked/topic/571417/Sudan.

2. But the war in Sudan is much more complex than this; the war began even before the Egyptians and the British left the country when Sudan became independent in 1956. For an insider's perspective on the conflict in Sudan, see Madut Jok, *Sudan: Race, Religion and Violence* (London: Oneworld Publications, 2015).

3. The war in Sudan has been scrutinized by many news media organizations and agencies. Information on the brutalities and atrocities committed by the warring sides can be obtained from https://www.hrw.org/africa/sudan. Other sources include the following: Central Intelligence Agency, "The World Factbook: Sudan," accessed February 18, 2016, www.cia.gov/library/publications/the-world-factbook/geos/su.html; *Encyclopaedia Britannica Online*, s.v. "Sudan," accessed February 18, 2016, www.britannica.com/EBchecked /topic/571417/Sudan.

4. Some of the information about the history of filmmaking in Sudan was taken from Kushkush (2014).

5. See POV, "Press Release," accessed July 30, 2018, http://www.pbs.org/pov /beatsoftheantonov/.

6. See POV, "Film Description," accessed January 30, 2017, http://www.pbs.org/pov /beatsoftheantonov/film-description/.

7. Ibid.

8. Holocaust Memorial Day Trust Communications Officer Ben Small reviews *Beats of the Antonov* following its UK premiere at Human Rights Watch Film Festival on Thursday, March 26, 2016.

9. See POV, "Press Release," accessed July 30, 2018, http://www.pbs.org/pov /beatsoftheantonov/.

10. See POV, "Film Description," accessed January 30, 2017, http://www.pbs.org/pov /beatsoftheantonov/film-description/.

11. Ibid.

12. Ibid.

13. See POV, "Community Engagement and Education Discussion Guide to *Beats of the Antonov*," accessed March 26, 2017, http://www.pbs.org/pov/beatsoftheantonov/discussion -guide/.

14. See POV, "Press Release," accessed July 30, 2018, http://www.pbs.org/pov/ beatsoftheantonov/.

Filmography

All About Darfur, 2005, Taghreed Elsanhouri, Sudan / UK.
Beats of the Antonov, 2014, Hajooj Kuka, Sudan / South Africa.
Darfur Now, 2007, Ted Braun, USA.
Darfur's Skeleton, 2009, Hajooj Kuka, Sudan.
Homeless Childhood, 1952, Sudan Film Unit, Sudan.
Hope and Dreams, 1970, Ibrahim Mallassy, Sudan.
Lost Boys of Sudan, 2003, Megan Mylan and Jon Shenk, USA.
Mother Unknown, 2009, Taghreed Elsanhouri, Sudan.
Naitou l'orpheline, 1982, Moussa Kemoko Diakité, Guinea.
Song of Khartoum, 1955, Gadalla Gubara, Sudan.
The Spanish Earth, 1937, Joris Ivens, USA.
Sudanna al Habib, 2012, Taghreed Elsanhouri, Sudan.

References

Althusser, Louis. 1969. *For Marx*. New York: Pantheon Books.
Asante, Godfried. 2016. "Glocalized Whiteness: Sustaining and Reproducing Whiteness through "Skin Toning" in Post-colonial Ghana." *Journal of International and Intercultural Communication* 9 (2): 87–103. doi:10.1080/17513057.2016.1154184.
Azevedo, Mario Joaquim. 2005. *Africana Studies: A Survey of Africa and African Diaspora*. Durham, NC: Carolina Academic Press.

Blay, Zeba. 2015. "'Beats of the Antonov' Finds a New Perspective from Which to Explore Civil War in Sudan—Aug. 3 on PBS." Accessed January 27, 2017. http://www.indiewire .com/2015/07/beats-of-the-antonov-finds-a-new-perspective-from-which-to-explore -civil-war-in-sudan-aug-3-on-pbs-153195/.

Bordwell, David, and Kristin Thompson. 2009. *Film Art: An Introduction*. 9th ed. New York: McGraw-Hill.

Broga, Dominykas. 2016. "Loaded Guns, Smoking Barrels and the Proliferation of Arms in South Sudan." Accessed January 20, 2016. http://weareiguacu.com/the -proliferation-of-arms-in-south-sudan/.

Cabral, Amilcar. 1970. "National Liberation and Culture." Speech delivered at Syracuse University. Accessed January 27, 2017. http://sfr-21.org/cabral.html.

Fanon, Frantz. 1967. *A Dying Colonialism*. New York: Grove Press.

Kushkush, Ismail. 2014. "Reviving Sudan's Love of Cinema." *Al Jazeera*, March 1. Accessed January 30, 2017. http://www.aljazeera.com/indepth/features/2014/02/reviving-sudan -love-cinema-201422712624921265.html.

Mullen, Patrick. 2014. "Review: *Beats of the Antonov*." *Point of View*, September 8.

Nichols, Bill. 1991. *Representing Reality*. Bloomington: Indiana University Press.

Robotham, Keith, and Gerhard Kubik, eds. 2016. "African Music." *Encyclopedia Britannica Online*. Accessed December 27, 2016. www.britannica.com/art/African-music.

Stam, Robert, Robert Burgoyne, and Sandy Flitterman-Lewis.1992. *New Vocabularies in Film Semiotics: Structuralism, Post-structuralism, and Beyond*. London: Routledge.

Ukadike, N. Frank. 1995. "African Cinematic Reality: The Documentary Tradition as an Emerging Trend." *Research in African Literatures* 26 (3): 88–96.

———. 2003. *Questioning African Cinema*. Minneapolis: University of Minnesota Press.

13 Human Rights Issues in the Nigerian Films *October 1* and *Black November*

Osakue Stevenson Omoera

IN SPITE OF the controversies that Nollywood as a film tradition and as an industry has generated, its firm charisma as a truly African cinema is incontestable in contemporary global film discourse. In support of this claim, it suffices to point to titles such as the following: *Global Nollywood: The Transnational Dimensions of an African Video Film Industry* (Krings and Okome 2013), *African Film: Looking Back and Looking Forward* (Ogunleye 2014), *Auteuring Nollywood* (Afolayan 2014), the special Nollywood issue of *Journal of African Cinemas* (Haynes 2012), *Nollywood: The Creation of Nigerian Film Genres* (Haynes 2016), and *Film Culture and the Idea of Nation: Nollywood and National Narration* (Tsaaior and Ugochukwu 2017). In these top-notch publications on Nollywood, several intersections have been forged, and many more continue to emerge, including Nollywood's relation to gender, religion, migration, urbanity, and politics, among other culturally significant phenomena.

In a personal communication with the author (October 25, 2016), Peddie Okao, a frontline Nollywood filmmaker and owner of Prolens Movies Nigeria Limited, argued that for over twenty years, Nollywood has explored content that has the capacity to be turned around quickly. In this regard, Nollywood has reflected the capitalist priorities inherent in Nigeria's trade sector. Contributors to content did not have a ready market for such subjects as human rights. The industry did not accommodate the subject of social responsibility, nor did it engage with research and development focusing on stories. Unsurprisingly, then, the human rights element found in Nollywood has been limited to entertainment. What is more, it was often a matter of celebrating abuses rather than offering a progressive focus aimed at countering them. Okao's observations help explain why Nollywood content producers, critics, and scholars have found little interest in connecting Nollywood with human rights. At the same time, it is important to note that in some instances, a link can be discerned between the video phenomenon in question and human rights debates. This chapter contributes to knowledge by problematizing human rights issues through textual analyses of the Nigerian films *October 1* (2014, Kunle Afolayan) and *Black November*

(2012, Jeta Amata), two films that are of considerable interest within a human rights context.

The issue of human rights goes hand in hand with the eternal desire of all responsible government and nongovernment agencies and authorities to protect, uphold, and promote human life, dignity, and security. Human rights are rights considered by most societies, including Nigeria, to belong to everyone—for example, the rights to life, freedom, justice, and equality. Jacob Umoke affirms that "human rights are those liberties, immunities and benefits, which by accepted contemporary values, all human beings should be able to claim . . . in the society in which they live" (2014, 49). Human rights, that is, are those rights that belong to all human beings by virtue of being human, irrespective of nationality, religious conviction, ethnicity, race, gender, or class. However, the greatest threat to human rights comes when the state (i.e., government) that is charged locally and internationally with ensuring that they are respected and upheld turns its coercive institutions into instruments of gross human rights abuses or violations.

In today's precarious times, human rights are frequently violated, sadism and violence are perpetrated, and emerging democracies capitulate in the wake of insurgencies, ethnic cleansing, government insensitivity, extrajudicial killings, and emergency regimes, as we have seen in parts of the Americas, Asia, Africa, and the Middle East. These conditions produce the need to engage in critical reflection on our contemporary human situation. It is likely that Bonny Ibhawoh (2002) had such conditions in mind when he observed that human rights are not just about violations but also about the *legacies* of violations. Human rights are intrinsically tied to questions of social justice and the creation of inclusive communities. So, the future of human rights is one in which history and our understanding of the past will play a much bigger role, where we will have to pay as much attention to the legacies of past violations as we do to active violations. Based on analyses of selected Nollywood films, this chapter identifies different manifestations of violence, including past and present derogations of human rights, in Nigeria. These films are seen as either directly capturing or symptomatically expressing central aspects of Nigeria's history and contemporary situation.

Theoretical and Methodological Considerations

Scholars have variously acknowledged the dynamic interconnections between art practices, cultural studies, and activism (Morris and Hjort 2012, 1; Faris 2015, 43). Such links partly explain why Bamidele, in his influential book entitled *Literature and Sociology*, asserts that "literature, [whether written or visual], is a social institution around which there is a cluster of other traditions and institutions that sustain and maintain its growth and development" (2003, 21). It is the assumption here that such processes bring benefits to society more generally. Purveyors of the different forms of literature—dramatists, novelists, engravers, poets, and, in the case of this chapter, filmmakers—have a significant role to play, not least because they can be powerful advocates of the artistic and literary pursuit of particular social and political causes, including human rights issues, all for the improvement of the human condition. Niyi Osundare asserts that "[an] artistic creation involves the dialectically related triad of inspiration, choice, and aspiration. Choice is intensely influenced by aspiration, the social-ideological goal of the artistic product; inspiration is the enabling force that transforms choice into concrete artistic reality" (2007, 6). Although the fulfillment of an artist's aspiration is fraught with all kinds of problems, he or she has the option of deploying what Zoe Trodd (2009) has theorized as a "protest aesthetics," some kind of artistic activism or agitation propaganda aimed at achieving specific goals.

The concept of protest aesthetics, involving "the uses of language to transform the self and change society" (Trodd 2009, xii), is suggestive in the present context inasmuch as it posits connections between various forms of expression and change. As Trodd sees it, change rests on an initial transformation of the self, which in turn allows for transformation on the sociocultural level. Trodd asserts that "by language I refer not only to words, but to visual art, music, and film. Protest literature functions as a catalyst, guide, or mirror of social change. It not only critiques some aspects of society, but suggests, either implicitly or explicitly, a solution to society's ills" (2009, xii).

Aside from offering examples of verbal forms of performing protest, African narratives feature other aesthetical forms of protest, by pointing, for example, to the negative consequences of the actions and inactions of literary or filmic characters. In this sense, depictions of suicide, silence, civil demonstration, disobedience, self-immolation, remonstration, arson, and hunger strikes all potentially count as a form of protest. The varying forms of protest aesthetics that exist within any given culture must inevitably contend with a hegemonic superstructure, a resistive formation that counteracts the voice or demands of the "other." It is generally believed that society conditions its art forms, but it is highly ironic that in spite of widespread human rights abuses, Nollywood film culture has paid little attention to the relevant pervasive and deeply damaging practices in Nigerian society. The few Nollywood films that do acknowledge the importance of exploring human rights violations thus warrant careful scholarly consideration and far greater attention. This is so because "it is important in Africa, colonial [and post-colonial] terrors notwithstanding, to use cinema to 'convert' the masses to political action. The cinematographic experiment at its outset is ideological before being artistic" (Tcheuyap 2011, 16). Although human rights have not been a recurring or well-articulated topic in Nollywood, there is the need for a kind of reenvisioning by Nollywood filmmakers, and indeed scholars, one that aims to deploy film as a popular, informative medium for enlightening the Nigerian public, engaging state authorities, and mobilizing the populace to stand up against injustices, deprivations, and inhuman conduct, wherever and whenever they rear their ugly heads in Nigeria.

It is a matter of realizing the liberatory potential of film as a form of visual literature, of bolstering the intrinsic potential for a revolutionary aesthetics that lies within moving images, and of supporting the artistic option to engage with vital issues, including human rights. This kind of thinking probably informs Yvonne Foerster's view that "movies can tell us a lot about how we imagine humanity and its future" (2016, 48). Such ideas also speak to how films (for present purposes, Nollywood films) could be used to reach socially excluded or deprived persons, giving them platforms on which to ventilate their opinions and grievances, in terms of their natural rights and privileges. In this regard, Onuora Nwuneli and Alfred Opubor claim that "of all the media of mass communication, the motion picture has perhaps the most universal appeal and impact. Properly conceived and executed, a film can rise above the limitations of language and cultural barriers by the powers of its visual images, its use of music and sound effects, and can succeed in conveying much the same message to audiences of heterogeneous background" (1979, 1).

Using selected Nigerian films as templates to pinpoint and articulate central issues, this chapter illuminates the complex experiences of human rights abuses and how people have had to grapple with the issues they throw up. The findings are based on the qualitative research methods of content analysis, key informant interviews (KII), historical analysis, and nonparticipant observation. Qualitative research methods place special emphasis on how people understand, experience, and operate within milieus that are dynamic and social in their foundation and structure (Tewksbury 2009, 39; Meribe 2015, 205). Through the relevant research methods, I hope to provide insights into Nigerians' perspectives on how human rights issues are represented in the visual paradigms of *October 1* and *Black November*. The central claim here is that Nollywood films have the potential to become significant drivers of change and social transformation in Nigeria, a country that is at the crossroads of development.

Engaging the Nigerian Films *October 1* and *Black November*

October 1 is a murky psychosocial film that is set in colonial Nigeria, just a few days before independence. It is about the serial killings that have been going on in a remote Yoruba village, Akote (western Nigeria). The film opens with a girl being raped to death by an unknown male assailant. This prompts the British colonial authorities to send a police inspector, Danladi Waziri (Sadiq Daba), a northerner and a Hausa by ethnicity, to Akote to unravel the mystery behind the raping and killing of young girls. Danladi meets Sergeant Afonja (Kayode Aderopoko), who briefs him on the situation on the ground as a way of helping his investigations. Coincidentally, Danladi comes to town the same day Prince Aderopo (Demola Adedoyin), the heir-apparent to the Akote throne, comes home. One of the guards of Prince Aderopo is believed to be responsible for another case of

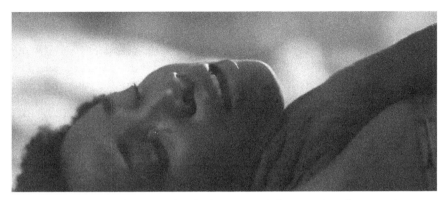

Figure 13.1. A young girl being raped to death. Framegrab from *October 1* (2014, Kunle Afolayan, Nigeria).

rape and murder. Yet, in some kind of miscarriage of justice, the guard's crimes are blamed on Usman Dangari, an innocent northerner and a Hausa traveler. The latter is accused simply because he is said to have been present at the scene of the crime and is a "nobody." The Hausa man gets sentenced to jail for what he really knows nothing about.

Okafor, the late girl's father, who is an Igbo man (played by Kanayo O. Kanayo), is not comfortable with the turn of events and decides to take the law into his own hands by stabbing the Hausa man to death on his way to the prison. Although the Igbo man is taken in by the police and the Hausa man is dead, the mysterious killings continue, with the viewer eventually being led to the crux of the matter through a series of flash-forwards and flashbacks. We learn of how Agbekoya (Kunle Afolayan) at the age of fourteen and Prince Aderopo at the age of twelve had to leave for Lagos in order to get a secondary education. While under the tutelage of Reverend Dowling (Colin D. Reese), they were sexually abused and molested every Thursday night in what their guardian euphemistically called "evening prayers." In the end we witness Prince Aderopo preparing to rape and kill his last victim, his childhood friend and classmate Bisi Tawa (Kehinde Bankole). We thus learn that the prince is behind the mindless killings because he feels that the village of Akote allowed Reverend Dowling to do all he did to him. As well, Agbekoya develops an anathema for Western education and forbids his own son from going to school; he prefers his son to work at the cocoa farm.

Black November tells of environmental degradation and the spoilage of aquatic and terrestrial ecosystems occasioned by the oil exploration and exploitation activities of Western Oil, an oil firm that actually operated in the Niger Delta region of postcolonial Nigeria. By Niger Delta I mean those parts of Nigeria (officially nine states) where there has been intense oil exploration, starting in 1958 at

Oloibiri, a town in the Ogbia area of local government, in Bayelsa State, Nigeria. In the movie, Ebiere Perema (Mbong Amata), a young, intelligent Niger Deltan, graduates from the university and subsequently becomes an activist after seeing her family consumed in a conflagration precipitated by an oil spillage caused by Western Oil. She protests with her people when officials of the company (both Nigerians and foreigners) try to bribe some elders in the community. She finds solace in Dede (Hakeem Kae-Kazim), another victim of circumstance, who also loses his family members in the civil protests aimed at drawing the world's attention to the government's and multinational oil corporation's indifference to human rights violations in the Niger Delta. Tamuno Aliabe (Enyinna Nwigwe) and his men (all of them police) initially beat and manhandle the protesters following a directive from "above." Yet, through a series of flashbacks, we see how the policeman Tamuno turns a new leaf and resigns from the force after seeing how the government unjustly manages the despoliation of the environment in the Niger Delta.

Tamuno joins Dede and other agitated youths of the community to form a transnational "agitation-propaganda" group, the United People's Front for the Emancipation of the Niger Delta People of Nigeria, which organizes intercontinental demonstrations (in Warri, Nigeria, and Los Angeles, United States) to the consternation of the government, the oil company, and their local colluders. This compels the government and Western Oil to call for a peace discussion with the revolutionaries. Ebiere is able to convince Dede to attend the peace talk, but the forces of the state and the oil firm use the occasion as a ploy to kill many of the "rebels." The thinking is that such killings will definitively defeat the group. Hell is let loose, and the center can no longer hold. Ebiere, who is sentenced to the gallows by the government of the day, is like a carrier in the mold of Eman in Wole Soyinka's *The Strong Breed* (1964). She has to carry the troubles of the community in the liberatory struggle to free her people from the fetters of bondage and oppression.

Human Rights Violations and Protest Aesthetics in *October 1* and *Black November*

The two films, *October 1* and *Black November*, which I have chosen for analysis in this chapter, illustrate the severity of human rights violations in Nigeria. Also, in pinpointing pervasive ills, they both have elements of protest aesthetics, which underscores the potential of Nollywood film narratives to help lift the Nigerian masses out of the socioeconomic and sociopolitical torpor to which the state authorities and their colluders (both local and international) have perennially tried to reduce them. The titles of both films have iconic or symbolic signification. *October 1* tells of the birth of a new country, the attainment of independence by Nigeria in 1960 from the British colonial power; *Black November* recalls the military junta of the maximum ruler, Sani Abacha, who killed a frontline environmentalist and human rights activist, Kenule Saro Wiwa. The latter was killed along with eight other activists under very questionable circumstances on November 10, 1995. A global plea for a fair hearing and a proper trial in a court of law did little to protect these victims of extrajudicial violence. Interestingly, the titles remind us of the Roman calendar months of October and November, which are coincidentally conterminous and belong to the last quarter of the year.

Black November is a revised and improved remake of *Black Gold* (2011, Jeta Amata, Nigeria). Although the film is a work of fiction, its story is based on actual events related to a Niger Delta community's struggle against the government and a multinational oil corporation to save the environment that is being destroyed by excessive oil drilling. At the height of the mass protests, the film flashes back to twenty-one years earlier during the military era, as Tamuno narrates the people's ordeal to a global public via Kristy's (Kim Basinger's) camera. Ebiere is born in Warri during the military era; she finishes high school and is offered a scholarship by Western Oil to study overseas. A few years later, an oil pipe in the Niger Delta bursts, and the people of the community go to fetch petrol from the pipe. Dede, a fisherman, discovers that fish in the river have been killed by the oil spillage. The police arrive at the spillage site and demand that the villagers vacate the area, but no one listens to them. When the site subsequently explodes, everyone, including all Ebiere's family members, is killed. At the core of *Black November* is the question of environmental human rights, which is also at issue in the Hollywood movie *On Deadly Ground* (1994, Steven Seagal). In the latter, an oil-company troubleshooter, Forrest Taft (Steven Seagal), fights the operators of an unsafe refinery in order to redress serious environmental human rights violations in a number of Alaskan communities in the United States.

Incessant gas flares loom over the Niger Delta communities, and farming and other economic activities in the area are hampered to the extent that the people have to devise means, whether right or wrong, of surviving. Ebiere's mother's (Mama's) conversation with the police officer before the spillage site explosion is instructive. It reminds us of an actual event that cost hundreds of lives and occurred in Jesse near Sapele in the Delta State of Nigeria. The conversation in the film is as follows:

POLICE OFFICER: You're all under arrest.

EBIERE'S MOTHER: What's our crime?

POLICE OFFICER: Stealing.

EBIERE'S MOTHER: Stealing?

POLICE OFFICER: This fuel is the property of the federal government of Nigeria.

EBIERE'S MOTHER: So, what would you rather we do? Stand by and watch the fuel of the federal government of Nigeria spill and spoil our land?

POLICE OFFICER: It is your duty to report any leakages in the pipelines.

EBIERE'S MOTHER: But we did, last week and no one came here to do anything about it.

POLICE OFFICER: I warn you not to go near the pipelines . . .

EBIERE'S MOTHER: What will you do? Shoot me? Which is worse? Watch the fuel flow past your house and yet in three days you cannot get one gallon of what your federal government cannot make available, ahn! [To the crowd that is scooping the fuel] Abeg! Continue. Take this fuel! Take fuel!

The unfolding events driving this tense conversation point to real-world conflicts and provide support for Lee Soyoung's claim that "film, especially, is a most hybrid form of cultural product that encompasses the spirit and historical determinants of the times. It shows a society in its most intensive form: Not only is it an imaginative reflection of life, but the society's production mode and economic issues are all integrated into the film's various forms, conflicting and in negotiation" (2016, 99). In fact, it is increasingly the case that politically powerful elites are monopolizing and manipulating the allocation of resources in ways that deny the needs of others, including those that form the basis for communal belonging. This has arguably fueled problems associated with identity politics in Africa (Mano 2015, 3).

Furthermore, we see officers of the state (soldiers) molesting, beating, maiming, and killing innocent children and men, while also raping women, both old and young, in the presence of their husbands. This they do in response to the slightest provocation or problem in the area. The persistence of such violations in the region is what makes the Dedes and Ebieres of real-life situations resort to self-help and take up arms to fight for their rights to freedom of expression, a decent life as part of God's creation, and fair treatment as bona fide citizens. Their aim is to liberate themselves from oppression and to halt the devastating exploitation of their environmental resources. In this regard, Paulo Freire (2000, 44) recounts that the determination of the oppressed to pursue liberation is motivated by a desire not to become the oppressors, but to liberate both themselves and the oppressors. He argues further that "the oppressors, who oppress, exploit and rape by virtue of their power cannot find in this power the strength to liberate the oppressed or themselves. Only the power that springs from the weakness of the oppressed will be sufficiently strong to free both" (2000, 44).

The character of Ebiere appears in the fiction to be living in the consciousness of Freire's postulation, trying to free both her people (the oppressed) and the multinational oil companies and corrupt leaders in the Niger Delta (the oppressors). In the conversation between Ebiere and Chief Kuku (Zack Amata) during a supposed truce meeting between the local oil-producing communities and Nigeria's oil interest groups, Ebiere evokes a strong commitment to the kind of liberation noted above, just as she opposes the denigration of women, which is rife among the Niger Delta people in Nigeria.

CHIEF KUKU: Is there no man to speak for your family?

EBIERE: I wish the fires had kept them alive. Besides, do men feel pain differently from women?

CHIEF KUKU: This is not a matter for women.

EBIERE: Then you will have to regard me as a man. Good show! Good show you put up here! Another wonderful way of pitting family against family . . . You come here, enriching yourselves from the spoils of our land. In the process, wiping out families and generations yet you keep the fuel burning . . . Give the people unrest, they would rely on you. What they do is give us sickness and then treat us. They make us hungry and then feed us. They kill our loved ones and then offer us money for burials. Can you not see their plan? It's high time you started thinking of the people rather than your selfish fat pockets and that of your goons and cohorts. If you do not change your ways the people will rise . . .

In the foregoing dialogue in *Black November*, Jeta Amata uses the case of the Niger Delta to tell us that in spite of Nigeria's enormous wealth of natural resources, the balance between resources, the environment, and development has deteriorated. And, by extension, the harsh reality in many parts of the country is that the quality of life has nose-dived to an abysmal level, respect for the human person having apparently been entirely lost. In agreement with the foregoing observation, Ehiemua, Okhiria, and Ehiemua contend that "the Nigerian environment is plagued by myriads of environmental problems and abuses of human and environmental rights. This includes drought and desertification, wind sheet and gully erosion, flooding, gas flaring, poor and absence of access roads, incessantly irregular power supply and lack of good potable water, amongst others. The situation has engendered pervasive poverty, loss of life and property and disillusionment. Some community members have lost faith in the 'Nigerian project' and justice delivery system" (2015, 201).

In view of the massive environmental degradation in the Niger Delta, the land can no longer sustain life (fishes in the river, food crops, animals on the farms, and even human beings are dying or being stunted as depicted throughout the film). This brings to the fore the question of sustainability or sustainable development, even as the oil companies promise some kind of El Dorado, a "heaven on earth" for local oil-producing communities. And when the companies fail to deliver, social instability is the result. In *Black November* there is a scene, for example, in which women are brutally beaten and molested by soldiers on behalf of the government and Western Oil tycoons.

Another angle on the issue of human rights in *Black November* is that of political thievery and corruption among community leaders and state authorities who ought to uphold societal values and a sense of human decency and dignity, but choose to engage in vicious practices and a primitive accumulation of wealth. We see this being portrayed by Gideon White (Fred Amata), the odiously corrupt community liaison officer who fleeces both the Western Oil officials and the local oil-producing communities of their money through doublespeak. We see it also in Chief Kuku, Chief Gadibia (Isaac Yongo), Chief Okon (Emmanuel Okhakhu), and other community elders who ignominiously share the compensation money that is meant for the development of the community while their people put up with misery. The point to note here is that internal agents (community elders) readily collude with external forces (oil companies and government authorities) to undermine the humanity of the toiling masses in the oil-producing communities. Scenes in the film speak to how ingrained human rights abuses are in the region and by extension in Nigeria.

It must be underscored that, to date, human rights violations in Nigeria are as alarming as they are appalling. Examples include the government's response to the killings of Shiite Muslims in Kaduna State or to the activities of pro-Biafran supporters as they peacefully protested the continuous detention of Sheik Ibrahim Yaquob El-Zakzaky of the Islamic Movement of Nigeria (IMN) in the North West region or in Nnamdi Kanu in the South East region of Nigeria. Strikingly, it is the diegetic motif of the people "doing themselves in" that forms the crux of the matter in *Oloibiri* (2016, Curtis Graham, Nigeria / Canada / USA), a film in which Gunpowder (Richard Mofe Damijo) engages in a fierce mêlée with Timipre (Olu Jacobs) over who controls the creeks and transacts "business" with the oil exploration companies. As is often the case in reality, the conflict leaves many innocent persons either dead or maimed for life. It is little wonder that there is an emerging literature (both visual and written) in Nigeria focusing squarely on the contemporary happenings in the Niger Delta.

Nwachukwu-Agbada (2009, 1) claims that the people of the Niger Delta labor in pain to eke out a living from a land and environment that has been devastated by years of prospecting for oil by powerful nonlocal companies. They had made their grievances known over time, but their leaders worked at cross-purposes with them and instead aligned themselves with the interests of the federal government of Nigeria and those of the oil conglomerates. The creation of states in 1967—the Rivers and Cross-Rivers States were carved out of the former Eastern region— seemed to have assuaged the people temporarily, although oil exploration continued, possibly with even less regard for the environment and its indigenous peoples. By the time the people, led by Kenule Saro Wiwa, returned to talk about the devastation of their environment in the early 1990s, they met with stiff opposition from Sani Abacha, an authoritarian leader who tolerated no opposition of any kind.

Kenule Saro-Wiwa, the Ogoni environmental activist, physically engaged eyeball-to-eyeball with the establishment monsters who were responsible for the poor social and psychological conditions of his people. As noted earlier, in what

Figure 13.2. Women demonstrating against Western Oil's environmental despoliation and human rights abuses in the Niger Delta. Framegrab from *Black November* (2012, Jeta Amata, Nigeria / USA).

looked like an extrajudicial killing, Saro-Wiwa and eight other activists were hastily executed, the aim being to ensure that they could no longer hinder the exploitation of the land's resources. However, the plan was unsuccessful, for the Niger Deltans responded both intellectually (through literary and other writings) and with an abrasive militancy that seems to have been entirely unexpected at the time. The people woke up to ask why "in spite of the huge revenue accruing from the exploitation of the oil under their feet, their region had been overly ignored in developmental terms while the resources realized from the sale of their crude oil had been used to develop certain cities in the other parts of the country as well as feathered the nests of certain individuals of a particular class in both the Niger Delta and elsewhere" (Nwachukwu-Agbada 2009, 1). Jeta Amata in *Black November* seems to be telling us that everywhere we look, we see the scars of poverty occasioned by environmental despoliation. The average Nigerian lives on less than two US dollars per day, and the average life expectancy in Nigeria is forty-seven years. Bribery and corruption in the corridors of power and political ineptitude have damaged the nation's fabric; hence, the fight no longer needs kid gloves, but organized and sustained civil engagements and mass protests geared toward redressing injustices, deprivations, and inhumanity.

October 1 is a subtle but powerful film that uses history as a screen on which to unfurl a number of human rights issues that have been glossed over or trivialized in Nigeria's sociocultural and historical evolution as a country. There is a probing search in this intensely psycho-physiological film: a search for the cause of the frequent female murder cases in the Akote community. From here emanates a range of human rights violations within the diegesis of the film. The case of Reverend Dowling is telling in this regard. He is a sexual pervert who frequently molests the boy children under his care, including Prince Aderopo and Agbekoya. What is more, he repeatedly engages in discriminatory behavior toward girls with educational aspirations, as depicted in his rejection of Tawa, even when she emerged as the best in her standard six examinations at St. David Primary School in Akote.

Apart from sexually violating Prince Aderopo and Agbekoya, Dowling stole their right to enjoy childhood and violated their right to protection. These violations are shown in the film as having had knock-on effects for other characters, including their own children. For instance, Agbekoya, having developed a strong hatred for Western education because of the abuses he suffered in the hands of Reverend Dowling, returns to Akote to become a farmer and insists that his own son will never pursue a Western education. The negative impact of the sexual molestation of children on society cannot be measured because it typically extends beyond the generation of the molester or the victim. We see an intergenerational educational backwardness being played out in the lives of Agbekoya and his son, all because Agbekoya was sexually abused and traumatized by the Reverend Father. This is happening "in an age that is characterised by technological and scientific literacy, [where] there is very little or nothing one can do if one lacks access to information" (Omoera and Ake 2016, 127). Thus, as Inspector Waziri puts it, Agbekoya and his illiterate son will end up being nobodys. We are given insight into the extent of the cruelty that Prince Aderopo and Agbekoya suffered in the hands of Dowling in the emotion-laden conversation between Agbekoya and Inspector Waziri:

> INSPECTOR WAZIRI: Primary education is free in the Western region of Nigeria. Why don't you allow your son to go to school?
>
> AGBEKOYA: Western education is bad.
>
> INSPECTOR WAZIRI: Hence, you become a farmer . . .
>
> AGBEKOYA: Is it a bad profession? Maybe you should ask Awolowo where he gets money for free education. It's from cocoa industry [*sic*].
>
> INSPECTOR WAZIRI: Reverend Father Dowling take[s] the two most intelligent boys to Lagos. One ends up attending King's College and graduates from the university. The other returns to farm the land. O! That's strange. What happened to you in Lagos, 'Koya? [touching Agbekoya].
>
> AGBEKOYA: Don't you touch me. Don't you ever touch me . . .
>
> INSPECTOR WAZIRI: Is that what he did to you. Did he flog you? Was he cruel to you? What kind of a man leaves King's to come back to the farm. 'Koya, you had every opportunity of becoming somebody but you're nobody. Your illiterate son will end up being nobody.
>
> AGBEKOYA: [Attempts to machete Inspector Waziri but breaks down emotionally and talks amidst sobs] I was fourteen and Ropo was twelve when we left for Lagos. During the day time, we attended school, but on Thursday night Father would beckon . . . The man will do unspeakable things to

me in that room. Things I could not understand. Things that destroyed my soul. . . . Then it will be Ropo's turn. . . . That man violated me every Thursday for five months. I had five months of violation but Ropo had six years . . .

INSPECTOR WAZIRI: And you said nothing.

AGBEKOYA: How could I speak the unspeakable?

In the Nigerian context and in most cultures of the world, sexual molestation is awful, but pedophilia (the sexual abuse of children), which is what Reverend Dowling engaged in, is worse. But we also have to acknowledge the painful, albeit unspoken, truth that pedophilia among Catholic priests, Muslim imams, and other priests of traditional religions is as rampant today as it was in the past. While specific cases have been uncovered, mostly because of whistleblowers and a high level of awareness in the Western world and some other places, abuse continues. What is more, its effects remain deeply buried in the wounded and ravaged minds of its victims—Prince Aderopo and Agbekoya in *October 1*—just as it continues to shape the sick and distorted minds of its perpetrators and those who covered it up in Africa, and, indeed, continue to do so. In the film Reverend Father Dowling is a placeholder for real people of his ilk in various African communities. The hushed stories about the revered village priest, or about the cute altar boys who turn into raging bulls brimming with anger and hate, are unfortunately still pervasive in different parts of Nigeria (Omoera 2004, 75).

The point to take away from this is that we all (parents, guardians, or adults) must be very careful about the issue of whom we entrust with our children because of what sexual molestation does to a child, especially in the areas of confidence and self-worth. Omoera and Akinwole argue that "forced sex is intended to abuse, humiliate, and dehumanize the victim" (2012, 168). An abused child becomes subdued morally and otherwise as a result of the molester's violence, leaving the child afraid to tell his or her parents or guardians and also fearful of saying no to the molester. Here too the roles of Prince Aderopo, Agbekoya, and Reverend Dowling in *October 1* are instructive. The molesters could be the children's uncles, aunts, teachers, church members, neighbors, caregivers, pastors, or imams, all of whom may come bearing gifts apparently intended to make the child feel loved. Of course, it is not the well-being of the child that is sought through various tricks and advances of a pedophile and sexual pervert, as is amply underscored in the figure of Dowling. Yet in the film, the Akote people do not see Dowling for what he is, because he is a "revered godly person." The boys who know of his evil abuse cannot speak up; instead, they bottle up their trauma and anguish, which they eventually release through horrible acts. The latter speak loudly of their anger. Consistent with the concept of protest aesthetics, these acts are indeed a form of protest against the situation. The dialogue between Tawa and Prince Aderopo further illuminates the kind of traumatic experiences that mold the warped outlook that the boys end up having on life:

> TAWA: Reverend Dowling! You must have missed him . . . Unlucky for me . . . Lucky for you.
>
> ADEROPO: Lucky for me! He violated me. You've no idea of what I went through. This whole town has no idea of what I went through in the hands of that monster for six years, but you will all suffer.
>
> TAWA: But why?
>
> ADEROPO: Because. I am in pain. You must all feel my pain . . . with six virgins for the six years of pain I suffered . . . in the hands of Reverend Dowling for six years. You all will suffer for what I went through in his hands. Six Akote virgins for the years I endured.

Onikoye (2016, 235) surmises that Aderopo's evil acts partly bring back memories of a historical-political past. For instance, Aderopo's view about the recurring ethnic antipathy, and his dispassionate prediction of an imminent war "in seven years," remind us of the Nigerian Civil War of 1967, although political independence is fast approaching during the period in which the film is set. The scriptwriter (Kunle Afolayan) deliberately puts the prediction in Aderopo's lines, perhaps to implicate him in the possibility of ethnic conflict. His singular act of murdering an Igbo girl puts Usman Dangari, a Hausa man, in a difficult situation. The fact that Inspector Waziri, who is Hausa, interrogates and detains Usman Dangari, is enough to elicit some feeling of animosity among the Igbo settlers in Akote, for they come to nurse the belief that the inspector might be protecting Usman Dangari on account of ethnic sentiments.

Indeed, the ethnic politics, rivalry, and cleansing that we see in the sociopolitical and socioeconomic spaces of today's Nigeria have a history. Nigerians, be they political leaders or ordinary citizens, tend to hide under the veil of ethnicity, committing crimes or violating the rights of others and expecting their own ethnic groups to shield and protect them against the "other." The British colonialists who are on the cusp of leaving the country in the film knew all this and used these dynamics against the peoples of the emergent nation. For instance, through Inspector Waziri's activities in *October 1*, we learn of how a white man flogged an Igbo man to death in Enugu for stealing chicken from a pot. This incident precipitated the killing of the white man by another Igbo man, who was in search of justice for his murdered brother. Okafor (an Igbo man) killed Usman Dangari (a Hausa man) under the erroneous notion that Usman killed his daughter; the outgoing British authorities preferred to lay the blame of the killings of virgin girls in Akote on Usman in their official reports because it was convenient for them to do so; Sergeant Afonja disagreed with Inspector Waziri when the latter's investigations pointed to the fact that Prince Aderopo—heir to the throne of Akote and of the same ethnic ancestry as Afonja—was the killer of the virgins.

The actions described above have elements of human rights violations, to lesser or greater degrees. The point here is to highlight a miscarriage of justice based on ethnic sentiments. It is a matter of justice for the highest bidder or the most connected because a poor person or a nobody cannot buy justice. Meanwhile, wealthy or influential people commit all sorts of crimes, including murders, heists, treasury lootings, money laundering, police brutality, and political assassination—to name but some of the practices rampant in Nigeria—and still get away with it.

These injustices continue in many parts of Nigeria. For example, in a country facing an unprecedented economic recession, one with extreme poverty and a government that has been unable to pay the salaries of civil servants for many months, the legislative arm of the Edo State government approves, among other things, the sum of 200 million naira for the outgoing governor, Adams Oshiomhole, and 100 million naira for his deputy, Pius Odubu, for them to build houses in any place of their choice. Clearly, such a legislative step is morally wrong and a clear instance of the most egregious greed and indifference to the plight of the masses in the context of a state that purports to be cash-strapped. It is not surprising, therefore, that a nongovernmental organization (NGO), the Socio-Economic Rights and Accountability Project (SERAP), has vowed to mobilize the masses and other civil society groups against the deeply immoral legislation in question. According to SERAP, the irksome legislative rascality is "coming at a time [when] the Edo State government cannot even pay its pensioners and [the] salaries of workers [.] [T]he amendment by the Edo State House of Assembly is immoral, unfair, unconstitutional, unreasonable, and a rip-off on a massive scale" (News360.info 2016).

Another telling example of egregious violations is the case of a Nigerian visual artist, Jelili Atiku, who was arrested in Lagos by the Nigerian police on the order of a traditional ruler in January 2016, for publicly posting art works that indict the corrupt activities of those in power. For this, he was said to have committed a felony. But the responsibility of art ought not to be restrictive and partial to the all-powerful in a society. The point is that the tropes of injustices, corruption, and the various attempts by reactionary forces to stifle the voices of protest are part of the thematic and artistic concerns of the film *October 1.* No matter the bleak picture that art may paint of a society, art and creativity are pro-people. More often than not, art takes the side of the oppressed or the defenseless.

With specific reference to filmmaking, Bonny Ibhawoh, a Nigerian professor of human rights history at McMaster University, Canada, in a personal communication with the author on November 1, 2016, affirmed that movie producers and directors should frame the themes of movies more explicitly around international human rights norms. For example, he explained that films should begin to focus on antihuman issues such as the Osu caste system, which is still prevalent among the Igbo people of Nigeria. This system, he claimed, is socially and morally unacceptable, and not just because it is against Christian teachings and values. Rather, the practice should be rejected on the grounds that it contravenes international legal human rights guarantees against discrimination that Nigeria and other African countries have supported with their governments' official signatures. What is more, the practice also contravenes the human rights guarantees in the Nigerian constitution, a fact that is also well worth evoking in films that reach large audiences, as Nollywood titles do. The thinking here is that such deliberate framings of human rights issues *as* human rights issues in Nollywood films can prompt Nigerians, and indeed Africans more generally, to become more aware of their rights and obligations, and, indeed, of their humanity. Nollywood can encourage capacious and neighborly attitudes, ones aimed at living fuller lives, in part as a result of treating others with dignity and respect.

Postscript

Nollywood content producers would do well to highlight the quiet work of human rights activists and NGOs that focus on a number of critical human rights issues: girl child marriages in northern Nigeria, police brutality, political corruption, gender discrimination, mistreatment and sexual abuse of internally displaced persons (IDPs), and the mindless killings of vulnerable Nigerians by the terrorist group Boko Haram, among others. This is because human rights are at the core of effective human security management (Imobighe 1998). Specifically, Peddie Okao, in a personal communication on October 25, 2016, insisted that Nollywood could get more involved in human rights issues in Nigeria by developing well-researched scripts on known cases of human rights abuses, and developing strong themes based on the relevant subject matter. The issue of entertainment is, of course, one that needs to be considered carefully in the context of human rights stories. Yet the elements that drive narrative can easily be accommodated by human rights storytelling. The resolution of conflicts, so central to storytelling, can be focused, for example, on the righting of abuses. Generally speaking, the industry could, by way of social responsibility, use the strong voice of Nollywood to crusade against human rights abuses at film festivals, seminars, conferences, and various media engagements, and, of course, on the many small screens where the films are typically watched.

The work of human rights activists often goes unreported or underreported in the local and international media. Examples here include the Nigerian Television Authority (NTA) and Cable News Network (CNN), both of which tend to focus on sensational human rights abuses and violations. We also need to tell uplifting stories about those committed artists-cum-activists who work tirelessly to uphold human rights in the country. Such stories will foster hope that all is not lost and encourage others to join the struggle for human rights. For example, films about the struggles against the Sani Abacha and Ibrahim Babangida dictatorships by prodemocracy groups in the 1990s would sit well with the

Nigerian film audience. So would films that would celebrate heroes and heroines such as Kudirat Abiola (a prodemocracy activist who was murdered in Nigeria for campaigning for the actualization of the democratic mandate Nigerians gave to her husband, M. K. O. Abiola, in an election that was regarded as free, fair, and credible in 1993); Gani Fawehimi (a frontline Nigerian lawyer and human rights activist who was severally incarcerated and tortured by the Nigerian government for publicly challenging the repressive policies and political highhandedness of those in government); Dora Akunyili (an internationally renowned Nigerian pharmacist and former director-general of the National Agency for Food and Drug Administration and Control [NAFDAC] who fought fake drug cartels in Nigeria to a standstill); and Gamaliel Onosode (a consummate industrialist and a humanitarian who initiated and executed many social projects geared toward the uplift of the Nigerian masses). Many of these personalities, among other worthy Nigerians, are, regrettably, not yet immortalized in Nollywood movies. Yet on the screen they would be able to inspire and educate a new generation of human rights activists and motivate larger groups to stand against injustice, corruption, and the impoverishment of the Nigerian populace.

In spite of the fact that we have demonstrated that *Black November* and *October 1* explore human rights issues, the need for an increased exploration of human rights discourses in Nollywood films remains. This is so because films are universally acknowledged platforms for advocating on behalf of sociopolitical and sociocultural causes. A noteworthy irony is that the government has yet to work out a clearly defined manner of reaping dividends from this burgeoning industry by systematically integrating it into its development objectives—and thereby into the new sustainable development goals (SDGs). The concept of sustainability relates to the continuity of economic, social, institutional, and environmental aspects of human society as well as the nonhuman environment. At a minimum, sustainability implies paying attention to the full spectrum of the effects of actions, insofar as they can be anticipated at present. At its most ambitious, the sustainability agenda is a means of configuring civilization and human activity so that society (in this case, Nigeria), its members, and its economic sectors are able to meet certain needs and reach their greatest potential in the present, while preserving biodiversity and natural ecosystems, and planning and acting for the ability to maintain these ideals in a very long term—typically at least seven generations (Jegede 2015, 204–205).

Hence, a blueprint on how to use film as an instrument for human rights education on a grand scale should be designed and implemented by concerned authorities in Nigeria, including the government, civil society organizations, Nollywood practitioners, and scholars. The point is to achieve the deliverables needed to redress the pervasive human rights violations in the country. Without an iota of doubt, films are potent narrative media for social causes. Given the searing poverty among the growing and adult populations, expansive accounts of how political corruption and a culture of impunity and brigandage can be replaced by integrity, accountability, and transparency, all of which are essential ingredients in development, should begin to take the center stage on the filmic chessboards of Nollywood content creators.

OSAKUE STEVENSON OMOERA is Senior Lecturer in the Department of Theatre and Media Arts, Ambrose Alli University, Ekpoma, Nigeria.

Filmography

Black Gold, 2011, Jeta Amata, Nigeria.
Black November, 2012, Jeta Amata, Nigeria / USA.
October 1, 2014, Kunle Afolayan, Nigeria.
Oloibiri, 2016, Curtis Graham, Nigeria / Canada / USA.
On Deadly Ground, 1994, Steven Seagal, USA.

References

Afolayan, Adeshina, ed. 2014. *Auteuring Nollywood: Critical Perspectives on* The Figurine. Ibadan, Nigeria: University Press PLC.
Bamidele, Lawrence O. 2003. *Literature and Sociology*. Ibadan, Nigeria: Stirling-Horden.
Ehiemua, Roseline O., Regina J. Okhiria, and Kingsley I. Ehiemua. 2015. "Creating Awareness of Laws and Environmental Justice through Drama: Lessons for Clinical Legal Education." *Iroro: Journal of Arts* 16 (1): 197–215.
Faris, Phoebe. 2015. "Art and Activism: Defining the Homeland." In *The Map Is Not the Territory: Parallel Paths—Palestinians, Native Americans, Irish*, edited by Jennifer Heath, 43–53. Boulder, CO: Baksun Books and Arts.
Foerster, Yvonne. 2016. "Singularities and Superintelligence: Transcending the Human in Contemporary Cinema." *Trans-Humanities* 9 (3): 33–50.
Freire, Paulo. 2000. *Pedagogy of the Oppressed*. 30th anniversary edition. New York: Continuum.
Haynes, Jonathan, ed. 2012. *Journal of African Cinemas* 4 (1). Special issue on Nollywood.
Haynes, Jonathan. 2016. *Nollywood: The Creation of Nigerian Film Genres*. Chicago: University of Chicago Press.
Ibhawoh, Bonny. 2002. "Between Culture and Constitution: Evaluating the Cultural Legitimacy of Human Rights in the African State." *Human Rights Quarterly* 22 (3): 832–60.
Imobighe, Thomas A. 1998. *The Management of National Security*. Inaugural Lecture, Series 10 of Edo State University, Ekpoma. Ekpoma, Nigeria: Edo State University Publishing House.
Jegede, Emmanuel. 2015. "Urban Centres and the Question of Sustainable Development: A Case for Strategic Transformation of Nigerian Cities." *Iroro: Journal of Arts* 16 (2): 198–215.
Krings, Matthias, and Onookome Okome, eds. 2013. *Global Nollywood: The Transnational Dimensions of an African Video Film Industry*. Bloomington: Indiana University Press.

Lee, Soyoung. 2016. "*Jane Eyre* in Our Times: Fukunaga's *Jane Eyre* in Dialogue with Two Film Adaptations." *Trans-Humanities* 9 (3): 99–125.

Mano, Winston. 2015. "Racism, Ethnicity and the Media in Africa." In *Racism, Ethnicity and the Media in Africa: Mediating Conflict in the Twenty-First Century*, edited by Winston Mano, 1–27. London: I.B. Taurus.

Morris, Meaghan, and Mette Hjort. 2012. "Introduction: Instituting Cultural Studies." In *Creativity and Academic Activism: Instituting Cultural Studies*, edited by Meaghan Morris and Mette Hjort, 1–20. Hong Kong: Hong Kong University Press.

Meribe, Nnaemeka. 2015. "Reappraising Indigenous African Communication Systems in the Twenty-First Century: New Uses for Ancient Media." *Journal of African Media Studies* 7 (2): 203–16.

News360.info. 2016. "Withdraw N300m Mansion Package for Oshiomhole, SERAP tells Obaseki." Accessed November 17, 2016. http://news360.info/2016/11/17/withdraw -n300m-mansion- package-oshiomhole-serap-tells-obaseki/.

Nwachukwu-Agbada, J. O. J. 2009. "Oil, Soil and Foil: Isidore Okpewho's Tidal Victims in his Niger Delta Novel of Environment." *Madonna Journal of English and Literary Studies* 1: 1–13.

Nwuneli, Onuora, and Alfred Opubor, eds. 1979. *The Development and Growth of the Film Industry in Nigeria*. Lagos: National Council for Arts and Culture (NCAC).

Ogunleye, Foluke, ed. 2014. *African Film: Looking Back and Looking Forward*. Newcastle upon Tyne: Cambridge Scholars Publishing.

Omoera, Osakue S. 2004. "Child Abuse and the Media: A Survey of the Oredo Local Government Area Situation." MA dissertation. University of Benin, Benin City.

Omoera, Osakue S., and Kehinde O. Ake. 2016. "Extreme Violence and the Media: Challenges of Reporting Terrorism in Nigeria." *Trans-Humanities* 9 (3): 127–46.

Omoera, Osakue S., and Omolola T. Akinwole. 2012. "A Review of Literature: Rape and Communication Media Strategies in Nigeria." *Benin Mediacom Journal* 6: 164–84.

Onikoyi, Babatunde. 2016. "Kunle Afolayan's *October 1*: A Review." *African Studies Review* 59 (1): 234–5.

Osundare, Niyi. 2007. *The Writer as Righter: The African Literary Artist and His Social Obligations*. Ibadan: Hope Publications.

Soyinka, Wole. 1964. *The Strong Breed*. Oxford: Oxford University Press.

Tcheuyap, Alexie. 2011. "African Cinema(s): Definitions, Identity and Theoretical Considerations." *Critical Interventions: Journal of African Art History and Visual Culture* 5 (1): 10–26.

Tewksbury, Richard. 2009. "Qualitative versus Quantitative Methods: Understanding Why Qualitative Methods Are Superior for Criminology and Criminal Justice." *Journal of Theoretical and Philosophical Criminology* 1 (1): 38–58.

Trodd, Zoe F. 2009. *The Reuseable Past: Abolitionist Aesthetics in the Protest Literature of the Long Civil Rights Movement*. Cambridge, MA: Harvard University Press.

Tsaaior, James T., and Francoise Ugocghukwu, eds. 2017. *Nigerian Film Culture and the Idea of the Nation: Nollywood and National Narration*. London: Adonis and Abbey.

Umoke, Jacob C. 2014. "The Status of Nigerians' Rights to Life and the Environment: A Comparative Critique of the Nigerian Constitution." *Nigerian National Human Rights Commission Journal* 4: 45–77.

14 The Antiecstasy of Human Rights

A Foray into Queer Cinema on "Homophobic Africa"

John Nguyet Erni

As a result of the triumph of the Anti-homosexuality Act in Uganda in 2014, the country has been portrayed by the international press and human rights organizations as the epicenter of state political homophobia sweeping across the African continent. Although the Constitutional Court of Uganda nullified the act on procedural grounds, there remain concerns that a similar bill or equivalent repressive measures could become law. David Bahati, the legislator who is the chief architect of the act, promised to bring forth an amended bill to Parliament again. In Uganda, there is widespread homophobia and transphobia; traditional moral beliefs that queer rights violate the "dignity of all Ugandans" are still held. In law, same-sex conduct remains punishable with life imprisonment under Uganda's colonial-era law prohibiting "carnal knowledge against the order of nature." Above all, as Michael Bosia and Meredith Weiss (2013) have suggested, *political homophobia* is in fact a purposeful state strategy, something "as embedded in the scapegoating of an 'other' that drives processes of state building and retrenchment; as the product of transnational influence peddling and alliances; and as integrated into questions of collective identity and the complicated legacies of colonialism" (1).

Aside from the continuous flurry of debates and condemnation that took place in the media domestically and internationally, as well as dismay expressed at multiple levels of the international human rights bodies, critical voices from political theorists, anthropologists, sociologists, African historians, art critics, and legal specialists have provided much-needed cogent analyses of this troubling trend of state political homophobia in Africa (e.g., Awondo et al. 2012; Boyd 2013; Cheney 2012; Coly 2013; Makofane et al. 2014; Matebeni 2014; Oliver 2013; Rice 2007; Wahab 2016). At the core of the many questions raised, the most puzzling has to do with the difficult matter of explaining the rise of a blatant antirights configuration of the "gay menace" at a transnational scale, against a general, equally transnational euphoria around the triumph of queer rights in the world today. Approaching this from a postcolonial cultural studies perspective, we may say this presents a perplexing "conjunctural" moment of struggle, constellated by multiple agents weaving a discursive network of contradictory relations of power, imagery, practices, and influence (Grossberg 2010).

If there is indeed a "conjunctural Africa" to speak about in relation to queer persecution today, one can mark this conjuncture as a crossroads of human rights global politics. In other words, the disavowal of queer existence in countries like Uganda reminds us of the contradiction between "the end of human rights" as proclaimed by many (witness the refugee crisis, Islamophobic wars, extreme environmental degradation, securitization, and all forms of social and economic exploitations; see Douzinas 2000; Erni 2009; Hopgood 2013; Luban 2003; Kennedy 2004), and the ethical-political renewal of global rights accountability (marked by constitutional reform movements everywhere, and all scales of resurgent political organizing and protests; see Boyle 2006; Erni 2010, 2012; Zembylas and Bozalek 2014). These two opposing views of human rights, I want to suggest, are in fact arising in tandem with the "worlding" of the global queer figure. More specifically, I suggest that an analytical response adequate to the political crisis over the intensification of queer hatred in recent times (in Africa, or anywhere for that matter) is to ask how this particular crisis is throwing up a discursive worlding—that is, putting into the world and creating the world at the same time—of a queer political predicament that fuses despair and ecstasy, correlating to the twin discourses about the death and renewal of human rights at a conjunctural scale.

My interest in this chapter, therefore, is to map out some of the elements in the worlding process that produces the instability of queer rights, and to do so through a study of the crisis of homophobia in the specific context of Uganda. I do not presume to know what the "whole map" looks like, if ever such a thing is possible. But in the context of the intellectual interests of this volume, I take cues from Karl Schoonover and Rosalind Galt's recent book *Queer Cinema in the World* (2016) to ask how cinema in general intersects with cosmopolitan notions of diversity, geopolitics, and aesthetics. My aim is to toss up a scope for a world that allows us to understand queerness as a site of both despair and ecstasy, at a time of mounting ambivalence about the usefulness of human rights. I am therefore most interested in the worldliness of the queer, acknowledging that the queer has in so many instances already trekked the world over, through global human rights campaigning, legal reform, intersectional social movements, artistic interventions, and media discourses. Here, I am simply adding to it the sphere of the cinematic, through which the queer figure enacts its worldly trekking.

To direct our attention to the cinematic is to invite an understanding of it in a worldly fashion, as (a) contextualization, (b) textuality and aesthetics, and (c) consumption and campaigning. I therefore jump into Schoonover and Galt's project of mapping queer worldliness through these three important lenses, using their approach of queer cinematic globalism to attend to the crisis of homophobia in Uganda. The political objective of such an exercise is, to echo Schoonover and Galt, to disrupt the kinds of normativities that structure the ways of being in the world for queers as a result of the fears of persecution in the thickening moment of queer hatred, as seen in Uganda and elsewhere. To trace this map through films, I turn specifically to two well-known works as impetus for contextualization, queer textual reading, and consideration of international consumption in the human rights circuit. The two documentary films are Roger Ross Williams's *God Loves Uganda* (2013) and Malika Zouhali-Worrall and Katherine Fairfax Wright's *Call Me Kuchu* (2012). The former is an American production, directed by an African American director, whereas the latter is an American-Ugandan production, directed by two American women. The convergences and juxtapositions presented by this pair of works, I will argue, afford a critical understanding of African queer worlding.

"Homophobic Africa"?: A Postcolonial Critique

In both the opening and ending of Roger Ross Williams's *God Loves Uganda*, we are presented with the specter of a distressed future for Uganda. This international hit delivers an exposure of the long-term and ever-intensifying indoctrination of homo-hatred by the American evangelical movement onto the soil of Uganda. The film opens with a narrator speaking about something frightening happening to his beloved Uganda that has the potential to destroy it. This distress is paired with imagery of Ugandan children playing in the field, unaware of the ideological perils festering around them, as signified by the presence of a church in the background of the playing field. The narration clearly implies that these children—and their future—are in danger. Toward the ending of the film, after having worked through the exposé of the American evangelical indoctrination, the tragedy of Uganda is represented by young men hitting each other in fist fights, shown in uncomfortable slow motion. A scene of bullying against queers in open air, this ending projects a distressed future for Uganda, as a place ripe for violence and disintegration.

Director Williams recalls the jubilance in Kampala where thousands of people were celebrating the passage of the antihomosexuality bill in ways comparable to how they celebrated Uganda's independence. About this, Williams says in an interview: "I totally felt this sort of impending genocide. And you can feel that. It's the same way they dehumanized the Tutsis. They're dehumanizing the LGBT community in this sort of witch-hunt. They say things like, they're worse than animals, they're worse than dogs" (Farley 2014, 13). Here, Williams made the chilling comparison between the Rwandan genocide of 1994 and the reveling in the passage of the antihomosexuality bill in Uganda as creating a poisonous environment ripe for an enflaming imagination of gay death. These two moments in the opening and ending of the film present a narrative arc, a movement through which the innocence of a beloved Uganda has tragically devolved into the darkness of hatred and a looming sense of genocide.

What does homo-hatred look and feel like? In this section, I approach this question as an important link in the discursive worlding of queerness in Africa. *God Loves Uganda* presents the idea that this world is toxic: the queer person or body is almost entirely absent from the film (except for a brief scene toward the end of the film, showing the funeral of slain Ugandan gay activist David Kato); there is only the toxicity of ideological indoctrination. In other words, the work of contextualization in *God Loves Uganda* is performed through examining the nature, practice, and impact of a particular type of brainwashing poison. What is presented to the viewer is, indeed, the question of what homo-hatred looks and feels like. This contextualization is thus highly affective: in Uganda, God is angry. In the hands of the local clergy and the parliamentary political culture, the unbiblical practice of the homosexual lifestyle in the country is translated into un-Africanness.

But how do the local church and political system turn against their own queer citizens? If the broad political machine here is the American evangelical church (specifically the International House of Prayers based out of Kansas), then the nuance in the delivery of the indoctrination lies in the affective bodies of Christian youth. Awed by an angry God but believing in his redemptive nature, the youth received evangelical training, passionately living out a dream of traveling deep into the heart of Africa to deliver God's message. As one of the young evangelists espouses, echoing the charismatic American Christian crusader Lou Engle: we are here to "disciple the nations"; "Africa is a firepot of spiritual renewal and revival." I will have much more to say about the film's treatment of the evangelical youth later in the chapter.

In contrast, for Malika Zouhali-Worrall and Katherine Fairfax Wright's *Call Me Kuchu*, the answer to the question of what homo-hatred looks and feels like is given through the depiction of the activist life and brutal murder of Uganda's most prominent queer activist, David Kato (1964–2011). At the beginning of the film, it is explained that "Kuchu," a word of Swahili origin, is a term that refers to queers in Uganda. Throughout the film, the viewer is led to witness what hatred looks and feels like through the eyes of Kato and his activist community.

Whereas *God Loves Uganda* pins the source of homo-hatred on longstanding evangelical indoctrination by the United States, intimating an imminent genocide of queer people in Uganda, *Call Me Kuchu* zeroes in on the local Ugandan newspaper *Rolling Stone*, under the editorial management of twenty-two-year-old Giles Muhame. A weekly tabloid newspaper published in Kampala with a small circulation, *Rolling Stone* relied on a readership that was apparently excited to read anything about queer people in Uganda. Muhame admits to this in the film. As if presenting key evidence to indict the paper for inciting homo-hatred, the film exhibits two front-page stories. One is entitled "100 Pictures of Uganda's Top Homos Leak," published on October 9, 2010, which listed the names, photographs, and addresses of one hundred queers in Uganda alongside a yellow banner that read "Hang Them." Holding up the paper to the camera, Muhame spoke about the insert of "Hang Them" with a nonchalant attitude and a grin on his face. In a manner totally different from that of the fanatical Christians shown in *God Loves Uganda*, the persona of Muhame in the film displays an understated calmness; he is not fussed up about anything in the world. Repeatedly, he is seen speaking to the camera in an informal style, cool in his composure and tone, unconcerned, it seems, at the potential impact of the stories that he prints. This relaxed posture transmits an underlying code of "journalistic ethics," if you will, that serves the function of guarding Muhame's own moral ground against homosexuality, all the while profiting from the curiosity of a homophobic public that reads his paper. The "Hang Them" story also alleged that gay people aimed to "recruit" Ugandan children, replaying the fear of the monstrosity of the queer sexual predator.

The second front-page story of *Rolling Stone* that is exhibited in the film carries the headline "Homo Generals Plotted Kampala Terror Attacks." The story alleges a connection between the Somali terrorist group al-Shabaab and Ugandan gay people in a complicitous terrorist suicide attack in Kampala in July 2010. If the evangelical force seen in *God Loves Uganda* elects Africa to be the "firepot of spiritual renewal and revival" (in the words of Lou Engle, the charismatic American antigay crusader), then the hatred-fanning local media such as *Rolling Stone* in *Call Me Kuchu* would construe Africa as a space contaminated by the obscenity and even terror of homosexuality (see Nyong'o 2012). Both films, in the end, converge on raising in the minds of the viewers the cancer of homophobia spreading across Africa.

Around 2011, the news of the Anti-homosexuality Act in Uganda was widely reported (dubbed the "Kill the Gays bill" by the Western mainstream media), prompting international debate about a homophobic Africa. A wave of homophobia was sweeping across the whole continent, it was alleged. The frenzy of debates branded the entire continent of Africa as the undifferentiated space of homohatred. In the thick of the imminent recriminalization of queers in Uganda in 2014, David Smith of the *Guardian* wrote: "Western liberals eager to see the best in Africa must face an inconvenient truth: this is the most homophobic continent on Earth. Same-sex relations are illegal in 36 of Africa's 55 countries, according to Amnesty International, and punishable by death in some states. Now a fresh crackdown is under way" (Smith 2014).

Earlier in 2010, the Associated Press had already run stories that proclaimed the spread of the potent force: "A wave of intense homophobia is washing across Africa, where homosexuality is already illegal in at least 37 countries. In the last year alone, gay men have been arrested in Kenya, Malawi, Sierra Leone, and Nigeria. In Uganda, lawmakers are considering a bill that would sentence homosexuals to life in prison and include capital punishment for 'repeat offenders.' And in South Africa, the only country that recognizes gay rights, gangs have carried out so-called 'corrective' rapes on lesbians" ("Even after Death," 2010). In addition, Coly (2013) talks about BBC's *The World's Worst Place to Be Gay?*, a 2011 documentary on homophobia in Uganda that similarly extends the sweeping notion of "homophobic Africa" as the overarching ideation for the entire continent (Alcock 2011).

While *God Loves Uganda* does not provide a direct response to the all-encompassing blanket claim, it does present homophobia as something more complex: homophobia in Africa is an American-African coproduction. This is the worlding power of the documentary film in question, for it offers a contextualization of the hybridity of forces, albeit formed through the evangelical importation of fear and anxiety toward queers from the United States to Uganda and other African nations. Journalist Keguro Macharia (2010) puts it pointedly: "Homophobia in Africa is a problem, but not as *African* homophobia, a special class that requires special interventions. And certainly not the kinds of special interventions that reconsolidate old, ongoing and boring oppositions between a progressive west and an atavistic Africa" (in Coly 2013, 22; emphasis his). Remembering Valentin Mudimbe's *The Invention of Africa* (1988) and *The Idea of Africa* (1994), Achille Mbembe's *On the Postcolony* (2001), and the works of many other African thinkers, we need to assert that the ideological prescription of homophobia as a conceptual cognate for Africa at large in fact stems from colonial and neocolonial framings of the West *about itself* (see also Ekine 2013; Hoad 2007). Every postcolonial intellectual has made a similar argument that the construction of Africa, be it good or ugly, euphoric or decrepit, in fact pertains to the self-construction of the colonial West through demarcation and disavowal of "absolute Africa" as radical otherness.

Curiously though, in both home-grown and imported evangelicalism, homo-hatred is produced through the designation of homosexuality as both "deeply African" (recall the cynical history of "African AIDS" in the 1990s) and un-African at the same time (see also Tamale 2007). While colonial framings insist that homosexuality in Africa is primordially strange (as opposed to civilized respectable sexuality in the West), local religious and political voices stress the disintegration that homosexuality brings to the primordially sacred African social and moral order. This curious combination—the coproduction suggested above—is displayed in *God Loves Uganda* through scenes of local Ugandan men preaching the sin of homosexuality on the streets of Kampala. Waving Bibles and dressed in Western suits, these men, we are told, have undergone special training by the team of young American evangelicals from the International House

Figure 14.1. Young evangelical soldiers as walking zombies or mental patients. Framegrab from *God Loves Uganda* (2013, Roger Ross Williams, USA).

of Prayers (and by Jo Anna Watson, an American missionary living in Uganda). In the street scenes, the figure who embodies the coproduction of homophobia in Africa is neither the white colonizer nor the local African clergy, but the ordinary young black men as preachers. No other scene in the film makes this point about hybridized religiosity more chillingly than the one showing black youth, men and women, in a large empty room crossing each other, each mumbling scriptures out loud. Their eyes are cast downward, never exchanging contact with one another. They walk briskly in lines, keeping their bodies moving and passing each other, as if absorbed in a personal conversation with their Savior. In showing how the young Africans prepare themselves fanatically through self-drilling over Bible verses, the scene displays them as walking zombies, reminiscent of patients in a mental facility. This fervent, exaggerated religiosity is a combination of imported and home-grown passions, coproducing the black subjects as warriors in an intensifying culture war.

What this insistence on coproduction does is remind us of the strange predicament of the local LGBTI movement in Uganda, one that fights for queer rights in the country on the one hand, but does so on the other hand by touting the same assertion of "homosexuality is un-African" as the reactionary preachers, in order to boost its persuasiveness in the eyes of potential foreign donors in the West. This dependence on outside resources also forces the movement to use Western gender and sexual identity terminology in African LGBTI activism. Coly (2013) cautions: "Ultimately, the need for proficiency in Western identity categories, acronyms, and strategies bolsters the dominance of African homophobia" (24).

It also bolsters the dominance of Western-style LGBTI activism through its own export to other parts of the world. John McAllister (2013) is right in suggesting that precisely because both modern notions of LGBTI identities and universal human rights *are* Western constructs and imports, they allow reactionary forms of nationalism to play on complex postcolonial feelings, dragging LGBTI activism in Africa into the mud, as it were.

Meanwhile, Joseph Massad (2002, 2007) is perhaps best known for his fierce criticism of global gay activism—what he calls the formation of the "Gay International"—for promoting an agenda and political tactics that force a replication and assimilation of Western sexual epistemology in non-Western contexts. In this way, the complexity of the coproduction of homo-hatred in Africa is unwittingly exacerbated by the success of global queer activism, if not the mainstreaming of the human rights movement itself (see Awondo et al. 2012). However, this kind of inescapable irony is entirely lost in *God Loves Uganda*, because unfortunately the film does not engage with LGBTI activism in Uganda or international queer activism at all.

In contrast, LGBTI activism, with all of its mortal trials and tribulations, is central to the narrative of *Call Me Kuchu*. There is a certain simplicity to the narrative and imagery in the film. "Activism is ordinary" might be a way to describe the narrative and imagery, resonating with the political ethos of Raymond Williams, who underscores through his famous statement of "culture is ordinary" that cultural life is mundane. But it is more to the uncharted nature of everyday cultural life embodied in Williams's statement that I want to turn to here. The argument I want to advance at this point about *Call Me Kuchu* is that it unfolds a kind of global worlding of ordinary queer life and activism, the worldliness of which pivots on the anxiety and uncharted dangers of everyday spaces. The film shows us a queer worldliness that stems merely from ordinary queer people's mundane search for happiness and basic personal safety. Yet this banality is replete with everyday anxiety, indeed rife with mortal danger under the diabolical atmosphere of homo-hatred fanned by papers like *Rolling Stone*.

Two divergent kinds of contextualization of the notion of "homophobic Africa" are presented in *God Loves Uganda* and *Call Me Kuchu*. Each connects to an empirical world out there, and enacts its own worlding, thereby returning cinema itself to the primary function of being political. In these instances, cinema as political discourse and practice engages with the vexed problem of human rights. Since the subject matter of these films is queerness (and the necropolitics surrounding it), the political foundation of cinema in this instance has had to confront an important question—namely, how would cinema about queers or queer cinema engage with the dominant human rights epistemology, as a product of Western history and moral politics? We may quickly assume that the universal and Western-inflected human rights paradigm frays at the edges in the context of

Africa. We may take for granted a certain postcolonial impulse of resistance that exists in an engagement with African matters. However, if we take a closer look, we may discover the contrary.

Whereas *God Loves Uganda* blatantly exposes the evil of Western religious rites as these are enacted to fan homo-hatred in Uganda, *Call Me Kuchu* flags the significance of sexual minority freedom and dignity as it is conceived in the Western human rights paradigm. Both films work within the parameter of this stable, universalizing Western model of rights; the difference is that the former criticizes it while the latter embraces it. This recuperation of the Western human rights model in these films can be explained by three major factors. First, there is the sheer fact that both films involve American participation (*God Loves Uganda* is an American production; *Call Me Kuchu* is an American-Ugandan production). Second, the itinerary with which they travel from film festivals to art house cinemas to other educational spaces—mostly in the West—also dictates the way human rights are to be read and adopted according to broad global understandings of rights and freedom. Third, as mentioned before, both the actors within the diegesis of the films (especially the evangelical church in *God Loves Uganda* and the queer activists in *Call Me Kuchu*), as well as the agents who enable these films to travel as human rights films, depend on a Western audience, if not Western donors. This strongly suggests a degree of connectivity with the legibility of Western human rights thinking and practice in the films about Africa.

Returning to the theme of (queer) worlding, we may say that in a broad sense both films recuperate the West and its human rights ideals, and they do so through the narrative work done around the very question of homophobia. Whether homophobia as framed in these films spreads like a contagious virus (in the story of *God Loves Uganda*) or literally kills queers (in *Call Me Kuchu*), it is a subject matter that instantly activates the dominant human rights moral epistemology. It also activates a dominant sense of queer worlding. Put more simply, we do not find in these films alternative or *indigenous* queer worldings, or their political sense of freedom and rights. In this way, Schoonover and Galt (2016) are right to point out that even in designating queer cinema as "promi[sing] to knock off kilter conventional epistemologies," they "use the term 'worlding' to describe queer cinema's ongoing process of constructing worlds, a process that is active, incomplete, and contestatory and that does not presuppose a settled cartography. Any utterance about the world contains a politics of scale that proposes particular parameters for that world, and we insist on de-reifying the taken-for-granted qualities that these parameters often possess" (5).

On a broad scale, therefore, both *God Loves Uganda* and *Call Me Kuchu* succeed in raising considerable global attention to the dire issue of homo-hatred in Uganda, leading to strong campaigns that put pressure on local politics and legislature. However, this broad scale of politics cannot guarantee a reorganization of dominant understandings of queer rights. To be sure, there are competing lines of force in the world-making that these films produce. In the following sections, I discuss two specific lines of force that compete to produce queer worlds through the two films. One line focuses on textuality, while the other centers on an institutional analysis. Together with the work of contextualization, a third line of force, these emphases form a good part of the sort of methodology proposed by Schoonover and Galt in their *Queer Cinema in the World*.

Queer Ecstasy

In this section, I attempt to animate the way queerness circulates in the two films concerned. I keep the analytical structure of the three axes of queer worlding produced by the films: contextualization, queer textuality and aesthetics, and consumption and market circulation. It has been suggested that cinema produces worlds and worldliness. Contextualization is the first axis with which we can trace this worlding—in this instance, the worlding that gives shape to the discourse on homophobia in Africa. Both *God Loves Uganda* and *Call Me Kuchu* contextualize the dark worlds of homo-hatred, by narrating the euphoric evangelicalism and despondent activism, respectively; in doing so, they recuperate the dominant worlding that is the world of human rights. Moving into the second axis here, I want to open up a discussion on the queer sensibilities of the films, a dimension that, while emanating from the site of textuality, is actually elusive but supple with imagination.

I am especially interested in the question of ecstasy as exhibited in *God Loves Uganda* and endeavor to read ecstasy as queer sensibility. In the film, the demonization and fear of homosexuality emits from the ecstatic bodies of the young evangelicals, thereby drawing a curious, and even surprising, connection between an organized religious practice bent on destroying homosexuality in Africa and a set of highly charged, semispontaneous, and ecstatic bodily performances that sensualize the whole evangelical experience. The word "evangelical" is synonymous with "zealous," "intense," and "fervent," suggesting a state of being, and not only an organized institutional practice. It is not that the ecstasy renders these young evangelicals gay, nor is it the case that Christianity is somehow subterraneously gay. I suppose there are plausible arguments to pursue on these grounds, but I think those considerations are misguided. Rather, ecstasy— as intense affect, as that which circulates between and across bodies-in-a-crowd, and as encounters amassing over time into more heady ideological convictions— mediates the relation between the evangelical institutions and the evangelizing bodies *as a relation of queerness*. I shall illustrate what I mean through examples from *God Loves Uganda*. But let me first say something briefly about the notions of "queer" and "affect."

Schoonover and Galt (2016) write: "The queer worlds we explore are made available through cinema's technologies, institutional practices, and aesthetic forms, which together animate spaces, affective registers, temporalities, pleasures, and instabilities unique to the cinematic sensorium" (6). They emphasize an approach that sees cinema as an *apparatus*, with representational, technological, sensorial, and affective components, all moving together to produce worlds. They go on to say: "It is crucial to affirm that cinema is not simply a neutral host for LGBT representations but is, rather, a queerly inflected medium," and "the dynamism of the cinematic image pushes against the reification of meaning, as it keeps the signifier in motion, never fixing terms of relationality" (6–7). Schoonover and Galt point out examples of those who have provided the queer cinematic prototypes indicating the fluidity of signification: Laura Mulvey's ([1975] 1999) use of the term "transvestite" to refer to Hollywood films' requirement that the female spectator mediate her identification through the male gaze; Maria San Filippo's (2010) suggestion of "the bisexual space of cinema," again as a spectatorial potentiality of reading across gendered selves and desires in cinema; and so on. Besides spectatorial identification, the queerness in cinema happens when contexts, narratives, political messages, and circuits of exhibition and reception do not abide by any linear or normative assumptions. In all, the queer potentials in the cinematic apparatus stem from a *denaturalization* of taken-for-granted, normative relations (in technologies, institutional practices, aesthetic forms, and spectatorships). To inflect a Foucauldian perspective here, we may say queer cinema produces *heterotopic worlds*.

One of the reasons why queer theory and affect theory share an intimate common ground is that they both attend to the body (and bodily reactions). They also both attend to the qualities of the unusual, the surprising, the vital, the intense—in short, to processes of *becoming*. In addition, they build understanding of the social and material world from aside, from the space of the "other than," from in-betweenness. I quote Seigworth and Gregg (2010) at length below, in order to (queerly) press their description of affect as always already a description of queerness:

> Affect is found in those intensities that pass body to body (human, nonhuman, part-body, and otherwise), in those resonances that circulate about, between, and sometimes stick to bodies and worlds, *and* in the very passages or variations between these intensities and resonances themselves. Affect, at its most anthropomorphic, is the name given to those forces—visceral forces beneath, alongside, or generally *other than* conscious knowing, vital forces insisting beyond emotion—that can serve to drive us toward movement, toward thought and extension, that can likewise suspend us (as if in neutral) across a barely registering accretion of force-relations, or that can even leave us overwhelmed by the world's apparent intractability. Indeed, affect is persistent proof of a body's never less than ongoing immersion in and among the world's obstinacies and rhythms, its refusals as much as its invitations. (1; emphasis theirs)

The core of queerness is affectivity, just as the most delicate properties of affect tend to be queer. The body is the chamber for affectively queer and queerly affective resonances alike. In this way, we approach the film text, not merely as a site of signification, but as something far more complex. We approach it as part of the cinematic apparatus that assembles a heterotopic sense of worldliness. Films like *God Loves Uganda* and *Call Me Kuchu* may not readily appeal to film critics or queer scholars as very queer works. Other than the home parties with drag performance shown in *Call Me Kuchu*, one is hard-pressed to consider the two films as queer cinema. But I intend to change this perception, especially for *God Loves Uganda*. When considered from the perspectives of queer and affect theories, *God Loves Uganda* exhibits a strange queer energy, and as such, it does a few interesting things, politically speaking. I shall argue that reading the film queerly can disrupt the normative understanding of the hegemonic practice of missionary Christianity, deliver a new understanding of homophobia, and provide a different understanding of the human rights violation concerned.

In *God Loves Uganda*, strong emotions circulate, as represented again and again by the trembling bodies of born-again Christians. Whereas homophobia is displayed as a looming, deteriorating atmosphere generating fear of queer persecution in *Call Me Kuchu*, in *God Loves Uganda* it is seen and felt through the imagery of hand-waving, wall-banging, whimpering, mumbling evangelicals. Some of them gyrate to the rhythms of the gospels with intense zealousness; others fall to the floor in half-rapturous, half-wretched movements. I have already mentioned the particular scene in *God Loves Uganda* in which the African youth preparing for evangelical work resemble figures of the zombie or mental patient. I consider them as ecstatic bodies, as potentiality, with the capacity to affect and to be affected.

The thinking that allows us to attend to the link that enfolds zealous Christianity, ecstasy, and perhaps even queerness helps open up the scope and texture of the worlds projected from the film. In fact, according to Seigworth and Gregg (2010) in *The Affect Theory Reader*, this way of thinking constitutes one of the main analytical orientations of research on affect. They state: "[There are] critical discourses of the emotions (and histories of the emotions) that have progressively left behind the interiorized self or subjectivity . . . to unfold regimes of expressivity that are tied much more to resonant worldings and diffusions of feeling /passions—often including atmospheres of sociality, crowd behaviors, contagions of feeling, matter of belonging . . . that forcefully question the privilege and stability of individualized actants possessing self-derived agency and solely private emotions within a scene or environment" (8). Crowdedness and the diffusion of feeling are main textual features of *God Loves Uganda*. While there is a political explanation of homophobia and of human rights violations that is centered on the transnational organizational efficacy of the church, particularly of the powerful church that is the International House of Prayers, I believe there is an alternative explanation for the production of homophobia and human rights injuries that requires us to attend to *the queer energy / potentiality of ecstasy as a political force.*

Figure 14.2. Faithful followers in ecstasy. Framegrab from *God Loves Uganda* (2013, Roger Ross Williams, USA).

In looking at the imagery of the frenzied crowd in evangelical sessions in both *God Loves Uganda* and *Call Me Kuchu*, we have reason repeatedly to note the power of emotional manipulation and indoctrination and to explain the formation of homophobia in Africa in these terms. Such an explanation is in fact correct and must be provided again and again. There are moments that clearly attest to the neocolonial impulse of the evangelical operation. For instance, in *God Loves Uganda*, Lou Engle calls Africa "the firepot of spiritual renewal and revival"; Robert Kayanja, a Ugandan pastor profiting from the mission, asserts that "the best thing the American missionaries can do today is to continue evangelizing in order to reap the maximum harvest out of Africa." In addition, one of the evangelical leaders from the International House of Prayers appearing in the film preaches that the holy spirit is there to "disciple the world," while another asserts that "we can multiply ourselves in these young people, and they can reach multitudes, they can reach nations." And when homophobic crusaders like Martin Ssempa exhibit slides of gay men engaging in sadomasochistic sex (as shown in *God Loves Uganda*) and Giles Muhame, the managing editor of *Rolling Stone*, displays in front of the camera the centerfold of his paper showing photographs of gay men in sexual poses (as seen in *Call Me Kuchu*), we must condemn these actions as spawning damaging stereotypes that stir fear and homo-hatred. The assertion of these as human rights violations relies largely on shaming these individuals and their actions.

However, something is lost in the kind of critique laid out above. A political critique of homophobia as human rights violation that centers on shaming the perpetrators and documenting victimhood, while necessary, misses the affective force that appears to produce a contagion of "positive feelings." A counterintuitive, if not queer, reading of *God Loves Uganda* is that this film focuses on positive feelings! The affective force of ecstasy generates an expansive ambience of unambivalent love for the corrective, restorative, and ultimately salvational power of Christianity.

In reviewing Judith Butler's famous argument of "critically queer" as the preferred political epistemology for queer politics, Tyler Bradway (2015) points out that much of the work of queer politics invests in the study of melancholia, grief, and ambivalence. In other words, queer politics focuses on, and even honors, negative feelings. I do not intend to enter into this debate about feelings (negative or positive) for delineating a direction for queer political critique. But I want to draw attention to the way in which an ethically queer relationship to the homophobic symbolic order can nonetheless be built by giving attention to the affective work done by positive feelings. I imagine pressing a consideration of the frenzied ecstatic evangelicals *as a queer community*, and that what they display is in fact queer exuberance (cf. Isherwood 2015; Mitchell 2016). I also imagine Martin Ssempa's and Giles Mahume's display of images of gay sex as queer approval and approbation. Could this kind of imagination be "critically queer," by leaving aside the emphasis on negative feelings and instead spotlighting affirmative feelings? I raise this question by referencing Bradway's (2015) own query: "What forms of queer community can be imagined through the discourse of positive affect? Despite recent interest in affect, queer scholars have been reluctant to explore the critical agencies of positive affect" (184). To this, I add: would a critical stance with which to analyze homophobia that unpacks the complexity of ecstasy be seen as politically naïve, and even as condoning the neocolonialism and fascism of certain forms of ecstasy, such as evangelicalism? More generally, is the exuberance of the body—one that carries the capacity to affect and to be affected—an inherent political enemy to the queer sexual commons? (see Osinubi 2016). On the one hand, there is by now a wide acceptance in queer critical work of the argument made by Lauren Berlant (2011) of "cruel optimism" as critical queer assessment of neoliberalism. On the other hand, there are works like Michael D. Snedliker's (2008) *Queer Optimism*, which refuse to reject affects such as happiness and exuberance, but instead consider them as complex political objects without presumed political meanings. Must cruel optimism and queer optimism be so stridently opposed?

I suggest that the real queer political potential of *God Loves Uganda*—again seen not just as a singular film but as a worldly and world-making object—lies in the presentation of born-again missionary Christianity as a queer system, in the sense of it being a productive affective machine that manages to generate hatred through the positive affects of unadulterated devotion, high-pitched optimism, and piercing joy. It is through this kind of critique that the world that is distressed about the wildfire spread of homophobia and human rights violations across Africa can pinpoint the source of the problem. What is it? Let me put it this way: in evangelical sessions and in concentrated preparation sessions, the ecstatic identification of the crowds with charismatic leaders like Lou Engle and Martin Ssempa delivers *a visceral form of fascism*. A queer critique of homophobia in Africa needs to pay attention to the positive feelings embodied in the electrifying ecstasy of evangelical fascism.

The cinematic apparatus has the capacity to figure (other) worlds. Sometimes we are surprised, while at other times we are more familiar with the itinerary, as it were. For films like *God Loves Uganda* and *Call Me Kuchu* that have achieved high international acclaim, a familiar itinerary of their politics might involve the way they are circulated and received. To be sure, as these were framed as human rights films, they were instantly inserted into an international moral community of viewers and critics. But what exactly were the dynamics of reception, and what (other) worlds might they open onto?

The Marketization of Human Rights?

In the aftershock of David Kato's death, Malika Zouhali-Worrall and Katherine Fairfax Wright, co-directors of *Call Me Kuchu*, went into high anxiety about how to deal with a documentary film that they had been working on for months, only to receive news of the brutal murder of Kato. How, for instance, would they be able to "tell the nuanced story of David and Kampala's Kuchus as they worked to change their fate" (Zouhali-Worrall et al. 2015, 8), when that fate turned out to be profoundly tragic? In 2015, Zouhali-Worrall and Wright worked with a group of international observers and activists to design *Call Me Kuchu: A Discussion Guide for Activists*, taking the consumption of the shock to a space for possible action and continued mourning for Kato. Knowing full well the shock at the international level, they crafted their tagline as an appeal to the world for a complex understanding of basic rights: "In telling this crucial story, we explore the paradox of democracy in a country where a judiciary recognizes the civil rights of individual Kuchus, yet the popular vote and daily violence threaten to eradicate those rights altogether" (ibid.).

As for *God Loves Uganda*, the focus of the film's international acclaim seems to be about casting a harsh light on what one reviewer has called "an unsettling sort of *déjà vu*: watching these white missionaries arrive on African shores, bearing a warped version Christianity, both saviors and oppressors" (see "Raves and Reviews"). Another reviewer calls the film "a compelling portrait of a volatile situation that is, at heart, fueled and financed by American cultural wars" (see "Raves and Reviews"). On the film's website, an appeal is made to American people to get involved, by questioning whether the money they donated to their churches went to support gay hate, sorting out the bad apples like Scott Lively, the antigay crusader, and so on. The Center for Constitutional Rights (CCR) has filed a federal lawsuit in the United States against Scott Lively, on behalf of Sexual Minorities Uganda (SMUG), the nonprofit umbrella organization for LGBTI advocacy groups in Uganda previously headed by David Kato (see *SMUG v. Lively* 2016).

Conceived as a cultural apparatus consisting of film texts, institutions, financing, audiences, and critiques and reviews, cinema binds spaces together: the diegetic space, the screening space, and the space of public organizing and action. The queer cinematic apparatus often binds the geopolitical with the world of aesthetic practices, hoping to produce counterpublics (see Warner 2002). The same apparatus has also become weary of being a tool for the proliferation of Western hegemonic queer worldviews and politics. As such, queer cinema could serve homonationalist purposes. Schoonover and Galt (2016) remind us that "queer film festivals seem particularly eager to proclaim *both* that queers make films more worldly and that films make the world more queer" (80, emphasis theirs). There seems to exist, in other words, a fine line between producing queer counterpublics (e.g., showing how queers can live publicly, opening the queer local to the world, building solidarity, etc.) and queering the world as an expansive globalist project. Queer film festivals are particularly interesting spaces in which to examine the tensions and negotiations for queer worlding, treading between visibilizing queer lives and succumbing to global market forces for proliferating those queer lives as consumables.

We recall a similar kind of tension in the controversy surrounding the by-now infamous global tour of the 2004 film *Born into Brothels* (Zana Briski and Ross Kauffman, USA), a film showing the harsh conditions of life for kids who had had to meander through seedy spaces of commercial sex in Calcutta, India. The main controversy has to do with the very question of worlding for films on society's disadvantaged minorities. In analyzing the film, Sarah Brouillette (2011) writes:

> I read the 2004 film *Born into Brothels* as a paradigmatic instance of an increasingly prevalent and transformative intertwining of the human rights market (which packages and sells causes to potential donors, investors or consumers) with the human rights culture market (which produces and consumes texts and images depicting struggles and movements, often narrating the experiences of individual beneficiaries of actions and organizations). Interlinked with media companies and aid agencies, and attended by websites, exhibitions, books, postcards and calendars, the film reveals some of the defining ways these markets operate, while evincing considerable nervousness about directly addressing their potential ethical implications. (169)

The ethical pressure points for *Born into Brothels* are considerably different from those for *God Loves Uganda* and *Call Me Kuchu*. The latter ones are not about framing and promoting an outside (white) hero performing a rescue narrative on film (as in the role of Zana Briski in *Born into Brothels*), or about the promotion of victims' self-representation as consumables in the international art market. Yet many queer films, especially when they enter into the international film festival circuits, are about the inception of a larger, transnational humanitarian program that is often entangled with processes of humanitarian consumerism. Upendra Baxi (2002) is perhaps the human rights thinker best known for suggesting that human rights violations "must be constantly commoditized to be combated," just as successful outcomes need to be "ledgered, packaged, sold and purchased on the most 'productive terms'" (124–5). The commodification argument may be valid, but if we overplay it, then it does tend to obscure the cultural integrity of human rights films and their capacity to imagine new worlds. No doubt, since the 1990s, human rights film festivals have been faced with the pressure to reconcile a globalizing mission with local politics. Programmers wrestle with the funders' request for more cosmopolitan films, pushing programming toward the indus-trial models associated with "global art cinema" and "world cinema."

In Africa, queer film festivals are a relatively new phenomenon, and they emerge under the twin pressures of having to navigate carefully, first, the colonial impulses imposed, directly or subtly, by Western queer institutional practices and identity politics, and second, the widespread domestic deterioration of rights that plagues local queer communities and their activism. As a result, it is no small feat to pull together a public queer film festival in Africa. Issues of marketization do exist in entanglement with Western funding and international media cover-age, but they pale in comparison with the dire political task of instituting the festivals as spaces much needed for building queer counterpublics within Africa. Many African societies remain deeply divided over views on homosexuality. The launching of queer film festivals to provide a platform for education, dialogue, and empowerment is no less than a heroic act of world-making. For instance, such an activist impulse is evident in the statement of what gets explored in the 2013 Batho Ba Lorato Film Festival, Botswana's first-ever LGBT film festival:

> This film festival, coined Batho Ba Lorato (People of Love) will . . . explore interrelated issues that plague the African continent:
>
> - How Christianity has exacerbated the violence directed at LGBTQ communities.
> - Homosexuality as "UnAfrican" and unnatural.
> - And whether the anti-sodomy laws that persist in Botswana are justifi-able. (cited in Schoonover and Galt 2016, 97)

Issues such as these raised by the festival embody both the universalizing and minoritizing, global and local impulses, a "hybrid approach [that] resonates in Batho Ba Lorato's local impact (where it has played an essential role in the legal struggles of local activists) and its global perspective (arguing for the relevance of film programming to human rights debates and black internationalism)" (98).

Indeed, in Africa, talks of the hybrid approach, of navigating the global / local dynamics, may sometimes be too lofty when the sheer act of organizing a queer film festival is outlawed and invites threats of arrest. Ruby Pratka (2016) chronicles the first-ever LGBTQ film festival in Uganda, which took place in December 2016, and stresses the very fact that this festival took place in a country where homosexuality is illegal. Pratka emphasizes: "There will be no red carpet, no palm trees, and no billboards, just a series of text messages directing the guests to a series of otherwise undisclosed locations. . . . Even though the organizers of Queer KIFF [Queer Kampala International Film Festival] dream of holding a public event, after a wave of arrests at this summer's Kampala Pride event, they have decided to release the list of screening venues only to a select group of pre-cleared supporters." Pratka notes especially the predicament of Kamoga Hassan, the lead organizer of the Ugandan festival, by recounting Hassan's fears:

> Kamoga has lost contact with relatives and friends, been evicted, and faced harassment from family members and strangers, a situation that's far from unusual in the Ugandan queer community. "You speak to some people and you assume they'll be understanding, but then they talk to other people, who might be your business associates," said Kamoga, who identifies as queer. "I can't get those contracts because no one wants to associate with a gay person. I can't stop speaking out, because professionally I've already lost everything." [He continues:] "Sometimes I'm worried to be in my country. I have to be careful every day, and there are certain places that I'll never go. I had to leave my old neighborhood, and I'm staying at a new address which I don't disclose. There are all [the] sorts of things you have to do to function in that sort of environment. You can't go on the streets with rainbow flags. Even when we have parades and festivals, they are underground. We were hoping we could count on the police to provide security for the festival, but after what happened at Pride, we realized we couldn't. We're going to screen each guest and keep the venues secret until the day before."

Hassan's words recall, almost verbatim, those uttered by characters appearing in *Call Me Kuchu*, especially David Kato, who was slain because of his outspoken queer activism in Uganda, and Stosh Mugisha, a Ugandan transgender activist who, after enduring a "corrective" rape at a young age, spent years feeling lonely, confused, and suicidal.

One critical question for queer film festivals in Africa, it seems, has to do with the temporal difference of what is allowed to go public, and what may progress into and be counted as a counterpublic, in different national contexts across Africa. Temporally, South Africa, Botswana, and Kenya have progressed farther than places like Uganda. The Out in Africa South African Gay and Lesbian Film Festival has been running since 1994, and this festival has enjoyed the most visibility and arguably enabled the most advanced theoretical discourse around the formation of queer identity politics and visual culture in Africa. Everyone knows

South Africa's unique situation, which emerges from the dismantling of apartheid and the production of new models for equitable citizenship. This exceptional situation has allowed the nation to become an international leader of sorts in securing queer rights. In commenting on Out in Africa, Nodi Murphy explains,

> We must be seen to be believed. The Film Festival helps people come out, in all senses of the word. . . . [It produces] a safe space, full of light even if part of it takes place in a dark room. The Festival has claimed very public spaces—in cinemas and newspapers, on television and radio, within an arts community and among civil society and activism organizations. . . . Large groups of people gather in what are essentially straight places, and claim them for themselves, for us. Films are powerful, and generally powerfully straight, so it's important that we are acknowledged and affirmed on film. We must be included; seeing ourselves helps belief in ourselves. (In Ma and Juhasz 2013, 386)

Yet, the "seeing = believing" equation is a temporally relative condition for queers and their film festivals. It is also a politically relative condition. As Hassan's statement above makes clear, queer visibility for Ugandans robs queer people of their self-belief due to the fear of persecution invited by visibility itself.

Katharina Lindner (2015) suggests that in general, we may temporalize the development of queer film festivals into a few landmark phases. In the late 1970s and 1980s, queer film festivals in the United States and Western Europe emerged as grassroots and oppositional events aimed at building the nascent sense of "gay and lesbian" identities. Yet it is worth remembering that this was enabled by a wider sociopolitical movement against minority oppression that resulted in women's and black film festivals in the same era. In the early to mid-1990s, queer cinema became a credible cinematic movement with the rise of "new queer cinema" in the West, drawing in that period a closer relationship between festivals and the commercial film industry. Subsequently, queer globalization through film festivals was articulated as a conceptual construct in the late 1990s to early 2000s. Queer film festivals began to take place in Eastern Europe and Asia. By the mid-2000s, queer film festivals started attracting larger corporate sponsorship deals, sharing more financial interests with the mainstream media. The same period also saw the growth of queer film festivals in Latin America. By now, we notice the rise of "niche" festivals, coinciding with a period of greater and more diverse representation of queer culture in the mainstream. In this temporal classification (which is, one must admit, constructed from a Western vantage point), we may place African queer film festivals across different periods, with South Africa participating in the queer globalization phase.

But how might we place Uganda in this temporal frame? With wide international acclaim, films like *God Loves Uganda* and *Call Me Kuchu* vied to be seen as part of the global queer moment of cultural visibility through their circulation in film festivals. Yet the political condition and basic rights for queers in Uganda lag far behind the kind of queer visibility that is ostensibly being celebrated in the global film festival arena. Caught between two temporalities, or between two world-making processes, these films about Ugandan queers clarify the tension between the commodification impulse pointed out by human rights thinkers like Upendra Baxi and the political impetus of building a queer counterpublic embraced by film scholars such as Schoonover and Galt.

Conclusion

In this chapter, I have examined the convergences and differences between *God Loves Uganda* and *Call Me Kuchu* in their construction of queer worldings. Considerations of this kind require us to take cinema as an assemblage, constellated by a set of textual, contextual, and institutional forces. The representation of the struggle against the poisonous homophobia in Africa in those films is by no means linear. At the level of contextualization, *God Loves Uganda* transnationalizes homophobia in Uganda but renders the Ugandan queers almost invisible, whereas *Call Me Kuchu* centralizes the existence of the suffering queers but fails to point out the transnational nature of the suffering they endured. At the level of the text, whereas a depressive affect pervades *Call Me Kuchu*, an intensive display of evangelical exuberance characterizes *God Loves Uganda*. Finally, at the level of reception, both films have had to tread a delicate line between a global commodification of human rights suffering and the galvanizing of a queer counterpublic through circulation in film festivals and on the internet. All the while, it remains unclear whether their circulation can withstand the dominance of Western appropriations of the films.

Through the analysis, I want to observe the ways in which queer suffering, and queerness in general, is complexly embedded in the spaces of human rights cinema. In fact, queerness is an intrinsic part of the development of human rights cinema. Queerness is not merely one of many sites of the "undeath" of human rights—the way in which the end and renewal of human rights are entangled in public discourse, in the media, and in geopolitics—it provides the discursive lens through which to mark this ambivalence. Put in another way, human rights is complexly queer, just as cinema has always already been a queer assemblage. Human rights have failed, but there has also been "success" in varying scales and at different stages of nations' development. They are particularistic, especially under intense pressure from different geopolitical actors and critics to resist the universalism of human rights. Within this conjuncture of human rights as ambivalent moral geopolitics, queer necropolitics—the ways in which various forms of governmentality have instigated the demise of queer individuals and communities—should be understood as a fusion of despair and ecstasy.

State political homophobia in Africa is no exception, and in fact should be understood in this way. State political homophobia helps build authoritative notions of national collective identity in more and more African nations, but in the process it helps produce more and more queer publics far beyond the queer hub of South Africa. Policy and organizational repression both locally and globally tend to reconstitute new sexuality-based movements where queer rights had not been invoked before. Finally, state political homophobia also helps impede oppositional or alternative collective identities that might or might not relate to sexuality, but in the process multiplies the queer presence of the born-again Christians with their queerly performed ecstasy. In short, state political homophobia invites new forms of queer worldings through queer affects materialized ironically through antiqueer politics and religiosity. I hope this range of ambivalence, as analyzed through an assemblage theory of queer cinema, can help us navigate the global incongruity that is the human rights imagination itself.

JOHN NGUYET ERNI is Fung Hon Chu Endowed Chair of Humanics and head of the Department of Humanities and Creative Writing at Hong Kong Baptist University. A recipient of the Rockefeller, Lincoln, Gustafson, and Annenberg research fellowships, Erni has published widely on international and Asia-based cultural studies and human rights legal criticism.

Filmography

Born into Brothels: Calcutta's Red Light Kids, 2004, Zana Briski and Ross Kauffman, USA.
Call Me Kuchu, 2012, Katherine Fairfax Wright and Malika Zouhali-Worrall, USA / Uganda.
God Loves Uganda, 2013, Roger Ross Williams, USA.

References

Alcock, C. 2011. *The World's Worst Place to Be Gay?* Television broadcast, February 15. London, UK: British Broadcasting Corporation.
Awondo, Patrick, Peter Geschiere, and Graeme Reid. 2012. "Homophobic Africa?: Towards a more nuanced view." *African Studies Review,* 55 (3): 145–68.
Baxi, Upendra. 2002. *The Future of Human Rights.* Oxford: Oxford University Press.
Berlant, Lauren. 2011. *Cruel Optimism.* Durham, NC, and London: Duke University Press.
Bosia, Michael J., and Meredith L. Weiss. 2013. "Political Homophobia in Comparative Perspective." In *Global Homophobia: States, Movements, and the Politics of Oppression,* edited by Meredith L. Weiss and Michael J. Bosia, 1–29. Urbana: University of Illinois Press.
Boyd, Lydia. 2013. "The Problem with Freedom: Homosexuality and Human Rights in Uganda." *Anthropological Quarterly* 86 (3): 697–724.
Boyle, Kevin, ed. 2006. *A Voice for Human Rights: Mary Robinson.* Philadelphia: University of Pennsylvania Press.

Bradway, Tyler. 2015. "Queer Exuberance: The Politics of Affect in Jeanette Winterson's Visceral Fiction." *Mosaic* 48 (1): 183–200.

Brouillette, Sarah. 2011. "Human Rights Markets and *Born into Brothels*." *Third Text* 25 (2): 169–76.

Cheney, Kirsten. 2012. "Locating Neocolonialism, 'Tradition,' and Human Rights in Uganda's 'Gay Death Penalty.'" *African Studies Review* 55 (2): 77–95. doi:10.1353 /arw.2012.0031.

Coly, Ayo A. 2013. "ASR Forum: Homophobic Africa?" *African Studies Review* 56 (2): 21–30.

Douzinas, Costas. 2000. *The End of Human Rights: Critical Legal Thought at the Turn of the Century*. Oxford: Hart Publishing.

Ekine, Sokari. 2013. "Contesting Narratives of Queer Africa." In *Queer African Reader*, edited by Sokari Ekine and Hakima Abbas, 78–91. Dakar: Pambazuka Press.

Erni, John N. 2009. "Human Rights in the Neo-liberal Imagination: Mapping the 'New Sovereignties.'" *Cultural Studies* 23 (3): 417–36.

———. 2010. "Reframing Cultural Studies: Human Rights as a Site of Legal-Cultural Struggles." *Communication & Critical/Cultural Studies* 7 (3): 221–9.

———. 2012. "Who Needs Human Rights: Cultural Studies and Public Institutions." In *Creativity and Academic Activism: Instituting Cultural Studies*, edited by Meaghan Morris and Mette Hjort, 175–90. Hong Kong and Durham, NC: Hong Kong University Press and Duke University Press.

"Even after Death, Abuse against Gays Continues." 2010. *The Associated Press*, April 11. Accessed November 2016. http://www.nbcnews.com/id/36376840/ns/world_news -africa/t/even-after-death-abuse-against-gays-continues/#.WGyqhU2wqp0.

Farley, Jim. 2014. "Uganda in the Hands of an Angry God." *The Gay & Lesbian Review Worldview* 21 (4): 12–6.

Grossberg, Lawrence. 2010. *Cultural Studies in the Future Tense*. Durham, NC, and London: Duke University Press.

Hoad, Neville. 2007. *African Intimacies: Pace, Homosexuality and Globalization.* Minneapolis: University of Minnesota Press.

Hopgood, Stephen. 2013. *The Endtimes of Human Rights*. Ithaca, NY: Cornell University Press.

Isherwood, Lisa. 2015. "Christianity: Queer Pasts, Queer Futures?" *Horizonte* 13 (39): 1345–74.

Kennedy, David. 2004. *The Dark Sides of Virtue: Reassessing International Humanitarianism.* Princeton and Oxford: Princeton University Press.

Lindner, Katharina. 2015. "No Longer Niche: How LGBTI Film Festivals Came of Age." *The Conversation*, September 24. Accessed November 2016. http://theconversation.com /no-longer-niche-how-lgbti-film-festivals-came-of-age-48054.

Luban, David. 2003. "The War on Terrorism and the End of Human Rights." In *War After September 11*, edited by Verna V. Gehring, 51–64. New York: Rowman & Littlefield.

Ma, Ming-Yuen S., and Alexandra Juhasz. 2013. "Queer Media Loci—South Africa." *GLQ: A Journal of Lesbian and Gay Studies* 19 (3): 381–403.

Macharia, Keguro. 2010. "Homophobia in Africa Is Not a Single Story." *The Guardian*, May 26.

Makofane, K., J. Beck, M. Lubensky, and G. Ayala. 2014. "Homophobic Legislation and Its Impact on Human Security." *African Security Review* 23: 186–95.

Massad, Joseph. 2002. "Re-orienting Desire: The Gay International and the Arab World." *Public Culture* 14 (2): 361–85.

———. 2007. *Desiring Arabs*. Chicago: University of Chicago Press.

Matebeni, Zethu. 2014. *Reclaiming Afrikan: Queer Perspectives on Sexual and Gender Identities*. South Africa: Modjaji Books.

Mbembe, Achille. 2001. *On the Postcolony*. Berkeley: University of California Press.

McAllister, John. 2013. "Tswanarising Global Gayness: The 'UnAfrican' Argument, Western Gay Media Imagery, Local Responses and Gay Culture in Botswana." *Culture, Health and Sexuality* 15 (1): 88–101.Mitchell, Gregory. 2016. "Evangelical Ecstasy Meets Feminist Fury." *GLQ: A Journal of Lesbian and Gay Studies* 22 (3): 325–57.

Mudimbe, V. Y. 1988. *The Invention of Africa*. Bloomington: Indiana University Press.

———. 1994. *The Idea of Africa*. Bloomington: Indiana University Press.

Mulvey, Laura (1975) 1999. "Visual Pleasure and Narrative Cinema." In *Film Theory and Criticism: Introductory Readings*, edited by Leo Braudy and Marshall Cohen, 833–44. New York: Oxford University Press.

Nyong'o, Tavia. 2012. "Queer Africa and the Fantasy of Virtual Participation." *Women's Studies Quarterly* 40 (1/2): 40–63.

Oliver, Marcia. 2013. "Transnational Sex Politics, Conservative Christianity, and Antigay Activism in Uganda." *Studies in Social Justice* 7: 83–105.

Osinubi, Taiwo Adatunji. 2016. "Queer Prolepsis and the Sexual Commons: An Introduction." *Research in African Literatures* 47 (2): vii–xxiii.

Pratka, Ruby. 2016. "Film Is My Tool." *Vice News*, November 12. Accessed November 2016. https://news.vice.com/story/a-queer-film-festival-comes-to-uganda-where-homosexuality-is-illegal.

"Raves and Reviews: God Loves Uganda." Accessed December 2016. http://www.godlovesuganda.com/film/raves-and-reviews/.

Rice, Lavon. 2007. "Queer Africa." *Colorlines* 10 (3): 38–42.

San Filippo, Maria. 2010. "Unthinking Heterocentrism: Bisexual Representability in Art Cinema." In *Global Art Cinema: New Theories and Histories*, edited by Rosalind A. Galt and Karl Schoonover, 75–91. Oxford: Oxford University Press.

Schoonover, Karl, and Rosalind Galt. 2016. *Queer Cinema in the World*. Durham, NC, and London: Duke University Press.

Seigworth, Gregory J., and Melissa Gregg. 2010. "An Inventory of Shimmers." In *The Affect Theory Reader*, edited by Gregory J. Seigworth and Melissa Gregg. Durham, NC, and London: Duke University Press.

Sexual Minorities Uganda v. Scott Lively. 2016. Center for Constitutional Rights. Accessed December 2016. http://ccrjustice.org/home/what-we-do/our-cases/sexual-minorities-uganda-v-scott-lively.

Smith, David. 2014. "Why Africa Is the Most Homophobic Continent." *The Guardian*, February 23. Accessed November 2016. https://www.theguardian.com/world/2014/feb/23/africa-homophobia-uganda-anti-gay-law.

Snedliker, Michael D. 2008. *Queer Optimism: Lyric Personhood and Other Felicitous Persuasions*. Minneapolis: University of Minnesota Press.

Tamale, Sylvia. 2007. "Out of the Closet: Unveiling Sexuality Discourses in Uganda." In *Africa after Gender*, edited by Catherine M. Cole, Takyiwaa Manuh, and Stephan F. Miesescher, 17–29. Bloomington: Indiana University Press.

Wahab, Amar. 2016. "Homosexuality / Homophobia Is Un-African"?: Un-Mapping Transnational Discourses in the Context of Uganda's Anti-Homosexuality Bill / Act." *Journal of Homosexuality* 63 (5): 685–718. doi:10.1080/00918369.2015.1111105.

Warner, Michael. 2002. *Public and Counterpublics*. New York: Zone Books.

Zembylas, Michalinos, and Vivienne Bozalek. 2014. "A Critical Engagement with the Social and Political Consequences of Human Rights: The Contribution of the Affective Turn and Posthumanism." *Acta Academia* 46 (4): 29–47.

Zouhali-Worrall, Malika, Katherine Fairfax Wright, and Amie Bishop. 2015. "Call Me Kuchu: A Discussion Guide for Activists." Accessed December 2016. https://callmekuchu.files .wordpress.com/2015/12/callmekuchu_discussion_guide.pdf

15 Refugees from Globalization

"Clandestine" African Migration to Europe in a Human (Rights) Perspective

Eva Jørholt

WHEN IN OCTOBER 2013, a fishing boat carrying over five hundred people, most of them Africans, sank off the Italian island of Lampedusa, the "clandestine," "illegal," "irregular," "undocumented," or "covert" African migration to Europe made the international news headlines. Since then, the African "boat migrants" have become a staple of global television news, typically through images of swollen black bodies washing up on Europe's southernmost shores, or of exhausted, dehydrated, hungry, disillusioned, frightened, and humiliated survivors being rescued by Europeans in protective white suits.

"Clandestine" African migration to Europe did not begin in 2013, however. It goes back to the 1970s when the oil crisis and subsequent economic downturn prompted most European countries to put a halt to immigration. But there were still people out there, not least in the former colonies, who dreamed of a better future in Europe, and if they could no longer obtain "legal" access, they found other, "irregular" ways of entry. Since the Schengen agreement abolished internal border checks within the European Union in the early 1990s and, by the same token, strengthened the control of the EU's outer borders, clandestine migration to Europe has become more dangerous. The crossing of the Mediterranean in overloaded, dilapidated fishing boats or small rubber dinghys has claimed numerous lives. According to a report from the International Organization for Migration (IOM), "between 2000 and 2017 (30 June), 33,761 migrants were reported to have died or gone missing in the Mediterranean during their journeys" (Fargues 2017, 1). Not all of these are Africans, of course, but in a so-called risk analysis, Frontex, the agency charged with securing the EU's external borders, reports that the vast majority of those migrants who come via the extremely dangerous Western and Central Mediterranean routes—from Morocco to Spain, and Libya to Italy, respectively—are in fact African, so it would seem reasonable to assume that most of the dead and missing are too.[1] In addition, many Africans have lost their lives while trying to climb over the fences to the two Spanish enclaves in

Morocco, Ceuta and Melilla, or while defying the Atlantic Ocean in an attempt to reach the Canary Islands.

Africans, however, constitute only a relatively small minority of the total number of migrants to Europe. Frontex detected 1,822,337 illegal crossings of the EU's external borders in 2015, only 161,110 of which were via the Western and Central Mediterranean routes. And yet, the harrowing images of African "boat migrants" seem to have gained a particularly prominent place in global media coverage, perhaps due to their horrific spectacularity. But if these images are sure to shock most spectators, at least initially, it is doubtful that they will also elicit any true understanding of what is at stake for the Africans who choose to set out on these journeys.

The main argument of this chapter will seek to highlight how African films—especially narrative fiction films—can offer a much-needed counterweight to Western representations of African migration, including many European films that, however well intended, tend to portray the migrants as (pitiful) "others." The African films, on the other hand, present "the lion's point of view"—to borrow the Senegalese rapper Didier Awadi's expression from his documentary *Le point de vue du lion* (2010, Senegal), which reverses the POV from that of the "Great White Hunter" to that of the "lion," metaphorically speaking. Crucially, the African films do not depict miserable, anonymous "migrants" or victims but human beings with names, agency, hopes, and desires—usually quite modest hopes and desires that cannot be realized in these people's home countries.

Distant Suffering and the Dehumanization of "the Sufferer"

To television viewers around the world, the plight of the African migrants has become a never-ending "spectacle of misery" (Arendt [1963] 2006)—a spectacle that the international audience follows at a comfortable distance. But, as convincingly argued by Lilie Chouliaraki (2006), the media coverage of what she refers to as "emergency news" tends to dehumanize "the sufferers," in this case the African migrants.

Chouliaraki emphasizes the importance of agency for any definition of human beings, and while the news coverage of African migrants rescued at sea does attribute some action to the migrants themselves, mainly in that they are seen jumping from their sinking boat to the rescuing coast guard vessel, "action is largely focalized on the figure of the benefactor—the coastguard crew rushing to the rescue" (2006, 125). Also, she points to the television spectators' position as voyeurs, in relation to the high-adrenaline "spectacularity of the rescue mission" that "tends to move this piece of news from the domain of the historical world on to the domain of cinematic entertainment" (ibid., 128–9). She further foregrounds the visual representation of the rescuers in their protective suits, which she sees as a key element "in the 'othering' of the African sufferers. Not only are these refugees cultural aliens, they are also polluted. . . . This is the primordial and unreflexive belief of our culture, that the racial 'other' contaminates and threatens our own 'purity'" (ibid., 130). Indeed, the African migrants are "today's ultimate pariahs" (Andersson 2014, 25).

If the migrants are rarely given a voice in these news stories, they are also seldom individualized. Usually, no names are mentioned—other than those of coast guards, other rescuers, and the reporters. On the world's television screens, the African migrants are reduced to a mass of anonymous black "sufferers." The fact that the migrants are both deindividualized and dehumanized makes it impossible for the spectators, who are typically more fortunate, to relate to their "distant suffering" (Boltanski [1993] 1999) with anything other than pity or, eventually, indifference. Indeed, the heavy media coverage of suffering people in general and African migrants in particular may lead to a kind of "compassion fatigue" or apathy in many spectators (Chouliaraki 2006, 112–3).

Chouliaraki is, however, convinced that emergency news also "has the potential to introduce the option of social solidarity to the public life of spectators," an option that, she argues, "can make a concrete difference to the sufferers' lives" (ibid., 197). Such acts of social solidarity can, for instance, take the form of more or less activist films that try to go behind the news headlines.

Pity the Poor Migrant: European Documentaries

To this day, a host of especially documentary films have been produced on the subject of clandestine African migration to Europe, most of them by European filmmakers. Typically, these films focus on the horrors encountered by the migrants during their journey, including the month- and sometimes yearlong involuntary stays in desert transit towns along the way, and the Africans' subsequent half-life as "illegal" immigrants on European soil. Examples of such films are *Bab Sebta* (2008, Frederico Lobo and Pedro Pinho, Portugal / Morocco), *Hotel Sahara* (2008, Bettina Haasen, Germany), *Under den samme himmel* (*Days of Hope*, 2013, Ditte Haarløv Johansen, Denmark / Italy / Mauritania / Sweden), *Ceuta, douce prison* (*Ceuta, Prison by the Sea*, 2013, Jonathan Millet and Loïc H. Rechi, France / Portugal), *The Land Between* (2014, David Fedele, France / Australia / Morocco / Spain), *Les messagers* (2014, Hélène Crouzillat and Laetitia Tura, France), and *Les sauteurs* (*Those Who Jump*, 2016, Moritz Siebert, Estephan Wagner, and Abou Bakar Sidibé, Denmark), but there are many more. Compared to the "emergency news" coverage, these films have, more often than not, the merit of presenting individual, named migrants who are allowed to tell their own stories, at least in part, but of course always within an overall framework controlled by the European filmmakers.

If the purpose of many of these "journey films" is to raise (political) awareness of what the migrants are going through, other European documentaries are more explicitly political in their critique of the way asylum seekers and (especially African) migrants are handled by European authorities. Particularly noteworthy in this respect are Fernand Melgar's *La forteresse* (*The Fortress*, 2008, Switzerland) and *Vol spécial* (*Special Flight*, 2011, Switzerland), both of which are scathing dissections of secured detention centers in Switzerland, where migrants are stored while awaiting their inevitable, forced deportation to their countries of origin—an extremely violent and humiliating procedure that has again and again been denounced by Human Rights Watch and Amnesty International. Also worth mentioning are the Italian *Come un uomo sulla terra* (*Like a Man on Earth*, 2008, Andrea Segre and Dagmawi Yimer) and *Mare chiuso* (*Closed Sea*, 2012, Stefano Liberti and Andrea Segre), both of which address Italy's less than humanitarian treatment of refugees and migrants under Silvio Berlusconi, culminating with the shady "treaty of eternal friendship" that Berlusconi signed with Libya's Colonel Gaddafi in 2008. Following this agreement, Italian ships were ordered to push African boat migrants back to Libyan waters and an uncertain destiny in Libyan jails, in violation of both the migrants' human rights and the laws of the sea.

While the strength of many of these films is that they present actual migrants whose faces, bodies, and stories testify to the harrowing experiences of their journeys, the films' POV remains distinctly European, which is, of course, neither surprising nor in any way reprehensible as such. In fact, one of the most accomplished of these documentaries, *Fuocoammare* (*Fire at Sea*, 2016, Gianfranco Rosi, Italy), does not even pretend to give the migrants a voice but simply, and perhaps sardonically, contrasts their desperation and sometimes violent deaths with the quiet, almost static lives of the inhabitants of Lampedusa.

Overall, however, it can be objected that the films' unequivocal focus on the migrants *as* migrants plays into the "sufferer" label promoted by mainstream media, arguably even subjecting them to a kind of "epistemic violence" (Nicholas de Genova in Andersson 2014, 12) by reducing their individual identities to that of "illegal migrants." Like the "emergency news" described by Chouliaraki, most of the European documentaries can thus be said primarily to elicit pity toward the migrants. And as much as pity may potentially entail solidarity, at heart it remains a feeling of superiority in the fortunate toward the less fortunate—a hierarchical distinction that can hardly be said to serve African interests.

Notwithstanding the quality and good intentions of many of these documentaries, it is debatable whether they actually contribute toward a more profound understanding of African migration and the reasons Africans may have for leaving their home countries. According to Susan Sontag, "harrowing photographs do not inevitably lose their power to shock. But they are not much help if the task is to understand. Narratives can make us understand" (2004, 80). Although news stories and documentaries obviously differ from the still photographs Sontag is speaking of, in that they unfold over a certain length of time, what they share, at least in this particular case, is the power to shock as well as certain failings when it comes to "making us understand." Narrative films, on the other hand, have the capacity not only to present their characters as individual human beings with goals and agency, and invite the spectators to empathize with them, but also to present them in a context that clarifies their choices. In fiction films, these characters will be fictional, of course; still, they may exemplify and embody some of the dilemmas with which real individuals are faced.

Sontag's use of the word "us," however, reveals that she—like Boltanski and Chouliaraki, who also highlight the advantages of narratives (Boltanski [1993] 1999, 85–95; Chouliaraki 2006, 38)—is primarily concerned with "our," the distant observers', understanding of "the pain of others" (see the title of Sontag's book, *Regarding the Pain of Others*). Arguably, it is indeed Europeans and other non-Africans who need to understand—the Africans already know—but the othering process inherent in the very concept of "understanding the pain of others" should not be ignored. And when it comes to narrative films on the subject of clandestine African migration, while they may all enhance the spectators' understanding in one way or another, there is a crucial difference between European approaches, which typically rely on this distinction between "us" and "them / the sufferers," and African films, which are more concerned with depicting an everyday reality that, for various reasons, drives people to leave their homes.

Shocking Encounters: European Narrative Fiction Films

Although European narrative fiction films on African migration do invite the spectators to empathize or at least form an allegiance with their protagonists, it should be noted right away that these protagonists are usually Europeans who in some way or other are brought into contact with African migrants. The "sufferers" have become too close for comfort, and the crux of these films is usually the shock that such encounters provoke in the European protagonists. In many cases, the shock is staged as a contrast between sunbathing tourists on the beaches of southern Europe and exhausted—or dead—Africans who wash up on the shore and disturb what was meant to be a carefree vacation. In *Implosion* (2007, Sören Voigt, Germany / Spain) and *Die Farbe des Ozeans* (*Color of the Ocean*, 2011, Maggie Peren, Germany / Spain), for instance, we have well-meaning German tourists who, under the sway of this shock, try to somehow offer their help to individual migrants. Other films—like *Retorno a Hansala* (*Return to Hansala*, 2007, Chus Gutiérrez, Spain), *Terraferma* (2011, Emanuele Crialese, Italy / France), and *Le Havre* (2011, Aki Kaurismäki, Finland / France / Germany)—address the moral dilemmas faced by Europeans whose everyday lives are affected by these encounters and who, in some cases, even resort to civil disobedience against the local authorities because they cannot turn a blind eye to other people's sufferings. The encounter, however, may also provide a framework for a critique of European racial stereotyping, as in *Bwana* (1996, Umanol Uribe, Spain). Like most of the European documentaries, these kinds of narrative fiction films typically stage the African migrants as objects for a European gaze, only here the European perspective is highlighted even further, while the role of the migrants is largely reduced to that of catalyst for various kinds of reactions in the European protagonists.

Some European fiction films do, however, place migrants as the protagonists of their stories. I will not consider those that address the experiences of "illegal" immigrants *in* Europe—films like *Pummarò* (*Tomato*, 1990, Michele Placido, Italy), *Las cartas de Alou* (*Letters from Alou*, 1990, Montxo Armendáriz, Spain), *Après l'océan* (*Beyond the Ocean*, 2006, Eliane de Latour, France / UK), *Clandestin* (2010, Arnaud Bédouet, France), *L'envahisseur* (*The Invader*, 2011, Nicolas Provost, Belgium), and *Il villaggio di cartone* (*The Cardboard Village*, 2011, Ermanno Olmi, Italy), among others. Instead I will briefly discuss those films that focus primarily on the journey itself and, to the extent that this issue is addressed at all, on the migrants' motivations for leaving.

14 kilómetros (*14 Kilometers*, 2007, Gerardo Olivares, Spain)—the title of which alludes to the Strait of Gibraltar, the shortest distance between Africa and Europe—and *Hope* (2014, Boris Lojkine, France) are quite similar in that they both revolve around two migrants, a male and a female, who meet each other along the way and eventually fall in love. Not much is revealed about their backgrounds. Judging from the bonus material on the French DVD version of *Hope*, a scene explaining why the eponymous female protagonist left her home in Nigeria (she is the oldest of a single, unemployed mother's seven children) was omitted in the final cut, and all we are told about her male counterpart, Léonard from Cameroon, is that he wants to pursue his studies in Europe. While *14 kilómetros* does contain scenes of the two protagonists in their respective African surroundings (Mali and Niger) before each of them sets out on the journey, the film provides only clichéd explanations of their reasons for leaving: he wants to be a football champion; she flees a forced marriage to a much older man.

Whereas *Hope* and *14 kilómetros* thus seek to translate the plight of the migrants into pretty conventional entertainment fare, complete with both chilling drama and a love interest—in the case of *14 kilómetros* even presented in tourist brochure–like images of African landscapes—*Lettere dal Sahara* (*Letters from the Sahara*, 2006, Vittorio De Seta, Italy) and *Mediterranea* (2015, Jonas Carpignano, Italy / France / USA / Germany / Qatar) owe more to the observational documentary genre in their sober, quite adrenaline-free approach to the subject. Both are mainly set in Italy and, like the other European "postjourney films," primarily dedicated to depicting the migrants' difficulties in finding real jobs and the often racially motivated hostilities they face. Yet the first twenty minutes or so of *Mediterranea* do depict the Burkinabè protagonist's crossing of first the Sahara and then the Mediterranean. In *Lettere dal Sahara*, the journey itself is reduced to archival news footage of boat migrants arriving in Italy, but the film merits attention for the way it follows its protagonist, a student, back to his Senegalese village, where he is urged by his former teacher to convey the horrors of his European adventure to the local youth, in order to dissuade them from emigrating themselves. Neither of the two films offers many clues, however, as to why their protagonists decided to emigrate in the first place.

Despite some individual merits, the European films all tend to present an external, European perspective on the migrants who, by and large, are reduced to being exactly that: migrants. In the following sections, I will take a closer look at four African films that are more concerned with human beings who *become* migrants. All four films are from francophone West Africa, a region in which the individual countries face more or less similar economic challenges. Also, according to the earlier mentioned Frontex report, a significant proportion of the migrants on the West and Central Mediterranean routes are in fact from francophone West African countries.

The films focus on the conditions that prompt the protagonists to migrate and, in some cases, on the journey itself. While there are some quite important North African films on this subject (see Abderrezak 2016, for example)—not least *Frontières* (*Borders*, 2001, Mostefa Djadjam, Algeria / France), *Et après?* ("And Then?", 2002, Mohamed Ismail, Morocco), *Le chant de la noria* (*Melody of the Waterwheel*, 2002, Abdellatif Ben Ammar, Tunisia), *Tarfaya* (2004, Daoud Aoulad-Syad, Morocco / France), *Roma wa la n'touma* (*Rome Rather than You*, 2006, Tariq Teguia, Algeria / France / Germany / Netherlands), and *Harragas* (2009, Merzak Allouache, Algeria / France)—and probably even more sub-Saharan African films on African migrants *in* Europe (see Thackway 2003 for an excellent overview), these four films are the only West African ones I have been able to find with this particular focus. But there could be more.

As none of the films provide sociologal or political-economic analyses—they merely focus on the human consequences of larger societal and economic issues—I will begin by providing a brief overview of the region's economic predicaments and also present some thoughts on the human rights of those who flee these difficulties.

Outside the Realm of Human Rights?

Most West African migrants to Europe are commonly perceived by Europeans to be simple "economic migrants," "bogus asylum seekers," or "welfare tourists," unlike people fleeing war or personal persecution. Whereas the latter stand at least a chance of being recognized as refugees and may, eventually, be granted asylum in Europe, West Africans are routinely refused entry. Crucial in this respect is article 14 of the Universal Declaration of Human Rights (UDHR) from 1948: "Everyone has the right to seek and to enjoy in other countries asylum from persecution." In the UNHCR (United Nations High Commissariat for Refugees) Refugee Convention, a "refugee" was three years later defined as anyone who "owing to a well-founded fear of being persecuted for reasons of race, religion, nationality, membership of a particular social group or political opinion, is outside the country of his nationality, and is unable to, or owing to such fear, is unwilling to avail himself of the protection of that country" (Article 1A.2). A "migrant," on the other hand, is "any person who moves, usually across an international border, to join family members already abroad, to search for a livelihood, to escape a natural disaster, or for a range of other purposes," according to the so-called UNHCR Emergency Handbook.[2]

To human rights lawyers, this distinction between refugees and migrants is a false one. The British barrister Frances Webber, for instance, to whom I owe the title of this chapter, argues that "one way or another most of those who come to these shores without official permission are refugees from globalisation, from a poor world getting poorer as it is shaped to serve the interests, appetites and whims of the rich world, a world where our astonishing standard of living, our freedoms, the absurd array of consumer novelties, fashions and foods available to us, and thrown away by us, are bought at the cost of the health, freedoms and lives of others" (Webber 2012, 4). Article 13 of the UDHR grants any individual the right "to leave any country, including his own, and to return to his country," but if it is a human right to emigrate, there are no legal requirements for other countries to accept those who make use of this right, unless they qualify as refugees. Of course, as Catherine Wihtol de Wenden observes, "the right to emigrate does not exclude the right to stay at home. . . . But what good is this right if the potential emigrants have no hope of realizing their projects in their home countries, and if they do not have the right to education, health, work, freedom of expression and if they come from 'failed states'?" (Wihtol de Wenden 2013, 49, my translation).

Typically, the West African migrants are not among "the poorest of the poor": "Indeed, the poorest of the poor remain within the region; it is those with at least some access to contacts and cash—often family funds—who can set off on long, uncertain journeys towards the north" (Andersson 2014, 20). In addition to having some money, the majority of the migrants are young and strong, some of them quite well educated—"They are the most vital people in our countries" (Oumar Sy, in George 1992, 132)—and yet their countries offer them no, or very few, opportunities for creating a life for themselves and their families.

What has really impoverished many African states to the point of driving their "most vital" citizens abroad is, arguably, the so-called Structural Adjustment Programs that the International Monetary Fund (IMF) and the World Bank have imposed on African countries since the 1980s to secure economic growth—and a capacity to pay off their debt, primarily to those same two institutions (George 1992; Ferguson 2006; Traoré 1999, 2008a, 2008b). This economic horse medicine basically consists of reducing public spending by selling off areas like health care, education, transportation infrastructure, power plants, water works, garbage collection, and so forth to private, sometimes foreign operators, and of forcing African farmers to substitute export crops (cotton, for example) for the production of food. While structural adjustments have indeed made the national economies look better from a macroeconomic point of view, the price for this growth is paid by the ordinary citizens of the countries in question. To all those who cannot pay for an education, or who, if they did get an education, cannot get a job corresponding to their qualifications, who cannot afford proper health care, who cannot rely on the transportation systems or on an uninterrupted supply of power and internet access, and who have to bribe their way through the remaining public sector whose employees (the police, for example) are usually very poorly paid, if at all—to all these people, life in their home countries amounts to a kind of "social death" (Andersson 2014, 19). What is salient is a general lack of opportunities for forming and supporting families, for creating businesses, or simply for realizing each citizen's personal potential.

Abderrahmane Sissako's extraordinary film *Bamako* (2006, Mali / USA / France), which stages a fictional African lawsuit against the IMF and the World Bank, specifically links the Structural Adjustment Programs to the issue of migration. Aminata Traoré, the Malian sociologist, writer, and former minister for culture and tourism, appears as one of the witnesses for the prosecution, and she does not mince her words, neither in the film nor in her books. In a response to European leaders' alleged fear of an invasion of migrants (see Bauman 2016 and Andersson 2014), she writes, for example: "Neoliberal globalization . . . has turned African migrants into political and economic refugees, not invaders" (2008a, 53, my translation). In the film, she asks, "Why should the fate of a people depend on their ability to produce and sell abroad?" She goes on to vehemently refute the defense attorney's claim that globalization is synonymous with an "open world": "We do not live in an open world. . . . Today, we see Africans who opt for emigration, who are economic refugees, arrested, handcuffed, deported, humiliated and sent back home. How can you claim, given that terrible situation that shocks the whole world, that we live in an open world? It's clearly open for whites but not for blacks" (Blaq Out DVD translation).

Another witness for the prosecution, Madou Keïta, a young Malian who never went to school or received any training, nor anything else from his home country, gives a first account of such humiliations: like many others he crossed the Sahara only to be bounced back and forth between Morocco and Algeria, shot at, and finally left in the desert. Out of his group of thirty migrants, only ten survived.

If the migrants' home countries cannot fulfill their own citizens' economic and social rights—to a fairly remunerated job, to decent living conditions, to social security, to good health and education—and they are denied entry to countries that do have the means but not the willingness to offer them what they lack at home, the migrants seem to be stuck in a kind of no-man's-land when it comes to human rights. A somewhat paradoxical situation perhaps, given the fact that the very issue of "illegal" migration can be boiled down to trespassing the land of other nations. In this no-man's-land, however, they are stripped of most human rights, not only in relation to the abuses many of them encounter along the way, but also in a more profound, structural sense. The title of an IOM report prepared by Bimal Ghosh—*Elusive Protection, Uncertain Lands: Migrants' Access to Human Rights* (2003)—pinpoints how migrants are not naturally included in the allegedly universal human rights; they need to gain access!

The four films, to which I will turn now, do not take up the issue of human rights as such, at least not as defined in the Universal Declaration of Human Rights. But through their depiction of various aspects of African everyday life under the sway of global neoliberalism, they do invite their audiences to ponder both the meaning and the scope of human rights.

A Modern-Day Slave Route: *Bako, l'autre rive*

Bako, l'autre rive (*Bako, the Other Shore*, 1979, Jacques Champreux, France / Senegal) is somewhat different from the other three films under consideration here, not only because it was made before the advent of structural adjustments and at a time when the gates of Europe were not as tightly closed as they are today, but also because Jacques Champreux, who is credited with directing it, is French.[3] He did, however, team up with the Guinean actor and, later, director Cheik Doukouré for the writing of the script—according to one source to "lend more authenticity to his project" (Chansel 2001, 149, my translation), but another source (*L'Avant-Scène Cinema* 1979) has Doukouré, who also acts in the film, as the actual instigator of the film. In any case, Doukouré has since taken ownership of the film. In an interview made for the Amiens film festival in 2008, he says, "I consider *Bako, l'autre rive* to be my most significant film," and adds that it "depicts my long journey towards Europe" (Jézéquel 2008, my translation). He has even named his production company "Bako Productions."

Leaving aside Djibril Diop Mambéty's wonderful *Touki Bouki* (1973, Senegal)—which does tell a story about a young couple's less than legal attempts at realizing their dream of going to Paris, but without addressing clandestine migration—*Bako, l'autre rive* is probably the first (more or less) African feature film entirely dedicated to the topic of "irregular" African migration to Europe. Indeed, "Bako" (i.e., "the other shore" in Bambara) is a code word for Paris among the clandestine migrants. Made in the late 1970s, the film testifies to the fact that there is nothing new about these journeys, but *Bako, l'autre rive* does differ from the other films I will look into here, partly in the protagonist's motivation for emigrating but also in the film's quite direct political critique of French immigration policies.

The year is 1972, a time when the Sahel region was struck by a severe drought. Boubacar (Sidiki Bakaba) is the son of Malian peasants, and when the family's only cow drops dead on the barren soil, the entire village decides that Boubacar should join his older brother Samba, who is already in Paris, from where he is sending money back home. In the early 1970s, France still had a fairly liberal immigration policy, one that allowed Africans to go there and work for a certain period of time. Yet, even though the entire village chips in to pay for his ticket, Boubacar has neither work nor a residence permit in France. Those can be obtained, to be sure, but only at a price that is far beyond the means at Boubacar's disposal. He therefore decides to try to reach France without the required permits and embarks on what will turn out to be an extremely long and hazardous journey by train, by bus, by truck, by boat, and on foot via Senegal, Mauritania, and Spain to Paris, where he finally arrives on May 15, 1973, a year and five months after his departure from Mali. Along the way he is robbed, mugged, cheated, and beaten up, as well as exposed to both the scorching sun of the Sahara and the icy cold of the Pyrenees, all of which takes a toll on his health. Without ever finding his brother, he expires alone and cold on the stairs of an abandoned Parisian building.

Bako, l'autre rive may, especially in hindsight, be accused of espousing a certain miserabilism, but it also adopts a quasi-documentary stylistic approach to its subject and shies away from compromises (it is shot on 16mm filmstock, with much of its dialogue in Bambara). As such it is quite disturbing, and compared to its (much later) European counterparts, it also provides a much more profound insight into its protagonist's reasons for leaving. Of particular note is the fact that Boubacar's journey is set against a collective background; the decision to leave is not his own—in fact, he has a girlfriend, Awa, in the village, and we are led to believe that he would have preferred to stay with her. Sending him to Europe is a choice made out of necessity by the entire village, despite the fact that he is the only young man left; after his departure there will be nobody to bury the elders.

Bako, l'autre rive thus inserts one individual migration story into a larger social fabric and touches upon its consequences for those who stay behind. It is also openly critical of French authorities who turned a blind eye to clandestine immigration at a time when extra hands were needed to secure the country's postwar economic boom, especially for jobs that the French would not take themselves, and at wages that did not meet any union requirements. The film opens with a montage of still photos of African immigrants in typical low-wage jobs—at car factory assembly lines, on major construction sites, and as street sweepers, for example—and just before the end credits, it presents a full-screen quote of then French labor minister Jean-Marcel Jeanneney, who in 1966 infamously declared that "clandestine immigration is not useless as such, for if we observed the international rules and agreements strictly, we might be in need of labor" (my translation). Few European politicians would probably put it as bluntly today, but in reality, not that much has changed for those African migrants who do make it to Europe and are forced to somehow make a living off the radar of the authorities.

The end credits of *Bako, l'autre rive* are presented against a monochrome bloodred drawing of slaveships, an unmistakable hint that even if the decision to migrate may now be taken by the Africans themselves, the way Europe, in this case the former colonial power France, cynically exploits their misery may be seen as a modern version of a bygone era's slave trade. Due to its ageing native populations, today's Europe also needs extra hands (see Alba and Foner 2015, for example), but instead of simply inviting people from places such as Africa, to come and work in Europe, Europe leaves the migrants—those who survived the journey, that is—to take care of themselves at the very bottom of society, some of them working off the books, while others face completely inhumane living conditions in camps such as the so-called Jungle near Calais in northern France.[4]

Yaguine and Fodé: *Un matin bonne heure*

Un matin bonne heure (*Early in the Morning*, 2006, Gahité Fofana, France / Guinea) is based on a true story that actually made the international headlines in 1999 when on August 2, two fourteen-year-old Guinean boys, Yaguine Koïta and Fodé Tounkara, were found dead inside the wheel-bay of a Belgian Sabena airplane at Brussels Airport. According to some reports, their bodies had made the trip back and forth between Conakry and Brussels at least three times. With them was a plastic bag containing their personal documents and a letter addressed on behalf of Africa's youth to Europe's leaders, begging for their help.[5] "Help us, we suffer enormously in Africa," the letter said, listing wars, famine, and illnesses as some of the continent's major challenges. Mainly, however, the boys asked the European leaders to do something to allow the youth of Africa to progress, through education of course, but also by giving them the opportunity to play football, basketball, or tennis like young people elsewhere in the world, for, as the boys emphasized in their best school French at the very end of the letter, "don't forget that it is to you we must complain about the weakness of our strength in Africa" (my translation), thus invoking a certain European responsibility for the situation they were fleeing. At the time, the letter was largely understood specifically to address the issue of debt relief, and it was actually quoted on the cover of an IMF press release sent out in December 1999 on the occasion of a joint IMF and World Bank assembly on the subject of debt reduction.[6] To James Ferguson, however, the letter is not about debt reduction in particular. To him, it rather

Figure 15.1. Fodé, Khésso, and Yaguine: Guinean teenagers with no future. Framegrab from *Un matin bonne heure* (*Early in the Morning*, 2006, Gahité Fofana, France / Guinea).

expresses "a haunting claim for equal rights of membership in a spectacularly unequal global society" (2006, 174–5).

Whereas some reporters did try to unravel the backgrounds of the real Yaguine and Fodé, Gahité Fofana, who is also an accomplished documentary filmmaker, deliberately chose a fictional format for his film.[7] In a personal email communication, he explains that his initial intention was indeed to make a documentary about the two boys, but as the people he talked to while researching for this film each had their own versions of what actually happened, "I decided to make a fiction and imagine my own truth." And he adds, "I did not want to meet the boys' families prior to making the film, as I wanted to avoid their rather miserabilist version of the events."

Indeed, *Un matin bonne heure* steers perfectly clear of any miserabilism in its portrayal of Yaguine and Fodé as two bright schoolboys who live in a green and inviting neigborhood of Conakry.[8] It is poor, to be sure, but nothing like the city's slum quarters, of which we also catch a glimpse. Yaguine is in love with a local girl, Khésso, whom he has known all his life, and Fodé is an accomplished kora player—in many ways they are perfect examples of the "vital" African youth mentioned above. And yet there is no future for them in Guinea.[9] Fodé dreams of becoming a pilot, but how will he ever be able to pay for the proper training? Their present school fees already pose problems—Yaguine's older sister, Salma, is paying for his tuition with money she has earned from offering certain sexual services to the local gangster boss. Even doing their homework after sunset proves difficult due to incessant power cuts (indeed, most of the pupils prepare for school at a spot right next to the airport where they can profit from the bright lights of the landing strip). Also, Yaguine will never be able to pay the dowry required for Khésso, whose parents end up choosing another husband for her, and despite his obvious talent as a kora player, Fodé cannot imagine succeeding as a musician in Guinea. A friend of theirs opted out from this deadlock situation by becoming a child soldier, which did endow him with a certain sum of money but also with deep-running traumas and a drug addiction—a trajectory that does not tempt Yaguine and Fodé.

From the gangster's Mercedes car by way of the international ships and airplanes arriving and departing from Conakry to the programs on the many television sets (probably foreign as well, and probably stolen) in the home of Khésso's family, globalization is staring them right in the face. But the world is definitely not open to boys like Yaguine and Fodé. As they make clear in their letter, all they want is a chance in life, an opportunity to grow up with sports and education— quite modest claims by the standard of most Western countries. At a certain point, Fodé sings out his despair on the beach, but the sound of his voice is, metaphorically as well, drowned in the roaring waves of the Atlantic Ocean.

Barcelona or the Hereafter: *La Pirogue*

Unlike *Un matin bonne heure*, which does not depict the two boys' journey at all (it just tells their story in a kind of flashback from their deaths, narrated by Khésso), a substantial part of *La Pirogue* (2012, Moussa Touré, France / Senegal / Germany) is focused on a motley group of thirty-one West Africans' attempt at reaching the Spanish Canary Islands in a traditional Senegalese fishing boat, a *pirogue*. The film is dedicated to the more than five thousand West African migrants who lost their lives in the Atlantic Ocean between 2005 and 2010.

The protagonist, Baye Laye, is a proud fisherman, as were his father and grandfather before him. Now, however, there are no more fish, and the small fishing village is struggling to survive. Some of the villagers have already left for Europe, and those who made it are now building new houses for themselves and their families in the village. Baye Laye himself is not particularly attracted by Europe, but many others are, including his younger brother Abou and his best friend Kaba, and out of concern for their safety, he finally agrees to be the captain of a pirogue bound for the Canaries.

While *La Pirogue* does not provide any explanation for the lack of fish—other than a remark by Kaba that it is now barely possible to see the horizon, which would seem to suggest pollution—*Cry Sea*, a documentary by Cafi Mohamud and Luca Cusani (2007, Senegal / Italy), unequivocally puts the blame on the Senegalese government's fishing agreement with the EU, which allows huge European, mainly Spanish, fishing vessels to practically vacuum Senegalese waters for fish that are then frozen and shipped off to Europe. *La Pirogue* is more concerned with the human consequences of this situation, without, however, presenting its characters as pitiful victims. Baye Laye is a strong and righteous man who loves his wife and son and acts like a father to the more irresponsible Abou, a musician who smokes despite his asthma, who gets laid off from his job because he is always late, but who does have an iPhone. Arguably, the film is as much about the relationship between the two brothers as it is about the journey as such, which works to test their relationship and reveal aspects of each of them that had hitherto been unknown to the other. Much as in *Un matin bonne heure*, the family's home is poor but nice, clean, and friendly, and short of being able to fish, the villagers do engage in other activities such as playing football on the beach and betting on wrestlers. If they are thus not depicted as passive "sufferers," it is, however, clear that their livelihood is threatened and their chances of improving this situation quite limited.

Farming too is under pressure. Among the passengers on the pirogue are two groups of Fulani farmers, one from Guinea, the other from Senegal. Again, the film is not explicit about their reasons for leaving, but it does make it perfectly clear that these men, some of whom have the status of village elders, are far from being "welfare tourists." If they set out on this journey without knowing how to swim and without any knowledge of European languages, it is because it is their only option. As one of them says: "If you stay at home, ten chances in ten that you are going to die"—that is, another way of expressing what has become a familiar saying in Senegal: *Barça walla barzakh*, which is Wolof for "Barcelona or the hereafter." It basically means that even though the chances of surviving a clandestine trip to Europe are slim, they are better than many people's chances of having a life in West Africa. Like the rest of the films under consideration here, and in stark contrast to the international news coverage, *La Pirogue* thus highlights the agency of the migrants: these are people who do not passively accept their situation but act to change it, despite the risks involved.

In addition, the film lets its spectators in on the diverse emotional reactions and moral dilemmas experienced by the passengers during the journey. One of the Fulani farmers, who has brought a live rooster with him, is so stricken with fear that the others tie him up and gag him, some because they find him to be a nuisance, others because they want to protect him from himself. When a female stowaway is discovered, some opt for throwing her overboard, while others insist that she stay. When they encounter another pirogue that has been drifting at sea for five days without food and water, some insist that they stop and offer their help, while others, including Baye Laye, realize that stopping would only jeopardize their own lives. And when eventually their own motors set out and the passengers die one after another, mainly from dehydration, Baye Laye is on the brink of giving up, whereas Abou rises to the occasion and encourages his fellow passengers by singing a song that has the others join in, in their respective languages. So, if *La Pirogue* eschews any political or economic analysis, it does present a poignant drama that invites audience members to align themselves emotionally with a set of morally complex characters and thus to put themselves in the place of those people in the boat.

In the end, the survivors are picked up by a Spanish Red Cross helicopter, only to be deported back to Dakar. On their way to the village, Baye Laye stops at a local market where he buys a Barcelona football jersey for his son. He had promised to bring one home from Spain, but other than pointing to the failure of their journey, the fact that he now buys it in Senegal may perhaps also be read as a subtle caveat against uncritically embracing the European mirage: Africa has its own Barça jerseys!

Stranded in the Desert: *Heremakono*

Whereas *La Pirogue* is structured as a pretty straightforward narrative with engaging characters, *Heremakono—en attendant le bonheur* (*Waiting for Happiness*, 2002, Abderrahmane Sissako, France / Mauritania) adopts an enigmatic, lyrical form that largely prevents the audience from empathizing with any of its characters. According to Roy Armes, it is "Sissako's most elusive film, a narrative . . . from which all the normal signposts have been removed, and where the boundaries between actuality and pure fiction are not immediately apparent" (2006, 197). Drawing on locals who largely play themselves as well as on a good deal of improvisation, *Heremakono* is a meditative poem in sound and images, but a poem that, arguably, is also a caustic comment on Africa's position in the neoliberal world order.

The film does have a kind of protagonist, though, whose arrival to and, possibly, departure from the Mauritanian coastal town of Nouadhibou frame the narrative: the seventeen-year-old Abdallah, who is on his way to Europe but stops over in Nouadhibou to visit his mother and fix some passport issue. While Abdallah is the film's narrative center, he is peripheral to the local community. He does not speak the local language, Hassaniya, but has to communicate with the others in French, the language of the former colonial power. Also, he spends most of his time alone, lying on a mattress in his mother's house looking out at the feet of the passersby, all he can see through the very low window. Interspersed by images of other feet getting rid of their shoes before entering people's homes; of a griotte teaching a young girl to sing; of a Chinese man singing karaoke and giving away the watches he was probably supposed to sell; of migrants waiting for a passage to Morocco; of a young girl, Nana, whose daughter died and who is now offering men her company; and, not least, of a couple of electricians—the former fisherman Maata and his young apprentice, Khatra, who work to install light in houses with no electricity of their own—the film draws a finely chiseled portrait of a very diverse group of people and a place of transit characterized by wind, sun, heat, and an endless desert but also by bright colors, rich cultural traditions, and a certain amount of dry humor.

Once Mauritania's busiest fishing port, the city of Nouadhibou is today primarily known for, on the one hand, a huge ship graveyard where the international community dumps its wrecks, and, on the other, its position as a hub for migrants hoping to reach Europe by way of Morocco; indeed, the town has been dubbed *la ville des clandestins* ("the town of the clandestines") (Andersson 2014, 69). In the film, these two defining characteristics of Nouadhibou are employed to metaphorically suggest Africa's place in the neoliberal world order: not only is the continent used as a dumping ground for the waste of rich countries (see Harrow 2013), the ships are also dead and therefore going nowhere. So while the town bears many of the marks of "incoming" globalization—in addition to the international shipwrecks, there are also French television programs, scarves in so-called Beijing or Swiss designs, Chinese karaoke, and, of course, the many nonlocal migrants who are just waiting, waiting, waiting—it is also implied that globalization is a one-way street. The migrants' journey stops here, where the Sahara desert meets the Atlantic Ocean. Indeed, when one of the migrants, Mickaël, does attempt to leave, the ocean soon spits him back up, dead. At night, a string of large vessels line up just off the coast, with glaring lanterns that make them look like savage predators. Neither their presence nor their identity is ever made clear in the film, but they could very well be European fishing trawlers—which would explain why local fishing seems as dead in Nouadhibou as it was in Baye Laye's Senegalese village—or they could be the Spanish coast guard on a long-distance mission to secure Europe's external borders.

To Sissako, it was important "to not depict a hopeless universe" (in Barlet 2003), and despite everything, *Heremakono* is far from espousing a pessimistic stance. In fact, the film seems to end on a note of hope as the boy Khatra apparently decides to stay. Also, a particularly beautiful scene toward the end of the film has him send a lightbulb off to sea among the huge, dark carcasses of the international shipwrecks. The lightbulb is the very one that his friend and mentor Maata was holding on to when he was found dead on the beach just before this scene, and to Sissako the two electricians' untiring efforts to draw cables—and spread light—in the village represent an act of pure generosity that shows "a will to give, to share: the dignity of a society in which humanism still exists" (ibid., my translation). If, in short, the scene captures a contrast between light, generosity, and humanism on the one hand, and, on the other, darkness, greed, and a disrespect for other people's lives—thus artfully reversing the stereotypical notion of Africa as "the dark continent"—it can perhaps also be seen as an expression of faith in the youth of the continent, and an emphasis on

Figure 15.2. The boy Khatra—Africa's future?—contemplating the huge international shipwrecks off the coast of Nouadhibou. Framegrab from Abderrahmane Sissako's *Heremakono* (*Waiting for Happiness*, 2002, France / Mauritania).

Africa's riches: how you can be rich without owning anything, and poor while having it all.

In *Bamako*, Aminata Traoré insists on not using the word "poverty" when speaking of Africa. Instead, she speaks of "pauperization," that is, a process through which Africa is *made* poor by the imposition of Structural Adjustment Programs and other external influences. To her, Africa is rich—"'We are rich,' that's the spirit the citizens of every African country should have" (Traoré 1999, 171, my translation)—rich in natural resources, rich in geographical surface area, rich in cultural traditions, rich in solidarity, and, not least, rich in men and women with great entrepreneurial potential. Migration thus only adds to the pauperization of Africa.

The Pursuit of Happiness: A Human Right?

With the arguable exception of *Bako, l'autre rive*, the films considered here represent Africa as rich in the sense pinpointed by Traoré. In stark contrast to the "spectacle of misery" promoted by international media coverage of Africa in general and African migrants in particular, the films focus on "vital" human beings who refuse passively to "wait for happiness"—and perhaps die while doing so—but set out on their own "pursuit of happiness."

"We hold these truths to be self-evident, that all men are created equal, that they are endowed by their Creator with certain unalienable Rights, that among these are Life, Liberty and the pursuit of Happiness" (Preamble to the American Declaration of Independence, 1776). To Thomas Jefferson and his coauthors, it was self-evident that all individuals have an unalienable right not only to life and liberty but also to the pursuit of happiness. The Universal Declaration of Human Rights, however, is concerned only with life and liberty, whereas the pursuit of happiness is apparently not considered a universal human right. Now, the concept of happiness is of course quite ambiguous and may mean different things to different people. In the American context, it has usually been understood in a materialist sense, wherefore "the pursuit of happiness" has by and large become synonymous with "the American dream" (see Arendt [1963] 2006). To the Indian economist and philosopher Amartya Sen, however, happiness, and the pursuit of it, has more to do with freedom of choice and is thus closely related to both life and liberty. What he proposes is "a serious departure from concentrating on the *means* of living to the *actual opportunities* of living" (Sen 2010, 233, emphasis in original), and while the latter does of course presuppose a certain level of means, his way of thinking provides an illuminating alternative to the textbook growth economics guiding not only the IMF and the World Bank but also many international aid programs, just as it counters the widespread European perception of African migrants as "welfare tourists": if they have the means to travel to Europe, surely they cannot be that needy.

To Sen, "an appropriate starting point for investigating the relevance of human rights must be the importance of the freedoms underlying those rights" (ibid., 366–7), and in his view, "the idea of freedom also respects our being free to determine what we want, what we value and ultimately what we decide to choose" (ibid., 232). From his philosophical perspective, freedom of choice and actual opportunities to carry out one's choices are as important as economic rights, or, to put it in another way, even a person who has the means to survive is not free in this very fundamental sense if denied the opportunity to pursue whatever he or she defines as happiness.

To many Africans like Boubacar, Yaguine and Fodé, the passengers aboard the pirogue, and the people stranded in Nouadhibou, this essential freedom is simply not available, and the films make palpably clear what it feels like to be deprived of it. Clearly, they are just films, and if films in general tend to have only limited social and political impact, African films have even less, as they are rarely seen, either in Africa or abroad. Of the films considered here, only *Heremakono* is out on DVD with English subtitles; *Un matin bonne heure* and *La Pirogue* are available on DVD with French subtitles, whereas *Bako, l'autre rive* is not commercially available at all. This is all the more regrettable given that especially Europeans, whose leaders continually portray African migrants as an unwanted and even dangerous invasion, could learn a lot from watching them. Not only might they get to understand the migrants, they might also realize that a viable European response to African migration is neither enhanced security measures nor more aid programs. What is called for is rather a different overall approach to Africa, one that helps open up opportunities rather than systematically blocking them. But if they are to make any difference at all, the films must of course be available. Hopefully, this chapter will have made a small contribution toward at least creating a demand for them.

EVA JØRHOLT is Associate Professor of Film Studies at the University of Copenhagen and former editor in chief of the Danish Film Institute's journal *Kosmorama*. She is coeditor (with Mette Hjort and Eva Novrup Redvall) of *The Danish Directors 2: Dialogues on the New Danish Fiction Cinema*.

Notes

1. *Risk Analysis for 2016*, accessed January 19, 2017, http://frontex.europa.eu/assets /Publications/Risk_Analysis/Annula_Risk_Analysis_2016.pdf.

2. *UNHCR Emergency Handbook*: "Migrant Definition", accessed January 19, 2017, https://emergency.unhcr.org/entry/44938/migrant-definition.

3. Many thanks to Alison Smith at the University of Liverpool for drawing my attention to *Bako, l'autre rive*.

4. The Jungle itself was bulldozed by French authorities in October 2016, but only a few days later many migrants returned to the Calais area—see "Migrants DITCH French asylum centres to head BACK to Calais and resume UK-bound mission" *Daily Express*, November 2, 2016, accessed January 19, 2017, http://www.express.co.uk/news/world/727763/Calais -migrants-ditch-French-centres-UK.

5. The letter is available both in its original French wording and in an English translation at *Wikipedia*, s.v. "Yaguine Koita and Fodé Tounkara," accessed January 19, 2017, https:// en.wikipedia.org/wiki/Yaguine_Koita_and_Fodé_Tounkara.

6. The press release can be found (in French) at IMF.org, accessed January 19, 2017, https://www.imf.org/external/am/1999/speeches/PR03F.pdf.

7. For a journalistic account of the real Yaguine and Fodé's backgrounds, see, e.g., "For a Pair of African Stowaways, Only Europe Held Hope of a Future" *Los Angeles Times*, March 19, 2000, accessed January 19, 2017, http://articles.latimes.com/2000/mar/19/news /mn-10355.

8. In his most recent film, *La lune est tombée* (2015, Guinea / France), Fofana further emphasizes the beauty of the country of Guinea and the entrepreneurial vitality of its citizens, which, however, is cut short by an amalgam of multinational corporations, power outages, and failing local politicians.

9. Already in his first fiction film, *I.T.—Immatriculation temporaire* (2001, Guinea / France), Fofana addressed "an African youth who has no future. During the day, these

young people try to get together some money; at night they go out and spend it on ephemeral pleasures, drinking, forgetting themselves . . ." (In Barlet 2002, 33, my translation).

Filmography

14 kilómetros (*14 Kilometers*), 2007, Gerardo Olivares, Spain.
Après l'océan (*Beyond the Ocean*), 2006, Eliane de Latour, France / UK.
Bab Sebta, 2008, Frederico Lobo and Pedro Pinho, Portugal / Morocco.
Bako, l'autre rive (*Bako, the Other Shore*), 1979, Jacques Champreux, France / Senegal.
Bamako, 2006, Abderrahmane Sissako, Mali / USA / France.
Bwana, 1996, Umanol Uribe, Spain.
Las cartas de Alou (*Letters from Alou*), 1990, Montxo Armendáriz, Spain.
Ceuta, douce prison (*Ceuta, Prison by the Sea*), 2013, Jonathan Millet and Loïc H. Rechi, France / Portugal.
Le chant de la noria (*Melody of the Waterwheel*), 2002, Abdellatif Ben Ammar, Tunisia.
Clandestin, 2010, Arnaud Bédouet, France.
Come un uomo sulla terra (*Like a Man on Earth*), 2008, Andrea Segre and Dagmawi Yimer, Italy.
Cry Sea, 2007, Cafi Mohamud and Luca Cusani, Senegal / Italy.
L'envahisseur (*The Invader*), 2011, Nicolas Provost, Belgium.
Et après? ("And Then?"), 2002, Mohamed Ismail, Morocco.
Die Farbe des Ozeans (*Color of the Ocean*), 2011, Maggie Peren, Germany / Spain.
La forteresse (*The Fortress*), Fernand Melgar, 2008, Switzerland.
Frontières (*Borders*), 2001, Mostefa Djadjam, Algeria / France.
Fuocoammare (*Fire at Sea*), 2016, Gianfranco Rosi, Italy.
Harragas, 2009, Merzak Allouache, Algeria / France.
Heremakono—en attendant le bonheur (*Waiting for Happiness*), 2002, Abderrahmane Sissako, France / Mauritania.*Hope*, 2014, Boris Lojkine, France.
Hotel Sahara, 2008, Bettina Haasen, Germany.
I.T.—Immatriculation temporaire (*Temporary Registration*), 2001, Gahité Fofana, Guinea / France.
Implosion, 2007, Sören Voigt, Germany / Spain.
The Land Between, 2014, David Fedele, France / Australia / Morocco / Spain.
Le Havre, 2011, Aki Kaurismäki, Finland / France / Germany.
Lettere dal Sahara (*Letters from the Sahara*), 2006, Vittorio De Seta, Italy.
La lune est tombée, 2015, Gahité Fofana, Guinea / France.
Mare chiuso (*Closed Sea*), 2012, Stefano Liberti and Andrea Segre, Italy.
Un matin bonne heure (*Early in the Morning*), 2006, Gahité Fofana, France / Guinea.
Mediterranea, 2015, Jonas Carpignano, Italy / France / USA / Germany / Qatar.
Les messagers, 2014, Hélène Crouzillat and Laetitia Tura, France.
La Pirogue, 2012, Moussa Touré, France / Senegal / Germany.
Le point de vue du lion, 2010, Didier Awadi, Senegal.
Pummarò (*Tomato*), 1990, Michele Placido, Italy.
Retorno a Hansala (*Return to Hansala*), 2007, Chus Gutiérrez, Spain.
Roma wa la n'touma (*Rome Rather than You*), 2006, Tariq Teguia, Algeria / France / Germany / Netherlands.

Les sauteurs (*Those Who Jump*), 2016, Moritz Siebert, Estephan Wagner, and Abou Bakar
Sidibé, Denmark.
Tarfaya, 2004, Daoud Aoulad-Syad, Morocco / France.
Terraferma, 2011, Emanuele Crialese, Italy / France.
Touki Bouki, 1973, Djibril Diop Mambéty, Senegal.
Under den samme himmel (*Days of Hope*), 2013, Ditte Haarløv Johansen, Denmark / Italy /
Mauritania / Sweden.
Il villaggio di cartone (*The Cardboard Village*), 2011, Ermanno Olmi, Italy.
Vol spécial (*Special Flight*), 2011, Fernand Melgar, Switzerland.

References

Abderrezak, Hakim. 2016. *Ex-Centric Migrations: Europe and the Maghreb in Mediterranean
Cinema, Literature, and Music.* Bloomington: Indiana University Press.
Alba, Richard, and Nancy Foner. 2015. *Strangers No More: Immigration and the Challenges
of Integration in North America and Western Europe.* Princeton: Princeton University
Press.
Andersson, Ruben. 2014. *Illegality, Inc.: Clandestine Migration and the Business of Bordering
Europe.* Oakland: University of California Press.
Arendt, Hannah. (1963) 2006. *On Revolution.* London: Penguin Books.
Armes, Roy. 2006. *African Filmmaking: North and South of the Sahara.* Bloomington:
Indiana University Press.
L'Avant-Scène Cinéma no. 229. 1979. "Bako, l'autre rive." Paris.
Barlet, Olivier. 2002. "Je vis à Conakry mais j'habite à Paris: Entretien avec Gahité Fofana."
Africultures 45: *Cinéma: L'exception africaine.*
———. 2003. "À propos de *Heremakono*: entretien d'Olivier Barlet avec Abderrahmane
Sissako, Cannes mai 2002." *Africultures*, May 1, 2003. Accessed January 19, 2017. http://
www.africultures.com/php/index.php?nav=article&no=2351.
Bauman, Zygmunt. 2016. *Strangers at Our Door.* Cambridge: Polity Press.
Boltanski, Luc. (1993) 1999. *Distant Suffering: Morality, Media and Politics.* Translated by
Graham Burchell. Cambridge: Cambridge University Press.
Chansel, Dominique. 2001. *L'Europe à l'écran. Le cinéma et l'enseignement de l'histoire.*
Strasbourg: Éditions du Conseil de l'Europe.
Chouliaraki, Lilie. 2006. *The Spectatorship of Suffering.* London: Sage Publications.
Fargues, Philippe. 2017. *Four Decades of Cross-Mediterranean Undocumented Migration to
Europe: A Review of the Evidence.* Geneva: International Organization for Migration.
Accessed July 25, 2018. https://publications.iom.int/books/four-decades-cross
-mediterranean-undocumented-migration-europe-review-evidence.
Ferguson, James. 2006. *Global Shadows: Africa in the Neoliberal World Order.* Durham, NC,
and London: Duke University Press.
George, Susan. 1992. *The Debt Boomerang: How the Third World Debt Harms Us All.* London:
Pluto Press.
Ghosh, Bimal. 2003. *Elusive Protection, Uncertain Lands: Migrants' Access to Human
Rights.* Geneva: International Organization for Migration. Accessed July 25, 2018.
publications.iom.int/bookstore/free/Elusive_Protection_Gosh.pdf.

Harrow, Kenneth W. 2013. *Trash: African Cinema from Below*. Bloomington: Indiana University Press.

Jézéquel, Yves. 2008. "Entretien avec Cheik Doukouré." Accessed January 19, 2017. http://www.filmfestamiens.org/?Entretien-avec-Cheik-Doukoure&lang=fr.

Sen, Amartya. 2010. *The Idea of Justice*. London: Penguin Books.

Sontag, Susan. 2004. *Regarding the Pain of Others*. London: Penguin Books.

Thackway, Melissa. 2003. *Africa Shoots Back: Alternative Perspectives in Sub-Saharan Francophone African Film*. Oxford: James Currey.

Traoré, Aminata. 1999. *L'Étau. L'Afrique dans un monde sans frontières*. Arles: Actes Sud.

——. 2008a. *L'Afrique humiliée*. Paris: Fayard.

——. 2008b. *Ceuta et Melilla. Mais pourquoi partent-ils?* Bamako: Éditions Taama.

Webber, Frances. 2012. *Borderline Justice: The Fight for Refugee and Migrant Rights*. London: Pluto Press.

Wihtol de Wenden, Catherine. 2013. *Le droit d'émigrer*. Paris: CNRS Éditions.

Index